■ Secularism and Religion

AAR
AMERICAN ACADEMY OF RELIGION

REFLECTION AND THEORY IN THE STUDY OF RELIGION SERIES
SERIES EDITOR
Theodore M. Vial Jr., Illiff School of Theology
A Publication Series of
The American Academy of Religion
and
Oxford University Press

Secularism and Religion-Making

EDITED BY

Markus Dressler

AND

Arvind-Pal S. Mandair

OXFORD
UNIVERSITY PRESS

OXFORD
UNIVERSITY PRESS

Oxford University Press, Inc., publishes works that further
Oxford University's objective of excellence
in research, scholarship, and education.

Oxford   New York
Auckland   Cape Town   Dar es Salaam   Hong Kong   Karachi
Kuala Lumpur   Madrid   Melbourne   Mexico City   Nairobi
New Delhi   Shanghai   Taipei   Toronto

With offices in
Argentina   Austria   Brazil   Chile   Czech Republic   France   Greece
Guatemala   Hungary   Italy   Japan   Poland   Portugal   Singapore
South Korea   Switzerland   Thailand   Turkey   Ukraine   Vietnam

Published by Oxford University Press, Inc.
198 Madison Avenue, New York, New York 10016

www.oup.com

Oxford is a registered trademark of Oxford University Press.

Library of Congress Cataloging-in-Publication Data
Secularism and religion-making / edited by Markus Dressler
and Arvind Mandair.
    p. cm.
Includes bibliographical references and index.
ISBN 978-0-19-978294-9 (hardcover : alk. paper)
ISBN 978-0-19-978292-5 (pbk. : alk. paper)
1. Secularism.   2. Religion and sociology.   I. Dressler, Markus.
II. Mandair, Arvind-pal Singh.
BL2747.8.S343 2011
211'.6—dc22   2010039997

1 3 5 7 9 8 6 4 2

Printed in the United States of America
on acid-free paper

CONTENTS

■ ACKNOWLEDGMENTS

We embarked on this project when we were both at Hofstra University. It was inspired partly by discussions between ourselves and other colleagues about the formation of a freestanding Religion Department. The collegial and stimulating environment that this new department, previously the Department of Philosophy and Religious Studies, provided was pivotal for the development of this project. Our discussions about religion and politics initially led to a panel that we organized for the American Academy of Religion convention in 2005, entitled "(World-) Religionization: Politics of Religion-Making" (cosponsored by the Critical Theory and Discourses on Religion Group and the Comparative Studies in Religion Program). The positive feedback we received encouraged us to deepen and broaden our discussion by means of an international workshop-style conference. This conference, which we named "Politics of Religion-Making," took place at Hofstra University, October 4–6, 2007, and was organized in cooperation with Hofstra's Religion Department and the Hofstra Cultural Center. A grant we received from the latter was decisive for the realization of the conference, which was cosponsored by the Sikh Research Foundation (UK) and the Center for Religion and Media at New York University (special thanks to Angela Zito), as well as further schools, departments, and programs from within Hofstra University. To all of these contributors we owe a debt of gratitude. While we are not able to thank each and every individual who helped to make the conference happen, special thanks are due to Athelene Collins and Natalie Datlof, from the Hofstra Cultural Center, and to Warren Frisina, the first chair of the Hofstra Religion Department and a never-ending source of support in the buildup and execution of the conference.

For his critical support in realizing this volume, which draws largely but not exclusively from the Hofstra conference (eight of the chapters in this volume originated as papers for the conference, and the three additional papers come from discussants of conference panels), we are indebted to Ted Vial, the editor of the Reflection and Theory in the Study of Religion Series sponsored by the American Academy of Religion. Working together with him toward the publication of this volume was a great pleasure. We further owe thanks to Oxford University Press, especially Cynthia Read and Lizbeth Redfield, for supporting this publication and leading us through the process of getting the manuscript in shape, as well as the anonymous reviewers, whose comments were extremely helpful in the final stages of (re)writing and editing the individual chapters. Last but not least, we want to express our gratitude to the contributors for their patience throughout the process of editing and above all for their excellent work that made this volume possible.

Markus Dressler, Istanbul
Arvind-Pal S. Mandair, Ann Arbor

Markus Dressler teaches at Istanbul Technical University. He has published extensively on Turkish Alevism, religion and secularism in Turkey, and Sufism in the West. His research engages in the work of concepts in the study of religion and Islam, as well as the dynamics between religious, secularist/modernist, and national discourses. He is currently finishing a book on the role of religion in the formation of Turkish nationalism.

Mark Elmore is an assistant professor in the Religious Studies Program at the University of California, Davis. He is currently finishing a book manuscript entitled *Secular Desires: Governance, Anxiety, and Modern Religion in Postcolonial India*.

Brian Goldstone is a Ph.D. candidate in the Department of Cultural Anthropology at Duke University, where he is currently a Mellon/American Council of Learned Societies Dissertation Completion Fellow and an Honorary Charlotte W. Newcombe Fellow.

Rosemary R. Hicks is a Mellon Postdoctoral Fellow at the Center for the Humanities at Tufts University and earned her Ph.D. in the North American religions subfield of the Columbia University Department of Religion with a dissertation titled "Creating an Abrahamic America and Moderating Islam: Cold War Political Economy and Cosmopolitan Sufis in New York after 2001." A three-time recipient of the Foreign Language and Area Studies Fellowship (Lebanon), Hicks was also a 2007–8 American Fellow with the American Association of University Women and a 2007–9 Mellon Fellow with the Institute for Social and Economic Research and Policy at Columbia University.

Greg Johnson is the chair of the Department of Religious Studies at the University of Colorado, Boulder. He studies contemporary indigenous traditions in moments of legal struggle, with specific attention to American Indian and Native Hawaiian contexts. His recent publications include *Sacred Claims: Repatriation and Living Tradition* (University of Virginia Press, 2007) and "Social Lives of the Dead: Contestations and Continuities in Native Hawaiian Repatriation Contexts," in *Culture and Belonging*, edited by Marc Ross (University of Pennsylvania Press, 2009).

Richard King is a professor of religious studies at the University of Glasgow and has published numerous books and articles on classical Hindu and Buddhist philosophy and postcolonial theory and religion. He is the author of *Early Advaita Vedanta and Buddhism* (1995), *Orientalism and Religion* (1999), *Indian Philosophy* (1999), and *Selling Spirituality* (2004, with Jeremy Carrette). He is currently editing a multiauthored introduction to classical and contemporary theories of religion for Columbia University Press and a monograph on apophatic mysticism in comparative perspective.

Arvind-Pal S. Mandair is Associate Professor and holds the S.B.S.C. Professorship in Sikh Studies at the University of Michigan. He is the author of Religion and the Specter of the West: Sikhism, India, Postcoloniality and the Politics of Translation (Columbia University Press, 2009) and coauthor of Teachings of the Sikh Gurus (Routledge, 2005). He is a founding editor of the journal Sikh Formations: Religion, Culture, and Theory and is assistant editor of the journal Culture and Religion, both published by Routledge.

Ruth Mas is an assistant professor of critical theory and contemporary Islam at the University of Colorado (UC), Boulder. She was a 2009–10 Fellow at the Society for the Humanities at Cornell University, a Visiting Fellow at Wolfson College, Cambridge University, a 2008–9 Fellow at the Center for the Humanities and the Arts at UC-Boulder, and a 2003–4 Post-Doctoral Fellow at the Institute for Advanced Study in the Humanities in Essen, Germany. Mas's research interests lie in the intersection between French secularism and contemporary Islamic thought.

Kerry A. Mitchell is an assistant professor and the Director of the Comparative Religion and Culture Program at Global College, Long Island University. He received his Ph.D. in religious studies from the University of California, Santa Barbara, specializing in the study of religion in America.

Michael Nijhawan is an associate professor of sociology at York University in Toronto. His work focuses on cultural practices, violence, suffering, and the politics of religion and secularism with a specific focus on Sikh and Ahmadiyya transnational religious communities. He is the author of *Dhadi Darbar: Religion, Violence, and the Performance of Sikh History* (Oxford University Press, 2006) and coedited *Shared Idioms, Sacred Symbols, and the Articulation of Identities in South Asia* (Routledge, 2009).

Alicia Turner is an assistant professor of humanities and religious studies at York University in Toronto. She specializes in the study of Buddhism in Southeast Asia with an emphasis on the period of British colonialism in Burma/Myanmar and the intersections of religion, colonialism, and nationalism. She is the editor of the *Journal of Burma Studies*.

Secularism and Religion-Making

1 Introduction: Modernity, Religion-Making, and the Postsecular

Arvind-Pal S. Mandair and Markus Dressler

The project out of which this volume emerged was initially framed under the title "Politics of Religion-Making." We conceived of "religion-making" broadly as the way in which certain social phenomena are configured and reconfigured within the matrix of a world-religion(s) discourse. In other words, the notion refers to the reification and institutionalization of certain ideas, social formations, and practices as "religious" in the conventional Western meaning of the term, thereby subordinating them to a particular knowledge regime of religion and its political, cultural, philosophical, and historical interventions.

From the outset the central aim of this project was to examine the consequences of the colonial and postcolonial adoption of Western-style objectifications of religion and its dialectical counterpart, the secular, by non-Western elites. By developing the concept of religion-making in a variety of different geographical, religious, and political contexts, we build on the relatively new field of thought that explores the thoroughly intertwined natures of religion and secularism in the modern period. In doing so we distance ourselves from the opposition between religion and the secular that has been so central for proponents and adherents of the secularization thesis and instead side with those scholars who are interested in exploring the various epistemological and political implications of the formation and codependency of "secular" and "religious" discourses.

The aim of this introduction is to articulate and deepen the methodological concerns and theoretical reflections that have since its inception accompanied this project on the politics of the religio-secular paradigm. The first part of this introduction is dedicated to an epistemological reflection on the major strands of scholarship that have a stake in critically reviewing modern discourses on religion and the secular/secularism. The purpose of this is to work out the limits of the existing paradigm by systematically questioning both religionist and secularist discourses as well as their respective historicizing negations (postreligious and postsecular, respectively). By means of this particular framing we aim at highlighting a set of continuities between these approaches—specifically the circular relationship among historical consciousness, the assumed secularity of critical thinking (or critique, the "critical attitude," etc.), and Western civilizational identity. Taken together, these continuities embody a historico–philosophical continuum that constitutes the intellectual and political heritage and investment in which projects of religion-making are grounded. It does so by simply improving or reforming the very structure that remains central to contemporary politics and theory, namely, the oppositional binary of self versus other. We suggest instead a notion of the post-secular that resists both the historico–philosophical continuum and the idea of religion as a historical and/or anthropological constant. Our alternative concept, which might be termed the *post-secular-religious*, tries instead to acknowledge the irresolvable contradiction, or *aporia*, that lies at the heart of the religio–secular paradigm and remains open to the questions raised in light of the experience of our postcolonial democracy. The second part of the introduction will turn to the more concrete work of religion-making, or religion-making politics, and distinguish between different modes of religion-making. The introduction will conclude with brief summaries of the individual chapters of this volume.

■ THREE STRANDS OF POSTSECULAR SCHOLARSHIP

In recent years there has been a rapid expansion of scholarship that has unpacked many of the connections between the secularization thesis and the work of religion-making, thereby offering fresh insights into the relationship between the twinned categories of "religion and the secular." While a comprehensive overview of this literature is beyond the scope of this introduction, we shall aim, for heuristic purposes, to point out several of the better-known strands of scholarship that continue to influence the debate. These strands are generated by a relatively diverse group of scholars whose insights have contributed to a rethinking of the categories religion and the secular—and by implication the academic study of religion—in such a way that their collective contributions have helped to redraw the map of the religion–secular debate, which, by and large, has tended to gravitate around the narrative of secularization. For the sake of argument, the three most easily identifiable strands include (1) the sociopolitical philosophy of liberal secularism exemplified by Charles Taylor (and to some extent shared by thinkers such as John Rawls and Jürgen Habermas); (2) the "postmodernist" critiques of ontotheological metaphysics by radical theologians and Continental philosophers that have helped to revive the discourse of "political theology"; and (3) following the work of Michel Foucault and Edward Said, the various forms of discourse analysis focusing on genealogies of power most closely identified with the work of Talal Asad.

All three of these schools of thought have responded in different ways to the challenges posed by the resurgences of religion and religious formations to the dominant framework of modern liberal secularism. Yet what connects the first two schools and thus distinguishes them from the third, apart from a difference in academic discipline, is a specifically *philosophical* investment in the constitution of what might be called the Western imaginary. As we shall argue below, this philosophical investment hinges on the belief that there is an essentially historical difference between the West and the non-West. The term *historical difference*, which we borrow from Dipesh Chakrabarty, can be envisaged as the structural basis of a comparative imaginary that links the West to the non-West, an imaginary that in turn depends on the belief in the notion of religion as a universal.[1] Accordingly, because secularism is *historically* associated with the West, it follows that any movement beyond or after the secular can only be framed from within this comparative imaginary. Taken completely for granted by both of these strands of scholarship, despite certain postliberal and/or postmodern leanings, is that the nature of this imaginary consists in the notion of a divided self-conscious subject—the modern form of critical self-consciousness and associated with this a certain mode of critical thinking—as a transcultural and transhistorical phenomenon. We shall return shortly to this link among subjectivity, critical thinking, and the religion–secular debate.

Both the schools of the liberal-secular and the postmodern/postsecular seem to affirm a particular notion of what comes *after* contemporary secularism. This convergence can be detected in the ontological affinity between their understandings of what constitutes history and the historical and what constitutes critique or critical thinking. That is to say, the very manner in which they continue to think about the transitions between religion, the secular, and the postsecular, indeed the possibility of thinking critically about these terms, is constrained by a particular notion of the historical that is forgetful of its own history as a history of foreclosure, if not exclusion, of the other. The question, however, is to what extent this claim might also be made in regard to the third school. Taking its cue from Foucault, the third school focuses on genealogical and discursive deconstruction of what one might call with José Casanova "knowledge regimes of secularism" and their respective religious others.[2] In doing so, it both challenges liberal secularism and attempts to revaluate religion through notions of the postsecular and political theology. However, important differences between this third school and the first two notwithstanding, one might ask whether there is not a subtle convergence among all of them in regard to their implicit conceptualization of historical time and the kind of rationality this conceptualization is associated with.

Before further delving into this criticism it will be helpful to more fully expound the differences among the three schools of thought by way of reference to their respective explanations of how the contemporary terrain of religion and the secular came about and how they envisage going beyond this terrain, especially where they employ the notion of the *post*secular. While fully recognizing the artificiality of grouping strands of scholarship in this particular way, we nevertheless continue to highlight this difference because it impacts the understanding of the notion of religion-making that is the main target of this book.

Critical Investments: (Post)Secularism, Historical Difference, and the Comparative Imaginary

In addition to sharing a similar disciplinary focus (post-Kantian Continental philosophy), philosophers who espouse liberal secularism and postmodernist advocates of political theology further share a common underlying assumption, which its different proponents hold to varying degrees. In its stronger version it consists in the belief that religion is a cultural universal, that all cultures have in varying degrees some understanding of religion. Where these philosophical schools diverge, however, is in their respective assessments of liberal secularism. Charles Taylor, for example, provides in his recent work *A Secular Age* a sophisticated reinterpretation of the framework of contemporary liberal secularism by distinguishing among three different forms of secularity: "secularity 1" and "secularity 2" corresponding to an older framework that designates the disappearance of religion from public spaces and declining belief and practice, respectively, while "secularity 3" indicates a shift "from a society where belief in God is unchallenged and indeed, unproblematic, to one in which it is understood to be one option among others." "Secularity 3" designates "a change in the very conditions of belief" and in the process provides more accommodation for religion. Taylor's "secularity 3" denotes less a reversal of "secularization" than "a time in which the hegemony of the mainstream master narrative of secularization will be more and more challenged."[3] Faced with increasing refutation of the secularization thesis by empirical evidence, Taylor's defense of the epistemic viability of the secular not only replicates a movement that is already there within the "mainstream master narrative of secularization" but at the same time seems to endorse the way in which secularism shifts from being a descriptive to a normative discourse. By remaining committed to an overall framework of the secular and to the exclusionary narrative of its origins, Taylor seems to be skeptical of labels such as "postsecular."[4] Despite this resistance, however, in recent replies to his critics Taylor also "argues for an analysis in which the religious and the secular (or secularist), far from being in exclusive competition, coexist and are subject to both social and ethical cross-pressures"—a formulation that does not seem too distant from the understanding of the "postsecular" that we shall be outlining later in this introduction.[5]

Effective critiques of the conventional understanding of religion and the secular have also been offered by philosophers and theologians who position their thought in the wake of the death of God as the key event that defines the closure of modernity and the opening of what is loosely called the postmodern age. Influenced by the "masters of suspicion" Marx, Nietzsche, and Freud, as well as later thinkers such as Heidegger, Lacan, and Derrida, the critical interventions of this movement range from the narrowly conservative group that calls itself "Radical Orthodoxy" to the loosely linked group of mainly Continental philosophers who locate their writings at the intersections of modern European philosophy, religion, and cultural critique.[6] By "unmask[ing] the modernist unmaskers," by growing "disenchanted with the idea of disenchantment," or by questioning "modernity's prejudice against prejudice," they show a weariness of the Enlightenment critique that does not, at first sight, sit comfortably with Charles Taylor's attempt to reform the secularization narrative.[7]

Despite their different attitudes toward liberal secularism, however, there is a consensus within the philosophically oriented schools of postsecular thought that religion and secularity are co-emergent and codependent. Indeed, they argue that these processes haunt each other, such that religion, as it has developed in the West, has always been present in all secular phenomena even when it appears to be absent and secularity, in turn, has covertly continued a religious agenda.[8] However, these oscillations between religion and the secular did not take place in a vacuum. Rather, they are tied to a complex of interrelated events that occurred in the wake of modernity. Such events include the rise of European cultural identity; various theological and philosophical shifts in the conceptual understanding of God, self, and the natural world; and not least the reformulation of the rules for what counts as proper or critical thinking. While these intricate events cannot be rehearsed here, it is nevertheless necessary to note in passing several of the key triggers within the philosophical imaginary of European modernity that have contributed to the contemporary map of religion and the secular and to the social imaginary that has organized itself around this map. At the very least these triggers would have to include the following:

1. Luther's invention of the divided self, that is, the form of consciousness that separates itself from itself.
2. Kant's discovery of the mechanisms of the human imaginary and his demarcation of critical thinking under the purview of the law of reason. One consequence of this is that any object of thought must separate itself from itself; in the case of religion this imperative to separate itself from itself constitutes its secularization. Through this mode of secularization the sanctity of religion is replaced by the sanctity of critique, which itself becomes inviolable.[9]
3. Hegel's incorporation and development of these ideas into a comprehensive comparative schema for organizing the ever-growing knowledge about other cultures in terms of the historical transition between religion(s), secularity, and the postsecular. It is with Hegel that the notion of historical difference becomes integral to the determination of the other. Hegel's peculiar genius was to integrate the possibility and definition of critique with the notion of historical difference. That is to say, traditions can be defined as critical if from their very beginnings they are able to contest their own origins, separate themselves from themselves (= secularize). The degree to which a culture can make this self-separation at its origins not only defines history (and secularity) but also determines the degree to which it is different from other traditions and cultures.[10]

As we argue below, these developments were inherited by the three strands of discourse that define the current map of religion and the secular right up until the work of Foucault and his successors and in a sense also limit the possibilities for thinking otherwise than in terms of the trio of concepts: religion/secular/postsecular.

Luther's Divided Self and Its Trajectories in Religious and Secularist Discourses

Most commentators on the cultural and intellectual history of Europe agree that Luther's Protestant Reformation is a pivotal event that set the currents of modernity into motion. According to Mark C. Taylor, in the process of reformulating Christian doctrines of salvation, "Luther discovered or more accurately invented the modern subject.... [B]y privatizing, deregulating and decentering the relationship between believer and God, Luther initiated a revolution that was not confined to religion but extended to politics and economics."[11] The subject that Luther invented, however, was fundamentally divided insofar as the "Christian man is both righteous and sinner, holy and profane, an enemy of God and yet a child of

God."[12] Among the implications of this are that faith is primarily a personal relation between an individual self and an individual God. It does not need to be
mediated by a third party—it can be direct. More important, though, this relationship to God is not just individual but also private, that is, subjective or interior.
Thus, because the individual is both sinner (through its capacity to act freely) and
justified, the self is never simply itself but is something other than what it is. It is
therefore possible for the subject of faith to confess: "*I am what I am not*," signaling
that the self who says "I am" is inherently contradictory, since it contains within
itself its other ("I am not").

However, Mark C. Taylor's assessment that the inward turn of the contradictory, divided, and infinitely restless subject led to the self-legislating subject,
without which the political revolutions of the modern era would have been impossible, needs to be tempered by a somewhat different observation.[13] The route
toward the modern era does not run quite so directly from theological speculation
to political changes that occurred in Europe. What tends to be conveniently omitted (or repressed) in the recounting of Europe's intellectual and cultural history is
the memory of imperialism as an event that might have influenced the development
of critical thinking and cultural identity of the West (Europe and North America).
Our argument is that modern intellectual history, the development of its thought
process, is inextricably linked to the history of its encounters with non-Christian
cultures, which can by no means be limited to the encounter with Islam and the
Crusades. A different sort of imperial encounter begins with the colonization and
conquest of the New World, inauspiciously marked by the planting of the royal
standard of the king of Spain in 1492. Our argument is that this sort of act—which
inaugurates the "conquest of America and a history of the West whereby knowledge,
ownership, subjectification and subjection become intertwined through incredible
violence"—cannot simply be separated from Luther's discovery of the rupture in
human consciousness that is elucidated, significantly, in the decades immediately
following 1492.[14] Luther's divided self entails an epistemological violence that has
important consequences for the political and epistemological fate of the other.
This link between philosophical speculation and colonial adventure can be illustrated by way of reference to Luther's *Thesis 95*, which is tied up with the privilege
that Luther accords to faith as exemplified by the love of the self for God. *Thesis 95*
states:

> It is a subtle evil to say that the love of God is, even in intensity, *the same kind of love as
> that for creatures.*[15]

What Luther specifically rejects with this thesis is that the love for God and the
love for other beings implied each other. Gone is the idea that in loving God one
should also love God's creatures, including nonbelievers, as the basis of charity.
The breakage of this link between the love for the other and love for God is total.
By relating the agency of grace and the meaning of charity in the act of loving God
for Himself, Luther draws the (Christian) subject further into the solipsistic knot
of individualism. As the other recedes from the acts of charity that the Christian
was meant to perform as part of the experience of love for God, from there on,
Protestantism loosens the responsibility the subject might have felt for the other.

Humanity is disaggregated into singular individuals who must look to themselves and their individual consciences for their salvation. By the time that this new proposition reached the thinkers of the Enlightenment via Calvin, Protestantism had transfigured the *viator* principle in Christianity into a personal journey of redemption involving oneself and an unknowable, transcendent God. According to Couze Venn, by "reconstituting the relationship between faith and reason Protestantism seemed to want faith to be the outcome of rational consideration while ensuring salvation by anchoring faith to a regime dictated by the application of reason."[16] In short, by simultaneously insisting on devotion to an absolutely transcendent, unknowable God *and* on the absolute interiority of faith, Luther's divided subject inadvertently prepared the way for the shift from theological foundation to rational (secular) foundations of the modern world.

However, the wider implications of Luther's self-contradictory subject were not fully articulated until the turn of the nineteenth century, when religion, art, and politics began to intersect through the evolving notion of the autonomous self-representing subject.[17] Between Luther's Reformation and the nineteenth century, the notion of the autonomous subject is refigured, as philosophers from Descartes to Kant and Hegel reconstructed the idea of "consciousness" and the self-conscious subject, replacing the conflicted devotional self of Luther (and his predecessors such as Augustine) with "a sovereign, self-possessed, dispassionate 'thinking being,' fully in charge of its potencies and possibilities, surveying the contents of its mind to sort out which among them represents something objective, out-there in the external world and which should be written off as merely internal and subjective."[18] Perhaps the most important development in this trajectory was Kant's transcendental faculty of mind—the imagination (*Einbildungskraft*)—whose operative mechanism he termed "the schematization of the categories." The purpose of the transcendental schema was to organize the manifold of human experience and to create the world we know, understand, and dwell in it today. In short, Kant's schema unified diverse objects of understanding through what he labeled as three interrelated ideas of reason—God, self, and world—and in so doing laid the groundwork for the disclosure by his successors of the self-reflexive structure of self-consciousness. A self-conscious subject is one that "turns its back on itself by becoming an object to itself. As a result self-as-subject and self-as-object are reciprocally related in such as way that each becomes itself through the other and neither can be itself apart from the other."[19] Paradoxically, therefore, the self-conscious subject is noncoincident with itself, and the structure of self-relation proper to this contradictory self presupposes the activity of self-representation.

In his "Age of the World Picture," Heidegger notes that through this mode of self-relation man places imagination at the center of the world.[20] What Heidegger alludes to is that this peculiarly modern form of thinking gradually produces the birth of the West as a self-referential system of thought, universalizing its position and discourse, claiming objectivity about human societies and cultures, on the same basis as the natural sciences. Through the work of this imaginary, which projects itself as a universal structure of human consciousness—the self-representing subject—not only does Europe become West, and thought become Western, but, in the very same process, *religion becomes secularity*. As mentioned above, this is most evident in the work of Hegel, for whom the representational model of self-conscious subjectivity explains not only the relationship among God, self, and world but equally the relation between religion and secularity (qua history). For Hegel, the field of self-consciousness—that is, the field on which the self represents itself to itself—mirrors exactly the conceptual structure of the Incarnation and the Trinity. To quote Mark C. Taylor once again: "the triadic structure of Father-Son-Spirit is isomorphic with the triadic structure of self-consciousness: Self-as-subject [= Father], self-as-object [= Son] and the inter-relation of the two [= Spirit]."[21] Moreover, since the figure of the Father (symbolizing transcendence, separation as attributes of secularity) is transfigured into that of the Son (symbolizing incarnation and immanence as attributes of religion), it is possible to see how the oscillation between religion and secularity is mediated through the activity of the spirit. And because spirit is described as that substance that is able to separate itself from itself in the moment of its origin (or what Hegel calls pure elevation, pure movement),[22] the work of spirit consists in nothing less than a pure relation, a perfect or "generalized" translation that is able to move between self and other, subject and object, religion and secularity, infinitely and at will.

However pervasive and influential this argument may have been, what philosophers and theologians tend to have forgotten is that the imaginary, which, in constructing the frame of intelligibility of the West, so conveniently universalizes its self-referential mode of subjectivity, was not framed in a cultural vacuum. Consequently it could never have been an imaginary in the singular. Given that its cultural and historical backdrop was the encounter between European and non-European cultures, followed almost immediately by colonization of the latter, *the imaginary was from the outset a comparative imaginary* "that functioned according to a structured-structuring process."[23] At the very moment that the comparative imaginary was "inscribed in and thereby came to structure the signifying practices that described, classified, annotated, analyzed, represented, prescribed and ordered the cultural and material world of its colonial subjects, in ways that have too often become naturalized," *in that very moment and through the work of comparison*, the very same imaginary was busy fleshing out the identity of European culture.[24] The contours of the West and the non-West were thus codependent and co-emergent, that is, mutually fleshed out (translated) within this model of self-representation. It is possible to suggest that the comparative relation between West and non-West was and continues to be isomorphic with the relation between self-as-subject and self-as-object—the only difference being that the actual movement or translation between West/non-West and self-as-subject/self-as-object was in fact a universalized or "generalized translation" in which the other was either reduced to the same (self-as-object) or cast out of the purview of human consciousness altogether.[25] Through this generalized translation that constitutes the comparative relation between self and other (say, Europe and Asia/Africa), "the difference of the other no longer appears as a threat; a hindrance maybe, and a source of resistance to be quelled, certainly a source of evidence and experiences for reflection on the human condition and for forging the policies and the means for the transformation of the world."[26]

To briefly summarize the above, the historical co-emergence and codependence of religion and secularity, leading up to the contemporary map of these two categories, is inextricably bound to the development of the modern Western imaginary, with its constitution of a particular structure of human consciousness that in turn privileges a particular type of critique or critical thinking as universal (the one that grounds itself in self-separation). Our point in the foregoing analysis has been to suggest not simply that the postsecular move as made by prominent philosophers, theologians, and theorists of religion cannot be restricted to its identification of the mutually imbricated natures of religion and the secular but, more importantly, that it continues to bring into play one of the key aspects of the secularization thesis, namely, the concept of religion as a cultural universal—that religion exists everywhere. The problem, therefore, is not Christianity per se but the direct linking of structures of Christianity (especially as they are found in classical Christology going back to the fourth and fifth centuries C.E.) with the modern structures of rational self-consciousness and thought itself (critique as self-separation), which of course determine the possibilities of action at individual, social, and political levels.[27]

In other words, unless it incorporates a move beyond the presumption that religion is a cultural universal, the very idea of a *post-* of secularism appears to be a chimera. It means little more than a return to Christian thought disguised as the postsecular. This has been particularly evident in the strange recent convergences between different strands of the Western political and intellectual spectrum (the global Left, the center, and the global Right) in response to the "threat of Islam" and similarly perceived forms of global religious violence and terrorism. While this might be expected from intellectuals on the Right, and even center-Left liberal secularists, the intellectual response of the global Left has been more surprising.[28] Indeed since the retreat of Marxism and the rampancy of neoliberalism that followed the end of the Cold War, leading thinkers of the Left have conspicuously returned to the religious sources of Western culture in their efforts to rethink the nature of politics.[29] Faced with the triumphalism of American global power in the 1990s, the massive resurgence of religion into the heart of national and global politics (indeed into the project of democracy itself), and the abject failure of the "traditional" Left, many prominent leftist thinkers have in different ways called for a renewal of Western/European political thought—a "renewal of Left Eurocentrism"—by reconnecting to the wellsprings of its culture, namely, religion and specifically Christianity. For them, the legacy of Western thought is endangered not only by the scourge of cultural relativism, New Age mysticism, and paganism that has afflicted contemporary Western thought and culture but also by a global economic shift associated with the rise of an authoritarian China and the politico-cultural consequences that are feared to come with it. Translated into vernacular languages, the culturalist normativity that comes with this line of thought has also lined up nicely with post-9/11 European fears of Islamization and added to Western Islamophobia. What is endorsed through the implicit juxtaposition of legitimate (= secular) and illegitimate (= fundamentalist) religion is a particularly European/Western/Protestant notion of modernity/civilized culture.

Though not always obvious, calls for a return to and reinheritance of Christian sources remind us of the logic of reform that was embedded within the Protestant Reformation.[30] For it is in relation to this logic of reform (specifically the "drive to make over the whole of society to higher standards"[31]) that, on the one hand, helped to shift Christianity away from corporeal practices toward states of mental interiority and doctrinal propositions and, on the other hand, helped to inaugurate the rise of modern secularism. As Jonathon Sheehan argues, reform can be regarded as the stipulated agent that transforms a prior age centered on religion into the presently secular age.[32] It was just such a logic of reform that helped to rupture the intimate connection between society and religious life and in turn forced the kind of rupture in consciousness that then generated the "individuated religion of devotion" (Protestant interiority) that is so integral to our understanding of the secular age. In other words, the recent calls for renewing the heritage of Eurocentrism are best seen as part and parcel of a certain tradition of apologetics that combines a return, reinheritance, and reform of religious sources within a historical frame. Sheehan usefully reminds us that this "historical logic of apologetics works . . . to ensure . . . that Christianity is preserved as a history whose presence the present can ignore only at the price of its own authenticity."[33]

The key here is the historical—the notion of time central to the task of inheriting (i.e., reforming) tradition—that is built into the perceived codependency of religion and the secular.[34] As we have noted above, insofar as the idea of history and the historical is tied to a concept of subjectivity as divided, and thus to a *critical* exercise of division and separation from religion (which can be traced within its Greek, Christian, and modern European traditions of thinking), this also adequately describes the work that is performed by secularization and secular critique. Moreover, given that the logic of reform that gives rise to the secular "represents the dynamic of religion's own unfolding," it is possible to suggest that the secular is contained within religion *from the very moment* that human consciousness itself emerges as a divided subjectivity. In other words, the relationship between religion and secularity is maintained by a particular notion of history, and this notion of history is nothing other than the moment of emergence of a particular form of self-consciousness as the so-called critical attitude that not only comes to define the very nature of modern Western man as the relational center of the world but also constitutes itself as universal insofar as the codependent and interchangeable notions of religion, the secular, time, and consciousness are then inscribed onto every other culture through the work of imperialism.

Hume, Hegel, and the Universalization of Religion

In this way, even before imperialism became a political reality, all other cultures of the world (indeed the very possibility of pluralism) were mapped within a framework of historical development in such a way that Christianity provided the essential blueprint for the map and the historical evolution of world cultures inscribed within it. Through this emerging narrative arrangement of cultures on a world grid, Christianity came to occupy all of the available sites of intellectual responsibility—"to possess the past . . . as the originary author of the secular age and yet to disavow responsibility for it."[35] The clever part in all of this is the narrative itself. For it is the narrative that, on the one hand, recognizes other cultures as religion(s), and in that very moment of recognition sets them apart in a proper place, and, on the other hand, inasmuch as it coincides with the transparent movement that is time (or history), ensures the Christian claim (1) to the present (the secular age that we all live in), (2) to its past (the history of the world's religion(s)—or the religious history of the world), and perhaps more importantly, (3) to its postsecular future, which would entail a renewal of the secular by returning to its religious sources.[36]

Of course, what underpins this narrative of the movement from religion to the secular to the postsecular, connecting the world spatially and temporally, is the concept of *religion as a universal*. Indeed the dependency of the philosophical interpretations of the religion–secular–postsecular relationship on the ability to conceptualize religion as a universal should not surprise us. Its antecedents can be found in the work of major thinkers of the Enlightenment such as David Hume in the mid–eighteenth century and, even more so, G. W. F. Hegel in the early nineteenth century.

One of the key problems for both Hume and Hegel was to find a reliable intellectual solution to the problem of pluralism and cultural difference as it was manifesting itself in the reports of explorers, missionaries, and Orientalists. Although they both worked in different contexts, in different time periods, and with different materials at their disposal, for both Hume and Hegel the only proper solution to the problem presented by the increasing variety of non-Christian cultural beliefs and practices was to assimilate them to a category of religion modeled on a Protestant understanding of religion with "belief and practice at its conceptual center."[37] The closest that Hume comes to entertaining the idea of religion as a universal category can be seen in his *Natural History of Religion*, in which he traces the origin of religion to peculiarly human experiences of hope and fear, arguing that the "first obscure traces of divinity" grow out of "ordinary affections in human life."[38] But even in this influential treatise Hume is very clear to point out that while religion is common (all men potentially have religion), it is not necessarily universal.

While arguments for or against a universally applicable model of religion remain implicit in Hume's accounts, they are far more rigorously theorized by Hegel. In his Berlin lecture courses on the philosophy of history and religion Hegel effectively constructed just such a model in the form of a comparative schema that could frame empirical and explanatory knowledge of other cultures within a historicist vector much the same as the one recounted above. Hegel's main concern in the Berlin lecture courses was to counter the philosophical influences of deism and the debates about natural religion. As Hegel saw it, discourses such as these, especially when deployed by the early Orientalists, provided a potentially safe haven for Asian cultures, a means whereby they could adversely influence the European intellectual mind-set and in so doing could possibly displace or undermine the dominant vantage point of Christian European cultural identity. The problem for Hegel was how to differentiate between Christian religion as properly historical (and therefore capable of self-critique and secularization) and other, especially Asian, *religions* as lacking history. Hegel's answer was to establish a firm theoretical standpoint, the concept of religion-in-general, that could be used as a means for *comparing* Oriental cultures (particular religions) by means of an ontotheological framework. The term *ontotheology* refers to an essential continuity of different moments in the Western philosophical and theological traditions (specifically the Greek [-*onto*], the medieval-scholastic [*theo*-], and the humanist [*logo*- or *logic*]), a continuity that challenges the dominant secular Enlightenment story in which modernity and humanism constitute a radical break with prior religious tradition.[39]

Hegel's genius was to incorporate both *religion* (by means of ontological proofs for God's existence) and *secularity* (through the vector of historicism) into the work of *comparing* different cultures. According to the rules of his schema, the degree to which any culture can think coherently and clearly about "the transcendent" corresponds to its ability to emerge into history, that is, to elevate itself from a purely natural existence. This in turn is a measure of that culture's ability to think *critically* as measured by its ability to separate itself from itself—and it also measures its degree of secularity. What becomes clear in any close reading of Hegelian narrative is that the concept of religion-in-general is being fleshed out with the simultaneous inclusion-exclusion of Asian cultures within history (i.e., inclusion within the domain of religion*s*, which is simultaneously exclusion from the domain of history/secularity). Furthermore, the concept of religion as universal is fleshed out in a process that is paralleled by the refinement of a specific mode of thinking, the so-called critical attitude that is characteristic of the modern West, in which the operation of thought becomes indistinguishable from *generalized translation* as the ability to translate infinitely and at will between the universal and the particular.

In short, Hegel's ontotheological schema identifies reason with Christianity and thus closes the circular relationship between historical consciousness, the assumed secularity of critique, and Western civilizational identity more securely than at any point in the history of philosophy. But more important, he can implement this circularity among history, critique, and secularity by identifying tangible others (Asia, Africa, etc.) as "religious," followed by their inclusion-exclusion within the order of knowledge and existence. In other words, by means of the law of history/critique/secularity Hegel is able to constitute a relation between Europe/Christianity and its others, but it is a relation in which the other is excluded through its inclusion within the orders of knowledge and existence. This simultaneous exclusion-inclusion becomes a means for rendering the encounter with non-Western cultures politically harmless. This was achieved by installing these cultures at the lower end of a vertical axis that represents the development (self-elevation) of cultures of the world from religion through secularity and eventually into the postsecular.[40] The dual purpose of this installation was to give them a comparable and recognizable identity while through that very gesture subverting their potential for contributing in any way to modernity.[41] The results of this new comparative schema were far reaching. Deploying for the first time the terms *pantheism, monotheism*, and *polytheism* as "world historical" or comparative categories, the schema provided an intuitive comprehension of the "meaning-value" of each culture that happened to be plotted on the axis.[42] The insidious aspect of this schema is not simply the representation of diversity, plurality, difference, time, and other(s) through a configuration of the "world" but more accurately, the fleshing out and preservation of the particular constellations "Europe," the "West," "Christianity," and "the secular" through the category of universal religion.[43] It is this move that allowed Hegel, and after Hegel a host of Orientalists, missionaries, philosophers, anthropologists, historians, economists, and religionists, to apply models that recognized the diversity of world cultures in terms of similarity and difference. Non-Western cultures could be recognized as *religions* (and therefore similar to "our own," i.e., Christianity and as part of a broad human unity) but at the same time served to differentiate between humans/cultures precisely on the basis of their different religious elevation (= incompatibility with secular cultures of Europe). This ambivalent schema that simultaneously *produces religions* of the world as a measure of their *historical* difference from the West even as they are denied the ability to overcome or reform themselves except through a developmental process based on Western patterns, was put to use intellectually and practically during the colonial and postcolonial era.

Obviously, variations of this Eurocentric schema were located within the broader imperialist politics of modernization understood as a civilizing mission when referring to the "Rest." Intellectually, aspects of it were incorporated into hermeneutic explanations about the essential nature of non-Western cultures that would eventually become seamlessly incorporated into the system of the emerging human sciences. Within an emerging world-religions discourse, the schema provided an intuitive comprehension of the "meaning-value" of cultures through a principle of "generalized translation"—a mechanism for bringing different cultures into a taxonomic system of equivalence, in which the relative meaning-values could be assigned to each culture in order for them to be exchanged/compared. By bringing the meaning-value of different cultures into a system of exchange-comparison, this approach effectively replaced the tangible problem of translation (and hence the anxiety of real encounter) with the work of representation proper to the political economy of the sign. Within the context of cultural exchange and comparison that begins to parallel commodity exchange in the political economy of empire, the system of exchange-comparison that is intrinsic to the comparative cultural imaginary of the West can be seen parallel to the system of global monetary exchange that, as Karl Marx pointed out, developed at roughly the same time.

In practice, the principle of "generalized translation" (which combined the twin assumptions that critique is secular and that religion is a universal category[44]) was transferred almost invisibly from philosophical texts into the work of Orientalists and missionaries as the privileged interpreters/translators of key indigenous texts and cultural practices. From there it passed, again seamlessly, into the policy-making decisions of administrators, lawmakers, and educators during the colonial period and then crucially into the reformist-cum-nationalist (religionizing and secularizing) projects of native elites in various parts of the colonial world.[45] Of course, as we know only too well today, the work of the schema of generalized translation did not stop with the colonial era but can be seen in the centrality of historicism and secular critique that continues to underpin the contemporary human sciences in such a way that it continues to theoretically exclude non-Western cultures, to "ban them from entering signification (the realm of human intellectual and physical contact and interaction)" and yet at the same time to "retain, rename and elevate them in a benevolent second-order gesture as signification's spectral other."[46]

Because it is born out of a particular religion (Christianity), and in order to justify its claim to be a universal discourse that can maintain its promise of peace, the secular-historicist regime has to be able to *produce* religion in other cultural sites. Yet this could be done only by the assumption of religion as a universal. That is, religion has to have a logic that requires the translation of itself, which means that it performs an invisible violence toward every culture it encounters. Only then can it be desired by all and accepted without the imposition of direct colonial violence. Consequently, as Dingwaney and Rajan point out, the normative and dominant diagnosis of a West that is secular (and/or postsecular) versus a non-West that is nonsecular (and/or religious) remains persuasive even when recast in tones of politically correct self-reproach and postmodern interrogation among intellectuals in the Western academy, as, for example, in the following statement issued at a recent major Euro-American conference on "political theologies":

> Imagined to be universal in both relevance and application, the rigid boundaries by which secular social structures divide the public sphere of political processes from private commitments to the values inculcated by religious and spiritual traditions have proved, instead, a source of mounting resistance on the part of cultures in which the superiority of such structures is not self-evident.
>
> The statement continues to insist on the urgency of understanding the "religiously informed resistance to pressures of secularization and cultural-political assimilation implicit in the continuing sources of tension between the 'secular' West and the developing societies imagined in the West as the 'beneficiaries of globalization.' "[47]

What Dingwaney and Rajan usefully draw attention to is the phenomenon of *religion-making*—the fact that "religion is still called on to serve as the distinguishing mark of such minority identity struggles. Even though the globalizing West may be blamed for such a development, it implicitly remains the secular [or postsecular] party in this narrative."[48] As we have argued above, this phenomenon of religion-making derives ultimately from the intertwined notions of historical difference, secular critique, and its concomitant, the belief in religion as a cultural universal.

Resisting the Concept of Religion as Universal

This brings us to the third strand of scholarship that has contributed to a rethinking of religion and the secular. This significant group includes scholars with an interest in the history of religious studies as a discipline,[49] as well as scholars focusing on the colonial history of religions in areas as diverse as Africa and South Asia.[50] A major impact on this branch of scholarship has been the work of Talal Asad.[51] Hent de Vries has argued that, in a way that clearly separates him (Asad) from those strands of scholarship described above as liberal-secular and postmodern advocates of political theology that insist on the universality of religion, "Asad's interest is less hermeneutic than that of the anthropologist-grammarian. He follows Wittgenstein's recommendation to look for 'use,' not for 'meaning,' steering clear of all attempts to essentialize either 'religion' or its supposed counterpart, 'the secular,' and insisting instead on seeing both as something 'processual' rather than, say, a 'fixed ideology.'"[52]

Many of the scholars associated with this influential and rapidly growing field have applied Foucault's genealogical analysis of power and through this have explored ideological uses of the construction of the term *religion* in the Western knowledge system. A major implication of this genealogical approach, and one that links them together, is a strong suspicion of religion as a universal category. What they all agree on is that "religion" as commonly understood today is a modern phenomenon that emerged in the West and which is tied to formations of the "secular." Consequently, there are no universals of "religion" or the "secular."[53]

As discourse analysts have pointed out, there are cultures and societies for whom "religion" has not been part of their native lexicons, at least not until the colonial era, and it is perfectly possible to organize societies without the concept "religion" or religious–secular interventions. Japan, China, and India are perfectly good examples of such cultures. There is increasing empirical evidence that what we today call Hinduism, Sikhism, and Buddhism only became part of the "world religions" group as late as the nineteenth and early twentieth centuries.[54] It is therefore worth asking why "we" continue to speak of Indian, Japanese, or Chinese *religions*. At least one of the answers to this has to do with our institutional and intellectual anchoring within modern academia, which was thoroughly implicated in the theoretical creation of languages of universalism, such as the discourse of "world religions" and their application to colonial policy making and the projects of sociopolitical reform in the colonial and postcolonial era. Indeed, the dependence of scholars of religion, especially those working within religious studies departments, on maintaining a discourse on "religion" as something isolatable and worthy of study in its own right constitutes an important institutional constraint for advancing the epistemological and genealogical deconstruction of religion and the secular-liberal discourses in which it is embedded. Beyond the institutional constraints of academia there are also nonacademic forces that remain heavily invested in maintaining the hegemonic discourse of the religio-secular. We suggest seeing the university's discourse about religion and religions not simply as a reflection of the discourse of the nation-state (which of course it is) but more importantly as an exercise of coloniality. Coloniality, as Bobby Sayyid argues, cannot simply be equated with colonia*lism*. Rather, coloniality refers to a global "logic of governmentality that not only supports specific forms of historical colonialism but continues to structure a planetary hierarchy in terms of the distinction between West and the Rest."[55] Again, the "logic of governmentality" does not refer merely to governance per se but to the existence of a globally secured liberal-secular epistemology that in principle also comprises the sociopolitical imaginary of Charles Taylor's "secular age."

In light of the above it may be possible to suggest that the historicization and deconstruction of religion as a universal that is carried out by the genealogical school can also be seen as a contribution to the idea of the *post*secular in the sense that the *post* is at once a demand that the modern secular-liberal epistemology should account for itself and at the same time suggestive of the possibility of alternative epistemologies. Based as it is on a loss of faith in the myth of political modernity—namely, that the liberal-secular state is necessary to save us from the violent consequences of religion entering into the public domain, a myth that eventually emerged from the idea of religion as a universal concept applicable to other cultures (Hume, Hegel, etc.)—this particular version of the postsecular questions the role of the modern secular state and its functionaries the modern university and the media as forms of technology that invest in the production of religion and religious subjects in order to maintain the sovereign integrity of the state. In bringing to light the often hidden function of secularism as a religion-making machine, this notion of the postsecular helps to release the space of the political from the grasp of the secularization doctrine. Or as Asad states toward the end of his *Formations of the Secular*: "If the secularization thesis no longer carries the conviction it once did, this is because the categories of politics and religion turn out to implicate each other more profoundly than we thought, a discovery that has accompanied our growing understanding of the powers of the modern nation-state."[56]

The Aporia of Post-Secular-Religion

Although Asad clearly diagnoses the problems associated with the liberal imaginary by pushing us to understand the "ambiguities" of the moral-political language of our secularism, it would appear that he is unwilling to go beyond just examining these ambiguities. But as Ananda Abeysekara asks, is it enough to go on problematizing and thereby inheriting such ambiguities in the name of secularism?[57] This question is pertinent since Asad also believes that we can neither simply receive the heritage of secularism nor just abandon its legacy. At this point it would seem that Asad comes tantalizing close to acknowledging the nature of contemporary religio-secular as an aporia, an irresolvable contradiction: "As a value-space, liberalism today provides its advocates with a common political and moral language (whose ambiguities and aporias allow it to evolve) in which to identify problems and with which to dispute."[58] So Asad recognizes the aporetic nature of the problem, but this is as far as he goes. He does not go so far as to actually grasp the nettle of aporia. This is partly because Asad's dominant method of inquiry remains restricted to a genealogical critique in the style of Foucault, and partly because this mode of critique appeals to the notional practice of history. In a way that echoes our critique above of the circular relationship among history, secular critique, and the liberal imaginary, Abeysekara in his *Politics of Postsecular Religion* argues that "both these positions [secularist and those critical of secularist politics] are animated by the belief that answers to the problems of our political present are available within our present.... That is, they are available at the end of a defense of the history of secularism or a critique of that history, by way of a defense of a nonsecular history in our present itself."[59]

In this volume we aim for an approach that draws on many of the insights from the three main strands of scholarship on religion and the secular outlined above. In addition, though, we also strive for an approach that is cognizant of the aporia at the heart of the religion/secular problematic by simultaneously inheriting and uninheriting its legacy. Coined by Abeysekara, the notion of un-inheriting suggests a path of thinking that treats any heritage (e.g., religion, the secular, democracy, etc.) as an irresolvable contradiction, an impossible inheritance, an aporia. Bearing this in mind we therefore retain a certain usage of the term *postsecular*, not as a means to revalorize religious epistemes but as a way of abandoning-embracing religious and secular epistemes as mutually contaminated and contaminating. In other words, we argue for a perspective that is postsecular as well as postreligious and, to the extent that the religious and the secular are epistemologically and semantically linked, for a perspective that is *post-secular-religious*. The focus needs to be shifted away from one that inquires and thus, consciously or not, reifies the dialectic of the religio-secular construct and the politics in which it is embedded. Trying to grasp the aporia outlined above we strive for a metaperspective that scrutinizes the religio-secular construct in all its epistemological and theologico-political facets.

Approaches that subvert and transgress the secular–religious paradigm have helped to foster alternative ways to question the manner in which these apparently universal concepts were translated during the nineteenth and twentieth century into non-Western contexts and indeed continue to be translated in contemporary geopolitics. One of the key contributions of this book is that it brings together (a) perspectives that show how religion is produced discursively rather than objectively found, and how religion is produced in relation to rather than in separation from secularism, with (b) (historicizing) perspectives that work out the extent to which the origins and contemporary forms of modernity/secularity are theological/Christian/metaphysical and so on. The unlikely convergences between these two approaches are rapidly changing the field of religious studies. The combination of discursive and historical perspectives makes visible the way in which the religio-secular emerges as evident episteme in the normalization of cultural sameness and difference. The task that this book undertakes is to explore the claims of the religio-secular paradigm and their implications through specific examples of "world religions" or "world secularisms" in a variety of contexts (India, France, Turkey, Germany, Burma, and the United States). The urgency of such a task is underscored by the fact that varieties of the secularization thesis continue to thrive in public discourses, among indigenous non-Western practitioners and also within certain lines of scholarly analysis. The tension between theoretical analysis and practical reifications of the secularization thesis at the local level remains a challenge for critical scholarship even as the latter points to its limits within global and local political contexts.

In response to this tension the contributors inquire into the theory and politics behind local and transnationally operative reifications of the religious and the secular. Each chapter, in different ways, voices intellectual and political suspicion of the modernist paradigm and particularly secularization theory as an explanatory model interconnected with the various forms of religio-secularism. The dismantling of the different subtheses of secularization theory (the privatization, differentiation, and decline theses, respectively[60]) has been based on historical, epistemological, and normative grounds.[61] Without totally denying the heuristic value of certain elements of secularization theory, the essays in this volume analyze particular historical contexts and compare the various trajectories of the secularizing processes—specifically their connections to particular knowledge regimes of secularism. Moreover, the contributors all take as their point of departure a need to interrogate the liberal assumption, historically rooted in a particular reading of the European Wars of Religion, that secularization in terms of differentiation between religious (church) and political (state) domains would be a necessity for the establishment and maintenance of religious tolerance and freedom. Taken together, they reflect a major shift in thinking about religion and the secular that has been taking place in recent years.

These reflections evolve, broadly speaking, in a post-secular-religious frame, which understands the public roles of religion not as explainable, and preliminary, phenomena (as the evolutionist paradigm of modernism would hold) or as regrettable aberrations that ought to be fought (as the liberal bias dictates). Rather, the post-secular-religious turn in the study of religion can be described as a scholarly attitude that not only is critically engaged with the assumptions and politics of the religio-secular paradigm but seeks to open up new spaces for the study of religion by self-consciously taking into account the historicity and thus perspectivity that such study necessarily entails. The post-secular-religious stance opens perspectives that allow for new epistemologies and methodologies with regard to the religious and the secular, freed from the monofocal, evolutionist, and Eurocentric assumptions of the modernist framework that links religion and politics as a binary pair and to that extent remains attached to organicist perceptions of division (between the religious and the secular/politics) or integrality (as evidenced in the discourse of the theologico-political). The contributions to this volume reflect such post-secular-religious awareness, point to new directions of inquiry, and hopefully will stimulate further reflection into the dynamics, genealogies, concepts, and sensitivities around the politics of religion and secularism.

■ POLITICS OF RELIGION-MAKING

The realities of global and local early-twenty-first-century politics put scholars critical of the religio-secular paradigm in a challenging position. While most of us engage in theoretical projects that take for granted the failure of secularism—indeed, many of us would question or reject most if not all of the premises of secularization theory—it has to be acknowledged that at the level of everyday politics the religio-secular discourse has, especially in times of a perceived "return of religion," not lost its pervasiveness (as, for example, Charles Taylor's designation for our "secular age", secularity 3, indicates). To the contrary, this "return" has reinvigorated secularist forces, which often respond with interpretations of the role of religion in political conflicts invoking pictures of a cultural if not civilizational clash. The political reality forces us, paraphrasing Talal Asad, to think about the conditions in which the dichotomies between "the religious" and "the secular" *do* (still) seem to make sense in so many public discourses.[62] Such inquiry needs to ask questions about political and epistemological hegemony: "How, when, and by whom are the categories of religion and the secular defined? What assumptions are presupposed in the acts that define them?"[63] In different ways, the chapters constituting this volume tackle these programmatic questions. They analyze cases where religion does seem to make sense and investigate how notions of religion and the secular are reified within specific, local and transnational, competitions for intellectual, material, and political resources.

The key concept or "critical term" that has guided the work of the contributors to this volume is *religion-making*. Broadly conceived the term *religion-making* refers to the ways in which religion(s) is conceptualized and institutionalized within the matrix of a globalized world-religions discourse in which ideas, social formations, and social/cultural practices are discursively reified as "religious" ones. Religion-making works, sometimes more and sometimes less explicitly, by means of normalizing and often functionalist discourses centered around certain taken-for-granted notions, such as the religion/secular binary, as well as binaries subordinated to it (such as sacred/profane, this-worldly/otherworldly, etc.).[64] We see the notion of religion-making not as a homogeneous analytical concept, but, rather, we see it as a heuristic device that allows us to bring into conversation a wide range of perspectives on practices and discourses that reify religion (as well as its various subcategories and associated others, such as, most prominently, the secular). Religion-making is thus a heuristic tool for analysis and deconstruction, and does not have any aspirations of reinstating notions of authenticity and essence through the backdoor by comparing different religion-making projects. The critical work done by the term *religion-making* is not concerned with the evaluation of authorizing and legitimating claims of any particular religion-making politics in a normative or normalizing sense. Far from aiming to endorse any particular religion-making processes, we rather want to foster perspectives through which these processes are contextualized and historicized within the frameworks of particular epistemes of religion and the secular, respectively.

The chapters of this volume incorporate and combine theoretical (philosophical/theologico-political) with descriptive-analytical (historical/sociological/anthropological) modes of critique. In this way the volume seeks to avoid the impasse between theory and empiricism that continues to be a hallmark of many books with a focus on the politics of religion and secularism. Without losing sight of the theoretical issues that are constitutive of this volume, in regard to the politics that we put under the critical lens, it is useful to distinguish typically among three different levels and discourses of religion-making, as well as the linkages between them: (1) *religion-making from above*, that is, as a strategy from a position of power, where religion becomes an instrument of governmentality, a means to legitimize certain politics and positions of power; (2) *religion-making from below*, that is, as a politics where particular social groups in a subordinate position draw on a religionist discourse to reestablish their identities as legitimate social formations distinguishable from other social formations through tropes of religious difference and/or claims for certain rights; and (3) *religion-making from (a pretended) outside*, that is, scholarly discourses on religion that provide legitimacy to the first two processes of religion-making by systematizing and thus normalizing the religious/secular binary and its derivates.

What we term *religion-making from above* refers to authoritative discourses and practices that define and confine things (symbols, languages, practices) as "religious" and "secular" through the disciplining means of the modern state and its institutions (such as lawmaking, the judiciary, state bureaucracies, state media, and the public education system).[65] While state institutions represent dominant positions of power within public discourse, other nonstate actors in the public sphere might also sometimes assume positions of normative efficacy, be it certain media (mainly print and television, possibly also the Internet), influential public personalities (opposition politicians, public intellectuals, showbiz and media stars), NGOs, or corporate enterprises. The example of neoliberal U.S. pundits arguing for a remaking of Islam may serve as an example to illustrate the often unabashedly political nature of such religion-making, revealing itself in very Foucauldian ways as an act of governmentality aimed at creating liberal-secular subjects. In a 2003 report published by the RAND Corporation, a conservative U.S. think tank, the "Islamic world" is depicted as in a severe crisis of identity posing a major threat to the "rest of the World."[66] Islam needed to be brought in line with Western/American interests. It is a difficult operation, as is frankly admitted: "It is no easy matter to transform a major world religion. If 'nation-building' is a daunting task, 'religion-building' is immeasurably more perilous and complex."[67] One of the heralds of neocon U.S. American dreams of civilizing Islam, Daniel Pipes, drove this language one step further.[68] In 2004 he remarked that the "ultimate goal" of the "war on terrorism" was "religion-building" in the sense of a modernization of Islam.[69] In his view, "only when Muslims turn to secularism will this terrible era of their history come to an end."[70] The imperialist tone of such statements is part of the rhetoric of the "new world order" and the "Middle East Project" envisioned by the conservative U.S. political circles that had been related closely to the Bush administration. To sum up the hardly concealed concern behind the arguments of the cited U.S. neocon pundits, the West/United States has to engage in a remaking of Islam, analogous to nation-building referred to as religion-building, with the goal to create a modern, that is, secular, Islam in line with American interests and a neoliberal, modernist frame for religion as secured by the doctrine of secularism.[71] The examples point not only to imperialist ambitions within U.S. politics, but more broadly exemplify drastically how political religion-making discourses can be. In line with the U.S. American tradition of liberal secularism, U.S. religion-builders are less concerned with keeping religion out of politics than with regulating its political manifestations.[72]

While scholars of postcolonial studies have discussed the role of religious and secular discourses in the legitimation and administration of the nation-state, less attention has been directed to cases in which marginalized sociocultural communities have adopted the language of religion as a means of empowerment vis-à-vis assimilationist politics directed against them. Such *religion-making from below* forms a dialectical relationship with religion-making from above, implicitly accepting the latter's hegemony to the language and semantics of which it responds. Whether perceived as acts of emancipation, appropriation, or subversion against hegemonic religious and secular knowledge regimes, religion-making from below has played important roles in local discourses of religion and secularism.[73]

Religion-making from below operates via processes of cultural translation. Translation here needs to be understood as a two-way relationship. Translation of the language of the religio-secular construct into new territories can be forceful

and violent, as evidenced amply in postcolonial studies. But one should not understand the appropriation of religio-secularist discourses as necessarily resulting
from coercion. Credit needs to be given to the more complex dynamics of agency
in the adaptation of these discourses in non-Western vernacular languages. Charles
Hallisey has discussed this dynamic as "*intercultural mimesis*—a phrase denoting
the cultural interchange that occurs between the native and the Orientalist in the
construction of Western knowledge about 'the Orient.'"[74] In other words, while it
is indisputable that the politics of translation of the concept of religion beyond the
Christian West were molded by the power imbalance that is characteristic of
Orientalist scholarship and its objects of study, analysis of this translation process
has to provide sufficient space for the agency of local appropriations of elements of
this discourse. We need to think the appropriation of the Western discourses of
religion and the secular in a manner that does not reduce local actors to the role of
passive objects but instead focuses on "local productions of meaning," that is, the
agency of locals in the encounter with Orientalist knowledge.[75]

Triggered by the emerging field of postcolonial studies following Edward Said's
Orientalism (1978), awareness of academia's complicity in the essentialization of
particular others has increased considerably. The work of Said and those who followed in his footsteps has forced those associated with historically "Orientalist"
disciplines to reflect on the history of these disciplines and their role within imperialist projects. The multifold implications of scholars in imperialist projects
unmasks pretensions of objectivity and reveals that *religion-making from the pretended outside* is often closely linked with more politically motivated religion-
making from above.[76] The academic study of religion in particular has been
implicated in imperialist projects and Eurocentric discourses more generally, and
it still plays, especially in the United States, where its institutional position is much
stronger than in Western Europe and despite an admitted increase in self-critical
reflection to this extent, an important role in the objectification of religion(s).[77]
Unraveling such entanglements, as an inquiry into the politics of religion-making
brings along, is therefore a challenging project particularly for the discipline of
religious studies, since it entails the theoretical and methodological deconstruction of the very concept ("religion") through which this discipline is legitimated.
World-religion courses are flourishing, and classes of this or similar kind belong to
the bread-and-butter courses of many religious studies departments. It will be
interesting to see in which ways the academic discipline of religious studies can
respond to the challenges that it will have to face once it recognizes and positions
itself more deliberately toward the historical biases that contributed to its creation,
as well as the religion- politics in which it is still involved.[78] The problem of course
is not new, and most of the readers of this volume will be familiar with J. Z. Smith's
controversial dictum "Religion is solely the creation of the scholar's study."[79]
Tomoko Masuzawa's recent work on the *Invention of World Religions* has further
increased awareness of the urgency to raise critical self-reflection on the involvement of the academic study of religion in the making and re-making of the concept of religion. Beyond the very existential problem that this constitutes for
institutions organized around religious studies an academic discipline, the relationship between this discipline and the genealogy of the religion and world-religion

concepts is itself an interesting and most important field of inquiry. In this context Peterson and Walhof have rightly asked about "what is the proper agenda for religious studies in a context in which the object of study, religion, has been invented or worked over by powerful economic, social, and political forces."[80] Such questions need to be addressed in order to understand better the role of both academic and political elites and institutions in the making and remaking of "religion" and the "secular".

■ CHAPTER OUTLINES

As part of his critique of liberal secularism, Talal Asad has pointed out that the "effort of defining religion converges with the liberal demand in our time that it be kept quite separate from politics, law, and science," in effect separating religion from power.[81] This volume takes Asad's criticism seriously and puts the focus exactly on those dynamics of power through which the discourses of religion and the secular have been historically formatted and are being maintained in the context of the hegemony of more and less liberal secularisms and the nationalist, culturalist/civilizationist, imperialist, as well as economic interests with which they have been aligned.

We have organized the chapters into groups according to common themes. The first group of chapters addresses the relationship between modernity and colonialism in the generation of discourses about Hinduism and Buddhism (Richard King), Sikhs and Hindus (Arvind-Pal S. Mandair), and Muslims (Ruth Mas) via the imposition upon indigenous discourses of a category religion duly separated from the secular. In his essay "Imagining Religions in India: Colonialism and the Mapping of South Asian History and Culture" Richard King focuses on the question of how we study and engage with Asian thought, traditions, and culture when their very representation and configuration have been so radically altered by the encounter with European colonialism and the processes of modernity. The colonial domination of the West over "the Rest" in recent centuries has caused many Western paradigms and categories to appear more universal and normative than they might otherwise have seemed. Echoing our earlier discussion of "generalized translation" that is so central to the cognitive mechanism of modern Western comparative imaginary, King argues that "religion" is a key feature in the colonial cartography that serves as a cognitive map for surveying, classifying, and interpreting diverse cultural and historical terrains and allows a distinction to be drawn between secular and religious spheres of life. King asks whether, by inverting the colonial move, new light can be thrown on features of Western culture if they were to be examined afresh in terms of the cartographic imagination of *other* cultures. But rather than doing away with the term *religion*, as some suggest, King argues for a double strategy, a "double move" that contests and interrogates but also actively rereads such taken-for-granted concepts of the Western cartographic imagination in new and imaginative ways.

In his essay entitled "Translations of Violence: Secularism and Religion-Making in the Discourses of Sikh Nationalism," Arvind-Pal S. Mandair continues to probe the role of generalized translation (or what Richard King has called the "macropolitics of translation") in the manufacture of parallel discourses of religious nationalism (in this case Sikh) and discourses of violence by the secular Indian state. Bringing attention to a general reluctance on the part of scholars to move beyond the language of secularism, Mandair shows how the strict opposition between religious nationalist and state secularist discourses has been sustained by a typology of violence that itself emanates from a Westphalian/Enlightenment interdiction against "religion" as a phenomenon that must remain outside the public realm, a gesture that has been repeated in state, mediatic, and academic discourses alike. Through a deconstruction of the conventional typology of violence Mandair points to a third form of violence, namely, "symbolic violence." This is a violence that is embedded within language (exemplified by the mechanism of "generalized translation") that had coerced Indian reformist elites during the nineteenth and early twentieth centuries into translating their cultural concepts through the category of religion during the colonial era. This translation into the category of religion involved a simultaneous interdiction of indigenous modes of enunciation and temporality and "conversion" into the secular time of empire and modernity (history). Mandair's essay concludes by asking what implications this unraveling of violence and secularism in the making of religious nationalist discourses might have for conceptually refashioning conventional models of secular democracy.

The "conversion" from indigenous to secular modes of time is also addressed in Ruth Mas's essay "On the Apocalyptic Tones of Islam in Secular Time." With the empirical focus on recent debates about the compatibility of Islam and *laïcité* in France, Mas discusses the role of reformist Muslim Franco-Maghrebi intellectuals such as Fethi Benslama and Malek Chebel in the subordination of Islam to liberal-secularist discourse. As she argues, these Muslim intellectuals are deeply entrenched in colonial apologetics, have basically accepted the civilizationist prejudices of French discourse, and have begun to endorse, at the expense of traditional Islamic conceptions of time, homogenizing secular temporalities. Mas shows how they have subscribed to a liberal-secular narrative that, relativizing apologetic renditions of the colonial past while simultaneously homogenizing violent Islamic otherness, semantically links notions of a barbarous Islamic past with secular apocalyptic visions projected onto Islam. Engaging a critical reading of Hardt and Negri's work on empire, she connects her argument about secular time to the homogenizing imperialist tendencies in the French secularization of Islam and argues, drawing on Asad, for a perspective that does not singularize historical experiences but allows for heterogeneous temporalities and Muslim subjectivities.

The second set of chapters interrogates the relationship between the liberal imaginary and the making of the modern category of religion as reflected in discourses of religious violence (Brian Goldstone), spirituality (Kerry A. Mitchell), and mysticism (Rosemary R. Hicks). In his essay "Secularism, 'Religious Violence,' and the Liberal Imaginary" Brian Goldstone interrogates the category of "religious violence" as it has been deployed by terrorism experts who offer causes and remedies for religiously motivated acts of violence. Resonating strongly with Mandair's earlier discussion of secular violence and religion, Goldstone examines the work of a variety of writers including Bruce Lincoln, Mark Juergensmeyer, Slavoj Žižek, and Charles Kimball, asking what place the category of religious violence holds in the liberal imaginary. What work does it perform, and what types of ethico-political formations does it necessitate? Following Talal Asad, Goldstone suggests that these questions are directly concerned with the concept of secularism, which in its liberal democratic version indicates a complex relationship to religion that cannot be reduced to an opposition between them. Rather, Goldstone argues, it is the case that "specific kinds of religion" are constantly being valorized and denounced, empowered and made redundant. Thus the demand of liberal democratic society is not so much that religious phenomena be removed from the public sphere but that religious beliefs and practices be calibrated in accordance with transcendent values of a particular way of life. In fact the modern secular state provides a mechanism for ordering and integrating individuals according to new forms and patterns. One of the author's main concerns is to interrogate not what "religious violence" means or why it happens but to ask what it does and, perhaps most urgently, what it stands for. For Goldstone there are distinct resonances between the discourses of religious violence and political formations such as secularism. These resonances include a concept of religion based on the opposition between a terrifying figure of the premodern past, on the one hand, and an Enlightened believer at home in the world, on the other. While the latter is rendered normative, the former has to be subject to correction or made extinct. The discourse of religion is what makes this project work.

One of the aims of Kerry Mitchell's essay "The Politics of Spirituality: Liberalizing the Definition of Religion" is to deconstruct liberal assumptions behind dominant strands in the North American scholarship on religion. Analyzing the writings on spirituality by writers such as Robert Wuthnow, Wade C. Roof, and Leigh E. Schmidt, Mitchell shows how they read liberal agendas into spirituality and thusly obscure the importance of the social practices in which discourses of spirituality are imbedded. He points to the methodological and theoretical problems posed by implicit concepts of freedom, self, and subjectivity in this literature. Alternatively, he argues for an approach that, informed by the work of Michel Foucault and Niklas Luhmann, would make explicit the social and political work of spirituality. In other words, Mitchell advocates a historically informed perspective that prevents a subjectivism that does not take into account the social relations in which notions of self are created (Luhmann) and takes seriously the power dynamics by which particular notions of the subject or the self, which form the subtext of the concept of spirituality, are evidenced (Foucault).

Rosemary R. Hicks's chapter "Comparative Religion and the Cold War Transformation of Indo-Persian 'Mysticism' into Liberal Islamic Modernity" aims at disentangling the complex connections between Cold War politics and academic institution-building as it unfolds in North American conceptualizations of Islamic mysticism. Historicizing the intellectual trajectories of a group of leading Western Islamicists, with a focus on Wilfred Cantwell Smith and Seyyed Hossein Nasr, Hicks traces their intellectual and political networks and their role in the evolution of a Sufism-biased school of Islamic studies in North America. Characteristic of these formulations of Islamic mysticism is their conceptual framework centered on notions of rationality, freedom, and individual faith with clear Protestant leanings. These notions are implicated in a differentiation between kinds of religion/Islam and are used in political projects of religion-making in line with Western/American interests. Hicks's analysis of the work and legacy of Smith in particular shows how his belief in the prevalence and necessity of faith made him uphold against believers of secularism a positive and prevailing notion of universal religion, that is, mysticism. Her contribution illustrates in an exemplary way the work of religious/Islamic studies in the (re)making of its subject and the way this reification is influenced by religious and political preferences.

The final set of chapters, by Greg Johnson, Markus Dressler, Mark Elmore, Alicia Turner, and Michael Nijhawan discusses contestations of the content and boundaries of religion between state institutions and particular communities. From different perspectives they address the role of state institutions such as the judiciary (Johnson and Dressler) and governmental administrations (Elmore and Turner), as well as the role of public discourse (Nijhawan) in the normalization of definitions of "religion" against potentially subversive local practices. The chapter by Greg Johnson, titled "Apache Revelation: Making Indigenous Religion in the Legal Sphere," discusses Apache claims regarding the religious quality of objects traditionally used in ritual contexts. Within a legal dispute with U.S. museums about the repatriation of these objects, Apache representatives invoked the theme of revelation and argue that the disputed objects constitute cultural patrimony, would therefore be inalienable, and could not be subject to property rights. Insinuating that the choice of language on the part of the Apache reflects a conscious appropriation of hegemonic tropes of religion, Johnson remarks that the "native representatives know more about how the category 'religion' works than many scholars of religion." As he describes, the Apache representatives were successfully drawing on both *majority-inclusive* and *minority-specific* discourses to strengthen their case. In their majority-inclusive discourse they employed an analogy to Jewish and Christian tropes, especially the finality of revelation, thusly creating a sympathetic audience for their claims. As Johnson stresses, the rhetoric of the Apache is successful not because of its content but because of its form, which "announces nonfalsifiable claims to authority" in line with the majority-inclusive discourse and metaphorically invokes Christian examples.

Markus Dressler's essay "Making Religion through Secularist Legal Discourse: The Case of Turkish Alevism" investigates into the dynamic relationship between knowledge regimes of secularism and notions of legitimate religion. Using the example of Turkish Alevis, he shows how laicist discourse can encourage the casting of communal identities in religious language. Dressler is particularly interested in how Alevi claims of difference from the mainstream Sunni community are negotiated in judicial contestations. While the Turkish courts are generally considered one of the strongholds of secularism, Turkish legal discourse is—and this becomes clearest when it defines and normalizes the boundaries of legitimate religion in the public—also drawing on notions of religion clearly shaped by Islam. Dressler's discussion of legal debates on the nature and legitimacy of Alevi symbols and practices provides both a window into the dynamics between conflicting trajectories of Turkish secularism and insights into the semantics of the concept of religion hegemonic in the Turkish public sphere. He points to the role of legal discourse in the institutionalization of particular knowledge regimes of secularism and shows how Alevis have learned to use the legal arena as a medium to advance their cause for recognition. The contributions by Johnson and Dressler exemplify the role of legal discourse in the normalization and contestation of the religio-secular. Additionally, the comparison between the ways in which concepts of religion are legally contested in the two countries points to interesting differences in the respective forms of secularism. While the evidentiary parameters of the Native American Graves Protection and Repatriation Act expressively acknowledge the validity of religious claims next to secular claims, in Turkish law and judiciary practice religious claims have no formal validity, and religious semantics enter secularist rhetoric in more indirect ways.

Similar to Dressler's, Mark Elmore's contribution, titled "Bloody Boundaries: Animal Sacrifice and the Labor of Religion," points to mechanisms by which the nation-state redefines legitimate religious practices and tries to endorse meanings of "religion" that help bolster agendas of "national unity" against regional or communalist particularisms. Elmore examines the debate over the legitimacy of animal sacrifice in the northwestern Indian state of Himachal Pradesh. This debate has come to redefine the meaning and function of religion in the region as it reflexively shapes Himachali self-understanding. The concern over the legitimacy of animal sacrifice hinges on the competition between alternative definitions of religion and how these definitions come to be inscribed within a particular configuration of human life. As a regime of truth this configuration provides the horizons of intelligibility against which religion becomes an object to be saved, reformed, or simply eradicated. Arguing that many of the recent conflicts over public religion and the definition of religion are simply misplaced, Elmore suggests that debates over the disappearance or return of religion deploy conceptualizations of religion that are not sufficiently nuanced. In contradistinction, Elmore adopts a different starting point. He assumes that the task of defining the boundaries between religion and its others—what he calls the "labor of religion"—is both historically conditioned and unstable and develops, moreover, in relation to specific regimes of truth and intellectual horizons. Indeed the conceptual and practical structures that make religion legible are themselves shifting. Elmore's task in this essay is not to recover essences around which formations of religion develop but to identify and analyze the regimes of truth, their strategic operations, and the politics that they legitimize. From this perspective, not only does the debate over animal sacrifice challenge the very foundations upon which discussions of secularism, modernity, and European hegemony are based, it also destabilizes the frames used to separate religion and the secular.

While much of contemporary scholarship in the field of religion and colonialism points to the rather successful production of secular and religious formations as universal categories of experience in former European colonies, Alicia Turner's chapter "Religion Making and Its Failures: Turning Monasteries into Schools and Buddhism into a Religion in Colonial Burma" investigates an example of the failures of the colonial category of religion. Focusing on Burmese Buddhism under British rule during the second half of the nineteenth century, Turner's essay brings attention to the British administration's unsuccessful attempts to transform

Buddhist pedagogy in monasteries. Burmese Buddhism presents an interesting anomaly, as Buddhism was central to the emergence of the concept of "world religions" in European discourse. Turner's essay explores how, in this instance, the colonial categories of religion failed to constrain Buddhist practices even when there were clear parallels to the European conceptualization of religion. Unlike Anglo-vernacular schools in India, which are considered the paradigmatic location in which new pedagogies were instrumental in replacing the indigenous forms of conceptuality (see Mandair's chapter), "religion" did not always succeed as a colonial ordering mechanism. In fact Burmese Buddhist monks rejected the colonial blueprint for primary education, which would have conflicted with Buddhist universal categories by facilitating the transfer and appropriation of religion and secular as universal categories. This chapter provides a interesting case demonstrating local resistance to European universals.

The final chapter by Michael Nijhawan, entitled "Precarious Presences, Hallucinatory Times: Configurations of Religious Otherness in German Leitkulturalist Discourse," investigates German "leitkulturalism" as a discursive mode of culturalist argumentation that links progressive-leftist and mainstream populist positions in reiterated gestures of identifying the religiously "weird" as the ultimate other(s). Focusing on the anti-mosque movement in Europe, Nijhawan charts out how especially within German civil society religious otherness becomes the locus not so much of a simple juxtaposition of the West and Islam(ism), but of a more contracted and refracted Orientalism that is nonetheless forcefully stigmatizing and exclusivist in its implications for specific immigrant subjects; in Nijhawan's case these are Ahmadi and Sikh subjects. Nijhawan illustrates how doctrinal forms and embodied practices of Sikh and Ahmadi subjects are translated as "abject" beings, a move which, particularly in the case of the Ahmadis, is produced through translations of a colonial language of heretic sectarianism. In his chapter, Nijhawan not only complicates how the religion-secular dichotomy is reconfigured in the European context (German having been pointed at as a counter-model to France in respect to the notion of laicism), he also traces out the internal fault lines and discursive ruptures in public framings of these dichotomies such as those of "moderate/fundamentalist" religion; as well as the modalities through which notions of taboo, blasphemy and transgression (see Asad) are negotiated both in distinction from and resonance with a more global configuration of such themes in Europe and North-America.

With this introduction we hope to have accomplished the following things. First, we have developed a framework for placing the historical and contemporary debate on religion and secularism within its epistemological and political contexts in a way that highlights the dependency of modern religio-secular discourses on a particular conceptualization of the historical and the way it is related to a particular kind of rationality. Second, we have made, as a reflection of this critique of the rationality of secular Western historicizing, a point for a reframing of the notion "postsecular" in a way that includes the religious in its conceptual criticism, adding up to a post-secular-religious perspective and thusly helping to shake the religio-secular paradigm. Third, we have provided an overview on the concrete politics of religion-making, or, in other words, the work of liberal-secular contestations and reifications of the religious and its various others. Finally, we hope to have shown—and this argument will be strengthened by the individual contributions of this volume—not only that important theoretical work has been done toward a debunking of conventional ways of conceptualizing religion and the secular within modernist frameworks but that this theorizing is based on and reflects new and ambitious empirical work on the formation of religio-secular discourses and practices.

■ NOTES

We owe thanks to Ted Vial and Elizabeth Shakman Hurd for their critical comments on an earlier version of this introduction.

1. See Dipesh Chakrabarty, *Provincializing Europe* (Princeton: Princeton University Press, 2000).

2. Casanova uses the expression "to point to the power of secularism as a historical idea that turned, at least in the case of Western Europe, into a self-fulfilling prophecy." He argues that "the secularization of Western European societies can be explained better in terms of the triumph of the knowledge regime of secularism, than in terms of structural processes of socio-economic development such as urbanization, education, rationalization, etc." José Casanova, "Immigration and the New Religious Pluralism: A EU/US Comparison," paper presented at the conference "New Religious Pluralism and Democracy," Georgetown University, April 21–22, 2005, 7, http://www.ipri.pt/eventos/pdf/Paper_Casanova.pdf (accessed: March 14, 2010).

3. Charles Taylor, *A Secular Age* (Cambridge: Harvard University Press, 2007), 534.

4. We see the persistence of this approach throughout the book. This is evident, for example, in one of the first claims advanced, where Taylor suggests that "we" who live in a secular age have reached a consensus about its secular nature: "Almost everyone would agree that in some sense we do [live in a secular age]: I mean the 'we' who live in the West, or perhaps Northwest, or otherwise put, the North Atlantic world—although secularity extends also partially, and in different ways, beyond this world" (ibid., 1).

5. Michael Warner, Jonathon VanAntwerpen, and Craig Calhoun, "Editors' Introduction," in *Varieties of Secularism in a Secular Age*, eds. Michael Warner, Jonathon VanAntwerpen, and Craig Calhoun (Cambridge: Harvard University Press, 2010), 23.

6. Some of the most prominent names associated with this school that has deployed the revived idiom of post-Kantian Continental thought in relation to the study of religion include John Milbank, John Caputo, Mark C. Taylor, Gianni Vattimo, Kevin Hart, Richard Kearney, Hent de Vries, and Slavoj Žižek.

7. John D. Caputo, *On Religion* (London: Routledge, 2001), 37.

8. A version of this can be seen in Mark C. Taylor, *After God* (Chicago: University of Chicago Press, 2008), 132.

9. A particularly useful source here is Ananda Abeysekara's recent paper "The Im-Possibility of Secular Critique. The Future of Religion's Memory," *Culture and Religion* 11, no.3 (2010): 213–246.

10. A more detailed version of this argument can be found in chapter 2 of Arvind Mandair, *Religion and the Specter of the West* (New York: Columbia University Press, 2009).

11. Taylor, *After God*, 55.

12. Ibid., 62.

13. Ibid., 64.

14. Couze Venn, *Occidentalism: Modernity and Subjectivity* (London: Sage Publications, 2000), 109.

15. Ibid., 130; emphasis added.

16. Ibid., 131.

17. For a wider treatment of this topic, see, for example, Andrew Bowie, *Aesthetics and Subjectivity* (Manchester: Manchester University Press, 1998); also Mark C. Taylor, *Dis-Figuring: Art, Architecture, Religion* (Chicago: University of Chicago Press, 1992).

18. Caputo, *On Religion*, 42–44.

19. Taylor, *After God*, 111.

20. Martin Heidegger, "Age of the World Picture," in *The Question Concerning Technology and Other Essays*, trans. William Lovitt (New York: Harper Torchbooks, 1982), 128.

21. Taylor, *After God*, 159.

22. G. W. F. Hegel, *Phenomenology of Spirit*, trans. A. V. Miller (Oxford: Clarendon Press, 1977), 21.

23. Venn, *Occidentalism*, 147.

24. Ibid., 147.

25. The term *generalized translation* is borrowed from Jacques Derrida (see "Theology of Translation," in *Eyes of the University: The Right to Philosophy II* [Stanford: Stanford University Press, 2004], 65).

26. Venn, *Occidentalism*, 147.

27. Although he does not refer to Hegel specifically, a similar point is made by Gil Anidjar in his recent book *Semites: Race, Religion, Literature* (Stanford: Stanford University Press, 2008). Anidjar argues that the secularization that is inherent within Christianity can be seen as a history in which "Christianity turned against itself in a complex and ambivalent series of parallel movements, continuous gestures and rituals, reformist and counterreformist, or revolutionary and not-so-revolutionary upheavals and reversals while slowly coming to name that which it came to ultimately oppose itself: Religion" (45). Christianity, Anidjar writes, "judged and named itself, re-incarnated itself, as 'secular.'" In so doing, Christianity became the "religion" in relation/opposition to its others, *religions*. The name religion is its secularized garb: "Secularism is a name Christianity gave itself when it invented 'religion,' named its other or others as 'religions'" (48). While agreeing with this assessment, we additionally point out the role of critique and critical thinking (the comparative imaginary) as essential to the production of religion and religions, that is, to the production of a universal concept of religion, all of which is worked out painstakingly in the writings of Hegel.

28. Samuel Huntington and Bernard Lewis are well-known examples on the Right. Representative of the center-Left position would be John Rawls and Jürgen Habermas, and, as for the study of Islam scholars such as Olivier Roy. In earlier publications Habermas tried to address the tensions between Western secularization and the Judeo-Christian ethico-religious heritage from which it arises, particularly in the aftermath of the demise of the Soviet Union and the rise in religious and ethnic nationalisms throughout Europe and other parts of the world. In essays such as "Citizenship and National Identity: Some Reflections on the Future of Europe" (*Praxis International* 12, no. 1 [April 1992]: 1–19), Habermas has indirectly drawn on John Rawls's recent work *Political Liberalism* (New York: Columbia University Press 2005), in which the latter outlines the idea of an "overlapping consensus" between different ethical-cultural perspectives, backed by "comprehensive" moral doctrines that can in turn give rise to a public space governed by a political culture, without any overt involvement of religion. More recently, though, Habermas has shifted his position to highlight the inescapable connection of Western political structures to the legacies and heritage of Western Christianity and Judaism. Indeed Habermas stresses that the role of "structures of consciousness," the "semantic potentials," and the "substance" of the Judeo-Christian

legacy must not be forgotten in contemporary secular political life. Underlying all of this is the influence of Max Weber's religious sociology as expounded in his classic study *The Protestant Ethic and the Spirit of Capitalism* (originally published in German in 1904-05). The central question for Weber was the historical influence of "world religions" on such "structures of consciousness" and whether certain religious worldviews hindered or enabled the rationalization of capitalist economics. While the influence of Kantian epistemology (especially his account of the imaginary) is evident in Habermas and Rawls, the key in understanding Weber's position is Hegel's notion of history and specifically the notion of *historical difference* that is so central to his understanding of the different capacities and motivations between world religions. See below.

29. Probably the best example is Slavoj Žižek, as well as Gianni Vattimo.

30. As Charles Taylor usefully reminds us, secularity in its modern Western sense can be considered the outcome of a "long history of reform movements within Christianity." While these reform movements began with efforts to purify Christianity of folk beliefs and practices, the reform effort was also responsible for the emergence of (1) an impersonal natural order in which God's intervention in nature became less frequent, (2) a purely natural science, (3) a transformation of the self as distanced from everything outside the mind, and perhaps most importantly, (4) a purification of the process of thinking as critique, that is, to a critical thinking that would become linked after the Enlightenment to atheism. But ironically, the reform movement started out by trying to improve Christianity. It is this effort to elevate and improve self, society, and thought that we term the "logic of reform." See Taylor, *A Secular Age*, 61–88.

31. Ibid., 63.

32. Jonathon Sheehan, "When Was Disenchantment? History and the Secular Age," in *Varieties of Secularism in a Secular Age*, ed. Michael Warner, Jonathan VanAntwerpen, and Craig Calhoun (Cambridge: Harvard University Press, 2009), 226.

33. Ibid., 238.

34. Ananda Abeysekara, *The Politics of Postsecular Religion. Mourning Secular Futures* (New York: Columbia University Press, 2008).

35. Sheehan, "When Was Disenchantment?" 240.

36. For similar arguments, see, for example, Sheehan, "When Was Disenchantment?"; see also Gil Anidjar's chapter "Secularism" in his *Semites*.

37. Robert Baird, "Late Secularism," in *Secularisms*, ed. Janet R. Jakobsen and Ann Pellengrini (Durham: Duke University Press, 2009), 165–66.

38. David Hume, *Natural History of Religion*, ed. A. Wayne Clover (New York: Oxford University Press, 1976), 33.

39. See Mandair, *Religion and the Specter of the West*.

40. This axis is, of course, entirely virtual, an imagined function of the narrative itself.

41. In one sense the comparative schema (underpinned by the religio-secular/postsecular) can be seen as part of a broader anxiety felt by European intellectuals about an originary diremption, a crisis of identity, at the heart of the intrinsically linked concepts of Europe, modernity, and Christianity. In other words, Hegel's response to this anxiety was not just epistemological but deeply political, a point that is echoed by Michael Hardt and Antonio Negri in their influential work *Empire*. According to Hardt and Negri, modernity was never a unitary concept but, rather, appeared in two ways. The first mode was a radical revolutionary process that broke with the past and declared the immanence of world and life, positing human desire at the center of history. For Hardt and Negri, the philosophy of Spinoza provides a good example of this tendency toward immanence. But it could also be discerned in the supposedly "pantheistic" philosophies of Oriental cultures, particularly those of India and China. Opposed to this, however, was a second mode of modernity,

which deployed a transcendental apparatus to suppress the potential for liberating the multitude. In the struggle for hegemony between these two modes, victory went to the second and hence to the forces of order that sought to neutralize the revolutionary effects of modernity. This internal conflict at the heart of European modernity was simultaneously reflected on a global scale in the form of external conflict. The same counterrevolutionary power that sought to control the potentially subversive forces within Europe also began to realize the possibility and necessity of subordinating other cultures to European domination. Eurocentrism was born as a reaction to the potentiality of a newfound human equality. See Antonio Negri and Michael D. Hardt, *Empire* (Cambridge: Harvard University Press, 2000), 74–77.

In many ways Hegel's reworking of the comparative imaginary of the West epitomizes this second mode of modernity. As Hardt and Negri point out, intellectual projects such as Hegel's "could not but take place against the historical backdrop of European expansion . . . [linked to] the very real violence of European conquest and colonialism." (ibid., 82)." However, the real threat for Hegel was not physical but intellectual—a threat to the very design of the *concept*. Hence the ontotheological schema can be considered a diagram of power that at the same time provided a mechanism of power for controlling the constituent and subversive forces within Europe that championed a revolutionary plane of immanence, as well as a "negation of non-European desire." During Hegel's tenure, the thought of his rivals, such as Schelling and later Schopenhauer, must be considered good examples of "non-European desire." For further details, see Mandair, *Religion and the Specter of the West*, 154–55.

42. The term 'meaning-value' is borrowed from Lydia Liu, "The Question of Meaning-Value in the Political Economy of the Sign," in *Tokens of Exchange: The Problem of Translation in Global Circulations*, ed. Lydia H. Liu (Durham: Duke University Press, 1999), 13–44.

43. See, for example, Tomoko Masuzawa, *The Invention of World Religions. Or, How European Universalism Was Preserved in the Language of Pluralism* (Chicago: University of Chicago Press, 2005). A detailed explanation of Hegel's epistemo-political schema can be found in Mandair, *Religion and the Specter of the West*, 147–60.

44. For a particularly helpful probing of the relationship between secularity and critique, see Talal Asad's recent essays in Wendy Brown, Talal Asad, Judith Butler, and Saba Mahmoud, eds., *Is Critique Secular? Blasphemy, Injury and Free Speech*, Townsend Papers in the Humanities, no. 2 (Berkeley: University of California Press, 2009).

45. We are by no means suggesting that Hegel's schema (or Hegelian ideology) was uncontested during the last two centuries. Far from it. All we suggest is that when one looks for a convergence of the key ciphers that constitute Western civilizational identity—as rooted in a convergence of Christianity, the "critical attitude," historicism, secularism, liberalism, democracy, freedom, etc.—it is Hegel more than any other thinker who brings them all together in a way that others were not able to do. And despite the fact that Hegelian thought was contested so vigorously, his basic schema, far from disappearing, seems to have morphed into what might be called the global/Western "social imaginary," partly through the more palatable and sophisticated renderings of his comparative schema, for example, by Karl Marx, Max Weber, Ernest Troeltsch, and any number of religionists during the twentieth century. Even today, if one looks closely at many of the postmodern and postsecular defenses of Western civilizational identity (e.g., Slavoj Žižek, Mark C. Taylor, and Charles Taylor, among others), Hegel is still a primary point of reference.

46. Rey Chow, *The Age of the World Target: Self-Referentiality in War, Theory and Comparative Work* (Durham: Duke University Press, 2006). For a fuller discussion on this, see also Mandair, *Religion and the Specter of the West* p. 40.

47. Anuradha Dingwaney and Rajeshwari Sundar Rajan, *The Crisis of Secularism in India* (Durham: Duke University Press, 2007), 3.

48. Ibid., 3–4.

49. One would have to include scholars such as Jonathon Z. Smith, Russell McCutcheon, Daniel Dubuisson, Timothy Fitzgerald, and Tomoko Masuzawa. See, for example, Jonathon Z. Smith, *Relating Religion. Essays in the Study of Religion* (Chicago: University of Chicago Press, 2003); Russell McCutcheon, *Manufacturing Religion. The Discourse on Sui Genesis Religion and the Politics of Nostalgia* (Oxford: Oxford University Press, 2003); Daniel Dubuisson, *The Western Construction of Religion* (Baltimore: John Hopkins University Press, 2003); Timothy Fitzgerald, *The Ideology of Religious Studies* (Oxford: Oxford University Press, 2003); Masuzawa, *Invention of World Religions.*

50. Prominent names include David Chidester, Richard King, Harjot Oberoi, Vasudha Dalmia, Saba Mahmood, and Peter van der Veer. See, for example, David Chidester, *Savage Systems. Colonialism and Comparative Religion in Southern Africa* (Charlottesville: University Press of Virginia, 1996); Richard King, *Orientalism and Religion: Postcolonial Theory, India and "the Mystic East"* (London: Routledge, 1999); Harjot Oberoi, *The Construction of Religious Boundaries: Culture, Identity, and Diversity in the Sikh Tradition* (Oxford: Oxford University Press, 1997); Vasudha Dalmia, *The Nationalization of Hindu Traditions* (Oxford: Oxford University Press, 1996); Saba Mahmood, *Politics of Piety. The Islamic Revival and the Feminist Subject* (Princeton: Princeton University Press, 2005); Peter van der Veer, *Imperial Encounters. Religion and Modernity in India and Britain* (Princeton: Princeton University Press, 2001). For additional recent critical literature on the concept of religion, see Richard King in this volume, pp. 54–55, n. 5.

51. Talal Asad, *Genealogies of Religion. Discipline and Reasons of Power in Christianity and Islam* (London: John Hopkins University Press, 1993); Talal Asad, *Formations of the Secular. Christianity, Islam, Modernity* (Stanford: Stanford University Press, 2003).

52. Hent de Vries, "Introduction: Before, Around, and Beyond the Theologico-Political," in *Political Theologies. Public Religions in a Post-secular World*, ed. Hent de Vries and Lawrence E. Sullivan (New York: Fordham University Press, 2006), 69.

53. There are, however, also voices from within this group of scholarship that argue that the trajectory of religion needs to be traced back into premodern times. An example is the work of late-antiquity scholar Daniel Boyarin, who locates the beginnings of the formation of the new kind of identity that we call religion in the differentiation of Christianity from Judaism in the fourth century. Daniel Boyarin, "Semantic Differences; or, 'Judaism'/'Christianity,'" in *The Ways That Never Parted: Jews and Christians in Late Antiquity and the Early Middle Ages*, ed. Adam Becker and Annette Yoshiko Reed (Minneapolis: Fortress Press, 2007), 65–85; Daniel Boyarin, *Dying for God* (Stanford: Stanford University Press, 1999), 7–19.

54. See, for example, Mandair, *Religion and the Specter of the West*; King, *Orientalism and Religion*; van der Veer, *Imperial Encounters.*

55. Bobby Sayyid, "Contemporary Politics of Secularism," in *Secularism, Religion, and Multicultural Citizenship*, ed. Geoff Braham Levey and Tariq Madood (Cambridge: Cambridge University Press, 2009), 193.

56. Asad, *Formations of the Secular*, 201.

57. Ananda Abeysekara, *The Politics of Postsecular Religion* (New York: Columbia University Press, 2008), 17–18.

58. Talal Asad, "Response," in *Powers of the Secular Modern: Talal Asad and His Interlocuters*, ed. David Scott and Charles Hirschkind (Stanford: Stanford University Press, 2006), 210.

59. Abeysekara, *Politics of Postsecular Religion*, 46–47.

60. See José Casanova, *Public Religions in the Modern World* (Chicago: University of Chicago Press, 1994), especially chap. 1.

61. The literature on this topic is abundant. For exemplary critiques of secularization theory and its subtheses from discursive-genealogical, historical-empirical, philosophical, and political perspectives, see Asad, *Formations of the Secular*; Rodney Stark, "Secularization, R.I.P.," *Sociology of Religion* 60 (1999): 11–39; Caputo, *On Religion*; William E. Connolly, *Why I Am Not a Secularist* (Minneapolis: University of Minnesota Press, 1999); Dubuisson, *Western Construction of Religion*.

62. David Scott, "Appendix: The Trouble of Thinking: An Interview with Talal Asad," in *Powers of the Secular Modern: Talal Asad and His Interlocuters*, ed. David Scott and Charles Hirschkind (Stanford: Stanford University Press, 2006), 298.

63. Asad, *Formations of the Secular*, 201.

64. Cf. Russell T. McCutcheon, " 'They Licked the Platter Clean': On the Co-dependency of the Religious and the Secular," *Method and Theory in the Study of Religion* 19 (2007): 173–99. For a critique of binary concepts in the study of religion, see also Markus Dressler, "How to Conceptualize Inner-Islamic Plurality/Difference: 'Heterodoxy' and 'Syncretism' in the Writings of Mehmet F. Köprülü (1890-1966)," *British Journal for Middle Eastern Studies* 37.3 (2010): 241–60.

65. As Peterson and Walhof have argued, "[m]aking and remaking religion is a political enterprise, intimately linked to the imagination of new social and intellectual communities" (Derek R. Peterson and Darren R. Walhof "Rethinking Religion", in *The Invention of Religion. Rethinking Belief in Politics and History*, ed. Derek R. Peterson and Darren R. Walhof (New Brunswick: Rutgers University Press 2002), 6). For interesting contributions to the debate on religion-making, mainly from the kind we qualify as "from above", see also the contributions in Peterson and Walhof, *Invention of Religion*. In this volume variations of religion-making from above are addressed in the chapters by Arvind Mandair, Alicia Turner, Markus Dressler, Michael Nijhawan, and Mark Elmore.

66. Cheryl Bernard, *Civil Democratic Islam: Partners, Resources, and Strategies* (Santa Monica: RAND Corporation, 2003), III.

67. Ibid., 3.

68. Pipes is the director of Campus Watch and one of the most notorious Islam critics in the United States. In 2003, President Bush nominated Pipes to the board of the federally sponsored U.S. Institute of Peace, where he served for two consecutive years.

69. Jim Lobe, "US: From Nation-Building to Religion-Building," *Asia Times*, April 9, 2004, http://www.atimes.com/atimes/Middle_East/FD09Ak04.html (accessed: March 14, 2010).

70. Daniel Pipes, "Fixing Islam," *New York Sun*, April 6, 2004, http://www.danielpipes.org/article/1704 (accessed: March 14, 2010).

71. For a sharp criticism of the liberal biases underlying the secularist rhetoric with explicit references to Bernard's report and the State Department's concurrent efforts in creating a "modern Islam," see Saba Mahmood, "Secularism, Hermeneutics and Empire: The Politics of Islamic Reformation," *Public Culture* 18, no. 2 (2006): 323–47. Elizabeth Shakman Hurd has extended this line of critique to the recent report of the Chicago Council titled "Engaging Religious Communities Abroad: A New Imperative for U.S. Foreign Policy." She argues that the report, which tries to establish principles for legitimate U.S. government engagement of religious groups abroad, amounts to what she qualifies as a "securitization of religion." Hurd points out that "in tacitly sanctioning a protestant understanding of religion as the (only) legitimate way to be religious and modern, it forecloses upon a range of understandings of religion and arrogates to the NSC [National Security Council] the authority to decide who is 'civil' enough to be allowed into the public sphere, and who isn't." Elizabeth

Shakman Hurd, "The Global Securitization of Religion," *Immanent Frame*, March 23, 2010, http://blogs.ssrc.org/tif/2010/03/23/global-securitization/ (accessed: April 17, 2010). For further critical discussion of the cited Chicago Council report, see *Immanent Frame*, http://blogs.ssrc.org/tif/category/religious-freedom/ (accessed: April 17, 2010).

72. It has to be acknowledged that reformist politics directed toward Islam with the aim to make it "compatible" to Western notions of secular-liberal modernity are not particular to U.S. neocons. The European debates on Islam as a problem of secularity, be it of the liberal or the laicist kind, show this very clearly. See Ruth Mas, "Compelling the Muslim Subject: Memory as Post-colonial Violence and the Public Performativity of 'Secular and Cultural Islam,'" *Muslim World* 96, no. 4 (2006): 585–616 ; see also the chapters by Dressler and Nijhawan in this volume.

73. Chapters in this volume that discuss cases of religion-making from below are especially those by Mas, Greg Johnson, and Dressler.

74. Charles Hallisey, as paraphrased in King, *Orientalism and Religion*, 148. On the force of translation in colonial and postcolonial contexts, but also the opportunities it offers for local resistance, see Tejaswini Niranjana, *Siting Translation: History, Post-structuralism, and the Colonial Context* (Berkeley: University of California Press, 1992).

75. King, *Orientalism and Religion*, 149–50; see also King's chapter in this volume.

76. Chapters in this volume investigating cases of religion-making from the pretended outside are those by Kerry Mitchell, Rosemary R. Hicks, and King.

77. See King, *Orientalism and Religion*; McCutcheon, *Manufacturing Religion*.

78. There are certainly more and more steps in this direction. See, for example, Linell E. Cady and Elizabeth Shakman Hurd, "Comparative Secularisms and the Politics of Modernity: An Introduction," in *Comparative Secularisms in a Global Age*, ed. Elizabeth Shakman Hurd and Linell Cady (Hampshire: Palgrave, 2010), 3–24.

79. Jonathon Z. Smith, *Imagining Religion: From Babylon to Jonestown* (Chicago: University of Chicago Press, 1988), XI.

80. Peterson and Walhof, *Rethinking Religion*, 14.

81. Asad, *Genealogies of Religion*, 28.

2 Imagining Religions in India: Colonialism and the Mapping of South Asian History and Culture

Richard King

> Modern politics is a chapter in the history of religion. The greatest
> revolutionary upheavals that have shaped so much of the history of
> the past two centuries were episodes in the history of faith—moments
> in the long dissolution of Christianity and the rise of the modern
> political religion. The world in which we find ourselves at the start of
> the new millennium is littered with the debris of utopian projects,
> which though they were framed in secular terms that denied the truth
> of religion were in fact vehicles for religious myths.
> —John Gray, *Black Mass: Apocalyptic Religion and the Death of Utopia*

The characterization of modern politics as a chapter in the history of religion by British political scientist John Gray (see quote above) is one way to deploy the category of "religion" to unsettle the easy separation of "the secular" from "the religious" in contemporary discourses. Another approach would be to call into question the usefulness of the category of religion itself as a discourse through which modern, universalist accounts of history have been written. Both strategies render the secularist separation of "politics" from a domain known as "religion" problematic, the former by totalizing the category of religion (even supposedly "secular" realms like "politics" and "economics" are now deemed to be a specific mode of "religiosity"), and the latter by challenging a totalization of the concept of religion by focusing upon its cultural specificity—its ethnocentric provenance as a key explanatory category of the Christian/secular West. Gray's approach, despite its many redeeming features, reflects a challenge to conventional liberal histories of the West that remains firmly *inside* the cultural experience of the Atlantic West. As Daniel Dubuisson has argued, it is through the language of religion that the West has spoken—and continues to speak, both about itself and about "the other."[1] In contrast to such strategies, a comparativist approach that seeks to suspend Eurocentered accounts of the world through an engagement with non-European worldviews is one that is better equipped to displace the prevailing discourse of religion, grounded as it is in the experiences and worldviews of the West. In this essay I wish to explore both approaches, with an emphasis on the importance of *comparison* in the development of a form of cultural critique that would denaturalize conventional (Occidentalist) accounts of human history and the discourse of religion that has served as the conceptual platform upon which such mythic narratives have been built.

The latter half of the twentieth century saw the end of the era of formal colonial rule of much of the planet by European powers, though not (yet?) the end of Western domination. We have been living through a period of history that Cornel West has called "the passing of the Age of Europe," and it has begun to exercise a profound impression on what counts as knowledge in the global circulation of ideas. Indeed, for macrohistorians such as Andre Gunder Frank, the dominance of Europe in recent centuries should more accurately be seen as a small phase within a larger historical trend of an Asian-centered world.[2] This is important, since as the age of European imperialism has faded, so increasingly has the belief that European worldviews and epistemologies constitute a normative (and potentially universalizable) way of understanding the world and our human experience of it. In many circles, the Enlightenment master narrative of European ideas and values as the apex of "civilization"—an attitude that undergirded the European imperial project—is now being seen for what it is—namely, as only one of a number of alternate cultural constructions of reality. In other words, in a cross-cultural and "postcolonial" context the *provinciality* of European ways of understanding the world is increasingly being thrown into relief with reference to the historical specificity of their origins and provenance. At the same time, the Euro-American West remains culturally, politically, and militarily dominant (even if in the economic sphere the much vaunted rise of China and India as global economic players suggests that this too may be in decline). The continued (if contested) hegemony of Euro-American forms of knowledge presents a challenge to those of us who wish to explore and understand the rich history of South Asian thought, traditions, and culture. How does one study and engage with such traditions when their very representation and configuration have been so radically altered by the legacy of the Asian encounter with Western colonialism and the processes of modernity?

■ THE MAP OF "RELIGION"

One thing is clear from this context. The colonial domination of the West over "the rest" in recent centuries has caused many Western categories, ideas, and paradigms to appear more universal and normative than they might otherwise have seemed. The category of "religion" is one such category and could be described as a key feature in the imaginative cartography of Western modernity. The concept serves as a cognitive map for surveying, classifying, and interpreting diverse cultural and historical terrain and allows a distinction to be drawn between "secular" and "religious" spheres of human life.

However, as Jonathan Z. Smith reminds us, "map is not territory." A key factor in the *claimed* universality of certain Western concepts and the resultant confusion between map and territory, I will suggest, is the recent history of European imperialism and the effect that this has had upon the cultures of the colonized. Maps are powerful things. As J. Brian Harley notes in the context of the 1947 British partition of India, "We can see how the stroke of a pen across a map could determine the lives and deaths of millions of people."[3] What effects do our cognitive maps of cultures have upon human lives and identities?

As a number of scholars have pointed out, both our *modern* understanding of "religion" as a "system of beliefs and practices" and the academic field of religious studies are a product of the European Enlightenment, though of course the term has a long classical heritage in the West with roots and rival etymologies going back to Cicero and Lactantius.[4] In recent decades a growing body of academic literature has called into question the central unifying concept of the discipline of the history of religions—the category of "religion"—itself.[5] In *Orientalism and Religion* (1999), I argue that the category of religion is the product of a culturally specific discursive history characterized by the imprints that Christian theology, the Enlightenment, and secular modernity have left upon it. As such its continued unreflective use cross-culturally, while opening up interesting debates and interactions over the past few centuries (and creating things called "interfaith dialogue" and "the world religions"), has also closed down avenues of exploration and other potential cultural and intellectual interactions.

Perhaps the first Western academic to draw attention to problems with the category in a systematic fashion was Wilfred Cantwell Smith in his 1962 book, *The Meaning and End of Religion*. Smith argues that the term 'religion' is confusing, unnecessary and distorting.... [P]rogress in understanding—even at the academic level—of the traditions of other people throughout history and throughout the world, are both seriously blocked by our attempt to conceptualize what is involved in each case in terms of (a) religion."[6] Despite this, Smith remained an eager advocate of "interfaith dialogue" throughout his career. He proposed replacing the category of "religion" with "cumulative tradition," on the one hand, and "personal faith," on the other. For Smith what links these two dimensions is "the living person." Faith is a kind of "inner religious experience" or "quality": "To be religious is an ultimately personal act."[7] In emphasizing this, Smith underplays the role of community identity and perpetuates the Protestant/post-Enlightenment privatization of the religious as an inner state or feeling, a characterization established by figures such as Schleiermacher, William James, and Rudolph Otto.[8] This characterization feeds into one important strand of interreligious dialogue and the comparative study of religion in the twentieth century—namely, the emphasis placed upon "religious experience" as the locus of religiosity and therefore also the ground for the meeting of different traditions in the search for a common mystical core to the various world religions.[9] However, the emphases upon experience and the concept of "faith" are also culturally loaded. Critiques of the modernist "rhetoric of experience" have been put forward by Denys Turner, Grace Jantzen, Robert Sharf, and myself on a variety of grounds,[10] but especially for the way in which medieval Christian mystics and ancient South Asian traditions have been translated by the psychologizing prism of Western modernity into what sociologist Paul Heelas has called "self-spiritualities."[11]

The privatization of modern notions of mysticism, inspired by the seminal work of William James, similarly ignores the shifting meanings and constructions of "the mystical" throughout its largely Christian history.[12] Scholars interested in exploring what has been called "Asian mysticism" need to pay more attention to the ways in which a number of constructed stereotypical images of the East—in D. T. Suzuki's "Zen Buddhism," Vivekananda's (or even Sankara's) Advaita Vedanta,

Patanjali's "Yoga," Laozi's *Daodejing*—have been pressed into service in the last century as token representatives of something called "the global phenomenon of mysticism." Whether colonized and homogenized by the perennialists or essentialized and segregated by the constructivists, such stereotypes of "the Mystic East" have been used to make a variety of competing claims about the "mystical," spiritual, or otherworldly nature of Asian cultures. Contemporary debates within the field have also served to locate certain aspects of Asian and Western cultures within a modernist and psychologized framework that misreads the phenomenon captured by the term *mysticism* on a number of levels.[13] The ongoing significance of the modern "psychological turn" can be seen not only in the emphasis that is placed upon "experience" as the locus of religiosity within the study of religions (and *especially* the study of mysticism) but also in the contemporary shift in certain circles away from the term *religion* and toward a privatized and consumer-oriented notion of "spirituality."[14]

There are similar problems with an emphasis upon notions of "faith" and the "world faiths." Faith may be an important determinant of identity within the Christian "cumulative tradition," but even here it is less significant historically than the Protestant Reformation might suggest. In medieval Europe most people were "Christians" not through an explicit self-willed faith but through their allegiance to the traditions and practices of their kin. For scholars such as Gabriel Le Bras it is not even clear that we can talk of Christianity as the religion of prerevolutionary France except in the limited sense of being so deemed by the monarchial constitution. Similarly, the notion of "faith" itself has gone through a number of shifts in meaning, most notably the shift from "being 'faithful' to" to "having faith in" something. As Rustom Bharucha has argued, the pluralities and ambivalences captured by the English term *faith* have yet to be properly theorized in either a South Asian or social scientific context.[15] More important for my argument, faith in the modern sense of adherence to a particular set of propositional beliefs (a creed) has not been a central feature of identity construction in most of the traditions with which Christianity has come into contact.

Rustom Bharucha's little known and short work *A Question of Faith* (1993) is a brilliantly nuanced and in many ways transgressive discussion of the importance of "faith" in contemporary India. At first sight, the emphasis the author places upon the concept of faith as a central aspect of Indian culture might be read as a rebuttal of my suggestions about the inappropriateness of the concept of faith when applied to Indic traditions. However, Bharucha's stance, in the emphasis placed upon the pluralities and ambivalences connoted by the term *faith* (illustrated through examples such as the *kumbh mela* and *līlā* celebrations), acts precisely as a means of contesting essentialized, universalist, and normative readings of faith by paying attention to ambivalence and the resistance of closure with regard to dichotomies such as "secular/religious" or "believer and nonbeliever." This is a good example of the strategy of opening up heterogeneous meanings within a discourse and in that sense reading its "commonsenseness" (which is always the commonsenseness of a particular community—in this case an Anglophone and modern Anglo-Indian readership) against the grain. Bharucha, however, often makes recourse to a modern notion of faith as private "belief" and also to the concept of "experience" (which he reads as the substratum of faith) without addressing the problems associated with such rendering of these ideas and their implication in a post-Enlightenment framing of "the religions."[16]

Let us consider further some of the problems in using the language of "faith" in an Indian civilizational context. *Śraddhā*, the Sanskrit term usually translated as "faith" in ancient Indian Buddhist texts, is not faith in the modern sense of assent to a series of metaphysical or theological propositions or in the earlier medieval sense of the term as a life of committed devotion and piety. *Śraddhā* traditionally means confidence in the teacher and the path, and it is often represented as a preliminary stage in the Buddhist tradition to be superseded by the wisdom or analytical insight (*prajñā*) that derives from mental cultivation (*bhāvanā*), the practice of the eightfold path.[17] In the ancient Buddhist traditions of India, what determined the nikāya you belonged to was how you practiced—the *Prātimokṣa*—that is, the set of monastic rules that you accepted, rather than your assent to a particular doctrine or set of beliefs. It is not so much that Buddhists did not differentiate on the basis of different doctrinal interpretations of the Dharma, or that beliefs were not important to them, but, rather, that this was not the *key* feature in determining affiliation and nikāya identity. My point is not that Buddhists do not "have faith" in things. I would venture that we all adopt a variety of views that we would be hard pushed to prove to a committed skeptic. Rather, it is that, with the possible exception of strands like the Pure Land Shin traditions, faith has not been a *determining* factor in establishing traditional Buddhist *identity*. Even here, as Galen Amstutz and others have noted, the representation of Shin in terms of Protestant notions of faith is far from unproblematic.[18]

Similarly, in the diverse traditions captured by the classification "Hindu," it might be argued that there are rough parallels to Christian devotionalism in the form of the various *bhakti* movements (particularly some strands of Śrīvaiṣṇavism, but these are hardly representative of the history and variety of Hindu traditions. Here again, we rarely find the same stress upon orthodoxy and "right belief" as a determining factor of one's allegiance or group identity. Moreover, bhakti encompasses a wide range of phenomena: Whose bhakti are we talking about—the contemplative devotion to Kṛṣṇa advocated in the *Bhagavad Gītā*, the later bhakti movements of medieval Śaiva and Vaiṣṇava traditions, or contemporary trends focusing upon the historicity of Rāma and promoting "Hinduness" (Hindutva)?[19]

As a number of scholars have noted, the construction of "religion" in terms of private belief is a peculiar feature of Western modernity.[20] The notion of Buddhism as a system of beliefs was introduced into modern Sinhalese consciousness through the activities of figures such as Col. Henry Olcott, one of the founding members of the Theosophical Society. In establishing the Buddhist Theosophical Society in Śri Lanka, Olcott expressed his commitment to his new "faith" by publicly taking the three refuges and publishing in 1881 a *Buddhist Catechism*, modeled, as he said, "upon the elementary handbooks so effectively used among the Western Christian sects."[21] Olcott's colonial-inspired desire to restore "true Buddhism" to a population that in his view was woefully unaware of its basic tenets was a countermove to the activities of Christian missionaries in Sri Lanka at the time. Olcott's approach, however, replicated basic Christian theological assumptions about the nature of religion just as much as it reproduced a colonial paternalism that prevented a full recognition of indigenous Sinhalese agency. As Donald Lopez notes in his discussion of this, "Belief appears as a universalist category because of the universalist claims of the tradition in which it became most central, Christianity. Other religions have made universalist claims, but Christianity was allied with political power, which made it possible to transport its belief to all corners of the globe.... Belief, then, or perhaps the demand that there be belief, is implicated both in the activities of Christian missionaries and in the 'native' efforts...to counter them. The question that remains, however, is what the Sinhalese gave up by giving credit to belief."[22]

I would suggest that one of the things that was lost in the nineteenth-century representation of "Buddhism" as a system of religious beliefs was a full recognition of Buddhist forms of life as a civilizational alternative to prevailing Western notions of what it is to be modern. In the act of its discovery as a "faith," *buddhadharma* or buddhāgama ceased to represent a complex and long-standing civilization—and one of the historical tributaries out of which the modern world has itself been constituted—and became instead a "religion." Indeed, as H. L. Seneviratne suggests in his critique of the modernist transformation of the Buddha-āgama in Sri Lanka, "The label 'Buddhism' itself symbolized this process of fixing, cleansing, and establishing boundaries, for 'Buddhism' had no such indigenous label, and existed only as a 'total social phenomenon' of pluralistic and unbounded beliefs and practices, a system with an 'open boundary' that allowed free movement of belief and practice between the total system's center and periphery."[23]

Moreover, *by representing Christianity, Buddhism, Hinduism, and Islam as "faiths" or "belief systems" in the modern sense, the role of faith in modern (so-called) secular and capitalist forms of life is occluded.* Through this process the secular is privileged as the "objective" common ground upon which the various religions or faiths meet, rather than as one of a number of divergent cultural models of what it is to be "modern." In this sense the creation of "interfaith dialogue" has led to a kind of enclavism, where the "wider" secular spheres of politics, philosophy, science, and economics are safely insulated from the need to engage with the perspectives of the great civilizations that many of these modern "religions" represent.[24] As Anouar Majid and William Hart have noted in different contexts, the Orientalist paradigm continues to be replicated for as long as one of its central presuppositions is left uninterrogated—namely, the postulation of a rigid dichotomy between the secular and the religious and the privileging of the former as constitutive of the real world "out there."[25]

The location of "the religious" within the private sphere of belief, however often highlighted as a key consequence of the European Enlightenment, has not gone uncontested.[26] Indeed, since the nineteenth century, and particularly after the collapse of the Soviet Union in the 1990s, the category of "religion" has provided the *main site for the framing and articulation of alternatives to Euro-American models of modernity.*[27] Such movements and modes of cultural resistance are translated, as Derrida suggested, into a *Latinized* frame of reference when they are represented in mainstream Western culture, or as Derrida himself puts it: "The world today speaks Latin (most often via Anglo-American) when it authorizes itself in the *name* of *religion.*" The process whereby expressions of cultural difference become translated as "religion" in the Western imagination is thus labeled by Derrida *mondialatinisation* (in "Anglo-American"—*globalatinization*).[28]

The role of "the religious" as a repository in the Western and Westernized imagination for movements with a strong degree of resistance to "secular" models of modernity has been somewhat masked from view by the tendency in Western liberal circles to relegate all that is placed in the category of "the religious" to the private sphere and to interpret any irruption of the religious into the public space as evidence of "religious fundamentalism." However, the attack on the World Trade Center in New York on September 11, 2001, and the ensuing "war on terrorism" have effectively contributed, in stark and horrific fashion, to an unraveling of this model of the religious in the public consciousness of the Western world. That this was already occurring can be seen from the work of José Casanova in his suggestion that at the end of the millennium we were witnessing a steady "de-privatization" of religion.[29] Of course in many parts of the world this "privatization" never really happened in the first place.

■ "RELIGION" AND THE SOCIAL IMAGINARY

The notion that the concept of religion is an "imagined category" has been explored by the Chicago historian of religion Jonathan Z. Smith. Like his namesake Wilfred Cantwell Smith, J. Z. Smith argues that the reification of the category of "religion" makes what is in fact a constructed notion appear as if it is a naturally occurring entity that exists "out there" in the world rather than simply an explanatory category located in the imagination of the scholar's mind. Smith makes the following statement at the beginning of his 1982 work, *Imagining Religion*:

> If we have understood the archaeological and textual record correctly, man has had his entire history in which to imagine deities and modes of interaction with them. But man, more precisely western man, has had only the last few centuries in which to imagine religion. It is this act of second order, reflective imagination which must be the central preoccupation of any student of religion.... *Religion is solely the creation of the scholar's study.* It is created for the scholar's analytic purposes by his imaginative acts of comparison and generalization. *Religion has no independent existence apart from the academy.* For this reason, the student of religion,... must be relentlessly self-conscious. Indeed, this self-consciousness constitutes his primary expertise, his foremost object of study.[30]

I agree with Smith in highlighting the constructed nature of the category of religion. His point of course is not that there are no traditions out there variously labeled as Islam, Judaism, Buddhism, and so on but, rather, that the decision to categorize or label them as religions is itself a classificatory act of the imagination. It is in fact a rather familiar habit, which some of us might feel quite reluctant to give up.

The continued unreflective use of the category of "religion," however, does not carry us forward in our attempt to understand better the diverse cultures and civilizations of the world. Nevertheless, I must admit to being uncomfortable with one reading of Smith's suggestion—namely, the suggestion that religion is a category located solely within the imagination of the scholar. This is for a number of reasons. First, religion is a socially constructed category. It is a constitutive element of the social, political, and economic world in which we live. To imply that the notion of religion exists only in the mind of individuals is to fall into the Cartesian trap of dividing the world up into empirically real facts, on the one hand, and an individually observing mind, on the other. This ignores the role that social and cultural conditioning plays in the manifestation of both and the inscribing of the discourse of religion on the body itself, in the form of disciplinary practices and what Foucault calls governmentality. In other words religion is not just in one's mind (if one wishes to continue to put it that way) but also exists as a structural and embodied feature of the way in which Western society has divided up the world. Such categories *are* imagined or constructed—they have particular discursive histories that we can plot, but we, as individual agents, do not imagine these categories in isolation from the wider social, political, and linguistic structures through which we make sense of reality. Moreover, Smith is also guilty here I think of indulging in a power fantasy, of overemphasizing the influence and importance of the scholar as the primary agent behind the cultural embeddedness of the category of religion. Religion exists not only in the scholar's imagination (not even *primarily* there if one wants to put it that way) but also in the collective imagination of the wider community. Its use is never "purely academic" and has been bound up, as Peterson and Walhof have argued, with the construction "of national identities and the exercise of colonial power."[31] Contemporary scholars of religion do not dream up this category; they inherit it and build upon it. To put this in a non-Western idiom, like the Yogācāra Buddhist philosopher, I wish to stress that imagined constructions (what the *Madhyānta Vibhāga* calls *abhūta-parikalpa*— "the imagination of the unreal") do in fact *exist* in the sense that they produce effects and structure our perception of the world. Such concepts, when reified and applied across diverse historical and cultural terrain, are, as Vasubandhu might say, collective illusions. They are no less "real" for that reason.

It is in fact "common sense" to the modern consciousness to think that various traditions, beliefs, and practices in the world are related to something called "the religions" and at the same time to classify others—pledging allegiance to the state, adoration of a celebrity, taking part in the May Day Parade in Moscow, supporting a football team, not walking under ladders, buying a lottery ticket, talking to your cat, deferring to the boss at work—as not "religious." "Common sense" is that which, as Clifford Geertz suggests, in its very taken-for-granted status requires the most rigorous interrogation. The dichotomy between the secular and the religious, unstable and problematic though it is upon close examination, is part of the cultural heritage—or "baggage," if you prefer—that Europeans have forcibly universalized through the last few centuries of colonialism. Now to be fair to J. Z. Smith, I do not think that he would wish to deny the socially embedded nature of the term *religion*. Indeed on the very next page of his work *Imagining Religion*, he appeals to the role played by Judaism in "our collective invention of western civilization."[32] Nevertheless, the rhetorical effect of distilling the category down to the level of individual agency (or representing it merely as a scholarly tool) is precisely to ignore its power. It is part of our social imaginary and structures our social reality.

One of the interesting issues that arise here is not so much whether or not Western notions of religion are accurate but, rather, a matter of documenting the historical process whereby such notions became self-evident even to those for whom they were an innovation. The classification of certain cultural phenomena as "religious" and its separation from a sphere known as the "secular" may well seem obvious to some, but it was not "common sense" at all to non-Europeans before the advent of colonialism.

However, attention to colonialism and that complex series of processes labeled "globalization" causes us to realize that although "map is not territory," the conceptual force (literally: *force*) of terms such as *religion* has meant that they have functioned not simply as descriptive taxonomies of cultural terrain; they have also led to *mondialatinisation*. In other words, "religion" and the related group of concepts and orientations that cluster around it have for some time now functioned as *prescriptive* models or blueprints that have transformed the terrain itself.[33] *Maps may not be territory, but through colonialism, European cognitive maps have reconfigured the very territory that they are purported to represent.* This is no more apparent than in the tendency in both colonial narratives and indigenous South Asian responses to locate "authentic religiosity" within the sacred texts of a tradition and in the interpretation of prescriptive statements within those texts as descriptive accounts of historical truth. This led to a widespread criticism of contemporary practices and a reformist spirit in both the colonizer and the colonized, grounded in both cases in an idealized "nostalgia for lost origins." To investigate this requires that we pay attention to the role that European colonialism has played in the reconfiguration of South Asian identities, as well as the multiple and complex agendas present and the politics of representation that they manifest. This also requires paying attention to what Talal Asad has called "the inequality of languages"—namely, the asymmetrical power relations present in the translation of concepts between "nonequivalent" languages.[34]

■ THE "DISCOURSE OF RELIGION" IN THE STUDY OF SOUTH ASIA

What have been the consequences of taking the European cartographic imagination too seriously—of using the map of "religion" to explain and classify the intellectual and cultural traditions of Asia? In the late eighteenth and nineteenth centuries, Western scholars and commentators began to coin a number of neologisms to denote the newly discovered "religions" of Asia: in particular "Hinduism" (a term apparently first used by the British evangelical Baptist Charles Grant in the 1770s and subsequently adopted by Hindu reformers like Rammohan Roy), "Buddhism" (1820s), and "Taoism" (1820s).[35] As Western accounts of Asian traditions benefited from their relatively easy circulation across colonial networks of power they became increasingly valorized in terms of the emerging global political system—a system dominated by Western nations and based upon the Westphalian model of the secular nation-state. The "religion versus secular" division of society came to function as the dominant template through which colonized and semicolonized Asian countries sought entrance to "modernity"—that is, to gain recognition as civilized and sovereign nation-states in a context of military, economic, and political encroachment into their regions by Western powers. Thus, in the late nineteenth and early twentieth centuries we see the rise of a variety of new "reformist" and "modernizing" agendas in various Asian countries, exemplified by the Meiji regime in Japan (1868–1912), the establishment of the Republic of China (1912–49), and trends such as the late nineteenth-century "Bengali Renaissance" in India, which sought, in their own ways, to respond to a Western-driven conception of modernity. These reformist trends sought to organize and reform indigenous traditions and polities in response to such demands. Thus, in the late nineteenth century new terms were coined such as the words *shukyo* and *tetsugaku* in Japan to translate foreign, Western distinctions between "religion" and "philosophy," or well-established but multivalented concepts (such as the Sanskrit term *dharma*) were adapted and translated in terms of Western notions of "the religious."

In this manner, some of the key cultural fault lines and traditional modes of identity construction are "written over" by an emphasis upon distinguishing features of the terrain that have been significant in a European Western context. In the history of intellectual thought this is no more obvious than in the exclusion of Asian intellectual thought from the history of philosophy. In the case of Indian traditions, this has usually been on the grounds that Indian philosophy is deemed "too religious" or "tradition-bound" to be philosophy in the purest (read: modern/Western/secular) sense. The contribution of Islamic thinkers to the history of philosophy, for instance, is often relegated to the role of medieval postal workers, safely delivering classical Greek philosophy to the medieval Europeans. As long as we continue to see Islam, for instance, as a "religion" in the modern post-Enlightenment sense of a "faith," we will fail to understand the significance of contemporary trends such as "Islamic science," and "Islamic economics," and crucially at the beginning of the twenty-first century, Islamic politics.[36] These simply cannot be adequately rendered in terms of the highly policed boundary between the secular and the religious that dominates Western post-Enlightenment descriptions of reality. The sense in which Islam, for instance, represents diverse communitarian, civilizational, and political dimensions is lost in translation if we focus upon it narrowly as a personal faith.

The real challenge, then, is to question the terms set by the dichotomy—that is, to challenge a conceptual map that draws a rigid boundary between the secular and the religious dimensions of human existence and to draw attention to the effect that this has had upon the classification and interpretation of non-Western intellectual traditions. It is this separation that maintains the marginality of non-Western perspectives and worldviews within the terms set by modern Western liberalism. In so doing their importance as the major site for the articulation of difference and resistance to *globalatinization* becomes severely curtailed. The distillation of "the religious" dimension of culture from other spheres of human activity causes such traditions to be cognitively and structurally segregated from the realms of politics, economics, science, and philosophy. This privileges modern Western ideologies and forms of life (such as economic neoliberalism, triumphalist secularism, scientific rationalism, and materialism) and insulates them from an open-ended engagement with the varieties of human attempts to articulate the nature of reality.

Moreover, the projection of anachronistic and highly reified notions of "Hinduism" and "Buddhism" onto South Asian history has also caused scholars to miss important points of connection and contestation between traditions. Overreliance upon the "map of religion" has led scholars to portray "Hindu" and "Buddhist" traditions as if they were wholly separate socioreligious systems with relatively fixed rather than porous boundaries. This has been reinforced by the tendency for scholars to specialize in one or the other but rarely both. As a consequence the complex interplay between these traditions in South Asia is often missed or at least underemphasized.

Despite the reconfiguration of indigenous subjectivities and communities during the colonial period and the relatively recent rise of the discourse of "Hindutva" and exclusivist Hindu movements with firmly demarcated boundaries, the dynamic and fluid nature of South Asian traditions remains to this day with Hindus, Buddhists, Jainas, and Muslims interacting on a number of different levels. Such interactions are of course complex and shift according to local context and history, but they are rarely well captured by the search for what might be called "the religious dimension." As Talal Asad has argued, the search for an essence of religion encourages us to abstract "the religious" from a wider cultural and political dynamic. *It points us away from culture and power rather than toward an appreciation of their mutual imbrication.* This has also helped foster the notion that the "religions," particularly the Indic traditions, are apolitical and "otherworldly" in orientation. From this perspective such traditions—and the scholars who specialize in them—would seem to have little to offer to broader discussions of politics, economics, and society and cultural critique more generally. As Ninian Smart once put it, "Having been dethroned as the *Queen of Sciences*, the study of religion has now become the *Knave of Arts.*"[37]

In the field of early Buddhist studies, the works of scholars such as Richard Gombrich, Steven Collins, and Joanna Jurewicz have demonstrated that we miss key features and allusions within early Buddhist thought and imagery if we ignore the social and ideological struggles being played out in the texts, particularly in terms of relations with the mainstream Vedic and Brahmanical traditions of the time.[38] Similarly, we cannot understand the specific form that early Advaita Vedānta took or the orientation of Patañjali's *Yoga Sutras* or Īśvarakṛṣṇa's *Sāṃkhya Kārikā* if we ignore their interaction with prevailing Buddhist traditions. In the study of "Indian philosophy," for example, there has often been a tendency to elide "Indian" with "Hindu" and to represent the various *darśanas* as if they were homogeneous and self-contained systems of thought. This occludes the history of interactions between the various Brahmanical and Śramanic traditions that have clearly been crucial to the historical development of the various *darśanas*.[39] It also underplays the significance of Buddhist contributions to the history of Indian civilization.

In *Orientalism and Religion* (1999), I attempt to highlight the ongoing replication of Orientalist presuppositions about "India" both in the neo-Vedāntic inclusivism of Vivekānanda and in contemporary discourses of Hindutva. In both cases appeal is made to a reified entity known as "Hinduism," and the history of South Asian philosophy and culture is mapped according to key features of the European cartographic imagination—most notably, the notions of "world religions" and the "mystic or spiritual East" and the search for a centralizing motif or theology of relevance to all Hindus. Again, as a number of scholars have noted, Dharmapāla's Buddhist modernism reproduces a number of key "Protestant" features, notably the notion of recovering "pure" Buddhism from its "decadent" and superstitious village forms, in the emphasis placed upon scripture as the locus of real Buddhism, in the claim that Buddhism is compatible with modern science, and in the idea that it is significantly different from other traditions in its nontheistic and nonritualistic emphases. Robert Sharf's work on D. T. Suzuki and the construction of "Zen nationalism" during the Meiji period is another case in point.[40]

Again, as Peter Gottschalk has argued (in his study of village life in Arampur, Bihar), there are multiple factors involved in identity formation that cut across a simple division of people in terms of an overdetermined "Hindu" or "Muslim" identity. These factors, related to gender, economics, caste, region, and familial relations, sometimes complement and sometimes cut across each other, making the question of identity and representation a complex affair. As Gottschalk himself notes, "Western scholars of the Subcontinent rely too heavily on *Hindu* and *Muslim* as descriptive adjectives and analytic categories."[41] The result has been that scholarly accounts, following the trajectory established by James Mill's *History of British India* (1817), tend to bifurcate India into two halves—*Hindu* and *Muslim*. While Western colonialists and Orientalists did not create these divisions ex nihilo, they certainly highlighted, inscribed, and authorized them through the census, education, and the strategy of "divide and rule." As Peter Van der Veer has noted, it is not so much that Orientalism is the cause of communalism but, rather, that "Orientalism and Indian nationalism both belong to the discourse of modernity. Indian nationalism, in its very anticolonialism, shares basic discursive premises with Orientalism and with the nationalism of the colonizing British."[42] The continuing presence of key Orientalist tropes in contemporary Hindu discourses of varying types is a good example of this ongoing legacy.

■ SHOULD WE THROW THE MAP OF RELIGION AWAY?

The "discourse of religion" of course structures and orders human knowledge and of course provides some semblance of unity for the academic field of religious studies. It also becomes inscribed in institutions and political structures that then become resistant to its interrogation. Given the problems highlighted should we, then, simply throw the map of religion away? Recognizing that *religion* is a mapping term—and the role of European imperialism in spreading and universalizing this category in the modern world—allows us to see both the problems with the term and its ongoing *significance*. To ask how many religions there are in the world is to confuse map with territory. Similarly, to ask whether "religion" is a *false* category is, in my view, a badly formed question since it implies that religion is more than a heuristic classificatory tool—a mental mapping term. Far more interesting is the question of the usefulness of the map and the effects of its deployment. Does the map cause us to miss interesting features of South Asian history and culture simply because they are not features of the map we are using?[43] What was lost, for instance, in the decision to translate terms like *āgama, sampradāya,* and *dharma* into "religion" in South Asian contexts?

Clearly, the tendency to take Western-derived terms like *religion* as representative of universal history as a whole, rather than viewing them as culturally and historically contingent conceptual tools for interpreting cultural landscapes, erases alternative indigenous terms—in the case of India, terms such as *dharma, sampradāya,* and *āgama* and their specific connotations. As Arvind Sharma has argued, the specifically Christian baggage of the term *religion* has led us to conceive of all traditions so designated in narrowly exclusionary and separatist terms. To be the member of one religion, then, is automatically to exclude you from any other. As Sharma points out this separatist model of religion, derived from the Christian history of the term, is presupposed in Article 18 of the Universal Declaration of Human Rights, which advocates the right to "change one's religion" but does not consider "religious freedom" in terms of the right to advocate one religion without renouncing one's allegiance to another. Sharma suggests that reconceiving "freedom of religion" in terms of the Indic term *dharma* would open up possibilities precluded by the emphasis upon "the religious" as understood in European cultural history.[44]

Indeed, I would suggest that the dominant Anglo-Protestant discourse of religion that was at play in the British colonial encounter with Asian traditions (and which continues to inform public discourse about "religion") involved a strong emphasis upon the following six basic and interrelated assumptions:

1. THE ROOT ASSUMPTION—THE UNIVERSALITY OF RELIGION AS A DISTINCT DOMAIN OF HUMAN SOCIETIES: that all societies have one or more "religions"—which constitute particular instances of a universal genus to which they belong—"Religion"—and which can be clearly distinguished from other cultural phenomena such as "science," "politics," "economics," and so on.

2. THE CREEDAL EMPHASIS (as in "the world faiths"): that religions (especially the so-called higher religions or what became known later as the "world religions") are primarily to be understood as systems of "beliefs" involving "faith in" or "assent to" a set of specific truth claims that all members of the community are expected to adopt.

3. SCRIPTURALISM: that each ("world") religion is fundamentally grounded in "scripture" and a closed canon and that such texts—treated primarily in terms of their cognitive meaning rather than as ritual artifacts—constitute the primary authoritative yardstick by which the beliefs and practices of each tradition are to be evaluated.

4. DISCRETENESS: that "religions" by definition are (or at least *should be*) discrete entities. Any evidence of "border crossing" or an "inappropriate" mixture of such "pure" essences is evidence of contamination and "syncretism."

5. THE PRIMACY OF PURE ORIGINS (mirrored in an Indian Brahmanical context by the belief that we are living in Kali Yuga): that religions that do not display the above characteristics either are primitive and underdeveloped or have devolved from a prior state of purity to which they should be

encouraged to return—usually through a process of reform designed to divest them of adventitious features, superstitious accretions, and foreign elements.

6. CENTRIPETALISM: that religious identities exhibit a profoundly centripetal dynamic that seeks to overcome difference and plurality and unify all members of the group under a common rubric.[45]

I would contend that there is much in the history of Indian civilization that presents a rather different model of social interaction and organization, one that frequently challenges all six of these core assumptions. The story of the translation of these Western assumptions into vernacular idioms and subjectivities and their naturalization (though again, neither universally nor evenly) is a case study of the cognitive imperialism embedded in mainstream accounts of "the birth of modernity." This version of history is a product of the last five hundred years of (unequal) relations between Asia and the West.

There is a need, then, to interrogate the historical processes whereby central features of the Western cartographical imagination become normative elements in the cultural terrain way beyond their original purview.[46] David Scott's work on Sri Lanka, for instance, highlights the role of the Colebrooke-Cameron reforms of the 1830s in restructuring indigenous subjectivities and institutions, thereby creating an Anglicized middle-class elite in Sri Lanka and providing the conditions for the emergence of new reform-oriented trends such as Dharmapāla's modernist Buddhism. As Scott notes,

> Concepts like "religion," "state," and "identity," are treated ahistorically insofar as they are made to refer to a set of timeless social-ideological formations as defining (or as *defining in the same way*) for say third-century inhabitants of the island as for contemporary Sinhalas. This conceptual/ideological projection of the present into the past (as a hermeneutic of the present) is possible only because these categories—religion, state, and so on—are the *authoritative* and *normalized* categories through which Universal History has been written, and through which the local histories of the colonial and postcolonial worlds have been constituted as so many variations on a common theme about the progressive making of modernity.[47]

What might be gained from a strategic and transgressive reversal of the translation process and the mapping of Western culture and history in terms of traditional Asian categories? Inverting the colonial move, might new light be thrown on features of Western culture if we examined them afresh in terms of the cartographic imagination of other cultures? If we see, for instance, the "European Enlightenment" as a loosely bound social and intellectual trend of the seventeenth and eighteenth centuries, originating in northern Europe but then increasingly universalized in the nineteenth and twentieth centuries through European colonial expansion, can this not be usefully compared in macrohistorical terms to, say, "Brahmanism" in northern India or "the Confucian tradition" in China some one thousand years earlier?

Accepting of course that the "European Enlightenment," Indic "Brahmanism," and Confucianism are heterogeneous cultural networks and systems, we are still able to examine the ways in which they functioned as the ideological and social backdrop for their respective societies at certain points in history. Are there not loosely defined *sampradāyas* and *āgamas* in the European Enlightenment traditions that provide the basis for our own modern academic lineages? Modern Western academics belong to their own *sampradāyas* and accept their own forms of authoritative testimony, as Gadamer has taught us, even if this is often effaced by the emphasis that is placed upon intellectual innovation and individual scholarship. When framed in this manner (that is, without privileging the binary opposition of "tradition versus modernity" and "religious versus secular," which itself undergirds one particular tradition—the Enlightenment tradition of Western secular modernity), European Enlightenment values, traditions, and forms of life do not seem nearly so different *in nature* from the so-called religious traditions of Asia.

■ READING "RELIGION" AGAINST THE GRAIN

If the *modern* concept of religion is (as I would argue) a *product* of secularization (that is, of the differentiation of spheres of human life in modern industrialized and postindustrialized societies), if it is in fact a *secular* concept (that is, an exclusionary label used by "secularist ideologies" to classify that which they claim not to be), might we usefully apply it within the supposedly secular sphere—as a transgressive move? What I have in mind here is an approach to comparative analysis that is prepared to transgress the highly policed boundary between the secular and the religious, between the traditional and the modern, between the Western and the Asian. Why not compare "Hail to the Chief" to a Vedic hymn praising Indra, or deity veneration to celebrity adoration, or the capitalist ideology of "market forces" to the Brahmanical ideology of *saṃsāra*? All of these comparisons would bring out interesting similarities and differences, but they all involve rethinking, unraveling, and transgressing the dichotomy between the secular and the religious, which *in its very sacredness in the modern Western consciousness privileges certain forms of life over others and sometimes even prevents certain questions from being asked or considered.* There are many interesting scholarly works that already explore cross-cultural themes, myths, and rituals in interesting and innovative places. Akhil Gupta's refreshing comparison of the reincarnation of souls and the rebirth of commodities is a good example of this kind of work.[48] Few studies, however, follow Gupta in directly challenging the construction of binary oppositions that make such comparisons appear unusual, often delightful, but always framed as exceptions to the rule.

Such strategic transgressions and inversions aside, one cannot simply wish the category of "religion" away. Not using the term will not erase the culturally embedded associations that derive from it or the related constellation of concepts and orientations that cluster around it. Rather, we need to pay renewed attention to the ways in which the term *religion* is being used, most notably the way in which it demarcates cultures, traditions, practices, and communities according to a number of competing (but at a deeper level, actually complicitous) ideological interests. For instance, the separation of "the religious" from the supposedly "secular" realms of politics and economics serves the interests of both secularists and those who wish to preserve the religious and insulate it from wider social criticism.[49]

There is a need, then, to be more *strategic* and sensitive to the diverse contexts in which the map of religion is being used. Because discourses are neither homogeneous nor unidirectional it is possible to enter the "discourse of religion" precisely as a means of contesting, reinterpreting, and reading its very "commonsenseness" against the grain.[50] What I am advocating therefore is a dual strategy—a "double move" that contests, interrogates, and denaturalizes the modern category of "religion," on the one hand, but which also actively rereads such taken-for-granted concepts of the Western cartographic imagination in new, imaginative, and transgressive ways. One might consider, for instance, applying the map of religion to an analysis of capitalist and consumerist ways of life, to secular rationalism, neoliberal ideology, nationalism, and scientism, as a means of challenging the normative effects and assumptions of the ideologies the category undergirds. Again, one might read "faith" as Rustom Bharucha does, as a complex and diverse set of phenomena that resists easy binary oppositions between "believer" and "nonbeliever" or "confessional" and "nonconfessional"—terms that have dictated the cultural wars of religious studies for too long already. The approach I am advocating requires an orientation to categories such as "religion," "faith," " experience," "mysticism," and "spirituality" (for example) that is more strategic and context-sensitive than either unreflective usage of the category as a normative given or simple abandonment of the category altogether. *It involves paying attention to "the politics of macrotranslation"—that is, the way in which entire worldviews, traditions, and forms of life have become translated through the universalizing "discourse of religion."* Fundamental to this approach is the realization noted by Cantwell Smith in his mature reflections upon his work:

> When I wrote *The Meaning and End* [*of Religion*] I knew that "religion" was a Western and modern notion. I had not yet seen, but now I do see clearly, that *"religion" in its modern form is a secular idea.* Secularism is an ideology, and "religion" is one of its basic categories.... The secular Weltanschauung postulates, and then presupposes, a particular—indeed an odd—view of the human, and of the world: namely the secularist view. It sees the universe, and human nature, as essentially secular, and sees "the religions" as addenda that human beings have tacked on here and there in various shapes and for various interesting, powerful or fatuous reasons.[51]

This is a crucial point to understand. "Religion" as a modern discourse is a product of the processes of secularization that took hold in Europe from the Reformation onward. It is a "secular" category in the sense that it provides an ideological contrast and platform for asserting, on the one hand, the distinctiveness of particular "religions" (keeping them isolated from certain forms of critique because of their claimed sui generis status but also restricting their public role); but perhaps more crucially, on the other hand, the discourse of religion maintains the claim for the *exceptionalism* of secular philosophies (privileged and raised above all other ideologies as the singular and *transcendental* discourse of Western modernity).

▪ REENGAGING THE COMPARATIVE STUDY OF RELIGION: THE LEGACY OF CULTURAL CRITIQUE

The category of "Religion" has of course also provided a point of orientation and a putative unity for the academic field of the study/history of religions.[52] What, then, is the future for the comparative study of "religions" in this context? Although most mainstream accounts of the history of the "history of religions" frame the emergence of the comparative study of religion as an ideological battle to free the subject from (Christian) theological influence, as scholars such as Hans Kippenberg and Wouter Hanegraaf have argued, the emergence of the history of religions as an academic field in Europe was also bound up with debates about the processes of modernization, industrialization, and diverse attempts by scholars to theorize "modernity."[53] Much of the classic scholarship within the field was concerned not just with defining a legitimate "science of religions" but also with defending and contesting different models of what it is to be modern through a comparative analysis of "the other" (whether conceived as "the Orient," "the archaic or primitive," or "the non-Western," etc.).[54] But what if, as Bruno Latour has suggested, we have never been modern?[55] What if the mythic ideology of modernity is simply that— the latest in a long line of assertions of Western exceptionalism, complete with its own millenarian tendency and missionizing drive to remake the world in its own image?

Much scholarship on the history of the study of religion has focused upon the claims to found a comparative "science of religion" that would seek to avoid the subjectivist pitfalls of "insider," theological positioning. This attempt to establish a field of study grounded in the empirical data and axioms of the social sciences explains, for instance, why figures such as Max Müller and William James have been so crucial to the historiography of religious studies since both figures grounded their claims on the attempt to develop a justifiably scientific approach to the comparative study of religion. However, both thinkers also participate in another important strand within the field—one that is too often neglected in the history of the field—namely, the role of the comparative study of religion as a form of *cultural critique*. This is the legacy within which I would seek to locate my own work problematizing Western categories when posited as universal truths. Rather than undermining the study of religion, challenging the *"religionization" of non-Western cultures* highlights the ongoing significance of comparativist forays in the development of cultural critique, as carried out by scholars within this field of study. As Müller famously said, echoing Goethe, "He who knows one, knows none." This basic axiom of the comparativist approach I would argue is even more appropriate in a tradition of cultural critique. One cannot develop a meaningfully critical perspective upon Western discourses of modernity without recourse to historical and *non-Western contexts* as sites of epistemological *difference*—of contrast—to those discourses. Otherwise it becomes all too easy to enter into culturally specific feedback loops, resulting in a rhythmic and cyclical production of binary oppositions and fixed positions within which intellectual thought is forced to oscillate. The colonial translation of diverse civilizations through the prism of the category of "religion" remains, in a Western context at least, the primary point of orientation and intervention for the comparative study of cultures. It is where the suspects are held for interrogation. That there are considerable problems in reading universal history in terms of the deeply embedded category of religion in the modern Western imagination is precisely a reason for its ongoing interrogation by scholars with specialist knowledge of non-Western cultures, if only because it remains the point of entry of so much that constitutes "cultural difference" into the Western *imaginaire*.[56]

In continuing the intellectual legacy within the study of religions of interrogating and challenging dominant models of modernity and Western identity there is an important and ongoing role for the comparative study of "religion" in a postcolonial context—acting as a kind of "foreign body" or "point of infiltration" within the university: a space for both the *specialized* and *comparative* study of cultures; a place for the articulation of cultural difference and the exercise of sensitive comparisons; and a site where the Eurocentric, theological, and secularist presuppositions of the academy can be thoroughly interrogated, explored, and debated alongside the study of non-Western wisdom traditions that have been subalternized and framed as "religious" by colonial epistemologies.[57] What better place to start than with the category of "religion" itself?

■ NOTES

1. Daniel Dubuisson, *L'Occident et la Religion: Mythes, Science, et Idéologie* (Brussels: Complexe, 1998); English translation, *The Western Construction of Religion* (Baltimore: Johns Hopkins University Press, 2003).

2. See Andre Gunder Frank, *Re-ORIENT:Global Economy in the Asian Age* (Berkeley: University of California Press, 1998). Frank argues that it is only Eurocentrism that causes us to see "Europe" as the focal point of world history. Directly challenging the received historiographical accounts provided by Marx, Weber, Polanyi, Braudel, and Wallerstein, Frank argues that the rise of the West from 1400 onward coincided with a period of partial decline in Asia and is tied, among other things, to the economic benefits gained by European expansionism. At the beginning of the twenty-first century, he suggests we are seeing the reemergence of Asia and a return to the Asia-centered global economy that preceded more recent history. For further discussion of the Eurocentric prejudices contained in mainstream accounts of world history (or even within the very nature of "History" itself), see J. M. Blaut, *Eight Eurocentric Historians* (New York: Guilford Press, 2000); and Dipesh Chakrabarty, *Provincializing Europe* (Princeton, NJ: Princeton University Press, 2000).

3. J. Brian Harley, "Maps, Knowledge, and Power," in *The Iconography of Landscape*, ed. Denis Cosgrove and Stephen Daniels (Cambridge: Cambridge University Press, 1994), 283.

4. For further discussion of this, see Richard King, *Orientalism and Religion: Postcolonial Theory, India and "the Mystic East"* (London: Routledge, 1999), chap. 2.

5. These works include Jonathan Z. Smith, *Imagining Religion: From Babylon to Jonestown* (Chicago: University of Chicago Press, 1982); Talal Asad, *Genealogies of Religion: Discipline and Reasons of Power in Christianity and Islam* (London: Johns Hopkins University Press, 1993); Russell McCutcheon, *Manufacturing Religion: The Discourse on Sui Generis Religion and the Politics of Nostalgia* (New York: Oxford University Press, 1997); Dubuisson, *L'Occident et la Religion*; King, *Orientalism and Religion*; Timothy Fitzgerald, *The Ideology of Religious Studies* (Oxford: Oxford University Press, 2000); Darren Peterson and Derek Walhof, eds., *The Invention of Religion: Rethinking Belief in Politics and History* (New

Brunswick, NJ: Rutgers University Press, 2002); William T. Cavanaugh, *Theopolitical Imagination: Discovering the Liturgy as a Political Act in an Age of Global Consumerism* (Edinburgh: T&T Clark, 2002); Talal Asad, *Formations of the Secular: Christianity, Islam, Modernity* (Stanford, CA: Stanford University Press, 2003); Arvind Mandair, "What If *Religio* Remained Untranslatable?" in *Difference in the Philosophy of Religion*, ed. Philip Goodchild (Burlington, VT: Ashgate Publishing Ltd., 2003), 87–100; Arvind Mandair, "Auto-Immunity in the Study of Religions(s): Ontotheology, Historicism and the Theorization of Indic Culture," *Sophia* 42, no. 2 (2004): 63–85; Arvind Mandair, "The Repetition of Past Imperialisms: Hegel, Historical Difference, and the Theorization of Indic Religions," *History of Religions* 44, no. 4 (2005): 277–99; Arvind Mandair, "The Politics of Nonduality: Reassessing the Work of Transcendence in Modern Sikh Theology," *Journal of the American Academy of Religion* 74 (2006): 646–73; Tomoko Masuzawa, *The Invention of World Religions or, How European Universalism Was Preserved in the Language of Pluralism* (Chicago: University of Chicago Press, 2005); Richard King, 'The Association of 'Religion' with Violence: Reflections on a Modern Trope," in *Religion and Violence in South Asia: Theory and Practice*, ed. John Hinnells and Richard King (London: Routledge, 2007), 226–57; Timothy Fitzgerald, *Discourse on Civility and Barbarity: A Critical History of Religion and Related Categories* (Oxford: Oxford University Press, 2007); Timothy Fitzgerald, ed., *Religion and the Secular: Historical and Colonial Formations* (London: Equinox, 2007); William T. Cavanaugh, *The Myth of Religious Violence: Secular Ideology and the Roots of Modern Conflict* (Oxford: Oxford University Press, 2009); Richard King, "Philosophy of Religion as Border Control: Globalization and the Decolonization of the 'Love of Wisdom' (*Philosophia*)," in *Postcolonial Philosophy of Religion*, ed. Purushottama Bilimoria and Andrew Irvine (Springer, 2009), 35–52. What is most intriguing about this body of published work interrogating the category of "religion" is that some works (notably Dubuisson, writing in French in 1998, and most of the authors in Peterson and Walhof, writing in 2002) were produced with little or no engagement with the wider debate going on in Anglophone religious studies on this question at the end of the twentieth century. Dubuisson's initial critique of the category of religion is largely independent of the already emerging Anglophone literature on this theme. Peterson and Walhof seem only to be aware of McCutcheon's 1997 work on this topic, writing as they do from the perspectives of the academic fields of history and political studies. This would suggest that wider cultural and political factors have acted to "pull the veil" from the eyes of scholars with regard to the naturalization of the category of "religion" in modernity. My suggestion in this essay is that the most significant factor in this "denaturalization" of the category in intellectual circles is the slow, but significant, impact of formal "decolonization" in the non-Western world that has been wrought by the end of European imperialism in the post–World War II period.

6. See Wilfred Cantwell Smith, *The Meaning and End of Religion* (New York: Macmillan, 1962), 50. Smith outlines the various shifts in the usage of the category of *religio* in the West from pre-Christian Rome to the present day. For a discussion of the significance of this shift, see King, *Orientalism and Religion*, chap. 2. Smith notes that in medieval Europe, the term was generally used by the Catholic tradition in the sense of "the religious life," that is, the life of monastic vows. The various *religiones* denoted the various monastic orders. However, it is with the Protestant Reformation that we find *religion* being used to denote faith or piety. This led the way for the seventeenth- and eighteenth-century uses of the term *religion* to denote a system of beliefs and the emphasis that theologians like Friedrich Schleiermacher and Rudolf Otto made upon "religious" as essentially about experience or a "creaturely feeling." In the late nineteenth and twentieth centuries we find the birth of a new goal—that of discerning the essence of "religion" and the religions. As Smith notes, "This is to carry the process of reification to its logical extreme: endowing the concepts that an earlier genera-

tion has constructed...with a final and inherent validity, a cosmic legitimacy" (*Meaning and End of Religion*, 47–48). Smith's overview of the history of the term in the West constitutes a single chapter of his work (chap. 2). For more detailed analyses, see Michel Despland, *La Religion en Occident: Evolution des idées et du vécu*, Héritage et Projet, 23 (Montreal: Fides, 1979); Ernst Feil, *Religio: Die geschichte eines neuzeitlichen Grundbegriffs vom Frühchristentum bis zur Reformation*, Forschung zur Kirchen- und Dogmengeschichte, 36 (Göttingen: Vandenhoeck and Ruprecht, 1986); and Ernst Feil, *Religio II: Die geschichte eines neuzeitlichen Grundbegriffs zwischen Reformation und Rationalismus (ca. 1540–1620)*, Forschung zur Kirchen- und Dogmengeschichte, 70 (Göttingen: Vandenhoeck and Ruprecht, 1997). See also Michel Despland and Gérard Vallée, eds., *Religion in History: The Word, the Idea, the Reality* (Ontario: Wilfred Laurier University Press, 1992); Dubuisson, *L'Occident et La Religion*; Fitzgerald, *Discourse on Civility and Barbarity*.

7. Smith, *Meaning and End of Religion*, 156, 171, 177.

8. For Smith's response to this and other criticism, see Wilfred Cantwell Smith, "Retrospective Thoughts on *The Meaning and End of Religion*," in *Religion in History: The Word, the Idea, the Reality*, ed. Michel Despland and Gérard Vallée (Ontario: Wilfrid Laurier University Press, 1992), esp. 14–15, 17–18.

9. See Steven Wasserstrom, *Religion after Religion* (Princeton, NJ: Princeton University Press, 1999), 240: "The dominance of mysticism in the History of Religions, more generally, remains regnant (not only genealogically) throughout the study of religion."

10. Denys Turner, *The Darkness of God: Negativity in Christian Mysticism* (Cambridge: Cambridge University Press, 1995); Grace Jantzen, *Power, Gender and Christian Mysticism* (Cambridge: Cambridge University Press, 1995); King, *Orientalism and Religion*; Robert Sharf, "The Zen of Japanese Nationalism," in *Curators of the Buddha: The Study of Buddhism under Colonialism*, ed. Donald Lopez Jr. (Chicago: University of Chicago Press, 1995), 107–60; Robert Sharf, "Buddhist Modernism and the Rhetoric of Meditative Experience," *Numen* 42, no. 3 (1995): 228–83.

11. Paul Heelas, *The New Age Movement* (Oxford: Blackwell, 1996). More recently Heelas has offered a spirited defense of progressive spiritualities against the charges of being reflective of consumerism, arguing that such "spiritualities of life" combine "inner-self" reflection with a socially engaged dimension. See Paul Heelas, *Spiritualities of Life: New Age Romanticism and Consumptive Capitalism* (New York: Wiley-Blackwell, 2008).

12. For a discussion of this, see Richard King, "Asian Religions and Mysticism: The Legacy of William James in the Study of Religion," in *William James and the Varieties of Religious Experience: Interdisciplinary Papers in Celebration of the Centenary of the Edinburgh Gifford Lectures* (a volume of papers delivered at the international and interdisciplinary centenary conference on William James's *Varieties of Religious Experience*), ed. Jeremy Carrette (London: Routledge, 2005), 106–23.

13. For a critique of the tendency to conceive of "Buddhism" as peculiarly concerned with the cultivation of "mystical experiences" and therefore as an archetypally "mystical" religion, see Sharf, "Buddhist Modernism and the Rhetoric of Meditative Experience." Sharf questions "the tendency to approach the compendious Buddhist *mārga* treatises (texts delineating the stages on the Buddhist path) as if they presented a phenomenological analysis of the experiences of seasoned meditators" (232). Rather, he argues, traditional references to meditation or mental development (*bhāvanā*) should be seen not in terms of the cultivation of extraordinary and private states of consciousness but as primarily liturgical and propadeutic in orientation. Such practice "consisted largely of the recitation of Pāli texts pertaining to meditation...chanting verses enumerating the qualities of the Buddha, reciting formulaic lists of the thirty-two parts of the body, and so on" (242). Moreover, in the modern period the "rhetoric of experience" functions as an empty category in which a

variety of Buddhist ideological positions can be placed and "Buddhism" as a spiritual phenomenon can be assigned a "transcultural, transhistorical reality." Such privatization of Buddhism allows for the construction of an idealized and ahistorical "world religion" amenable to both perennialist and secular interpretations and successfully divorces the traditional Buddhist meditative practices from the ethical, doctrinal, liturgical, and sociopolitical context in which they occurred.

14. For further discussion of this, see Jeremy Carrette and Richard King, *Selling Spirituality: The Silent Takeover of Religion* (London: Routledge, 2005).

15. Rustom Bharucha, *A Question of Faith* (London: Sangam Books, 1993).

16. Ibid., 10, 14.

17. For the distinction between a *śraddhānusārin* and the *dharmānusārin*, see *Abhidharmahrdaya*, 129–31. See also *Bodhisattva-Piṭaka*, chap. 11, in U. Pagel, *The Bodhisattva-Piṭaka*, 1995, especially 371. The Buddhist tradition lists the five faculties as "faith" (*śraddhā*), energy (*vīrya*), mindfulness (*smrti*), concentration (*samādhi*), and insight (*prajnā*). Although they are often ranked hierarchically by the tradition, Gombrich has suggested that the commentarial distinction between a "follower of the Dhamma" (*dhammānusārī*) and a "follower through *śraddhā*" (*saddhānusārī*) may not be present in the Pāli Suttas themselves. See Richard Gombrich, *How Buddhism Began: The Conditioned Genesis of the Early Teachings*, Jordan Lectures in Comparative Religion (London: Continuum: Athlone Press, 1996).

18. Galen Amstutz, *Interpreting Amida: History and Orientalism in the Study of Pure Land Buddhism* (Albany: State University of New York Press, 1997), 86–87, 180n, 181n.

19. See John Stratton Hawley, "The Nirgun/Sagun Distinction in Early Manuscript Anthologies of Hindi Devotion," in *Bhakti Religion in North India*, ed. David Lorenzen (Albany: State University of New York Press, 1995). Hawley argues that the modern tendency to read a distinction between *sagun* and *nirgun* traditions of *bhakti* actually derives from sixteenth-/seventeenth-century sectarian anthologies of poetry in Hindu produced in North India in the sixteenth and cannot be easily read back earlier. See also Karen Prentiss, *The Embodiment of Bhakti* (Oxford: Oxford University Press, 1999).

20. See Asad, *Genealogies of Religion*; Dubuisson, *L'Occident et la Religion*; King, *Orientalism and Religion*; Peterson and Walhof, *Invention of Religion*; Fitzgerald, *Ideology of Religious Studies*.

21. Henry Olcott, cited in Donald Lopez Jr., "Belief," in *Critical Terms in Religious Studies*, ed. Mark Taylor (Chicago: University of Chicago Press, 1998), 29.

22. Ibid., 33.

23. H. L. Seneviratne, *The Work of Kings: The New Buddhism of Sri Lanka* (Chicago: University of Chicago Press, 1999), 3.

24. The realization that challenging the universal applicability of the concept of religion also causes one to reflect upon the peculiarity of modern secularity as the condition in which the modern notion of "religion" arises has subsequently been noted, for instance, by Wilfred Cantwell Smith in his 1984 article: "Philosophia as One of the Religious Traditions of Humankind," in *Différences, valeurs, hiérarchie: Textes offerts a Louis Dumont*, ed. Jean-Claude Galey (Paris: Éditions de L'École des Hautes Études en Sciences Sociales, Maison des Sciences de l'Homme–Bibliotheque, 1984), 253–79; reprinted in *Modern Culture from a Comparative Perspective*, ed. John W. Burbridge (Albany: State University of New York Press, 1997), 35–49, 148–49; and again in *Wilfred Cantwell Smith: A Reader*, ed. Kenneth Cracknell (Oneworld Publications, 2001), 72–84.

25. Anouar Majid, *Unveiling Tradition: Postcolonial Islam in a Polycentric World* (Durham, NC: Duke University Press, 2000), 29; William D. Hart, *Edward Said and the Religious Effects of Culture* (Cambridge: Cambridge University Press, 2000).

26. As Talal Asad argues in *Genealogies of Religion*, the modern Western tendency to conceive of religion in terms of belief—located in the private state of mind of a believer— has led Westerners to think of religion as something that is essentially private and therefore *wholly* separate from the public realm of politics. Indeed, for Asad all attempts to find a universal definition or "essence" of religion are to be avoided because they imply that religion is somehow able to operate in isolation from other spheres of human cultural activity such as politics, law, and science (28). The privatization of the religious, characterized by the emphasis upon "the world faiths" simultaneously insulates such traditions from wider public criticism, but it also ghettoizes them by marginalizing their significance for debates in the public domain. Moreover, the sheer diversity of human cultures means that the search for universal definitions of terms like *religion* is fruitless. In its place Asad advocates an approach to the study of cultures that focuses upon embodied practices and the specific power relations in which they operate.

27. Indeed, since the collapse of the Soviet Union, it has become increasingly difficult to express cultural and political alternatives to Western liberal capitalism without such resistance being framed in terms of the post-Enlightenment category of "the religious." In the vacuum caused by the collapse of the communist bloc, Marxism itself appears to be going through a period of transition and reconfiguration "after the Age of Europe." In this new context, it is no surprise to find that it is the "culturalist" Marxists such as Althusser and particularly Gramsci who are proving of most interest to postcolonial and "third world" writers, if only because these strands of Marxist thought are better able to accommodate a dialectical space for indigenous intentionalities that are otherwise erased by universalist notions of "class" and a narrow emphasis upon economic determinism.

28. See Jacques Derrida, *Acts of Religion*, ed. and intro. by Gil Anidjar (London: Routledge, 2000), 64; see also 42, 45–46, 50–52, 66–67, 72.

29. José Casanova, *Public Religions in the Modern World* (Chicago: University of Chicago Press, 1994).

30. Smith, *Imagining Religion*, xi (emphasis added).

31. Peterson and Walhof, *Invention of Religion*, 1.

32. Smith, *Imagining Religion*, xii.

33. Frits Staal notes, for instance, that "the inapplicability of Western notions of religion to the traditions of Asia has not only led to piecemeal errors of labelling, identification and classification, to conceptual confusion and to some name-calling. It is also responsible for something more extraordinary: the creation of so-called religions." See J. F. Staal, *Rules without Meaning: Rituals, Mantras and the Human Sciences*, Toronto Studies in Religion Vol. 4 (New York: Peter Lang, 1989), 393.

34. See Asad, *Genealogies of Religion*, 190; Richard King, *Indian Philosophy: An Introduction to Hindu and Buddhist Thought* (1999; Washington, DC: Georgetown University Press, 2000), 237–38.

35. In his recent book *Imagined Hinduism: British Protestant Missionary Constructions of Hinduism, 1793–1900* (New Delhi: Sage Publications, 2006), Geoffrey Oddie establishes (following up on his 2003 article) that the earliest known use of the term *Hindoo-ism* was not in fact its adoption in the early nineteenth century by the Hindu reformer Rammohan Roy in 1816 (as I, following the work of Dermot Killingley, suggest in *Orientalism and Religion*) but, rather, in the personal correspondence of Charles Grant, an evangelical Christian, commercial agent, and the later director of the East India Company. Although Grant first uses the term in a letter dated September 1787, Oddie points out that "Grant seems to have assumed that an England-based recipient of his letter would already understand the meaning of the word" (71). Similarly, William Ward was already using the term in his diary in 1801. Thus, Oddie notes that Europeans employed the term *Hinduism* at least

twenty-nine years before Rammohan Roy used it in 1816. Furthermore, he contends, evidence that Hindu reformer Rammohan Roy met Yates (a Serampore missionary) in 1815 and visited Serampore in the following year leaves open the possibility that he borrowed the term *Hinduism* from the Baptist missionaries. Recent works by Oddie, Will Sweetman, and also David Lorenzen ("Gentile Religion in South India, China, and Tibet: Studies by Three Jesuit Missionaries," *Comparative Studies of South Asia, Africa and the Middle East* 27, no. 1 [2007]: 203–13) have shown that there remained an ongoing debate within Catholic and Protestant circles over the question of the unitary or plural nature of Hinduism as a phenomenon, despite the emergence of a dominant paradigm (represented, for instance, in the Protestant tradition by Ward and Carey), which emphasized the links between "Brahmanism" and "Hinduism," and a unitary model, based strongly on the paradigmatic example of (European) Christianity as the supreme religion and yardstick for all comparative analysis.

36. See John Esposito, *The Islamic Threat: Myth or Reality* (New York: Oxford University Press, 1992), 199–202.

37. In Eric Sharpe, *Understanding Religion* (London: Duckworth Co., 1983), 2.

38. Gombrich, *How Buddhism Began*; Steven Collins, *Selfless Persons: Imagery and Thought in Theravāda Buddhism* (Cambridge: Cambridge University Press, 1992); Joanna Jurewicz, "Playing with Fire: The Pratityasamutpada from the Perspective of Vedic Thought," *Journal of the Pali Text Society* 26 (2000): 77–103.

39. It is clear, for instance, that the *āstika–nāstika* distinction so often pressed into service to reinforce the separation of "Hindu" and "Buddhist" traditions is a fluid and changeable mode of classification with shades of meaning and application that shift according to context. The Buddhist philosopher Nāgārjuna, for instance, refers to the Vaiśesika school as one of several *nāstikas* (nonaffirmers) in his work the *Ratnāvalī* I, v. 60–61.

40. See Sharf, "Zen of Japanese Nationalism"; Sharf, "Buddhist Modernism and the Rhetoric of Meditative Experience."

41. Peter Gottschalk, *Beyond Hindu and Muslim* (Oxford: Oxford University Press, 2001), 3.

42. Peter Van der Veer, "The Foreign Hand: Orientalist Discourse in Sociology and Communalism," in *Orientalism and the Postcolonial Predicament*, ed. Carol A. Breckenridge and Peter Van der Veer (Philadelphia: University of Pennsylvania Press, 1993), 39.

43. Note that here I am explicitly resisting the tendency of "the modern consciousness" to equate the imaginary with the false. In that sense I am trying to reconnect with a more positive or perhaps "constructive" (in both senses of the term) understanding of the imagination in a manner that is consonant with pre-Enlightenment conceptions of the imagination, that is, before the imaginary came to mean "false" or unreal in the context of secular modernity. To see what is imagined or constructed as the 'false' is to fall into a trap set by post-Enlightenment thought, where the Cartesian dichotomy between mental and material existence is bolstered by an association of the "real" with "the empirical" and the material, as opposed to "the imagined," which is located in the mind of a human and therefore constitutes something that does not really exist "out there." Since the Enlightenment, imagination has often been the faculty that imagines that which does not exist (in the so-called real world). However, before secularization in medieval Europe the faculty of the imagination was not always seen as denoting the construction of the false but, rather, tended to be represented as a faculty of perception. Similarly in a traditional South Asian context, we should note the example of the Buddhist notion of *manas* as a sensory apparatus—that which apprehends ideas. When something is imagined— particularly at the social or conventional level—this does not make it false (a point well noted by those Indic philosophical traditions that promulgated a notion of two truths [*dvaya-satya*]). We should avoid treating the socially constructed as if it is unreal. It has effects.

44. Arvind Sharma, "An Indic Contribution towards an Understanding of the Word 'Religion' and the Concept of Religious Freedom," paper presented at "Completing the Global Renaissance: The Indic Contributions," organized by the Columbia Center for Buddhist Studies and the Infinity Foundation, New York, July 24–29, 2002.

45. For further discussion of these points, in particular the centripetalism that dominates modern conceptions of "religion," see Richard King, "Colonialism, Hinduism and the Discourse of Religion," in *Rethinking Religion in India: The Colonial Construction of Hinduism*, ed. Esther Bloch, Marianne Keppens, and Rajaram Hegde (Routledge, 2010), 95–113.

46. See David Chidester, *Savage Systems: Colonialism and Comparative Religion in Southern Africa* (Charlottesville: University Press of Virginia, 1996), 266.

47. David Scott, "Toleration and Historical Traditions of Difference," *Subaltern Studies* 11 (2000): 288–89.

48. Akhil Gupta, "The Reincarnation of Souls and the Rebirth of Commodities: Representations of Time in 'East' and 'West,'" *Cultural Critique* 22 (1992): 187–211. Gupta challenges the stereotypical dichotomy between Indian notions of time as "cyclic" and Western notions as "linear" with reference to the ongoing adoption of cyclic motifs in industrial and postindustrial Western societies. This does not lead to a kind of simplistic perennialism ("we are all basically the same") or to a rigid form of cultural apartheid ("we are all essentially different"); rather, it is a recognition that there are multiple registers to consider in comparative study and that a rigid separation of religious/secular, traditional/modern, preindustrial/industrial, and West/East causes us to miss opportunities to understand ourselves and others better. Such an approach, however, must take into account the multiple axes of domination—gender, sexuality, race, class, colonialism, etc.—and a recognition of differences both *between* and *within* the cultural phenomena under investigation.

49. Fundamentally, of course, the segregation of certain cultural traditions and movements as "religious" from "the secular" has functioned as one of the central platforms of secularism and its latest progeny, neoliberalism. Through this process, Islamic, Christian, and Buddhist (and so on) critiques of the social, economic, and political injustices of neoliberal policies, as promoted by groups such as the IMF and the World Bank, are portrayed as "religious," "tradition-bound," and (therefore) "dogmatic" and reactionary incursions in the otherwise secular realm of political and economic policy making. Secularist ideology requires the concept of religion precisely as a means of maintaining its own hegemony as "nonmetaphysical," which of course it is not.

50. One way to do this is to challenge the tendency to enter the terrain of "the discourse of religion" by exploring the tension between the Enlightenment tradition of locating religion in a privatized sphere of experience, belief, and "spirituality," on the one hand (Kant, Schleiermacher, James, Otto), and a more communitarian strand within the Enlightenment (probably best exemplified by figures like Robertson Smith, Mauss, and Durkheim) that locates the significance of "the religious" in the articulation of the values and perspectives of communities, societies, and cumulative traditions, on the other hand. The tension between these two Enlightenment strands can be seen, for instance, in W. C. Smith's choice of "faith" and "cumulative tradition" as dual alternatives to the category of "religion," thereby acknowledging both strands in his account.

51. Smith, "Retrospective Thoughts on *The Meaning and End of Religion*," 16 (emphasis added).

52. Indeed, one way to read the history of the study of religion is to consider it as a series of competing attempts to determine the precise locus of the religious—that is, to define the central focus of study. Is religion to be understood primarily in terms of myth (Müller), inner experience (Schleiermacher, James, and Otto), ritual (Robertson Smith), social fact

(Durkheim), belief in the supernatural (Tylor), or sacred text ("the Protestant assumption")? What one focuses upon is as much a consequence of the method or discipline that one is working within as it is a feature of the terrain itself.

53. Hans Kippenberg, *Entdeckung Der Religiongeschischte/Discovering Religious History in the Modern Age* (Princeton, NJ: Princeton University Press, 2002); Wouter J. Hanegraaf, "Defining Religion in Spite of History," in *The Pragmatics of Defining Religion: Contexts, Concepts and Contests*, ed. Jan Platvoet and Arie Molendijk (Leiden, Netherlands: E. J. Brill, 1999), 337–78.

54. See Hanegraaf's "Defining Religion in Spite of History," where the history of the "science of religions" is read as a battle between two competing intellectual trends (Isaiah Berlin's Enlightenment and "Counter-Enlightenment") and perhaps more significantly emotional responses to secular modernity—one positive, the other highly critical. The role of a Counter-Enlightenment and even "Romanticist" critique of secular modernity is no less obvious, for instance, in the birth of Orientalism and the clash between Anglicists and Orientalists over the nature of Britain's mission as imperial ruler of India. Within the study of Indic traditions, we should note that Western interest in Hinduism and even more so in Buddhism has often been motivated in terms of finding a receptacle for disillusioned and estranged Westerners to express what one might call countercultural, antimodern (or perhaps even "nonmodern") sentiments. Realizing this function of the category "Buddhism" in the Western *imaginaire* allows us to appreciate, as Richard Cohen has recently argued, the role that the study of Buddhism and Indology might play in exploring and contesting prevailing models of modernity (see Richard S. Cohen, "Why Study Indian Buddhism?" in *The Invention of Religion. Rethinking Belief in Politics and History*, ed. Darren Peterson and Derek Walhof [New Brunswick, NJ: Rutgers University Press, 2002], 34).

55. Bruno Latour, *We Have Never Been Modern*, trans. Catherine Porter (Cambridge: Harvard University Press, 1993).

56. For further discussion of this point, see King, "Philosophy of Religion as Border Control."

57. This can be done by drawing attention to the parochial or provincial nature of European and/or Western paradigms of knowledge, as well as to the ethnocentricity of some of its practices and theories. Such a project can be approached of course from a number of different disciplinary angles. My own particular interest tends to be what might be called in the West "philosophy" or the history of ideas, but this can be (and is being) done by anthropologists, sociologists, historians, geographers, cultural studies specialists, and so on.

3   Translations of Violence: Secularism and Religion-Making in the Discourses of Sikh Nationalism

Arvind-Pal S. Mandair

■ **THE DEMISE OF SECULAR CREEDS IN POLITICS AND THEORY**

While secularism has been integral to India's democracy for more than half a century, there has been increasing evidence in the last two decades of a crisis in the concept of secularism reflecting a similar crisis in relations between state and society. This has been amply demonstrated not only by the widespread and highly visible violence directed against ethnic and religious minorities by identifiable agents (Hindutva, Hindu nationalists, Sikh, Muslim separatists, etc.) but also by the more systemic and therefore less visible violence sponsored by the secular state. Following Slavoj Žižek I would like to designate the difference between these two kinds of violence as "subjective" and "objective."[1] Subjective violence is the kind of violence performed by a clearly identifiable agent such as the separatist or "religious" fundamentalist and enunciated, for example, as one's exclusive identity. Objective violence is the kind of violence inherent within the smooth functioning of political, intellectual, mediatic, and economic systems of the modern state; it treats any encroachment of the separatist/fundamentalist's subjective violence into the public domain as a violation of the legality of the state. Despite their apparent opposition, these two modes of violence are deeply complementary. In fact the correspondence between these two forms of violence sustains the very opposition between religion and secularism, society and state.

However, the inability to recognize this relationship between "subjective" and "objective" violence is one of the signs of the crisis in the concept of secularism discernable in the theorization of recent political events in South Asia. For example, until the late 1980s the dominant Left-liberal secularist position among Indian intellectuals—most of whom were either Nehruvians or Marxists—identified "religion," "sectarianism," "fundamentalism," and "separatism" (euphemisms for identifiable agents: Muslims in Kashmir and Sikhs in Punjab) as *the* threat to a fledgling Indian democracy. This perceived threat was usually instigated from outside the nation by a "foreign hand." Interestingly Hindu nationalism, though perceived as communalist, was not generally considered a threat to Indian democracy until relatively recently. The threat was always projected as non-Hindu. As the role of the Indian state had become more suspect by the early 1990s, evidenced by its suspicious neutrality toward Hindu nationalists, other voices began to make themselves heard. Prominent political psychologists and sociologists began to formulate a "communitarian" critique of secularism that advocated decentralizing policies based on their support for a pluralist democracy rooted in the recognition of the pivotal role of India's religious communities in the makeup of Indian democracy.[2]

For some years the debate between Left-liberal secularists and communitarians defined the polarized state of Indian theoretical responses. It was not until the Hindu nationalists led by the Bhartīya Janata Party (BJP) won the Indian elections in 1996, and thereafter began to redefine Indian democracy in terms of a "Hindu secularism" by way of influencing the writing of Indian history and the entire educational and pedagogical infrastructure of India, that a third position began to emerge. This alternative position was defined mainly by disaffected intellectuals of the Indian radical Left, many of whom were historians or literary theorists influenced by French poststructuralism and especially by Edward Said's postcolonial theory. When inflected into the scene of Indian polity, Said's "secular anti-imperialist critique" provided a way to think about democracy without succumbing to the myth of national belonging, that is, from the standpoint of those most vulnerable to the vagaries of majoritarian rule. Indian postcolonial theory has done much to deconstruct the religious effects of nationalism in addition to demonstrating that religion is not native to India but is a colonial imposition. What seems clear is that scholars in South Asian studies and postcolonial theory have been reluctant to move beyond the safety of the secular, specifically refusing any engagement with the "discourses of ontotheology and the postsecular" for fear of tainting their intellectual enterprises with the question of religion.[3]

It is here that we come across an important and revealing difference between theoretical responses to the crisis of secularism by Western (European American) and Indian academics. Much of the critique of secularism by Western academics has been performed mainly by those who are professedly religious or by those who write from the perspective of the academic study of religion and, insofar, keep a minimal distance from religion. Nevertheless Western academics generally share at least a minimal commitment to the idea that religion has been, for better or for worse, part and parcel of the cultural and philosophical frame of the history of the West. By contrast critiques of secularism by Indian academics are rooted in a strictly historicist perspective and rarely come from academics who either profess affiliation to a religion or indeed are part of the scholarly study of religion. Even within critiques of secularism that have been written from a postcolonial/historicist perspective, the absence of systematic questioning about the supposed universality of "religion" is somewhat surprising. This point is well illustrated by Anuradha Dingwaney and Rajeshwari Sundar Rajan in their volume entitled *The Crisis of Secularism in India*. The editors offer the following explanation for the absence of discussion about religion in the considerations of secularism in their book:

> Despite its crisis, secularism bears a normative status within and as constitutive of a modernity that remains the context from which we perform our critique. The critique of secularism is therefore obliged to be self-reflexive, an insider job by secularists

themselves. In the contemporary academy it would seem that few exercises of this kind are performed by the professedly religious. Or at least the discourses of the ontotheological and the post-secular today inhabit other spaces than that of the historical, social science, and cultural critiques of secularism such as this one. Writing about a conference on religion that he had convened in Capri in 1994, Derrida defined the (limits of the) participants' position as thus: "We are not priests bound in a ministry, nor theologians, nor qualified, competent representatives of religion, nor enemies of religion as such....But we also share a commitment to Enlightenment values." Some of these limits operate in the same way among the essays assembled here, even as a critique of secularism.

Religion, in these essays as well as in the broader discourse that constitutes them, is primarily addressed in terms of historical explanation or as a sociology of religion.... The "religious" is a concept that encounters a notable impasse in the work of contemporary postcolonial theorists who attempt to go beyond respectful or wistful acknowledgement of this "other" knowledge.[4]

What Dingwaney and Rajan seem to imply here is that to make a valid critique of secularism, the conceptual terms of this critique must not be tainted with religion or the religious. The terms of this critique, in order for it to be a critique, must acknowledge a strict separation of the religious and the secular. One cannot think in terms of religious ideas since this would be untrue to Enlightenment values. Echoing Said's "secular anti-imperialist critique" Indian postcolonial theorists see themselves as faithfully adhering to Enlightenment values because they are able to refuse any contact with religion. Western theorists by contrast have been able to blur the lines of separation between religion and secularism because they "inhabit other spaces" in the humanities such as theology or the study of religion.[5]

In this essay I question the logic of thinking about the twin phenomena referred to either as the crisis of Indian secularism or as the return of religious nationalisms (specially Sikh ethno-nationalism) through a notion of violence grounded in the conceptual opposition between religion and secularism. Continuing to do so leaves us with an either/or scenario: either the "subjective" violence of religious nationalisms or the "objective" normal and peaceful state of things promised by the secular state. Such a standpoint hinders any attempt to understand the nature of violence that simultaneously underpins these two domains. More important, it prevents us from locating the driving mechanism behind phenomena such as Sikh ethno-nationalism and why the resolution to it may not consist in measures that attempt merely to localize, pacify, or liberalize it but, rather, has to do with the very nature of democracy in India. What if the real nature of the problem is that we are trying to perceive subjective and objective violence from the same standpoint? And what if this very standpoint, either/or, is itself false? What if the seemingly irrational subjective violence (of religious nationalism, sectarian conflict, ethnic cleansing, etc.) is perceived as a disturbance of the "normal" state of things only from the either/or standpoint whereas, in fact, the "normal" state of things simply hides the reality of objective violence that constitutes the state?

Rather, and particularly in relation to Sikh ethno-nationalism, I argue that we need to bring into view a third kind of violence—one that is not yet recognized due to the standpoint from which we perceive the distinction between religion and secularism—that holds the subjective and objective, religious nationalism and the state secularism, together in India. This is a symbolic violence embodied in language and present in the forms of social domination reproduced in our customary forms of speech.

In order to make sense of this third form of violence, it is first of all necessary to outline the conventional schema for representing violence associated with Sikh ethno-nationalism and how this conventional representation of violence has been deployed to frame our perception of Sikh ethno-nationalism. I shall therefore begin with a brief description of the "subjective" (i.e., "religious") nature of Sikh violence before comparing it with the "objectification" of Sikh ethno-nationalism within the secular discourses of state, media, and academia. The final part of the essay will attempt to make a shift beyond the conventional representations of violence (subjective versus objective) by reaching back to a point prior to the representation itself in order to retrieve a more foundational form of violence (symbolic violence) that can help us understand (1) the inherent connection between the so-called crisis of secularism and the return of religion into Indian politics and (2) ways of understanding what really drives movements like Sikh ethno-nationalism.

■ SUBJECTIVE VIOLENCE: SIKHS AND THE INDIAN STATE (1978 TO 1998)

Of the three forms of violence being considered in this essay, subjective violence is the most visible. The term *subjective* suggests several markers that tell us something about the nature of the violence in question: (1) that it is performed by a clearly identifiable agent: the "fundamentalist," the "terrorist," the religious nationalist, and so on; (2) that it has clearly identifiable consequences: ethno-religious cleansing, civil unrest, sectarian or communal rioting, international conflict, violent insurgency, and so on; and (3) that the agent is able to identify a certain logic to the violence in the sense that the latter is intrinsic to the formation and maintenance of identity.

In many ways, the conflict between the Sikhs and the Indian state from the late 1970s to the 1990s exemplifies all three of the above markers. Since this conflict is reasonably well documented elsewhere,[6] I shall restrict myself to simply listing the key events, agents, and agencies associated with it:

(a) Between the 1970s and 1990s, the long-running political agitation by the main Sikh political party, the Akali Dal, against the ruling Congress, had two aims: on the one hand, to end Indira Gandhi's dictatorial state of emergency and, on the other, to attain a majority-Sikh Punjabi-speaking state in postindependence India.

(b) The formation of a political party, Dal Khalsā, funded by the Punjab Congress Party (Zail Singh), allowed fringe Sikh religious organizations such as Damdami Taksaal and Akhand Kirtani Jatha an entry into Punjab politics and ultimately helped to undermine the putatively secular stance of the main Sikh political party, the Akali Dal, turning the latter toward a more "religious" politics.

(c) The cynical engineering of confrontation and violent clashes between Sikh groups and the "heretical" sects such as the Nirankaris was carried out by the Punjab Congress and right-wing Hindu media controlled by Lala Jagat Narain. Following the Sikh–Nirankari clash, Sant Jarnail Singh Bhindranwale, as head cleric of Damdami Taksaal, emerged into mainstream Punjab politics, partly through his promotion by the then chief minister of Punjab and later president of India, Giani Zail Singh. Within a short time Bhindranwale became the most identifiable agent in the rise of Sikh militancy and "fundamentalism" prior to June 1984.

(d) During the Asian Games (1982–83) Sikh protesters were stopped from entering the capital and harassed or humiliated by the Haryana police; in response to this development the Akali Dal resurrected its agitation against the central government in the form of the Anandpur Sahib Resolution. In response to Sikh agitation the ruling Congress Party became more intransigent in the face of mounting pressure from Hindu nationalists. As Punjab politics became more polarized, this led Bhindranwale and the Akali Dal (Longowal) to join forces in their opposition to the government. By the beginning of 1984 Bhindranwale eventually broke with the Akalis and took up residence with his followers at the Akal Takht (Sikhs' highest seat of political sovereignty), a move that was calculated, on the one hand, to undermine the Akali Dal's and Shiromani Gurdwara Parbhandhak Committee's monopoly on political and religious authority within Sikhism and, on the other hand, to invite a violent attack on the Akal Takht by the state. Part of Bhindranwale's calculation was that any attack on the Akal Takht would constitute an attack on Sikh political sovereignty and would thus engineer a clash of sovereignties, thereby exposing a fundamental flaw within the institution of Indian secular democracy.

(e) Using the Akal Takht as a base Bhindranwale spearheaded a more extreme phase of resistance to the state including acts of retributive violence, including assassinations of police officers and others deemed to be "enemies of Sikhism." Between March and June 1984 there was a tense standoff between Bhindranwale in the Akal Takht and state paramilitary forces who had surrounded the Golden Temple complex with a view to curtail Bhindranwale's activities.

(f) This led directly in June 1984 to Indira Gandhi's fateful decision to remove Bhindranwale from the Golden Temple complex through a massive army operation code named Blue Star and fronted by Sikh battalions. In October 1984 Indira Gandhi was assassinated by her Sikh bodyguards, which in turn was followed by anti-Sikh pogroms in New Delhi orchestrated by elements close to the Congress Party.

(g) The period from 1984 to 1992 saw (i) the emergence and proliferation of a militant Sikh insurgency based within and outside of India for a separate Sikh state (Khalistan) and led by groups such as Babbar Khalsa International (BKI), All India Sikh Students Federation (AISSF), Khalistan Commando Force (KCF), and Bhindranwale Tigers Force (BTF); and (ii) a series of massive counterinsurgency operations by Indian paramilitary forces that systematically eliminated the "terrorist" threat and returned Punjab to a state of normalcy in the early 1990s.

What seems to stand out about this conflict, and justifies the labeling of Sikh agitation and politics as "subjective" violence, is the degree of conformity between Sikh self-representations, irrespective of whether this was by the democratically elected Akalis (who had, until the intervention of Bhindranwale and Dal Khalsa, maintained a resolutely secular politics for the betterment of the state of Punjab) or the more militant Khalistani organizations (such as All India Sikh Students Federation, Babbar Khalsa International, Damdami Taksaal, Bhindranwale Tiger Force, Khalistan Commando Force, etc.). Even a cursory perusal of the literature and rhetoric of these organizations reveals a distinctive logic of violence that justified their agitation in the public sphere, such as the relatively nonviolent (*morchas*) courting of imprisonment by breaking state law or the more overtly terrorist tactics of the Khalistani groups. This logic of violence derives largely from a particular interpretation of Sikh theology and history that in turn informs their broadly representative narrative of Sikh identity.

Their narrative goes something like this: The origin of Sikh identity lies in the personality and teaching of one man, Guru Nanak, whose philosophy broke with the Vedic heritage into which he was born, thereby violating the Brahmanic norms that governed non-Muslim or "Hindu" society in the fourteenth–fifteenth century. Before he died, Nanak founded his own community, chose a successor, and passed authority to the latter by bequeathing to him, and to eight other successors, the signature name "Nanak." During the reign of the fifth and sixth Gurus, who came into conflict with the Mughal Empire, the role of the individual Sikh was transformed from a purely spiritual aspirant (*miri*) to that of a spiritual aspirant fully immersed in temporal affairs (*miri/piri*). Although this transition was solidified through the creation of the Khalsa by the tenth and last living guru in 1699, the movement toward the immersion of politics and spirituality (or rather, the resistance toward the separation of these two realms) had already begun with Guru Nanak. In other words, violence—understood as an entry into and resistance to the sphere sanctioned by the Mughal state—became explicit through the creation of the Khalsa. The purpose of the Khalsa was therefore fourfold: (1) to resist political and religious persecution by the Mughal state, (2) to fight the social oppression of Brahmanism, (3) to remain involved in worldly and political affairs through a spirit of inner detachment, and (4) to live according to a code of conduct (*rahit*) that would help distinguish Khalsa identity from all others. From the early eighteenth century to the present day, this narrative goes, the Khalsa identity has remained sovereign and distinct from Islam and Hinduism. Although it suffered a decline in the nineteenth century, the Khalsa was able to revive its authentic (*tat*) form through the reformist movement known as the Singh Sabha.

As we know from recent scholarship,[7] however, this narrative of an unchanging identity from the late seventeenth century to the present day occludes two important facts: (1) that this identity was framed by scholars from the dominant Tat Khalsa faction of the Singh Sabha movement and, perhaps more important, (2) that the process of framing identity had itself changed in the colonial period through the adoption of a "Western" logic of identity.[8] Thus it is now possible to distinguish two modes of Khalsā identity—one prior to colonialism and another identity forged in the colonial era. Prior to colonialism, Khalsā identity was framed through a logic that allowed overlap with a broader "Hindu" or Indic sphere of meaning, but where Hindu had not yet been redefined in the modern (and colonial) sense of the term. Precolonial Khalsā identity could be described as conforming to a contradictory logic of "both-and" (or where A = B, Sikh = Hindu, etc.). In other words, Khalsā Sikhs had a sense of their own identity, but it was an identity that also admitted a relationality to a broader Indic universe. During the colonial period Orientalists and Brahmanic elites redefined the signifier *Hindu* as a religious signifier and specifically in contradistinction from the other as Muslim. In response to this Brahminization of the broader Hindu sphere of meaning (which absorbed Sikhs under a Vaishnava/Brahmanic umbrella), Sikhs in the nineteenth century responded by declaring a distinct Sikh identity that was *not* Hindu. This new framing of identity was based on a logic of absolute identity—"either-or," A ≠ B, Sikh ≠ Hindu, and so on—which effectively posited Sikh and Hindu as religious and therefore mutually exclusive signifiers. I will look more closely at this latter frame of identification, which had become hegemonic by the early twentieth century. For now it should suffice to note that subjective violence (both Sikh and Hindu) is driven by a logic of absolute identity (where identity is valued over and above difference), which not only is a response to "the violation of the self-same in its purity by an external other" but is also the means whereby the identity of the self is constituted and maintained.

■ OBJECTIVE VIOLENCE: RELIGION AND SECULARISM IN DISCOURSES OF STATE, MEDIA, AND ACADEMIA

In this section of the essay I shall focus on the *representation* of "religious" violence associated with Sikh militancy and terrorism during the 1980s. Part of the function of this representation is to reproduce the enunciation of religious identity by colonial elites and by religious nationalists in the postcolonial context (or what I referred to above as the "subjective" violence of religious and ethnic "fundamentalisms"). The reproduction of this enunciation is evident (1) in the work of media journalists and academic experts specializing in the study of "religious violence" and (2) in the political management of religious pluralism by the secular state (which can be considered as a systemic violence endemic to the legal function of the state). These discourses of religion-making not only subscribe to the doctrine of secularism but are connected by a process of "generalized translation," which can often create an unholy alliance among academia, media, and the state.

This connection among academic writing, media reporting, and statecraft has recently been subjected to closer scrutiny.[9] A number of scholars have recently criticized the conceptualization of religion in the work of Mark Juergensmeyer, who reinvented himself during the 1990s as one of the leading experts in religious terrorism and whose writing also reflects a general trend in academic literature about

Sikh "terrorism."[10] Juergensmeyer deploys a concept of religion that can be traced back to the early work of Orientalist historians of religion and native elite scholars, which has helped to construct a firm notion of "Sikh theology." This concept of religion in general and Sikh religiosity in particular captures and builds a static ontology of a privatized Sikh subjectivity that becomes axial to modern definitions of Sikhs and Sikhism. In the 1980s and 1990s this static privatized Sikh subject came to be deployed in numerous articles written by academics who became "experts" in Sikh "terrorism" literally overnight. Many of these articles appeared in national newspapers particularly within the Indian and Western presses. The question that I ask below is how a certain conceptualization of Sikh "religiosity" was translated from the work of historians of religions, into the work of academics who specialize in the study of "religious violence," and from there to the wider sphere of media journalism. My intention in the following discussion is not to exonerate the actual violence perpetrated by militants. Rather, I try to highlight the problem of adopting "a secularist position that privileges its own standpoint as *uniquely* positioned to promote tolerance, pluralism and protection of minorities in a modern society."[11] The irony here is that in the various attempts to exclude "religious" discourse from the public arena, the pluralistic ground championed by the secularist doctrine is itself undermined. The blind spot of secularism appears when it dogmatically sets itself up as the doxa, and thus authoritative center, of public discourse. Central to this doxa is the oppositional discourse of "religion" and violence and the process of identity politics that in turn serves to maintain a strict dichotomy between "religious" and "secular" worldviews.[12]

In the South Asian context, the role of the fiduciary and its link to constitutional law is clearly illustrated by the role of the state and its representations of "religious violence" between Hindus and Muslims, Hindus and Sikhs, and Buddhists and Hindus. In their recent work on war and democracy, Michael Hardt and Antonio Negri analyze this link between violence, the law, and state machinery. Hardt and Negri argue that once the state reserves for itself the exercise of violence as legal, all other social violence is deemed illegitimate.[13] Although religion does not specifically figure in their argument, it is not difficult to see that a perfect example of social violence would be the violence attributable to religion. According to this argument "religious" violence has by definition deviated from its proper place, namely, the domain of privatized interiority that corresponds to a static notion of the divine, which in turn constitutes the truth of religion.[14] Although the state's legitimation of violence is grounded in the structures of law, an adequate notion of legitimate violence is in turn dependent on the law's claim to morality. Violence is legitimate if it can be morally justified but illegitimate if its basis is immoral.[15] This is of course a circular argument, for the law's claim to morality is itself justified by the state's presentation through the media of an enemy with its attendant threat of indeterminate chaos. Ultimately, then, it is the presence of the enemy that legitimates the violence of the state. The figure of the enemy can be seen to function either as a schema of reason or as a schema of mythologization. Either way the schema sketches out in advance the very horizon on which is constructed the sphere of one's own (self) versus the sphere of what is radically different (other). Within the triangular nature of the schema that connects the representation of chaos–religion–enemy, (1) chaos names that which has fallen from the state of order, (2) the guarantor of order is the state of divine stasis exemplified by the truth of religion, and (3) the enemy is a figure of chaos that deviates and tempts into deviation from the truth of religion.

While this schema serves to demonstrate the state's need for maintaining security, it is in fact based on the two sources that constitute the phenomenon called "religion." As Derrida reminds us, these two sources are, on the one hand, the notion of sacredness exhibited by the experience of remaining unscathed or untouched by anything exterior and, on the other hand, the experience of belief (the fiduciary-*ity* of confidence, trustworthiness, faith, credit, etc.).[16] The signification of religious violence as radically different from the state's use of violence therefore depends on the very same fiduciary structure, such that when the other or enemy is confronted as other, the pure relation to other *is* faith. The state simultaneously *suspends belief* in the name of knowledge (religion must remain unscathed, untouched by violence by remaining privatized; religious identity must be conformed to!) and *reinforces it* (believe in the purity of public space that guarantees the structure of society!). By thus endorsing religious identity as the only state in which religion can exist socially, and at the same time manipulating a knowledge about the fiduciary structure of religious identity, the state demonstrates an almost transcendental ability not only to monopolize violence but, more insidiously, to manufacture violence and then switch it off at will.

In short, liberal humanism entails a very real correspondence (or "generalized translation") between the domains of academic theory and state politics insofar as both are able to manipulate the relationship between religious identity and violence.[17] This ability to translate between theory and politics, and hence the ability to switch the flow of violence on and off, which would also imply a seemingly facile connection to constitutional law, is clearly illustrated in contexts as different as India and the United States by the recent mediatization of "religious" conflict between Hindus and Muslims (Ayodhya, 1992; Gujerat, 2002), Hindus and Sikhs (Punjab and New Delhi, 1984), Buddhists and Hindus (Sri Lanka), and Muslims and the West (post-9/11). The term *mediatization* effectively names the mechanisms whereby academic theory fluidly translates into state politics and from there into the global circulation of the stereotype. Despite their different geographical and cultural contexts, it is not difficult to demonstrate parallels between the media representation of these conflicts in India during the 1980s and 1990s and the representation of religious violence in the US media post-9/11. For one thing both India and the United States are large democratic states with legal constituencies framed in the name of secularism but governed in reality by overwhelming religious majorities—Christian in the case of the United States and Hindu in the case of India.

Second, the main ideological vector in US and Indian media and academia during the 1980s and early 1990s with regard to the representation of religious violence largely echoed state policy, not only by attributing violence to some enemy of the state (turbaned and bearded Sikhs or Muslim fundamentalists with regard to India, Muslims with regard to the United States) but by narrating and displaying the spectacle of violence as a deviation of these troublesome minorities from the "truth" of the religions they purport to represent, where truth is contained in some kind of fiduciary structure. Of course, the truth of these religions, as both the media and academia have been so keen to portray, is peace, or non-resistance to the state law. It is the ultimate measure of a religion's compatibility with democracy. Clearly, what is elided in this representation is that the definition of religion in terms of peace/non-resistance is also a legal definition. It is framed by a juridical process that has predetermined the definition of religion as a renunciation of violence and violence as a deviation or fall from religion's truth.

Third, there is an interesting, though relatively unexplored, convergence between India and the United States during the early 1980s in their respective representations of religious violence. The early 1980s witnessed the development of an academic forum on terrorism and media to consider the growing problem of "terrorist theater"—a staged performance of violence in which the "terrorist" had become the "master of ceremonies at a media spectacle."[18] The major international forum for this was the Second International Conference on Terrorism held in Washington, DC, in 1984. This was an important policy-making event in which a new public figure, the "terrorism expert," joined with policy makers, journalists, and politicians in articulating the phenomenon of media terrorism. In a deft series of moves this conference (aptly named "Terrorism: How the West Can Win"), along with its published output, projected a somewhat different understanding of terrorism as (1) the broad targeting of civilians with a focus on an international event such as hostage taking that made extensive use of the media, (2) an infection whose main site and source was the Middle East, and (3) having a special relationship to "Islam," such that the "world of Islam" effectively came to be seen as having invented terrorism.[19]

Particularly interesting is the timing of this high-profile conference and the way its central message was adapted by the Indian state and media before and especially after 1984. During this period the Indian state invested heavily in propagating the idea of an imminent threat to the nation, primarily by Kashmiri Muslims but increasingly after 1982 by Sikh separatists, whose imagery was effortlessly reinvented as the new international terrorist sponsored by India's supposedly malign Muslim neighbor, Pakistan. This is an exemplary episode in modern Indian politics that demonstrates the state's ability to switch violence on and off, seemingly at will. Let me briefly elaborate on this ability to manipulate the relationship between religious identity and violence by referring to the secular Indian state's careful crafting of the phenomenon of "Sikh terrorism" and how this phenomenon was seamlessly incorporated into the academic domain. I will end this section by making reference to the post-9/11 wave of hate crimes in the United States motivated, again, by an overinvestment on the part of the state and popular imaginary in the connected signifiers *religion* and *violence*.

The Indian state's creation and successful deployment of the image of "Sikh terrorism" between 1982 and 1992 was in turn dependent on its ability to recognize and manipulate the relationship between two key signifiers of identity. The most important one was the master signifier *Hindu*, which became central to the fantasy of the national imaginary and formed the basis of identification with an image of totality: Hindu/Hindustan/Hinduism as a nation, a civilization, and a religion. A master signifier, as explained earlier, is any term that operates through the logic of identity—where identity in turn is defined as religious identity and as the condition for difference. Once the master signifier is defined and accepted as a universal, all other signifiers (e.g., Sikh or Muslim identity) work as particulars and in opposition to the master signifier. Thus, within the symbolic order of the nation, "Sikh identity" had to be enunciated by way of a subaltern relation to the master signifier, for example, "We are Sikhs *because* we are not Hindus."

This complex interplay between signifiers, perceived either as acceding to or resisting assimilation to the "National Symbolic" that operated at the level of language and law, is aptly illustrated by the political strategies of the ruling secular Congress Party and its think tank organ, the National Integration Committee, which was mainly responsible for manufacturing the fantasy of national unity and integration after 1958 and particularly in the early 1980s.[20] This was a period when Congress had to counter a dual threat to its electoral bases at the national and provincial level. The main threat came from the religious activities of the Hindu nationalist movement, the BJP, Rashtriya Swayamsevak Sangh (RSS), and Vishva Hindu Parishad. During the 1980s the VHP successfully organized its networks along religious lines by taking measures such as (1) mobilizing *sādhūs* and other notable activists and patrons by integrating the main strands of devotional Hinduism—Vaisnavites, Śaivites, and Tantrists—under a common slogan of Mother India; (2) organizing a series of unity conferences to highlight the dangers to Hinduism from "proselytizing" religions such as Islam and Christianity; and (3) holding a series of high-profile nationally televised marches such as the "Sacrifice for Unanimity" March (*Ekatmatā Yajna*) in 1983.[21] Emboldened by the success of these earlier measures, the VHP convened a large gathering of Hindu religious figures in April 1984 in the capital, New Delhi, for the purpose of issuing a resolution for the "liberation" of three temple sites in North India at Mathura, Varanasi, and Ayodhya. This temple liberation project was designed to link the calls for Hindu unity with an anti-Muslim rhetoric. To define and mobilize a Hindu religious identity, the VHP decided that it was necessary to identify an enemy. From then on, "Muslims would be cast as violators of the sacred homeland."[22]

Besieged by vocal minorities such as the Sikhs at the provincial level and by Hindu fundamentalists at the national level, the ruling Congress seemed to be caught in a serious dilemma. Muslims were part of an important vote bank for Congress as the self-styled party of "unity in diversity," but it could not afford to alienate mainstream Hindus, who constituted the vast majority of Indian voters but were increasingly affected by the upsurge of BJP/RSS/VHP activity and rhetoric.

Congress's solution to this dilemma was to divert the attention of the Hindu voting bloc by creating the figure of an alternative enemy: the Sikh. Ever since the imposition of emergency rule by Indira Gandhi in 1977, the main Sikh political party, the Akali Dal, had been a major thorn in the side of the Congress due to a sustained nonviolent campaign directed against the suspension of democratic rule. Throughout the early 1980s, the Akali leadership had kept up a series of economic and territorial demands designed to gain a certain measure of autonomy for the state of Punjab. These included a demand for increased water rights for

Punjabi farmers, for the return of Punjabi linguistic territories given to the neighboring state of Haryana, and for more open center–state relations.[23] The Akali opposition had succeeded thus far mainly because its tactics and conduct had remained within the limits of constitutional law and was therefore perceived to be entirely secular. In addition it was backed by an alliance with the Janata Party, a mainly Hindu political party and precursor of the future nationalist Bhartīya Janata Party. Congress's master stroke was to religionize the Akali Dal's ostensibly secular and nonviolent stance. It did this by promoting controversial and extremist elements within Punjab and in the Punjabi diaspora, whose combined presence would communalize the nature of the political scene. Among these elements was a new extremist Sikh political party (the Dal Khalsā); a former Congress minister and expatriate, Jagjit Singh Chauhan, who instigated the demand for a separate Sikh state (Khalistan); and notably the militant cleric Sant Jarnail Singh Bhindranwale. All of these elements were covertly supported by high-profile members of the Congress Party. As the head of a Sikh missionary institution, the Damdami Taksaal, Bhindranwale was brought into Punjab's state politics by prominent Congress figures such as Giani Zail Singh, then president of India and a former chief minister of Punjab, with the sole purpose of undermining the popular support base of the dominant Sikh political party, the Akali Dal.[24] The combined presence of the Dal Khalsā and Sant Bhindranwale was intended to further catalyze an already communalized scene.[25]

Although Bhindranwale soon discovered Congress's true motives and turned against his former promoters, party officials quickly found a new role for him. Through his portrayal in the media as the archetypal "Sikh fundamentalist" representative of the aspirations of all Sikhs, Bhindranwale's name became synonymous with the image of secessionism and as chief instigator of what was termed the "Hindu/Sikh conflict." By neatly packaging the image of Bhindranwale as the arch "Sikh terrorist" with the "Punjab problem" within India and the demand for Khalistan, which came mainly from outside India, the Sikh community as a whole came to be perceived as the "enemy within," ready at any moment to collude with the "foreign hand" of Pakistan and undermine the unity of the Indian nation. In this way Congress found an effective way of undermining a key component of the BJP's campaign strategy during the early to mid-1980s to project itself as the only party that championed the cause of the Hindu majority and national unity. Following the death of Bhindranwale and his supporters at the hands of the Indian Army in 1984, the state machinery continued to project Punjab as a chaotic or "disturbed region" infested with Sikh terrorists whose resistance was evidence of a deviation both from the essentially peaceful nature of Sikhism and from a key principle of the democratic state, namely, that it alone exercised a legal mandate to deploy violence for the protection of the peaceful majority.

In hindsight what remains most disturbing about the Indian state's handling of the "Sikh problem" is not so much the number of people who were killed over a twelve-year period nor even the controlled precision with which the state allowed the chaos of insurgency to proliferate before brutally and clinically exterminating it almost at will. What continues to disturb is the degree of unison—one might even speak of a circular relationship—among the secular state, the national and global media, and the academic domain that was generated in the aftermath of the events of 1984 and could easily be generated again, as was so evident following the events of 9/11.[26] I refer to the manner in which an avowedly secular democratic state was able to bet on the close fiduciary connection between the enunciation of religious identity (in this case Sikh identity) and the law as enshrined within the nation's constitution. Implicit within this constitution and thus within the structure of Indian law is an overlap between the signifier *Hindu* and national identity. In both secular and religious versions of Indian nationalism, the signifier *Hindu* names the closest proximity between the "I" of the nation and its "Oneness" or unity, hence its truth-value. Understood in this way, the signifier *Hindu* becomes the guarantor of a *Pax Indica* that is enshrined within the constitution. But when the "I" and the "One" coalesce in this manner, all other named identities, hence all manner of pluralism, must be deemed not-true or not *as* true. According to this logic, enunciations such as "Sikh identity" would be deemed suspect, an affront to the true identity of the nation. The state is always able to bet on this fiduciary structure and more important, win every time! The state's covert policy, it would seem, was to trap Sikhs (in this case the Akali Dal leadership) into enunciating their being as a *religious* identity. To remain within the *Pax Indica*, however, Sikhs could only enunciate this identity privately. Expression or enactment of this identity in the public sphere would constitute a violation of a public space so clearly defined by the nationalist master signifier *Hindu*. It would seem that Sikhs were constituted as violators of the *Pax Indica* ever since Bhai Kahn Singh first enunciated "Ham Hindu Nahin" ("We Are Not Hindus") as a retort to an earlier publication, *Sikh Hindu Hai"* (*Sikhs Are Hindus*), back in the late nineteenth century.

Once the fiduciary structure of this trap was set back in the colonial era, it continued to be used by the Indian state at various times and with devastating consequences for Sikhs in the 1980s. Confronted with the figure of the Sikh as "enemy," Hindus reacted by differentiating themselves from it, while Sikhs were forced into a dilemma: *either* to reject this enemy, thereby (1) affirming that militant insurgency was a deviation from "true" Sikhism and (2) renouncing the right to resist the state (a principle historically and "theologically" inscribed in Sikh tradition); *or* to identify with the enemy, thereby (1) affirming that Sikhism itself is not a true religion and is by nature incompatible with democracy and (2) affirming that Sikhs and Sikhism can never rightfully belong within the ambit of the Indian nation, hence justifying separatism, which would inevitably invite the morally sanctioned violence of the state. The moral of the story is that as long as minorities continued to respond to the demand for religion in a predictable way, the state could keep its finger on the fiduciary structure of religion. Consequently the fiduciary could be turned on or off at the whim of the state and milked not only to produce violence when and where needed but ironically to *legitimize* state violence by creating *spectacles* of violence in the eyes of international law.

But for Sikhs the effects of the fiduciary structure were not confined to India. Most people in Punjab who had directly experienced the violence of the 1980s and early 1990s breathed a sigh of relief with the cessation of the Sikh insurgency and the "normalizing" of the political scene in Punjab heralded by the return of an Akali

Dal–BJP coalition government in 1996. After the events of 9/11, things took a very different turn for diaspora Sikhs. The attacks of September 11, 2001, on the United States by radical Islamists linked to Osama bin Laden resuscitated the association of religion with violence and was brought into the forefront of public debate by the global media. Through the US media's overt sensitization of the American mind-set with the image of a bearded and turbaned bin Laden, the events of 9/11 created an unexpected and deadly problem of "mistaken identity" for many Sikhs and South Asians living in the United States and Europe. Mistaken for Muslims, turban-wearing Sikhs were targeted in a wave of hate crimes, which began with the murder of fifty-two-year-old Balbir Singh Sodhi, who was shot at a gas station in Mesa, Arizona, on September 15, 2001. The media quickly absorbed and distilled the dangerous religious and racial rhetoric deployed by the US political establishment, which began with George W. Bush's televised speeches to the nation. In laying out a fundamental civilizational divide between the secular West (but based on Christian ethical values) and the "Axis of Evil," which referred to those nations, regimes, and individuals who stood against the rule of Western democracy (implicitly referring to the Taliban, Al-Qaida, and other Islamist groups connected to the Palestinian struggle, Saddam Hussein, Iran, and North Korea), these speeches deployed the fiduciary nature of religion.

Within hours of the 9/11 attacks a frenzied US media was awash with images and posters of a bearded and turbaned Osama bin Laden. One newspaper front cover in particular—carrying a photograph of bin Laden with the title "Wanted: Dead or Alive"—was displayed by many Americans on cars and even on the front doors of their homes. Within this heightened atmosphere, male Sikhs in particular very quickly became substitute embodiments for "bin Laden" and "Islamic terror" and as such represented a socially and politically sanctioned hate crime target. Once sanctioned in this way, male Sikhs became a legitimate target for a "socially appropriate emotion" of revenge and retributive justice that was expressed in "socially inappropriate ways."[27] As Jasbir Puar notes, "These hate crimes became normalized within a refashioned post 9/11 racial landscape, but more significantly, they became immanent to the counter terrorism objectives of the state, operating as an extended arm of the nation, encouraging the surveillance and strike capacities of the patriotic populace."[28]

While Puar rightly brings attention to the heteronormative frame of white middle-class America that designated the turban-wearing man with a terrorist masculinity, what seems to be underplayed in her analysis is the religious grounding of this frame, a grounding that equally motivated liberal and conservative sentiments. Within this religio-heteronormativity, the turbaned man was not just a patriarchal figure who presented "a resistant antiassimilationalist stance" but a deviant figure of monstrosity, a barbaric evil that refused to become civilized: "The turban both reveals and hides the terrorist, a constant sliding between that which can be disciplined and that which must be outlawed."[29] Not surprising, the turban, in its capacity to invade the visual public space of an American citizenry of both religious and secular persuasions, becomes a source of contagious affect that continues to cause anxiety.

Sikh responses to the post-9/11 hate crimes were nothing if not predictable. One manifestation of the domestication demanded of those ethnic groups that did not conform to American-ness was that large numbers of Sikh men, particularly the children of new immigrants, chose to disrobe their turbans. In such cases, turban removal "functioned as a reorientation into masculine patriotic identity."[30] Other Sikhs who refused to disrobe their turbans adopted different types of self-preservationist but ultimately assimilative tactics. Candlelight vigils accompanied by group singing of the US national anthem became common. This was a way in which Sikhs could mark themselves as patriotic but victimized citizens. Sikhs increasingly began to hang American flags outside their homes, on their cars, or outside *gurdwara* premises. Public relations firms were hired, and Sikh advocacy groups sprang up to try to educate fellow Americans about Sikhs and to alleviate their anxieties about the turban. The real irony here is that many of these same Sikh organizations had been petitioning the US government about human rights abuses committed by the Indian state against Sikhs and to recognize that the Sikhs were a separate religious identity from Hindus.

A common response among Sikh communities throughout the United States was to engage in interfaith dialogues with neighboring Christian and Jewish communities. This was clearly driven by a desire to correct the "mistaken identity" and to inhabit the normative religious space that is part and parcel of American patriotism. A key component of these dialogues was the emphatic enunciations that (1) Sikhs were not terrorists, (2) Sikhs were not Muslims, and (3) Sikhism was a "world religion." Identification as a world religion ensured two coveted prizes: on the one hand, an admittance into the moral space governed by Christianity and as a result of this, safe passage and proper placement within secular public space on the other. The idea here is that proximity to Christianity accrued both religious and secular benefits.

In 2004, however, such attempts to negotiate the Scylla of religion and the Charybdis of secularism caused a different kind of dilemma for Sikhs living in France in the wake of the French government's widely publicized ban on the wearing of "religious symbols" in public—a ban that included the turban. For French Sikhs the problem was exacerbated by the fact that the American and British Sikh groups advocating on their behalf were divided about how to actually contest the French government's ban. While the London-based Sikh Human Rights Group opted for a more pragmatic argument (that Sikhism was not necessarily a religion but a culture and that it had become a religion through its entry into the colonial frame), the New York-based United Sikhs continued to argue that Sikhism was a religion, that the turban was a mandatory religious item, and that the French government was in violation of their fundamental religious rights. The secular nature of the British group's argument might have favorably impacted the French government had it not been for a well-publicized legal battle that was going on in New York at roughly the same time. Shortly after September 2001, a Sikh traffic enforcement officer, Jasjit Singh Jaggi, employed by the New York Police Department (NYPD) filed a lawsuit against his employer alleging that the NYPD had denied him numerous requests for a religious accommodation, that is, the right to wear a turban while on duty. In April 2004 the presiding judge ruled that traffic agent Jaggi was discriminated against on the basis of religious beliefs when the NYPD ordered him to remove his turban and beard or face dismissal.[31]

What seems to be noteworthy about the French and American cases, respectively, is that in order to argue their case for wearing turbans in public space, and thus to be integrated into secular liberal society, Sikhs found it necessary to formulate two different kinds of language that in turn recognized and negotiated between two different kinds of public space—the *religious* space of American secularism and the *seemingly nonreligious* space of French *laïcité*.[32] Despite the apparent differences among Indian, American, and French forms of secularism, Sikh identity ended up being cast as a violator of the public space. This violation was due to nothing more than the desire of many Sikhs to assert a secularization—the ability not only to be within the world but to make and remake this world in ways that would allow them to move beyond the limits of an installed and interiorized subjectivity and to escape a mode of repetition that kept them chained to the signifier religion.

■ SYMBOLIC VIOLENCE: THE EMERGENCE OF "RELIGION" IN (POST)COLONIAL ENUNCIATION

I believe that there is a more productive way of conceptualizing the seemingly opposed notions of subjective and objective violence, particularly as this opposition sustains the phenomenon of Sikh ethno-nationalism. The alternative I have in mind consists in shifting one's standpoint in order to bring into view a third kind of violence. Although this third form of violence is not immediately recognizable because of the standpoint from which we perceive the distinction between religion and secularism, it nevertheless holds the subjective and objective (religious nationalism and state secularism) together in India.[33]

This is a symbolic violence embodied in language and present in the forms of social domination reproduced in our customary modes of speech. For Sikhs, as for other North Indians, this symbolic violence of language took effect in the intellectual encounter between Indian and Western conceptuality, an encounter that produced one of the central paradoxes of Indian (post)coloniality. Such a paradox can be visualized in terms of the apparent opposition between the following phenomena: (1) the concept of religion (and the secular, as well as the opposition between them) may not have existed in the lexicons of Indian cultures prior to the encounter with European imperialism, but at a certain moment in the production of colonial discourses, it entered into the nationalist enunciation as if it had been an indigenous category all along; (2) the secular state's *response* to religious conflict—to keep religion out of the public sphere—is in fact premised not on what Carl Schmitt would call a "translation of theological concepts" but on what Derrida calls a "theology of translation." That is, the postcolonial state's objective response to subjective religious violence depends on this "theology of translation," which works by molding or reshaping religion as if it were essentially plastic. And yet this plasticity of religion, and hence the ability to mold it, is entirely dependent on the symbolic force of language that imposes an operation of translation into the nationalist enunciation of "religion."

By shifting our standpoint and thereby allowing symbolic violence to come into our view, it may be possible to think normally opposed categories such as religion and secularism, subjective and objective violence, as *aporia*, that is to say, something that is simultaneously possible and impossible, an irresolvable contradiction. Yet such contradictions must be held intact in order for us to make the required shift.

Let me explain what I mean by returning to the earlier arguments for removing religion from discussions of secularism, as put forward by Dingwaney and Rajan (see above). What they and many other Indian postcolonial theorists seem to be alluding to through this disavowal of religion, not only as a political alternative to secularism but as a theoretical influence on the formation of the secular, is that while religion is an intrinsic part of the cultural, historical, and intellectual experience of the West, this may not be valid in the Indian context. It could therefore be argued that "religion," *as a generalizable concept*, is more likely the result of a colonial transposition from a Christian/European context into an Indian context. Yet it now exists as though it were an indigenous concept.

Something similar to this is argued by the Indian sociologist T. N. Madan. Madan points out that "secularism...failed to make headway in India since Hindus, Muslims, Buddhists, Sikhs cannot and will not privatize their religion." Secularism for Madan is the "gift of Christianity to mankind and therefore part of the unique history of Europe."[34] The question that Madan seems to be raising here is that religion and secularism have been imposed on the Indian mind-set through the colonial encounter, and as a result of this encounter Indians have in some way come to accept them as universally translatable and therefore cross-cultural categories.

One must therefore differentiate between the gesture of simply refusing to be tainted intellectually or politically by religion and the rather different gesture of admitting that Indians, even as they describe themselves as secular, have been constructed by their entry into the Christian/European category of religion. Stated otherwise, India's entry into secular modernity happened, paradoxically, by its native elites acquiring a conceptual framework to respond to the concept of religion. Such a scenario presents nothing less than the aporia that marks Indian thinking about the relationship between religion and the secular. Perhaps the clearest manifestation of this aporia is the way in which Indians today engage the political through a mode of identification *that once did not exist yet which today is brought to life* through a response to the word *religion*. Yet the native elites' identification with religion (their enunciative response to this colonial category) was (and is still) based on an active repression of whatever within indigenous culture cannot count as religion.

However, few Indians today would stop to think that they are actively repressing anything whenever they use the word *religion*. Are Indians not sufficiently versed in English to understand the proper meaning of the term *religion*? As free agents today, are they not capable of entering into a dialogue about religion even if it happens to be conducted in the language of the ex-colonizer? And even if the language of dialogue belongs to the ex-colonizer, has not the world's general understanding of the word *religion* expanded because of this dialogue? Indeed as a result of this dialogue is it not the case that everyone can now assent to universally recognizable objective realities called Hinduism, Sikhism, and so on that make up the phenomenon called "world religions"?

Yet it is precisely when Indians reciprocate, confidently and without resistance, the word "religion", and its pluralized counterpart that circulates globally as part of a discourse of "*world* religions," that the need to question the seemingly inextricable connection between religion and response (where the response *is* religion and religion *is* the response) becomes especially pertinent to the South Asian experience. Indeed, the very idea that some kind of repressive force or "interdict" could link the subjective response as "religion" and the objectivization of this response as the discourse of *world* religions is supported by recent historical research on colonial and precolonial India.[35] As a result of these studies it is now increasingly recognized that when South Asians enunciate identity in terms of strictly defined religious traditions, such a response can be considered to be the outcome of a process of cultural and psychological transformation during their encounter with British imperialism.[36] It forms part of a history of response to the colonizer's demand for Indians to equivocate the concept religion. Central to this enunciation–response is the repression of indigenous cultural terms, initially in the linguistic transactions between colonizer and colonized, followed by a similar repression within the composition of nationalist literatures.

Although the work of repression can be discerned in most South Asian nationalist discourses during the late nineteenth and early twentieth century, it is particularly evident in the efforts of Sikh reformist scholars to reformulate the reception and understanding of their tradition texts and literatures within a modernist context.[37] The work of the scholar Bhai Vir Singh serves as a good example in this regard.[38]

Bhai Vir Singh introduced two main changes to traditional literatures. First, he introduced the genre of historical fiction in the form of the novel into Sikh and Punjabi literature. The immediate effect of this was to convince his readers that they were reading properly historical as opposed to fictional material, since the novels used extensive footnotes and annotations explaining the sources of data. These novels therefore helped to sow the seeds of the cultural translation that resulted in a conceptual transition from the indigenous multiplicity of narratives told in vernacular languages to the modern nationalized narratives that are fully attuned to the narrative time of empire, which carries the self-designation of "History." Second, Bhai Vir Singh wrote extensive commentaries on Sikh scripture, the immediate impact of which was to transform the receptive psychology of the native elites and popular understandings of tradition texts toward ethical monotheism. Thus the broadly nondual and temporal sense of terms such as *bhakti*, *Sikhī*, and *gurmat* is shifted under the purview of a dualistic framework in which the governing parameter is ontotheology (i.e., a combination of rational logic and monotheism). However, these conceptual shifts toward historicism and ontotheology could only have taken place through an operation of metaphysical violence, which subjected key terms in the indigenous language to a transcendentalization, thereby erasing their connections to time and temporality. Metaphysical violence therefore refers to the systematic erasure (or repression) of indigenous modes of time and temporality in the native understanding of their literatures. That is to say, what had to be repressed in the processes of intra- and interlinguistic translation (or what I refer to as enunciation) were indigenous meanings and values deemed incompatible with the dominant time and temporality of modernity. The most prominent example of this repressive symbolic violence of language is the shift from the intrinsically temporal term of self-designation *Sikhī* (to be on a path of learning grounded in finitude) to Sikh-*ism* (or the "Sikh religion"), signifying an unchanging system of beliefs and practices grounded in the notion of a static, immortal deity.

In order to further understand the sense of the violence of psychic repression that I am trying to convey—one that is associated with the symbolic violence of language that gives birth to the colonial-nationalist enunciation—and to explain how it differs from the subjective and objective modes of violence considered earlier, it will be helpful to draw upon Jacques Derrida's meditations on the relationship among violence, religion, and language. These meditations revolve around the work of symbolic repression that he terms the interdict.

From seemingly different angles Derrida argues that religion and violence are intrinsically connected to the question of law and the (im)possibility of experiencing justice.[39] Thus every time an Indian responds to the word *religion* she is obliged to speak (whether in English or Hindi) in another's language, breaking with her own and in so doing giving herself up to the other. "In this obligation the violence of an injustice has begun when all members of a community do not share the same idiom throughout. For all injustice supposes that the other, the victim of the languages' injustice, is capable of a language in general," that the other is a subject capable of responding and insofar, a responsible subject.[40] Furthermore, Derrida argues, to address oneself to the other in the language of the other is the impossible condition of all justice since I can speak the language of the other only to the extent that I am able to appropriate it according to the law of an implicit third, an appeal to a third party who suspends the unilaterality or singularity of all idioms, implying thereby the element of universality and specifically here the implied translatability/universality of the term *religion*.[41] Accordingly, every time an Indian responds, quite responsibly, "I am Hindu/ Hinduism is my religion," or whether one rejects this response in favor of a purely secular enunciation, what is never questioned, because it is always assumed, is the concept of religion operating in this case, indeed, the relation between religion and conceptuality. In responding one will always have conformed to a certain law according to which the meaning and concept of religion are universally known and accepted without resistance. In other words, the "symbolic" violence of language produces a subject of enunciation who is capable of reciprocating terms such as *religion* through a mode of translation that relies on the exchange of universal equivalents.

A strange scenario: Indian's have no exact word for religion, yet they cannot avoid answering to its call. As Derrida notes, "There is no common Indo-European term for what we call religion, no omnipresent reality that is religion. There has not always been nor will there always and everywhere be *something*, a thing that is *one and identifiable*, identical with itself, which whether religious or irreligious, all agree to call 'religion.'"[42] Why, then, do Indians continue to respond? And respond precisely in terms of something that is identifiable and one? More to the point, why do they feel obliged to respond in conformity with a law? To feel obliged is already to have interiorized that law, to have imposed the law on oneself, to have introjected as a self-censorship, the visible projection of which would be the response or enunciation: "I am Hindu/Hinduism is my religion" or "I am a secular Indian." The law itself is never seen. It is simply assumed. Indeed to make visible the law that obliges one to respond to religion would entail a trespass against the law, a violation of a meaning that all are supposed to know, whence its universality. Clearly, though, a universal that needs to be shown in evidence is no longer a universal since not everybody will have assented to its meaning.

Prior to even questioning religion, therefore, what needs to be interrogated is the invisible link or law that connects, on the one hand, religion as the response that conforms to the enunciation of an identity ("I am Hindu/Sikh, etc.) and, on the other, the violence that results *not* from simply not-responding but from a response that resists conforming to the law that demands identity and identification.[43] Derrida refers to this law as an interdict.[44] The interdict works by preventing a certain kind of speech from being articulated, instead specifying access to certain identifications while in that very moment actively repressing other identifications. Moreover, the interdict does not simply work at the level of language. It is the language of law: Language as Law. Though Derrida does not reveal his source, his notion of the interdict is indebted to Lacan's concept of the Unconscious structured like a language.[45] The relationship between religion and response can therefore be recast in a Lacanian frame as follows. By responding to the word *religion* in the form of a religious identity ("I am Hindu/ "Hinduism is my religion"), the Indian believes that he has already mastered the meaning of religion through a normal acquisition of English. But according to Lacan one cannot acquire language, one merely accedes to it, which means that one willingly agrees to submit to it as Law, such that one is first mastered by language. If the legitimate meaning of religion appears as an identity that is repeated as the same thing, always one and identifiable, then violence is a force that acts legitimately to remove this active repression that reproduces the universal meaning of religion with Indians.

■ THE PERFORMATIVE FUNCTION OF SYMBOLIC VIOLENCE: WHAT CAN IT ACTUALLY DO?

In contradistinction from subjective and objective violence (which together correspond to the dictionary definition of violence, namely, that religion constitutes an unlawful entry into public space), implicit within the symbolic violence inherent within language is the possibility of *resisting* the repression that comes about when the meaning of religion is determined exclusively in terms of identity. In fact, two forces of resistance are at work here. The first kind of force is effected by language-as-law, where an Indian speaker in acceding to the word *religion* actively identifies with certain meanings associated with the signifier *religion* (such as nonviolence) while repressing other meanings (such as violence). In this case the repressive force of the law is manifested not as the signifier *violence* but as the equation of "religion" with "nonviolence."

The second kind of force is effected when we actually become conscious of the self-censoring function of law. Becoming conscious of self-censorship enables the removal of repression through questioning the inevitability of the meaning of religion as "nonviolence." It would then be possible to entertain the idea that religion is simultaneously violent and nonviolent. This is the shift in standpoint that enables us to comprehend the "symbolic" nature of violence as performing a positive function that helps to push the analysis of phenomena such as Sikh ethno-nationalism beyond its objectivist framework and related to this, to push the sociopolitical enunciation of Sikhs beyond its current identification with a narrowly subjective ethno-nationalism. To do this it is necessary to understand that the very phenomenon known as Sikh nationalism exists only because of the translation-transformation of indigenous concepts into the category of religion. This "fundamental translatability" of religion, the suggestion that religion is a generalizable category, is inextricably related to the process of becoming modern (albeit under the guise of traditionalism), which means a simultaneous entry into and exclusion from the dominant symbolic order of late capitalism and secular democracy. By entering into the symbolic domain of secular democracy as a religious identity, Sikh ethno-nationalism is already foreclosed from enunciating any other way.

So my argument about symbolic violence is relatively simple. What symbolic violence makes visible is the interdict—as the very law that forecloses/excludes Sikhs by forcing them to translate themselves as religion. However, symbolic violence is not just an event that happened once and for all in the colonial past and which Sikhs have subsequently internalized into their modern imaginary. Rather, it is an event that is constantly repeated every time a Sikh enunciates as "Sikh religion," which means that what needs to be altered or broken is this very operation of enunciating/translation that results in the representation that in turn gives rise to the subjective versus objective framework. This operation can be radically changed by refusing to translate in terms of the concept "religion." Such a refusal constitutes a political decision taken at the very moment at which the self (re)makes itself. The point therefore is to retrieve the moment in this cycle of repetition that precedes the resultant representation as religion. What gets retrieved, in other words, is the excessive prenationalist kernel that has always accompanied the production of the nationalist subject. This retrieval is *not* a going back in time to some authentic past but, rather, the disenclosure of a subjectivity that does not answer either to the logic of secular modernity or to its attendant politics of religion-making but which had been trapped by and within an affect of shame. All along, it was this affect of shame that performed the violence necessary for the Sikh to emerge as an ethno-nationalist subject.

In contrast to discourses that try to merely domesticate the violent aspect of Sikhs by exposing them to the liberal imaginary, symbolic violence brings the Sikh back into dialogue with democracy but without the intervention of the interdict. In such an encounter, democracy itself is reexposed to cultural translation. If the interdict forced the Sikh to translate or enunciate as "religion," then symbolic violence simultaneously exposes the autoimmunity of democracy itself and the fact that the underlying problem in any encounter between Sikhs and democracy will always be the question of competing universals. In other words, is it possible for Sikhs to retain a notion of sovereign consciousness but still participate in democracy? Symbolic violence puts the onus on the role of Sikh leadership and intelligentsia to break away from the trap of identity politics (i.e., the politics of religion-making). What begins as a process of transformation within the individual Sikh (refusal to translate as religion) takes effect at the level of political community as a form of agonistic politics within the symbolic order that we know as democracy. It poses the following question: If what was interdicted in the colonial period (late nineteenth century) and then again with the Akali and Khalistani confrontations with the Indian state (1960s through to the 1990s), and even today continues to be interdicted every time Sikhs identify themselves with an ethno-nationalism—if what was interdicted was a sovereign Sikh consciousness that because it was deemed incompatible with modernity was forced to *translate* itself (and thereby interdict itself) as Sikh "religious" identity, then is it still possible for Sikhs to enunciate a form of consciousness that refuses to become a religious identity and ethnic identity? And could such a consciousness become the basis of political action?

In conclusion, let me restate the central issue toward which this essay has been moving: Is it possible for those who continue to be translated as "religious" subjects to lift the interdict self-imposed by nationalist elites in their transition to modern secularist democracy? To lift the interdict is to return to the moment of the colonized native elites' "original" entry into the symbolic order imposed by the colonizer, so as to relive, retranslate, and renegotiate that moment as though it had not yet taken place. If one could thus attain release from the interdict in this manner, might it be possible to retrieve through a different kind of enunciation those terms or concepts that were prohibited as nonmodern, non-Western, primitive, and so on or translated as "religion"? To put it differently, is it possible in the "moment" of accession to reread the meaning of religion/secularism, thereby allowing nonmodern forms of subjectivity to be articulated through indigenous concepts (such as *gurmat* or *bhakti*) that cannot simply be made to correspond to what is signified by the concepts "religion" and "secularism"? Can such different modes of enunciation open up new access to the political, thereby redefining the nature of democracy?

If democracy has thus far been determined by its proximity to a fiduciary structure rooted in a combination of Christian conceptuality and European languages (encapsulated in Derrida's neologism: *mondialatinisation*, or *globalatinization*), is it viable to imagine "different vernacular models of democracy" that might enable South Asian (and other) subjects to remake themselves otherwise than religion/secularism using foundational Indic concepts? Such a thought has usually been dismissed by mainstream political theorists in the West and by Indian thinkers whose enunciation of the political remains interdicted by the force of globa*latini*-zation. Given the shifts in the global political economy that are currently under way, however, such a possibility—of opening the doors of democracy to "non-Western" ideas and concepts—may not be so far-fetched.

■ NOTES

1. This typology of violence is borrowed from Slavoj Žižek. See Slavoj Žižek, *Violence* (New York: Picador, 2008).

2. See, for example, the work of Ashis Nandy, Sudhir Kakar, and T. N. Madan.

3. Anuradha Dingwaney and Rajeshwari Sundar Rajan, eds., *The Crisis of Secularism in India* (Durham, NC: Duke University Press, 2007), 22. This fear is best seen in the glaring lack of engagement between disciplines associated with theology and philosophy (such as the Continental philosophy of religion) and those associated with area studies, despite the fact that politics has recently become a theme of major interest to both of these fields.

4. Ibid., 22–23.

5. Ibid., 22.

6. See, for example, Gurharpal Singh, *Ethnic Conflict in India: A Case-Study of Punjab* (New York: Macmillan Publishers, 2000); Sanjib Baruah, ed., *Ethno-Nationalist Movements in India* (New Delhi: Oxford University Press, 2009); Rajiv Kapur, *Sikh Separatism: The Politics of Faith* (London: Allen and Unwin, 1986); Ghani Jaffar, *The Sikh Volcano* (Lahore: Vikas Publishing House, 1982).

7. Harjot Oberoi, *The Construction of Religious Boundaries: Culture, Identity and Diversity in the Sikh Tradition* (New Delhi: Oxford University Press, 1994).

8. See chap. 3, "Sikhism and the Politics of Religion-Making," in Arvind Mandair, *Religion and the Specter of the West: Sikhism, India, Postcoloniality and the Politics of Translation* (New York: Columbia University Press, 2009).

9. See Birinder Pal Singh, "The Logic of Sikh Militancy," in *Punjab in Violence and Prosperity* (Chandigarh: Institute of Punjab Studies, 1997), 138–156; and Cynthia Mahmoud, *Fighting for Faith and Nation: Dialogues with Sikh Militants* (Philadelphia: University of Pennsylvania Press, 1996).

10. Richard King, "The Association of 'Religion' with Violence: Reflections on a Modern Trope," in *Religion and Violence in South Asia: Theory and Practice*, ed. John Hinnells and Richard King (London: Routledge, 2006), 226–253. See also, William T. Cavanaugh's *The Myth of Religious Violence*, New York: Oxford University Press, 2009; and Timothy Fitzgerald's *Discourse on Civility and Barbarity*, New York: Oxford University Press, 2007.

11. Ibid., 251.

12. See ibid., 251–52.

13. Michael D. Hardt and Antonio Negri, *Multitude: War and Democracy in an Age of Empire* (New York: Penguin Press, 2004), 25.

14. This argument is discussed at length in the following works: Grace Jantzen, *Becoming Divine: Toward a Feminist Philosophy of Religion* (Manchester: Manchester University Press, 1998); Jeremy Carette and Richard King, *Selling Spirituality: The Silent Takeover of Religion* (London: Routledge, 2004); Mandair, *Religion and the Specter of the West*.

15. Hardt and Negri, *Multitude*, 29.

16. See Jacques Derrida, "Faith and Knowledge: Two Sources of Religion Within the Limits of Reason Alone," in *Religion*, ed. Jacques Derrida and Gianni Vattimo (London: Polity Press, 1998), 33–58.

17. See also Brian Goldstone's essay in this volume.

18. "Lost in the Terrorist Theater," *Harper's*, October 1984, 43.

19. Melanie McAlister, "Iran, Islam and the Terrorist Threat. 1979–1989," in *Terrorism, Media, Liberation*, ed. J. David Slocum (New Brunswick, NJ: Rutgers University Press, 2005), 151–57.

20. See Brian Axel, *The Nation's Tortured Body: Violence, Representation and the Formation of a Sikh "Diaspora"* (Durham: Duke University Press, 2001), 110–12. Axel provides a very useful discussion of the strategies used by the Indian state to produce national

integration and unity (*rashtriya ekta*). Particularly after the 1950s there were concerted attempts by the ruling Congress Party to bring about national unity. As Axel argues: "The repeated address of *ekta*, or integration/oneness, has been organized and mediated, historically, by the procedures of the National Integration Committee (NIC)....The NIC was initially convened by the Congress Working Committee in 1958, after the 1957 'Jabalpur riot,' to address the emerging problem of 'fissiparious tendencies in the body-politic of our country.'...In the 1970s, the NIC turned its efforts to the problems of 'internal dangers': casteism, communalism, and separatism. Between 1983 and 1992, the activities of the NIC were almost exclusively concerned with the threat of Sikh 'terrorists.'" Indira Gandhi often presided over the NIC between 1960 and 1984.

21. Christophe Jaffrelot, *The Hindu Nationalist Movement and Indian Politics: 1925–1990s* (London: Hurst and Co., 1993), 346–53.

22. Richard Davis, "The Iconography of Ram's Chariot," in *Making India Hindu: Religion, Community and the Politics of Democracy in India*, ed. David Ludden (New Delhi: Oxford University Press, 1996), 40.

23. For details, see, for example, Singh, *Ethnic Conflict in India*; Giorgio Shani, *Sikh Nationalism and Identity in a Global Age* (London: Routledge, 2008).

24. See, for example, J. S. Grewal, "Sikhs, Akalis and Khalistan," in *Punjab in Violence and Prosperity*, ed. J. S. Grewal and Indu Bhanga (Chandigarh: Institute of Punjab Studies, 1997); Shani, *Sikh Nationalism and Identity in a Global Age*; Singh, *Ethnic Conflict in India*.

25. Agitations against the Nirankari sect in 1978 and the assassination of their guru, Baba Gurbachan Singh, in 1980 are thought to have been organized by the Dal Khalsā, which it seems was supported by the local committee in charge of the Delhi *gurdwaras* and Congress Party officials connected to these *gurdwaras*. Another prominent event was the assassination in 1981 of Lala Jagat Narayan, the editor of a Haryana-based Hindu nationalist paper. Jarnail Singh Bhindranwale was implicated in this assassination, but the likely perpetrator was Dal Khalsā.

26. King, "Association of 'Religion' with Violence."

27. Jasbir Puar, "'The Turban Is Not a Hat': Queer Diaspora and Practices of Profiling," *Sikh Formations: Religion, Culture and Theory* 4, no. 1 (2008): 47–91.

28. Ibid., 57.

29. Ibid., 54.

30. Ibid., 56.

31. *India Abroad*, May 14, 2004.

32. The France–US comparison can be compared to similar situations faced by the Alevis in Germany and in Turkey (see Markus Dressler's essay later in this volume) or to the predicament of Muslims and Sikhs in Germany (see Michael Nijhawan's chapter in this volume). Both of these essays highlight the religion-molding force of particular secularist discourses.

33. I mean to suggest that the symbolic violence of language (the gaining of an ability to enunciate in terms of the religion/secular opposition) is perhaps the crucial factor behind India's transition from premodernity to modernity, with the attendant shift into the structures of secular democracy, on the one hand, and "religious" nationalism, on the other.

34. T. N. Madan, "Secularism in Its Place," in *Secularism and Its Critics*, ed. Rajeev Bhargava (New Delhi: Oxford University Press, 1998), 298.

35. Works that contribute, albeit implicitly, to this thesis include Oberoi, *Construction of Religious Boundaries*; Vasudha Dalmia, *The Nationalization of Hindu Traditions* (New Delhi: Oxford University Press, 1997); Gyan Pandey, *The Construction of Communalism in Colonial North India* (New Delhi: Oxford University Press, 1989); Brian Pennington, *Was Hinduism Invented?* (New York: Oxford University Press, 2005); Mandair, *Religion and the*

Specter of the West; and more recently, Esther Bloch, Marianne Keppens, Rajaram Hedge, eds., *Rethinking Religion in India: The Colonial Construction of Hinduism* (London: Routledge, 2010).

36. Ashis Nandy, *The Intimate Enemy: Loss and Recovery of Self under Colonialism* (New Delhi: Oxford University Press, 1983).

37. I have explored this at length in my book *Religion and the Specter of the West*. See especially chaps. 1 and 3.

38. For details, see Arvind Mandair, "The Politics of Non-Duality," *Journal of the American Academy of Religion* 74, no. 3 (2006): 646–73.

39. Jacques Derrida, "Force of Law: The 'Mystical Foundation of Authority,'" in *Deconstruction and the Possibility of Justice*, ed. Drucilla Cornell, Michel Rosenfeld, David Gray Carlson (London: Routledge, 1992), 3–67.

40. Ibid., 18.

41. Ibid., 17.

42. Derrida, "Faith and Knowledge," 36.

43. Particularly instructive here is Martin Heidegger's argument in *The Principle of Reason*, trans. Reginald Lily (Bloomington: Indiana University Press, 1992).

44. See Jacques Derrida, *Monolingualism of the Other* (Stanford, CA: Stanford University Press, 1998).

45. Jacques Lacan, "The Function of Language in Psychoanalysis," in *Speech and Language in Psychoanalysis*, trans. and ed. Anthony Wilden (Baltimore: Johns Hopkins University Press, 1991), 29–50.

4 On the Apocalyptic Tones of Islam in Secular Time

Ruth Mas

> Time was about to step out of time, and what they call the homeland
> sits on the edge of time about to fall.... I shout that time is punctured,
> that its walls have crumbled in my bowels. I vomited: I have no
> History, no present. —Adonis

Islam is out of time. A pressing matter, or so it would appear for the secular prophets who, in the clamor for its "reform," have questioned whether Islam, as a religious tradition, and Muslims have any place in correct historical or chronological time; they are anachronistic, out of harmony with the present, and in effect they belong to an earlier time that has no relevance to the secular politics of our historical present. Such is the position held by Fethi Benslama, a Muslim Franco-Maghrebi intellectual, who, inspired by Shakespeare's Hamlet's political urgency and the metaphysical skepticism of time in the sixteenth century (*The time is out of joint; O cursed spite! That ever I was born to set it right!*), tells us that Islam is out of joint.[1] It is? But, we may ask, whose time is he speaking about, and for whom is it out of joint? Can this be the same time that the Syrian poet Adonis refers to when, in the spirit of the mythic blind prophet Tiresias, he claims to stand at its razor's edge?[2] Is it also the time that, as Adonis puts it, is sobbing in the lungs of his forefathers, the time whose historical cries of tradition he would like to silence? I am curious about how the time of Islam and its tradition is agitating the seductive calm of secular waters. I also wonder what is mobilizing the secular imperative directed at Islam and Muslims, to "set time right," to temporalize and be temporalized along the fixed temporal architectures of "our" secular time that stratify Islamic histories, traditions, subjectivities, and sensibilities.

At the forefront of this issue of time as it relates to Islam is the affective shackling of apocalyptic dimensions to the secular present. What this puts into question for Muslims is the possibility for them to exist in relationship to the religious tradition of Islam in a secular context that perpetuates a structure of time maintained by the anticipation of an apocalyptic future. Since the Cold War, the positioning of Islam within the project of secular modernity and the latter's forward-propelling anticipation of the end of times have configured Islam as having the potential to bring about nuclear annihilation; Russia has been replaced as the biggest threat to world order by Islamic states now said to be developing biological, chemical, and nuclear weapons. The images of Saddam Hussein, once figured in the media as the

Anti-Christ, and then bin Laden, the new face of the "Islamic threat" poised to unify Islamic countries in a holy war against Israel and the United States, are now threading the political ideals of global unification and a new world order into tidy apocalyptic loops that lead the grasp on the world's oil resources. And yet, almost paradoxically, in the turbulence of the new millennium, axes of chiliastic appeals to crusade have staged the prophetic jettisoning forward of Islam to the end of time, a time of Islamic apocalypse. In the meantime, the political logic that ensues also posits an apocalyptic *regression* to the continual violence of a medieval Islam that anachronistically recruits its tribal barbarity.[3] Secular time, sustained as it is by apocalyptic properties, thus seems to function by making Islam the ontological terror of secularism dialectically tossed with clashing anticipation into forthcoming destruction.

The operation of secular time involves the imperial confrontation of dominant time (conceived as objective, without content, and everywhere and endlessly the same) with the complexity of those forms of time that are residual and emerging.[4] Anthropologist Johannes Fabian has discussed how the imperial currency of serial objective time and its effects are built into the "schizogenic" temporal distancing of the advantaged and authorized architectures and temporal rankings cataloged by anthropologists from their ethnographic subjects.[5] Crucial, then, to the historical act of discovering and encountering different cultures and peoples is an ideological distancing that, through repetition, reinscribes the seriality of dominant forms of time. In so doing, it displaces, constitutes, objectifies, and ultimately downgrades the anachronism of temporal breaks that it thereafter leaves in its imperial wake. By the extension of its secularity, one of the gestures of the imperiousness of time is to disjoint itself from what it conquers by considering what is religious as already dangerously anachronistic. In this way secular time is that which characterizes and enables the rule or authority of a sovereign state over its dependencies. Walter Benjamin has famously defined the idea of *empty homogeneous time* in *Theses on the Philosophy of History* as that which characterizes state sovereignty by ascribing universality to the uninterrupted continuity of time as progress. For Benjamin this has enabled state power to establish a certain continuum of the temporal by structuring life and producing repetitions and predictability.[6]

Conceptually, the coupling of the homogeneity of time to the birth of the nation-state has been importantly and convincingly developed by Benedict Anderson in *Imagined Communities*, in which he considers Benjamin's notion of the empty homogeneity of time to be a "precise analogue of the idea of the nation."[7] Anderson notes that Benjamin's challenge to the evacuating and homogenizing capacity of time with messianic time, one in which the simultaneity of the past and the future can be contained in the instantaneous present, is utterly foreign to our secular trajectories of thought.[8] Benjamin's ideal of messianic time offers us a comparative and productive point of departure for thinking about the place of the anachronism of certain forms of time in nationally contained secular society. It is precisely the effect of such a thinking that Talal Asad engages when he introduces us to the notion of secular time whose boundedness does not allow for the heterogeneity of nonsecular temporalities, that is, the "embodied practices rooted in multiple traditions, of the differences between horizons of expectation and spaces of experience—differences that continually dislocate the present from the past, the world experienced from the world anticipated, and call for their revision and reconnection." This complexity threatens the project of the nation-state or, as Asad puts it, "reduces the scope for 'national politics' with its exclusive boundaries and homogeneous temporality."[9] Asad duly notes how this scope is further complicated by the fact that global capitalism activates the competition for sovereign power among states. The empty homogeneous time that is nationally safeguarded by secular time is thus inflected with imperialistic ambition.

Following this line of argumentation, to speak of secular time is not an attempt to generalize or to reify how either secularism or time functions, nor is it to conceptually homogenize it. Instead, to speak of secular time addresses how secularism—as *the* form of state governmentality—provides and authorizes the structuring force and locus of control for the power that enables time to maintain its homogenizing capacities. That is not to say that the homogenizing and evacuating function of serial time—abetted as it is by secularism—is uniform or produces uniform results. This lack of uniformity is sustained by anticipatory expectations of apocalyptic futures that further raise the hegemonic stakes of secular time by affectively gathering different times into its serial grasp. What I do below is examine a specific instance or framing of a moment of secular governance in its project to serialize its history as the time that predates, establishes, and guarantees the continuity of its pasts and presents. Doing so does not confuse "uniformity" with its homogenizing capacities. Instead, it brings into focus how the homogenizing function of secular time depends on the production of anticipatory affects.

In this essay, the fearful talk around Islam by Franco-Maghrebi Muslim scholars is evidence of how the otherworldly anachronism of the "originary" moorings of Islam have not only spooked those "encountering the native other." Their discourse reveals how the stratifying action of imperial time avoids the political challenge posed by the disjunctive breaks and unordered crystallizations that coexist in different understandings of time. This challenge is cogently articulated by Asad in terms of the "temporalities of many tradition-rooted practices," which he glosses as "the time each embodied practice requires to complete and to perfect itself, the past into which it reaches, that it reencounters, reimagines, and extends."[10] These traditionalist understandings of Islamic time and the practices that they engender produces a fear and an apprehension of temporal instability and cultural collapse that is then amalgamated to a hope for an alterable Islamic future. This merger functions to put into place progressivist secular historical plans that are designed from the belief in the gradual perfectibility of human progress throughout history.[11] To do so, Reinhart Koselleck's contention that "prognosis is a conscious element (*Moment*) of political action" is especially useful in examining the secular faith of these Franco-Maghrebi Muslims, who, in assuming the role of prophetic seers, displace the skepticism of a political metaphysics of secular time onto Islamic metaphysics.[12]

For Koselleck, prognostication works from a diagnostic moment of rational forecasting that demands political intervention. The forecasting of a rational and liberal Islamic future by these intellectuals hence can be understood as modulated by and through the politics of secular governance whose judgment and verdict about traditional Islam are that it is irrational. Koselleck's argument is that prognosis "implies a diagnosis which introduces the past into the future."[13] I understand this as the apocalyptic characterization of traditional Islamic forms of time by these Muslim reformers whose secular prognostications select terrifying Islamic pasts. The corrective to these terrible pasts that beg even more terrible futures begins with the rational prediction of the secular political ideals that folds the repeated expectations of the apocalyptic unruliness of a wayward Islamic time into a temporally structured continuity of unforeseeable probability. For Koselleck, this produces the "excess of political controls on the world."[14] This excess is the issue at stake in this essay, most specifically in relation to the ways in which French secular governance makes Muslims its object by sustaining the hegemonic properties of secular forms of time.

The discussion of secular time as it predicates the permanency and presentness of the past into the future stems from, as Koselleck argues, a different experience of time at modernity's onset and the distinct ways of assimilating and gathering experience that it characterized. These are, as Asad has lucidly established, the "multiplicity of overlapping bonds and identities" that "medieval Christendom and Islam recognized."[15] Ever since, the gradual secularization of Church power has meant that the prophetic anticipation of the end of times has been prorogued for political aims, which depend on the type of diagnostic prognostics that ensure the repetition-with-a-difference of pasts tied futuristically to progress. More specific, Koselleck contends that modernity's promises and hopes of secular advancement have accelerated the experience of present time into ever-briefer intervals such that from the perspective of a chronological past, a lived and given present locates an anticipated, expected future that then becomes a former or past future or, ultimately, a "superseded former future."[16] The acceleration of the present that this involves is caused by the temporal abbreviation that ensues from a future that leaves behind the uniformity of history and becomes the past.[17] The newness of the modern experience of lived time is thus ceaselessly produced out of the transitory sunder between the past and anticipated futures. Within this break, *anticipation* is the index of the temporality contained in the relation and intersection of the past and future and emerges as what promises to accelerate the progressive achievement of freedom.[18]

Thus, to consider anticipation as the apocalyptically strained affective register of the dominance of modern time is to recognize how it activates the emptying capacity of the secular teleology of "our" time. It drives and smoothes out, conflates and squelches, the projected ominousness of religious difference. It allows the evacuating gestures of secular history to capriciously operate by marshaling the progressive drive toward the future and trussing its energies with chilling forecasts about the incongruity of certain forms of time, here, specifically traditional Islamic understandings of time. This means, for example, that in the context of the French state out of which the calls for the reform of Islam that I examine below arise, apocalyptic sentiment directed at Islam and Muslims puts into motion the emptying out of those historical traces no longer useful to the production of national memory. Concomitant to this national project of historical evacuation is the reinscription of those "positive" fragments of the past that serve as the justification for and indexing of its imperialism.

* * *

> To conceptualise the "contemporaneity" of our thought requires the
> reliance on a certain anachronism or untimeliness.
> —Jacques Rancière

The contemporary prognosticators of Islam considered here are Muslim Franco-Maghrebi intellectuals Fethi Benslama and Malek Chebel, who have, to different degrees, walked a very fine line through the frenzy of discourses compelled by the violence associated with Islam. Fethi Benslama, for example, has argued in other texts that Islamist movements do not constitute a "fatality" and acknowledges that the process of uprooting Muslims from traditional time can be attributed to, among other things, the colonial violence that has accompanied the project of modernity.[19] Malek Chebel, who also reminds us that Islam is not "intrinsically a religion of permanent war," would also want to resist the essentialization of Islam with violence.[20] These stances that seemingly contradict their initial concern with the violence associated with Islam bespeak the complexity of the positioning of such intellectuals. In other words, to say that the position of these Muslim intellectuals is complex is not to deny that they are reproductive of forms of power. However, the forms of power that they generate do not reproduce the nation-state in linear, *static*, and systematic undiluted continuity. Of interest here, then, is how admitting to the complexity of past historical contexts affords Chebel and Benslama the intellectual permission to deny that very complexity to traditionalist Muslims. Instead, they can extrapolate to explosive heights the one dimensionality to which they have confined the practices of traditional Muslims.

The stakes involved in Chebel's and Benslama's discussion of time and the importance of their appeals for a reform of Islam are located in the strong debate that arose over the teaching of French colonial history in France as "positive."[21] President Chirac's plans to legally enforce this casting of France's past intersected discursively and politically with an ongoing debate over the 2004 passing of a law that would ban the wearing of the *hidjab* in the French school system. In response, petitions were circulated and signed to support, identify, and set out a program for secular Islam within the context of the French state's deployment of a legal version of the past that secured the sedimentation of a specific casting of history.[22] In 2003, Chebel was one of the original signatories of "L'appel de mai," a petition organized by the Mouvement des musulmans laïques de France that identified with and supported a "secular Islam."[23] The motivations for signing the petition can be seen in his *Manifeste pour un islam des Lumières: Vingt-sept propositions pour réformer l'islam* (2004), which is an unabashed call for the reform of Islam. Benslama was also involved in the launching and signing of a petition, this time "Le Manifeste des libertés," which was published on February 16, 2004, in the French daily *Libération* and whose purpose was, among other things, to legitimate Islam as secular and cultural.[24] The subsequent commentary on and contextualization of this debate can be found in Benslama's book *Déclaration d'insoumission: À l'usage des musulmans et de ceux qui ne le sont pas* (2005). The breaks in time posed by traditional Islam are confronted in their acceptance of the continuity and repetition of dominant forms of time in these writings. This acceptance is nothing less than adherence to the continuity of structural violence, which is precisely what the French state also performs when it refigures violence as traditionally Islamic.

Malek Chebel's reaction to the professed untimeliness of Islam in his *Manifeste* reflects his interpellation by the dubious binaries and language used to describe Muslims in the French public sphere. His rejection of Islamic time therein is explicit; as he explains, the book "points to the anachronisms [of Islam] that need to be got rid of as quickly as possible."[25] Throughout *Manifeste*, Chebel's sense of what constitutes the proper movement of time stands in rigid opposition to the "fossilized" petrifaction or lack of movement that makes the time of Islam anachronistic. Chebel's contention that the time of Islam is anachronistic implies two different velocities of time: first, the movement that he posits as inherent to modern time and, second, the fixity of Islamic time, from which modern time bifurcates and whose origins are "nebulous, almost hallucinatory." He attributes to the latter the most problematic symptom of the "total apathy of some Muslims" (and the Islamic world), who are "frozen" or petrified in the dust of the past and who "give the impression of being catatonic." Since Chebel would have us believe that in gazing back at the origins of Islam, Muslims risk turning into calcified pillars in the Sodom and Gomorrah of time, we find him urgently arguing that being rhythmically synchronized to the movement, change, and unyielding transformational march and celerity of world events is the quality of a moderate Muslim attuned to the temporal scale of modern time. (When Chebel describes those "identitarian Muslims" as succumbing to the facile temptations of violence, one wonders, however, how he accounts for their incitement to action.) For Chebel, the harnessing of force and energy is crucial in order for "enlightened Islam" (*islam des lumières*) "to disengage from the vicious circles of impossibilities" that spin into violence.[26] Chebel's project of reform is accordingly imbued with the "new and energetic movement" of modern time, whose strength and daring can scare away the hostile specters of Islamic pasts.[27]

In turning to Fethi Benslama we find that many of the intellectual underpinnings of his *Déclaration d'insoumission* can be found in his earlier work, *La psychanalyse à l'epreuve de l'islam*, which was published shortly after the events of September 11 and which explicitly addresses the issue of modern time and Islam's role within it. Benslama explains the "crisis" of Islam in the last decades as a "break that cuts into its history and opens within it another possibility of history."[28] Here, the break that Benslama refers to is what he understands as the anachronism of the "other" time of Islam, which he locates within a temporal axis in which secular time progresses *away* from sacred original time: "Time," he explains, "is no longer that of cosmic and celestial movement around the origin.... [I]t is now no longer subjected to any condition but that of itself; it is in this way that the order of pure time is open to the order of interminable change."[29] Playing with the inevitability of secular temporal progress and "restricting" the abundance of time are the political mistakes of Islamic movements nostalgic for a religious past: "The present,"

Benslama writes, "was ceaselessly brought closer to the first events [of Islam] and perceived like a palimpsest of earlier time which, by rising to the surface of lived time, devoured the present."[30] And so, for Benslama, encroaching on the politics of secular time is a present that is rendered vulnerable by the endless reinscription within it of a nonsecular falsely authenticated past. When he later asks, "What does this *political desire for the origin* and the terror that accompanies it signify? What is this turning back [*retournement*] towards originary scenes and the battle to death that is engaged around them and in their name?" it is clear that Benslama's notion of time, however bountiful its array, does not afford the generosity initially promised by perpetual change to those threatening it with a turning back and away from onward movement.[31] Hence, the terror of incorrect time or of time in crisis proceeds from the "torment of the origin" around the Islamic and thus sacred exclusivity tied to the Quran, the hermeneutics and affects of which impede secular time from the model of the temporal plenitude of endless multiplicities that Benslama proposes as its replacement.

Benslama's lapse into the lexis of horror in speaking of time is meant to explain the violence of certain forms of political Islam, to which he links the former very closely. One can sense the anxiety in his earlier book when he states, "Let us remember the major crises experienced throughout the last ten years: the Rushdie affair, the Gulf war, the wars in Bosnia and in Algeria, the Israeli–Palestinian conflict, all this logic of intimidation and terror that has been made to rule by fanaticism, like the hidjab affair, the fatwas, the murder of intellectuals, and the massacre of civil populations."[32] But by the time of the 2005 publication of *Déclaration d'insoumission: À l'usage des musulmans et de ceux qui ne le sont pas*, Benslama's language around the question of violence and Islam is increasingly strained, even apocalyptic, and his focus on Islam as the source of violence is more pointed. "'In the name of Islam…,'" he begins, "such today, is the macabre invocation, the crazed litany that decrees for itself the absolute power to destroy. It spares neither human life, nor institutions, nor texts, nor art, nor words. When the strength of the name radiates so much devastation, we cannot take what occurs for an accident.… For what we need to question with utmost priority is the fissure that released in the sphere of Islam such a desperate will to destroy and to self-destruct."[33] It is not difficult to be sideswiped by the *singularity* with which Benslama attributes such horror to Islam. And well one should be—any reaction against this unilateral appellation could only ever be understated, however one wants to acknowledge that, yes, indeed, horrific acts are committed in the name of all sorts of things.

And yet my intention here is also to point out how the anxiety of this discourse is intimately connected to the imperative to secularize Islamic time. Even at Benslama's most mindful moments, one wonders what plane of consciousness he is privileging in his anxious statements, especially in reference to his contention that the Muslim subject is "precipitated into a historical mode [*un agir historique*] that surpasses the plane of consciousness" and "towards the unknown and towards the unthinkable, impelled by modern efficacies."[34] One also wonders what is unthinkable and for whom when he cautions that the impelling, accelerated, and propelling forces of modern time also lull Muslims into a "hypnotic state" of subjugation that noisily proclaims archaic anachronisms in the public sphere. The tensions in Benslama's work are also displayed in descriptors such as the "regression of human development" and the "infantile disposition of memory." His language carries with it the presuppositions of a secularized apparatus, which allows him to portray traditionalist Muslims as dizzied out of reality by the circumambulating spell of sacred time. Shades of dread do more than color Benslama's writing; they also risk short-circuiting his historico-political analysis of Islam with psychoessentialist determinism in whose secular junctures tenuously hangs Islamic subjectivity.

* * *

> History is the discourse of power, the discourse of the obligations power uses to subjugate; it is also the dazzling discourse that power uses to fascinate, terrorize, and immobilize.   —Michel Foucault

The secularist pressure to reform Islam that arose within the context of the debates over France's national memory of its past imperial formations locates Muslims and their relationship to the Islamic tradition within the obscured violence of its secularist pasts. In a milieu still resonating with the "Islamist" aftermath of the Algerian War, secularly ridding the nation of the "religious excess" of Islam refracted the state's own strategic trimming of its colonial overkill, that is, the "excesses" of its national history. And yet, with the impulse to secularly temporalize Islam comes the inevitable streamlining of the present horror-inducing "aberrancy of Islam" out of secular narratives of political governance and social cohesion.[35] For countless inhabitants of France, colonial violence is simply an anomalous blip in the history of the development and elaboration of French Republican values whose continuity with colonial Algeria existed only in terms of the purported welcome of those values by Algeria's natives. The durability of the structural violence of the state is hence propped up by whims of remembrance and denial that are textured with optimism about French governance as the permanent solution to the perpetual crises and future of Islamic violence.[36] At "best," the structural inequalities of the French colonial system and its continuities have been replayed as the face-off between competing memories—namely, those of "good" versus "bad" colonialism—that needed to be "fairly" balanced, the pretense being, of course, that the "balancing" of history entails de facto the balancing of power. At worst, the structural continuity of French colonial violence is "subterfuged," only to be revived as a Dickensian Islamic Ghost of Algeria Past menacing the futures of those who did not welcome the ongoing battle for secular hearts with sanguine equanimity. The question that consequently needs to be asked is how poised we can expect "Islam" to be in its balancing act if it is forced to walk a tightrope strung between frightful histories and apocalyptic futures and held by secular forces tipsy with imperial power.

The issue of the continuity of force has once again arisen in terms of the transitioning of a politics of empire to a global scale and has raised the stakes beyond the local context of ex-colonizing countries. The debate launched by Hardt and Negri in 2000 with the publication of *Empire* tackled the question of the stable reproduction of imperial force and power and its relation to time.[37] But many commentators have resisted the totalizing move that they propose in their account of the paradigmatic shift from European imperial sovereignty to its culmination in the new supranational and borderless order of "Empire" that embodies the infinite inclusivity of unitary power. If anything, the French case, where the secular politics of state governmentality curtail the excess of religious difference within national boundaries, illustrates that regardless of the grandiosity of imperial ambition, Empire and the globalizing stakes that it inflects can be put to work in a very local and territorialized scale.

Nonetheless, Hardt and Negri's argument also usefully draws attention to how very much tied to the horizontal conditions of empire is its *timely* process. Hardt and Negri exploit the idea of the hegemonic structural continuity of time in order to conceptualize the regulation of the function of time in relationship to the imperial production of power, and in this way they argue that Empire "encompasses all time within its ethical foundation." "Empire," they continue, "exhausts historical time, suspends history, and summons the past and future within its own ethical order. In other words, Empire presents its order as permanent, eternal, and necessary."[38] Here the example of the French state's attempt to streamline its national history makes evident the necessity to safeguard its moral position as a continuing center of governance in the context of an imperial past. That this also involves disaligning the subjectivities, affects, and temporalities of traditionalist Muslims brings into focus how such attempts depend on the hegemonic force of secularist time and its homogenizing potential, which in turn is supported by the national and even imperial ambition of the state. As such, Hardt and Negri would understand the disjointing of the traditional temporalities of Islamic time from the progressive time of modernity as the inevitable product of the way in which time is harnessed by the reins of power at its most industrious—the generating of time therefore implies the continual hegemonic action of power as the solution to repeated crises. It is in this way that one can think of the concept of secular time not as a generalizing or totalizing concept but as one that addresses the very totalizing mechanisms that it puts into place and that allow it to function, however discontinuously and asymmetrically.

To speak of imperial or even national strategies of governance as functioning in a uniform manner is to generalize the hegemony of state power into a consistent and unilateral act of force. Thus, the arguments against Hardt and Negri focus on how they problematically argue for a deterministic understanding of empire as an already set system of expansion whose aims are as teleological as they are absolutizing.[39] However, a Foucauldian step back from the horizontal looming of their claims can turn the durability of Empire for which they argue on its head. This more modest aim to examine the deep grammar and archaeology of the durability of Empire, that is, its vertical axis of materiality, avoids the totalizing tendencies of Hardt and Negri's claims. This involves first coming to terms with Michel Foucault's genealogical approach that understands history as making no reference to a transcendental subject that "runs in its empty sameness throughout the course of history" and whose repressive capacity plays out in a superstructural position.[40] In his *Society Must Be Defended* lectures, Foucault addresses the way in which force nevertheless organizes and *sustains* structures of power. Here he states that "power is the continuation of war by other means," implying that "power relations...are essentially anchored in a certain relationship of force that was established in and through war at a given historical moment that can be historically speci-fied....Politics, in other words sanctions and reproduces the disequilibrium of forces manifested in war."[41] Foucault's argument here is all the more relevant because the secondary talk about Foucauldian genealogical notions of power as "diffuse" or "everywhere" and as "subjective" as it is subjectifying has done much to relativize power and in so doing has flattened out our historical understandings of acts of force and their continuing material effects. The relativizing of power, which conflates force with power, also confuses the continuities of history (what the philosopher Ian Hacking has termed its ontology, or historical ontology, whose traces are *sedimented* into our present) with its atemporality.[42] In other words, to accept that historical structures are resilient is not to expect transcendental pat-terns of uniformity but to admit that certain structures do stabilize into cartogra-phies of material continuity.

In the context of the debates over the silencing of certain aspects of French mil-itary presence in the colonies, the Algerian War stands as the fulcrum of the perpetual relationship of force to power, in which war, as Foucault states, is "the point of maximum tension" of power whose "force relations [are] laid bare."[43] Taken with Foucault, Hardt and Negri's argument is useful to demonstrate how force, even at its clearest apogee, as in the case of the war of Algeria and the continued organization of its political effects and elaborations, cannot be confused with its totalizing unity or unifying capacity. This, however, does not contradict the fact that even though colonial structures are not uniformly replicated several decades later in the French context, the relationships of force that they systema-tized and harnessed are materially sedimented and reproduced even in their insta-bility. So, to those who decry as too facile the claims that French colonialism is alive in the postcolonial *métropole*, one can answer, "Quite." But one can also fault them for obfuscating the question of force in France's governmental strategies with simplistic denials of equivalence that do little to acknowledge the *timely* might of certain strokes of power, that is, those that underpin and sustain the hegemonic workings of secular time. Of course, this argument would not serve those needing to fill the "good" camp of the debate over the continuing legacy of French gover-nance because it is easier to claim innocence by denying sameness at one's convenience so that details can later be filled in at whim. It is also easier to resus-citate sameness in other forms by crying wolf so as to efficiently expedite equiva-lencies within the frame of secular time while pretending not to.

Moreover, the construal of time in the thought of Benslama and Chebel as inev-itably and positively progressing forward is forcefully played off against the violent anachronism of certain Islamic pasts. This dislodging from anachronism is a modern attempt to liberate a secular future by pushing these pasts back to the fur-thest recesses of normative history. Past anticipations of apocalyptic futures put into historical motion, so to speak, the political function and authority of secular liberalism, whose structural claims and ambitions unfold a particular concept of

progressive history. In this vein, Hardt and Negri challenge us to think more specifically about how hegemonic time is produced from and also produces the appre-
hensive shuffling and reordering of the irregularities of time and of pasts and
futures that stabilize and bolster the durability of its hegemony. Stoler, the most
articulate of critics of Hardt and Negri, has rightly described this process as the
historical *sedimentation* of "alternating density and absence of historical referents"
whose management Empire seeks when it collapses the differences in history and
time within it.[44] Hardt and Negri identify this process as Empire's ability to present
itself as perpetually in a crisis that needs to be overcome in order to allow Empire
to reconstitute its regime of possibilities.[45]

An examination of the work of these intellectuals suggests that apocalyptic sentiments function as the coefficient to the disjointing of traditional Islam from
modern secular time such that the collapsing of different historical referents and
the reordering of time that this entails are sustained by terror-producing discourses about the violence of Islam. The declaration of the "crisis of Islam" is consequently the declaration of Empire in crisis, each constitutive of the other for the
latter's prognostic anticipation of its role in the future. Significant to this examination of the production of secular Islamic time, therefore, is understanding how the
apocalyptic functions as a fundamentally self-stabilizing technique inherent to
modern secular projects, even as it implies destabilizing strategies of binding and
unbinding the present from its historical structures.[46] By liberally reorganizing the
past for the progressive sake of an idealized secular future, apocalyptic sentiment
in modern time ensures that the hastening of the latter's advancing intransience is
unsullied by the messes of certain histories. The catastrophic imaginary that emo-
tionally undergirds these Muslim reformers' interpretations of Islam involves, as a
point of departure, that their utopian attachment to secular liberal principles be
closely tied to an apocalyptic vision of Islam that cherry-picks its past. In this case,
the past in question, riddled as it is with the violence of the Algerian War(s) and
the subsequent rise of Islamist movements in North Africa or the Middle East,
requires an apocalyptic and anticipatory stance in the present that sheds historical
particulars and layers for it to be then carried forward into fears about the present
role of Islam in global politics.[47] In this way, the violence of the wars and conflicts
in Palestine, Algeria, Bosnia, and so on is restructured to support the introduction
of secularism and the values that it promises, and to which it pays lip service, and
to rehearse *in continuum* Islam as the legitimate container of violence. Securing
Muslims' past and future status as foe also secures the stabilization necessary to
the continuity of a secular politics determined and manufactured already by its
anticipatory judgment of irreconcilability with or irreducibility to Islam.

Furthermore, the secular Islamic twist on the modern secularist discourse of
apocalypticism lies in how its calls for the reform of Islamic tradition and history
promote the "destructiveness" of its *past* from which the (and its) future has to be
saved. This adoption of secular liberal ideals envisions both a renewal that will
enable Muslims to advance from such violence and a transformation of Islamic
traditional religious norms and the embodied practices, sensibilities, and affects
that have been historically connected to them. The apocalypticism that arises from
within the bounds set upon Islam depends on the *present* of these reformers, which

assembles and disassembles the reform of Islam with history. In doing so, it functions in relationship to the moral worth attributed to secular society as a new Eden of political and economic freedom that posits and exists in relation to a historicized Islam of a specific type, whose tradition is in line with secular post-Christian or atheistic ideals and the progressive march of utopic history. It is precisely because the utopian moment in the thinking of these intellectuals of Islam implies a possibility for morality (contrary to its strictly post-Christian or atheistic counterparts) that it strengthens what Koselleck would term "a utopia that sees itself compelled to constant reproduction" and which proceeds by "continually reproducing its foe [figured in these works as the Islamist] as the means through which it can remain permanent."[48] The apocalyptic moment is abstracted to the conceptual level such that these intellectuals propose the ongoing revolution/reform of Islamic thought that is necessary for the peaceful rebirth of Islam in secular society. For them, this involves the extirpation of what they see as extremist interpretations of Islam. Thus they bring to the present and future surface of history those lines of humanistic thinking (such as the pluralistic rationalism of the Mu'tazilah and the humanism of philosophers such as Averroes and Ibn Miskawayh) that have been buried in what they view as an Islamic teleology of ruin, decay, and violence.[49] Their calls for the reform of Islamic thought in light of Koselleck's concept of revolution contains a coefficient of movement that mobilizes history in terms of the prevailing prospect of the future. Hence the alteration of a prospective Islamic future changes the view of the past by positing a revolutionary break that dislocates the traditional space and time of difference (here that of Islamic tradition). The calls for Islamic reform therefore liberate a new future at the intersections of progress and catastrophe by fashioning a new and more catastrophic Islamic past.

The claims that these intellectuals make about the anachronism of Islam thus demarcate between the haves and have-nots of proper chronological time, depending on their place in the correct historical order of the present. The issue of anachronism, however, not only poses a problem about the lack of harmony between Islamic time and present time; to varying degrees, for these thinkers, modern time is also teleologically driven, such that it "needs" to dislocate itself from those past times that are considered to impede its progress. In this way, the supposed neutrality of secular time and its degrees of historical progress barely escape, if at all, the evolutionary principle of time that denies Islam the achievement of modernity. Temporally distancing Islamic pasts into a past that is *depassé* refuses the substantial basis and legitimacy of continuing pasts for Muslims. This does not allow the sequencing of Islam into the munificence of the harmonious or synchronizing secular time that they advocate. The apocalyptic efficiency involved in Benslama's overt agenda to assonate a plenitude of different histories and bring them up to speed, nevertheless inserts a syncopating process into a modern secular present that suppresses Islam's initial historical pulses. The effects that these engender are thus horrifically reduced to pure violence. Accordingly, the arguments of these intellectuals about the lack of synchronism between varying tempos of time and the fretful overtones of their reformist incentives reveal that what is at stake is more than just a problem about the dissonance of temporal continuums; these arguments inevitably locate Muslims historically in a catalepsy of inert subjectivity or, at the very most, situate them as caught in a paradox of stasis and violent action. Positioning Muslims as either passive subjects of Islam's "structural stasis" or hurled into the rhythm of modern mobilization allows both Chebel and Benslama to reinscribe Muslims as children whose temporal tantrums are noisily and violently interruptive of correct secular space. What is more, while they pay lip service to the colonial pasts as having negatively affected Muslim populations, these intellectuals remain resolutely mum about the ways in which they strain their compositions of secular time—however much still in the present, some pasts, it seems, are just past and are in no need of reform. Instead, with airs of objective homogeneity, the overtones of secular harmony are synchronized to streamline the violence of secular colonial histories out of secular temporality with ever-louder apocalyptic crescendos about Islamic pasts in futures. And so, if secular liberal political ideals function salvifically in their reconceptualizations of Islamic norms, it is because they are marshaled and galvanized by catastrophic fears about Islam *in displaced time* and Islam *displaced in time*. In this way, the efficacy of apocalyptic sentiment functions to produce a notion of time whose temporal dimensions folds past, present, and future into each other or redouble the past and future onto one another in an unequal manner. As a result, the reduction of Islam to violence is stabilized and labored in support of a framework of secular time that in the conviction of its political sufficiency reconsolidates Islamic subjectivity for its secular mobilization.

This analysis of the secular production of Islamic time has demonstrated how the imperial specter about which Hardt and Negri warn us is raised over secular time through its indexing of the assumptions of progressive time that are then built into the secular grounding of modern societies. Time is at the not-so-silent beck and call of power veiling and extinguishing its own by-products, strategically coating its grids of domination and reinvigorating its extremities and visceralities within a gridlock of history that is mired in structural disparities. Plagued with inequities inherent to its temporality, secular time maps imperial relations and sustains the disproportions of political landscapes. With claims to transparency and neutrality, it mortgages power structures in the present contexts of colonial pasts whose sovereign impulse is stubbornly sedimented, deposited, and built into the present. Its scaffolding contains and at the same time structures the proliferation of antagonisms, which reduces and obscures the complexity of power itself. By doing so it fixes temporal successions and sequences whose constitutive outside is reserved for glossaries of premodern nonsecular temporalities. In other words, hidden behind the binary antagonisms of Islamic violence and secular peace is the self-legitimating ruse of the ever-increasing largesse of liberal embrace, whose network of regulatory power produces and instrumentalizes the trope of Islamic violence to fabricate progressive histories. The time of Islam and its histories, and the traditions that inform the lives of Muslims, is not out of joint. Rather, much of it has been disjointed: at its most extreme, punctured, displaced from within and without; at its most perspectival, insidiously diffused and dissolved, coded and recoded within liberal lattices of secular power.

Politically our thinking about dominant time and the fractious complexity and assemblages that it has yielded is challenged by residual and emerging forms of times. This includes conceiving of time as the possibility of more than one time being at work, of there being more than one (or even more than two: modern or premodern) Islamic time(s) at work. But it also means *not* thinking of time simply in terms of multiplicities and their convergences, which often involves the forma-tive force of an unquestioned unitary framing that imposes its coherence. Models of time that do not deny its coercive qualities or simply grasp it as a continuous unfolding of unalloyed and self-sufficient secular histories of different cultures (which would not solve their disorientation or even their atrocious confrontation) require thinking the aperture of different temporalities *into* secular time and looking for their disjunctures, their discontinuous contact into and encounter with one another and the interruptive capacity of different pasts. Here, the resonance with Talal Asad's work is most clear. His invocations for the circuity of time, its overlapping nature in which heterogeneous temporalities dislocate presents from past to unfold different experiences, push us to think of the varying spheres of anticipation, expectations, and simultaneities that exist outside of the homoge-neous bounds of secular linear temporalities.[50] The conditions and possibilities that will steer us clear of the dyadic tensions between violent origins and cata-clysmic futures depend on our capacity to identify the displacement of the secular achievement of progress to the deployment of its own homogeneity. After all, is secular time not invested in maintaining and regenerating the anachronism of certain forms of time within which it feigns its unaltered functioning in order to justify its existence as nonreligious? Does not the best avoidance of the challenge of thinking an ontology of the present lie in stamping out its material and radical plurality through the fabricated rationale of a liberalism in which complex differences are compelled to function together? The rendering anachronistic of traditional Islamic time is the ultimate sham of apocalyptic castings and conclu-sions that makes possible a tearing into the present of the exercise of power. It is nothing but the self-preserving partitioning function of a secular time that trades in difference—the recovery of another existence of time as an event of the present—for the ever and constant obliteration of that present.

■ NOTES

This essay was first presented as an introductory lecture to "European Islam between Religious Traditions and Secular Formations" in Sublice/Frankfurt an der Oder, February 7–10, 2008. It bears the influence of Ann Stoler's thinking on questions of affect, and was initially formulated in her SCT seminar "The Logos and Pathos of Empire: Durabilities of Matter and Mind" at Cornell University. My thanks go to Ann Stoler, David Ferris and Natalie Rose for their engagement with the issues presented in this chapter.

1. *The Tragedy of Hamlet, Prince of Denmark*, I.V.211–12, Hamlet speaking to Horatio after a visit from the ghost of his father. Fethi Benslama, *La psychanalyse à l'épreuve de l'islam* (Paris: Aubier, 2002), 88 (translations of this text are mine).

2. Ali Ahmed Said Asbar, also known as Adonis, is a Syrian poet (b. 1930).

3. Bruce Holsinger, "Empire, Apocalypse, and the 9/11 Premodern," *Critical Inquiry* 34 (Spring 2008): 488.

4. Ronald Schleifer, *Modernism and Time: The Logic of Abundance in Literature, Science, and Culture* 1880–1930 (Cambridge: Cambridge University Press, 2000), 2. Schleifer argues that the ethnocentric ideology of objective progressive secularity is a result of and is sustained by the revolutionary, scientistic, progressivist nineteenth-century impetus that followed from the mechanicality of Newtonian orders of temporality. He states that the "secular humanism of our Enlightenment inheritance... manifested itself not as the detachment of the subject of knowledge from the vagaries of time... but in the impossibility of maintaining this detachment in light of its *timely* successes" (xi) that held back the religious metaphysics of time tied to the timeless atemporalities of transcendental theological truths.

5. Johannes Fabian, *Time and the Other: How Anthropology Makes Its Object* (New York: Columbia University Press, 2002), 21.

6. Walter Benjamin, *Illuminations: Essays and Reflections* (New York: Schocken, 1969). For a most lucid account of Benjamin's conceptualization of history, see David Ferris, *The Cambridge Introduction to Walter Benjamin* (New York: Cambridge University Press, 2008), 130–35.

7. Benedict Anderson, *Imagined Communities: Reflections on the Origin and Spread of Nationalism* (New York: Verso, 1991), 26. Anderson's statement is worth quoting in full: "The idea of a sociological organism moving calendrically through homogenous empty time is a precise analogue of the idea of the nation, which is also is conceived as a solid community moving steadily down (or up) history."

8. Ibid., 24.

9. Talal Asad, *Formations of the Secular: Christianity, Islam, Modernity* (Stanford: Stanford University Press, 2003), 179.

10. Ibid.

11. Daniel Wojcik, *The End of the World as We Know It: Faith, Fatalism, and Apocalypse in America* (New York: New York University Press, 1997), 4, 14. See also Schleifer, *Modernism and Time*, 6, 133.

12. Reinhart Koselleck, *Futures Past: On the Semantics of Historical Time*, trans. and intro. by Keith Tribe (New York: Columbia University Press, 2004), 19 (translator's italics).

13. Ibid., 22.

14. Ibid., 19.

15. Asad, *Formations of the Secular*, 179.

16. Koselleck, *Futures Past*, 3.

17. Ibid., 50.

18. Ibid., 246.

19. Benslama, *La psychanalyse*, 319.

20. Malek Chebel, *Manifeste pour un islam des Lumières: Vingt-sept propositions pour réformer l'islam* (Paris: Éditions Hachette Litteratures, 2004), 41 (translations of this text are mine).

21. At the time of his presidency, Jacques Chirac decided to pass a law on February 23, 2005, that called for the recognition in French schools of the "positive role" that the French played in its colonies. The French education system, a system that had been seen as carrying out the secularizing and civilizing ideals of the French Revolution, was to serve as the medium for the type of historical revisionism that could manage France's national memory. Strong objections were raised by many, especially those for whom the Algerian War was still fresh in their minds, warning that the law would abstract and silence the very historical context of the *laïcité* to be taught, namely, the structural violence that it exported in the detour that it took in colonies as the motor of the *missions civilisatrices*. Chirac eventually repealed the law on February 25, 2006, but this move was decried by many on all sides of

the political spectrum as undermining the "positive" aspects of colonialism, an argument that went hand in hand with the denial of the *longue durée* of structural violence of the French colonial system and its practices. For a discussion of the "*longue durée* of colonial violence and postcolonial ambition," see Paul Silverstein, *Algeria in France: Transpolitics, Race and Nation* (Bloomington: Indiana University Press, 2004), 16.

22. Ruth Mas, "Compelling the Muslim Subject: Memory as Post-Colonial Violence and the Public Performativity of 'Secular and Cultural Islam,'" *Muslim World* 96 (October 2006): 585–616.

23. In May 2003, the Mouvement des musulmans laïques de France launched "L'appel de mai: Appel aux citoyens musulmans de France épris de paix, justice, de liberté et de laïcité."

24. The petition can now be accessed at http://www.manifeste.org.

25. Chebel, *Manifeste*, 19–20.

26. Ibid., 10.

27. Ibid., 193.

28. Benslama, *La psychanalyse*, 317.

29. Ibid., 88.

30. Ibid., 29.

31. Ibid., 30.

32. Ibid., 26.

33. Fethi Benslama, *Déclaration d'insoumission: À l'usage des musulmans et de ceux qui ne le sont pas* (Paris: Flammarion, 2005), 1 (translations of this text are mine).

34. Benslama, *La psychanalyse*, 12, 317.

35. Throughout these debates, consolidating French sovereignty by rationalizing and thus legitimating the deployment of *laïcité* in France's colonies meant renovating its colonial past and recasting the violence of the colonizing missions in Algeria as an "exceptional" part of French national history. Indeed, the discourse of exception surrounding the security measures set up in France after September 11th follows a tradition firmly established in the colonies, where, for example, the state of emergency law was created and put into effect. Many who reacted to the 2004 law, such as those who signed the petition launched by the Marche des Indigènes in May 2005 and participated in demonstrations, saw the increased policing of Muslims as evidence of the ongoing colonizing of activities within the republic and the continuing effects of France's project of empire. When riots broke out in the Parisian suburbs in November 2005 and the state of emergency was applied for the first time within the *métropole*, the calls for the decolonization of the republic only increased and hardened the conviction that, though now being enacted internally, the French colonial project was alive and well.

36. See Benjamin Stora, *La gangrène et l'oubli* (Paris: La Decouverte, 2006), for his discussion of the nostalgia and melancholy of the French over lost French Algeria. Far less mirthful about the long-standing fugues of French historical consciousness and the possibilities for colonial resilience are the authors of *La fracture coloniale: La société française au prisme de l'héritage colonial*, published in 2005. Their book clarifies the ways in which the colonial context has been sustained in the *métropole* and advocates the development of a nonsystematic approach that uncovers how histories have been concealed and mutilated, how amnesia has been collectivized, how memories have been fractured, and how colonial history has been amputated. Pascal Blanchard, Nicolas Bancel, and Sandrine Lemaire, eds., *La fracture coloniale: La société française au prisme de l'héritage colonial* (Paris: Éditions La Découverte, 2005), 13.

37. Michael Hardt and Antonio Negri, *Empire* (Cambridge: Harvard University Press, 2000), xiii–xv.

38. Ibid., 11.

39. See Ann Stoler, "On Degrees of Imperial Sovereignty," *Public Culture* 18, no. 1 (Winter 2006): 125–46.

40. Michel Foucault, *The Order of Things* (London: Tavistock, 1970), 83.

41. Michel Foucault, *Society Must Be Defended: Lectures at the Collège de France 1975-1976* (London: Penguin Books, 2004), 16–17.

42. Much of the confusion centers on Foucault's break in the *Archeology of Knowledge*, trans. A. M. Sheridan Smith (New York: Routledge, 2002), with the Annales school's support of the continuities of history. But as Hacking reminds us, "At the height of his enthusiasm for abrupt changes in knowledge, [Foucault] never denied the importance of the *Annales* methodology with its search for underlying stability." Ian Hacking, *Historical Ontology* (Cambridge, MA: Harvard University Press, 2004), 83. According to Dreyfus and Rabinow, Foucault's point is that historical structures remain even though they cannot be considered atemporal. Hubert L. Dreyfus and Paul Rabinow, *Michel Foucault: Beyond Structuralism and Hermeneutics* (Chicago: University of Chicago Press, 1983), 15.

43. Foucault, *Society Must Be Defended*, 46.

44. Stoler, "On Degrees of Imperial Sovereignty," 127.

45. Hardt and Negri, *Empire*, 21.

46. Hacking, *Historical Ontology*, 193 ff.

47. For a discussion of the anticipatory policies developed within the rubric of security concerns in Europe, see Frank Peter, "Political Rationalities, Counter-Terrorism and Policies on Islam in the United Kingdom and France," in *The Social Life of Anti-Terrorism Laws: The War on Terror and the Classifications of the Dangerous Other*, ed. Julia Eckert (Bielefeld: transcript, 2008), 79–108.

48. Koselleck, *Futures Past*, 54.

49. For a discussion by Benslama and Chebel on the importance of Ibn Rushd's legacy, for example, to the reform of contemporary Islam, see Benslama, *Déclaration d'insoumission*, 81; and Chebel, *Manifeste*, 19.

50. Asad, *Formations of the Secular*, 178–80. Aren't the disjunctions of time precisely where we can best think about politics, the essence of which, as Rancière reminds us, is not Habermasian consensus but disagreement? See Jacques Rancière, Solange Guenoun, and James H. Kavanaugh, "Jacques Rancière: Literature, Politics, Aesthetics: Approaches to Democratic Disagreement," *SubStance* 92 (2000): 3–24.

5   Secularism, "Religious Violence," and the Liberal Imaginary

Brian Goldstone

For the past several years now, intellectuals spanning the political and disciplinary spectrum have become increasingly obsessed with identifying the causes and potential remedies for what are presumed to be religiously motivated acts of violence. Since September 11, 2001, these are the experts to whom many have anxiously turned in order to better comprehend the nature of "religious terrorism"— which, of course, was what the attacks of that day were immediately identified with.[1] Taking this burgeoning preoccupation as a point of departure, my aim in this essay is not only to take stock of the various and often incompatible positions assumed in these discussions but also to assess the figure and the category of religious violence itself: the uses to which it has been put; the modes of feeling and subjectivity it has called upon, authorized, opposed, or rendered unintelligible; and, above all, the political and ethical projects its invocation has been able to mobilize in the present. Dating from the sectarian clashes of post-Reformation Europe, the memory and feared reemergence of religious violence have featured prominently in the organizing rationale for a secular ethos and polity, with the malignancy and inhumanity of the former perpetually contrasted with the salvific (though in many instances no less devastating) potentialities of the powers that replaced it. But while such accounts of the relationship between religion and the secular state are in the annals of modern political thought both familiar and reassuring, less commonly has it been observed that what the latter seeks to redeem, indeed encourages and incites, is a uniquely recalibrated religious subject. And it is in light of this longer tradition of secular-liberal political discourse—a tradition characterized, with regard to matters of religiosity, by a distinctive confluence of *critique and commendation*—that the prescriptions proffered by those currently theorizing about religious violence can, I think, best be understood.

My purpose in what follows, then, is by no means to offer an improved theory of religious violence—why it happens, where it comes from, how it might be prevented—but neither is it merely to criticize those who choose to engage in such endeavors. In this regard, my reflections can be at least partly distinguished from those who have sought to call attention to the inconsistent and even incoherent means by which specific acts of violence are analytically ascribed to religious as opposed to nonreligious motives. For although their claims have come to constitute the conventional wisdom of a populace at war, these experts on religious violence have not been without their critics: some who have challenged their pretensions to quantifiability—the conjecture that *more* destruction has been wrought by religious than nonreligious institutions or that religion is *more* likely to produce pathological subjects—and others who have simply underscored what they take to be a discourse beset with a range of contradictions.[2] Notable among those who have pointed to such inadequacies is Christian theologian William T. Cavanaugh. In a series of recent articles, Cavanaugh's critical energies have been directed at, on the one hand, a radical reappraisal of the historiography surrounding early modern Europe's wars of religion and, on the other, an attempt to undermine the analytical sustainability of the "religion" in contemporary discussions of religion and violence.[3] Surveying the vast archive dealing with these issues, he convincingly shows that even the most sophisticated attempts to "separate a category called 'religion' with a particular tendency toward violence from a putatively 'secular' reality"—and hence to distinguish religious aggressions from those generated by supposedly secular commitments—are ultimately doomed to failure, leading him to conclude that such attempts comprise and contribute to the persistence of what he provocatively terms "the myth of religious violence."[4] And this myth, he goes on to argue, not only has long underwritten the modern nation-state's persistent contrast between irrational forms of violence and those more enlightened cruelties considered necessary to contain them but has also served to consolidate the secularist demand that religion be done away with, or at the very least be made private, so as not to infect public and political life.[5]

Cavanaugh is undoubtedly right to underscore these problems and in doing so to call attention to the ideological investments that accompany them. But in the end I find his account to be inadequate in some important ways, and it is along these lines that my own approach seeks to depart from it. For while I share his skepticism of the confidence with which many theorists have tried to distinguish religious from nonreligious phenomena, and agree that such comfortable binaries ought always to be challenged, it nevertheless strikes me as insufficient to simply discard categories like religious violence as analytically incoherent; rather, it seems we ought to attend to the contexts in which such categories *are taken to cohere* and are spoken and written about as such. For if the myth of religious violence is as deeply entrenched as Cavanaugh believes it is, it will not do to emphasize the lack of rigor by which the concept is construed. In Cavanaugh's work, this leads him to pay relatively little attention to the secularism that he claims is behind the myth and so also to neglect the distinctive sensibilities and affects—that is, the *modes* of secularity—that underlie the political visions of those who perpetuate it.

This essay tries to compensate for such neglect by following a somewhat different route. I propose that one way to think through the category of religious violence is to ask about the place it holds in the liberal imaginary, the work that it does, and the kinds of ethico-political formations it is taken to necessitate—and this brings me to ask about its connection to secularism. Following some recent attempts at reformulating the concept,[6] I point out that in its liberal democratic guise secularism indicates a complex relationship to religion that cannot be captured in terms of outright antagonism; rather, it seems that *specific kinds of religion* are always and for myriad purposes being valorized and denounced, empowered and made provisional, and that the demand of liberal democratic states is less that religious signs and subjects be evacuated from public spaces than that the beliefs and behaviors of those subjects be refashioned, by whatever kindnesses or cruelties the situation necessitates, in accordance with the transcendent values of a particular way of life.[7] Put otherwise, in terms borrowed from Foucault, the modern secular state can be seen as a highly sophisticated structure into which individuals and their various convictions, religious and otherwise, can by all means be integrated, but only on the condition that "this individuality be shaped in a new form and submitted to a set of very specific patterns."[8]

A significant part of secularism's claim to moral and political legitimacy, after all, was and continues to be linked to its claim not only to being able to provide space for the peaceable coexistence of a plurality of identities and beliefs but to being able to *secure* this space against anything or anyone that might stand to threaten it. To be sure, this double promise of public security, on the one hand, and individual liberty, on the other, relies on the regulatory and coercive power of the law to determine and eliminate such threats where they appear, but it also depends on the pedagogical apparatuses of the state to instill in subjects a particular understanding of liberty in conformity to which their commitments can be appropriately ordered. It follows that some commitments may subsequently need to be reconfigured (or else violently proscribed) for the sake of "the public good" and that, as Alasdair MacIntyre has observed, the moral calculus undergirding this vision of "the public good"—exactly a *liberal* calculus—will itself be rendered authoritative over against rival conceptions of social existence.[9] By this I am not suggesting that the modern secular state is in fact incapable of tolerating religious difference (a fallacy that recent scholarship on these matters has effectively disabused us of) but only that there are certain kinds of difference that will be deemed intolerable and, if need be, subsequently recast or extinguished altogether. A closer examination of this articulation of secularism with sovereign power will, however, need to be undertaken elsewhere; here I only seek to capture some of the ways in which religion—or more precisely "religious violence"—has been invoked to make certain political formations, with their attendant affects and rationalities, seem prudent and to an extent even inescapable. I must stress again that my concern in this essay is neither to explain religious violence nor to defend "religion" (however this happens to be construed) against the accusations leveled at it. Rather, it is to attend to the more basic question of *what it is we do* when we assign responsibility for violence to specific agents and traditions—in other words, not to interrogate what "religious violence" means or why it happens but to ask what it does, what it stands for, and, perhaps most urgently, who is made to answer for it.

* * *

I begin by looking at what has today become a highly visible and sensationalized perspective on religious violence. Those who espouse this view maintain that religion by its very essence fosters a predisposition toward intolerance and irrationality among its practitioners and that its violent pathologies only reveal the truth of its hidden logic. Of course, it is Islam that is seen as especially likely to inculcate such tendencies, with recent events like the Danish cartoon affair only serving to corroborate these suspicions. For many of those writing in its wake—from celebrity provocateurs to lesser-known scholars and editorialists—the Muslim reaction to the cartoons (at least as it was represented in the Western press) helped to confirm not merely the saliency of an "Islamic threat" or even the danger of allowing religious passions into the public sphere but, more importantly, the problem of an inherent, if not inevitable, penchant for violence built into the very constitution of "organized religion."[10] Thus Slavoj Žižek would opine in the editorial pages of the *New York Times* that "the lesson of today's terrorism is that if God exists, then everything, including blowing up thousands of innocent bystanders, is permitted—at least to those who claim to act directly on behalf of God, since, clearly, a direct link to God justifies the violation of any merely human constraints and considerations." He concluded: "Today, when religion is emerging as the well-spring of murderous violence around the world, assurances that Christian or Muslim or Hindu fundamentalists are only abusing and perverting the noble spiritual messages of their creeds ring increasingly hollow. What about restoring the dignity of atheism, one of Europe's greatest legacies and perhaps our only chance for peace?"[11] Notwithstanding his earlier writings, in which he found in Christianity a model par excellence for a revived political militancy—and in St. Paul a precursor to Lenin[12]—Žižek's comments can be seen to resonate with a long tradition of Euro-American thought stretching from the so-called radical enlightenment to the more recent polemics of pundits like Richard Dawkins and Christopher Hitchens. What these thinkers share is the conviction that those who persist in attributing religious violence to misappropriations of otherwise benevolent belief systems only obscure the reality of religion's naturally destructive inclinations. And, surprisingly or not, arguments such as these are to be found not only in popular diatribes but in a range of influential scholarly works as well.

Take Mark Juergensmeyer's *Terror in the Mind of God*, perhaps the most widely cited examination of the links between religion and violent militancy.[13] Juergensmeyer, a prominent sociologist of religion, discloses in the book's introduction that "although some observers try to explain away religion's recent ties to violence as an aberration, a result of political ideology, or the characteristic of a mutant form of religion—fundamentalism—these are not my views." Instead he sets out to "look for explanations...in a strain of violence that may be found at the deepest levels of the religious imagination"[14]—though, as I discuss below, he will later propose ways in which this imagination might be transformed from within. Regina Schwartz follows a similar yet somewhat narrower path, positing a link between the notion of identity exemplified by the Abrahamic tradition ("the chosen people") and the model of scarcity and intolerance it supposedly creates. This leads her to trace the roots of exclusionary violence to what she calls the "myth of monotheism";[15] and by so identifying what she considers to be "some key intersections between biblical identity and later secular beliefs about collective identity," Schwartz is able to hold monotheism responsible not only for explicitly religious acts of violence but for the atrocities fomented by modern nationalism as well.[16]

A recent book by Hector Avalos, inspired in large part by and in explicit reference to Schwartz's hypothesis, goes a step further. After bluntly asserting that "while it does not always cause violence, religion is inherently prone to violence," Avalos proceeds to accuse even those "pacifistic religions" conventionally associated with a commitment to nonviolence of harboring secret hegemonic aspirations.[17] Notwithstanding the dubious evidence mobilized to substantiate this charge, one might admire what appears to be Avalos's desire to excavate, so as to destabilize, the inchoate premises underlying all varieties of sanctioned violence— that is, until one reads a few pages later that a central argument of his book will be that "the lack of *verifiability* in religious belief differentiates ethically the violence attributed to religion from the violence attributed to nonreligious factors." Religiously motivated violence, he concludes, is "always ethically reprehensible, while the same cannot be said of nonreligious violence," the latter being acceptable "in self-defense or to protect the physical well-being of others."[18] If few of the aforementioned authors would be likely to put matters so brazenly, they neverthe- less share with Avalos the view that religiously motivated violence is not only cir- cumscribable but conceptually and morally dissimilar with regard to putatively secular aggressions.[19]

Whatever notoriety such assessments may currently enjoy, and without diminishing the degree to which they shape the contours of public debate, the analytic with which I will be occupied here is one that purports to render religious traditions subdividable according to a range of productive and degenerative poten- tialities and in so doing calls forth a decisive contrast between an enlightened, peaceful religiosity and what is taken to be its belligerent counterpart. Whether by making recourse to an essentialist notion of religion that simply reverses the claims of the critics cited above ("Religion *is* peaceful") or by deploying a more ambiva- lent conception ("Religion can *potentially* be a source of both peace and destruc- tion"), those who promulgate this perspective invariably go to great lengths to stress that they in no way oppose religion—only its misuses that result in intoler- ance, narrow-mindedness, and coercion. The implication is that religious commit- ments can enter into and even play a positive role in the public life of modern societies, just so long as they abide by a predelineated ("minimal") set of transcen- dent political values.[20]

For my purposes here it is worth noting, for example, that liberal democracies have rarely undertaken campaigns, whether inside of or beyond their borders, meant to bring about the wholesale eradication of "religion" (although particular religions, cults, sects, and so forth have been targeted); to the contrary, the secular ethic purportedly governing liberal societies mandates the mutual independence of politics from religion and guarantees its citizens the freedom to exercise both. In practice, however, this has not prevented the secular state from regulating, at times forcefully, those practices deemed to fall outside the purview of "proper religiosity"—a shifting category whose adjudication relies both on a profound asymmetry between religion and legal power and on some way of discerning those beliefs and practices that can be shown to *authentically* belong to a given tradition. This may require courts, legislatures, or administrative officials to directly engage with, interpret, or even endeavor to reshape the doctrines that are thought to com- pose a particular "religion," thereby causing agents of avowedly secular states to assume the interpretive duties of de facto theologians.[21]

But more fundamentally it entails the presupposition, crucial to liberal secu- larity, that there exist among and within specific traditions not merely a capacity for "good" but also, as Hent de Vries puts it, "the possibility, the reality, or the risk and threat of 'the worst.'"[22] Remaining mindful of and, indeed, vigilant against this specter of *the worst* has played a constitutive role in the structuring of modern subjectivities, authorizing new political arrangements and the array of preventative and punitive measures—from profiling and surveillance to intimidation and torture—intended to keep the danger of religious passions at bay.[23] Equally significant, though, are the ways in which visions of what might be thought of as religion's *best* possibilities—from helping to maintain civic virtues and morally buttressing ideas such as democracy and human rights to, at the very least, mandating that one's beliefs be held in a sufficiently modest and non-compulsory manner—have served to underwrite the brand of religiosity that a liberal culture normativizes and seeks to bring about or failing that, to marginalize and render obsolete. Which is only to say that it can no longer be assumed that secularism naturally resists all theologico-political formations, for it is precisely a distinctive—and often no less terrifying—political theology that it wishes to inaugurate.

✶✶✶

The idea that religion, or specific religious traditions, can be disaggregated according to a calculus of moderation and extremism, purity and perversion, is ubiquitous in contemporary discussions pertaining to the relationship between "religion and violence." Thus Charles Kimball will echo what has in many quarters become self-evident when he suggests that "distinguishing between corrupt forms of religious expression and authentic, life-affirming forms is essential if we hope to reduce the global threat."[24] Drawing on the theoretical writings of Paul Tillich, religious studies scholar Lloyd Steffen similarly explores "the moral meaning of religious violence" by way of a choice between what he calls "life-affirming and demonic religion."[25] Steffen defines the latter in terms of "irrational absolutism, fanatical obedience to authority, and an unfounded preoccupation with certainty" but hastens to add that demonic religion, while in fact *headed* toward evil, is "too complex and fluid…to be equated with a full realization of evil"—this in apparent contrast to the title of Kimball's book.[26] My interest here is not to parse the intricacies of such arguments or to decipher what are taken by their authors to be contributions to a theory of religious violence. It is only to point out that, notwithstanding Steffen's insistence on the "complexity and fluidity" of religious matters, he and Kimball agree not only that words like *demonic* and *evil* are useful ways of describing certain practices (they diverge only in their views of when they should be applied) or that such practices can be conclusively tied to specifically religious impulses (they take this for granted) but that the most important task facing contemporary observers of religion is to recognize the patterns of thought and behavior, even of reading and worship, that are most likely to produce them. Hence the extent to which debates surrounding religious violence often turn on the aptitude to discriminate life-affirming from insidious tendencies within and between specific traditions, with the accompanying assertion that, while the *capacity* for militancy is the monopoly of no religion in particular, there nonetheless remains an array of forces that render some believers particularly susceptible to corrupting influences—and that therefore mark them as particularly dangerous.[27]

Converging with this body of work, a growing number of experts have maintained—against those who would submit acts such as suicide bombing to the scrutiny of political, historical, or economic analysis—that the "war against terrorism" is, simply put, best understood as a *religious war*. They suggest, moreover, that ours is a war not of Islam versus Christianity or Judaism; to the contrary, as Andrew Sullivan famously argued in the *New York Times Magazine*, it is a war of "fundamentalism against faiths of all kinds that are at peace with freedom and modernity."[28] Be that as it may, it is Islam, not Christianity or Judaism, that is singled out as especially given to extremist tendencies, and various now-familiar appellations—Islamist, jihadist, Islamic fascist, and so on—are employed to mark those who have succumbed to this temptation.[29] "For the past two decades," Sullivan writes, "this form of Islamic fundamentalism has targeted every regime [in the Middle East] and, as it failed to make progress, has extended its hostility into the West." Echoing the diagnoses of Steffen and Kimball, he goes on to argue that what generates this current within Islam is "the blind recourse to texts embraced as literal truth, the injunction to follow the commandments of God before anything else, [and] the subjugation of reason and judgment and even conscience to the dictates of dogma."[30] It follows that because Muslims as of yet lack the means to differentiate the domain of politics from religion (or so we are told), they are more likely to pose a threat to a pluralist world whose inhabitants do not share their views.[31]

Of course, some theorists have tried to refute the notion that Islamism is simply a catalyst for and manifestation of unbridled religious aggression. In her book *Thinking Past Terror: Islamism and Critical Theory on the Left*, for instance, Susan Buck-Morss seeks to pry apart the association between religious extremism and Islamism by drawing attention to what she considers to be the largely atheological emancipatory ambitions of the latter. As part of a soon-to-be-realized "global public sphere," Islamists and critical theorists are, according to Buck-Morss, those who "speak different political languages, but whose goals are nonetheless the same: global peace, economic justice, legal equality, democratic participation, individual freedom, mutual respect."[32] Yet, for a theorist whose understanding of cultural translation avers that we do not "already know where we stand," her depiction of Islamism seems remarkably assimilated to the aims and desires of progressives such as herself. So even as she favorably cites and claims to be influenced by Talal Asad's assertion, inspired by Walter Benjamin, that acts of translation ought to "retain what may be a discomforting—even scandalous—presence within the receiving language," Buck-Morss nevertheless ends up (or rather begins by) depicting Islamism as little more than a variant of the multitude of political subjectivities that make up an emergent "Global Left."[33] I mention Buck-Morss's argument neither to dismiss nor to endorse her assertion that, as she puts it, "Islamism is not a religious discourse, but a political one"—that what *appears* to be one thing is *actually* another—but instead to inquire into the work accomplished by such assertions and the series of oppositions they manage to sustain.[34] In Buck-Morss's narrative, for instance, the liberatory potential of Islamism resides precisely in its ability to couch demands for political reform in theological language while concomitantly showing Western audiences that "Islamism as a political discourse embraces far more than the dogmatic fundamentalism and terrorist violence that dominate in the Western press."[35] Hardly a critical reappraisal of secular normativity, what we are left with is an "Islamist project" whose appeal for intellectuals such as Buck-Morss lies in its divergence from and willingness to confront both imperialist power and an aberrant religiosity.

To be sure, Buck-Morss is not alone in attempting to move beyond the prejudices that, particularly in the years since September 11, have typified the West's portrayal of the Muslim world. And seeing as how no scholarly account has done more to fuel such prejudices (and the policies derived from them) than the infamous "clash of civilizations" hypothesis, a multitude of writers have felt compelled to revisit the theory—some to modify it, others to discredit it altogether. It is to the former group that Martha Nussbaum's acclaimed book on sectarian violence in India belongs. Against the implicit triumphalism of Huntington's pronouncements, wherein a democratic West is contrasted to the intransigence of the Muslim world, Nussbaum argues that even within liberal democratic societies there exists a conflict between tolerance on the one side and intolerant dogmatism on the other: "We do see a 'clash of civilizations' in India, [but] it is not the one depicted by Samuel Huntington, between a democratic West and an antidemocratic Islam. It is instead a struggle between two 'civilizations' in the nation itself. One civilization delights in its diversity and has no fear of people who come from different backgrounds; the other feels safe only when homogeneity reigns and the different are at the margins.... One sees richness in inclusiveness; the other finds inclusiveness messy, unmanly, and humiliating.... The 'clash of civilizations' exists in every modern democracy."[36] While Nussbaum no doubt offers this reformulation as a corrective to a number of prevailing stereotypes, the implications of her claim for the current political moment can be differently assessed: whereas the clash Huntington prophesied would be one in which "we"—that is, we in the Judeo-Christian West—confront an enemy easily identified in spatial, religious, and even racial terms, the adversary in Nussbaum's scenario is much less immediately recognizable.[37] The traits that distinguish them belong to no "civilization" as conceived by Huntington; they are as likely to be discovered in our midst, at the heart of a liberal democratic polity, as among those external others thus far unreached by the freedoms of democratization. Far from doing away with the idea that certain cultural or religious characteristics separate "us" from "them," Nussbaum rather implores her readers to *rearrange* the boundaries by which Huntington's civilizational differences are delimited so as to better understand how, in India and elsewhere, the "ideals of respectful pluralism and the rule of law can be threatened by religious ideology."[38] In this narrative and others like it,[39] the idea of a discrete and morally superior West is demystified, to be sure, but only due to the realization that even "modern democracies" are susceptible to those qualities—religious intolerance chief among them—that define their ostensibly uncivilized others.[40] Left decisively intact is the danger of an immanent barbarism embodied in the figure of religious fanaticism, only now it is shown to threaten "the rule of law" both within and beyond the latter's jurisdiction.

Though it might easily pass unnoticed, it is important to note the extent to which Nussbaum's postulation of a clash within resonates with a recurrent thematic in modern political thought, one in which "the state of nature" is postulated not simply as a condition outside of or temporally prior to the founding of civil society but as a menace wholly internal to it. "In this vision of political life," write Veena Das and Deborah Poole, "the state is conceived of as an always incomplete project that must constantly be spoken of—and imagined—through an invocation of the wilderness, lawlessness, and savagery that not only lies outside its borders but also threatens it from within."[41] In a like manner Carl Schmitt considered it a vital responsibility of the state to decide on a "domestic enemy" who, along with those territorially external ones, could then be appropriately dealt with. And this decision, pertaining not only to matters of life and death but to the possibility of inclusion in the political community, was seen as a prime measure of sovereignty: "As long as the state is a political entity this requirement for internal peace compels it in critical situations to decide also upon the domestic enemy.... Whether the form is sharper or milder, explicit or implicit, whether ostracism, expulsion, proscription, or out-lawry are provided for in special laws or in explicit or general descriptions, the aim is always the same, namely to declare an [internal] enemy."[42] For Schmitt, as for Hobbes and Kant and so many others before him, the prospect that the state of nature (or the enemy taken to embody it) might reappear in contemporary political life elicited a fear that could be instrumentalized to encourage agents in submission to their sovereign[43]—and the force exercised by the latter in banishing this threat was, as legal and peacemaking violence, always to be distinguished from the lawlessness it was putting down.[44] The state of nature therefore comes to exist not only in the abstractions of political philosophers—although for many of these philosophers it had a decidedly empirical dimension—but in the way this abstraction is thought to be enacted in the actual spaces and behaviors of a given people in a specific historical moment.[45] If this was indeed the case, then perhaps it is not too much to argue that invocations of religious violence perform a similar function in our own time; neither would it be too much to suggest that by pointing to these contemporary states of nature—the so-called sectarian conflicts in Iraq and Afghanistan are these days the most popular example—liberal commentators are able to demonstrate that certain inhabitants of the modern world *embody in the present* a survival from Euro-America's own discarded past. According to the logic of this temporalization of difference, religious violence, and the ways of life from which it is thought to erupt, quite literally harkens to a former epoch.

This, at any rate, is one way of reading the confrontation Nussbaum poses between "respectful pluralism" and "religious ideology," along with the other clashes summoned thus far: between "Islamism" and "dogmatic fundamentalism" (Buck-Morss); between "corrupt" and "healthy, authentic" religious practices (Kimball); between "life-affirming" and "demonic" beliefs (Steffen); and between "fundamentalism" and "faiths of all kinds that are at peace with freedom and modernity" (Sullivan). And when Sullivan declares that "from everything we see, the lessons Europe learned in its bloody history have yet to be absorbed within the Muslim world"—by which he means that in the latter, as in sixteenth-century Europe, "the promise of purity and salvation seems far more enticing than the mundane allure of mere peace"—we are meant to be reminded, amid what he calls "our new Wars of Religion," of the conditions out of which the modern state emerged and if not for its legally protected principles of toleration, would be in perpetual danger of descending back into.[46] It is in this spirit that Bruce Lincoln, in a manner that rather epitomizes the story liberalism tells about itself, writes:

> Restoring religion to its dominant position within culture hardly puts an end to conflict; it simply ensures that a culture's most bruising conflicts will assume religious, rather than ethical or aesthetic character, *and in that form they can be more destructive than ever*. When one rejects the Enlightenment's values en masse and dispenses with its model of culture, one risks not just a return of the repressed, but novel Wars of Religion. Postmodern critiques have made us acutely aware of the many shortcomings associated with the regime of truth, style of culture, and practices of power introduced by the Age of Reason, and these are real enough. It is, however, worth remembering what the Enlightenment accomplished, which involves reading it in historic context and contrasting it with what came before, *also with what could come after*.[47]

What this suggests is that not only advocates for an absolutist state, such as Hobbes and Schmitt, but liberals as well have depended on the specter of religious violence for the legitimation of their projects—among them the construction of "religion" as anchored in personal experience, expressible as belief statements, and dependent on private institutions or, in short, as that which is *inessential* to our common politics and morality.[48] And by keeping the memory (real or imagined) of religious violence constantly at the fore, liberal democrats have been able to secure for themselves, and for the social orders they commend, a politics of redemptive—if at times extraordinarily destructive—necessity.

Thus liberalism's injunction against the entrance of "comprehensive doctrines" into political deliberation is considered to be a public good not only because it helps to maintain the integrity of an abstraction called "public reason" but because it is seen as a crucial means to warding off the possibility of what Rawls once referred to as "mortal conflict…over transcendent elements not admitting of compromise."[49] As political theorist Romand Coles puts it, "By repeatedly recalling the 'wars of religion,' Rawls believes he gets beneath our current conflicts: He recalls the tragic possibility that might fundamentally inform, orient, and limit our understanding of what is desirable in politics.... Political liberalism's vitality will thus require that we repeatedly remember such mortal and never-too-distant conflict."[50] Consequently, those for whom religious commitments predispose its bearers to intolerance and coercion will be alarmed by the rapid deprivatization of religious movements worldwide and will do anything in their power to prevent what they perceive to be the encroachment of religious signs and symbols, biases and interests, into the domains of policy making and public life. If, on the other hand, "religion" can be subdivided (as the above-mentioned authors believe it can) into a range of positive and negative capacities—or even posited as essentially beneficial or benign[51]—then it is not at all clear why religion, once it has been sufficiently reconstituted in conformity with the dictates of liberal citizenship, must as such be excluded from these domains.[52] And here we come to the prescriptive force of the discourse I have been exploring, which rests not, as critics like William Cavanaugh would have it, in a repudiation of religion or even in an insistence that it be separated from public life but in an argument for a normative religiosity against which visions of "the worst" can be juxtaposed and its life-forms justifiably undone. In closing, I consider such remedies as elaborated by one of the foremost scholars of religious violence and briefly explore what they might imply for a rethinking of secularism.

✳ ✳ ✳

Unlike some of the more virulent currents of criticism leveled at religion in the contemporary West, the discourse I have focused on—a discourse that, in my view, quite profoundly dovetails with present US imperialist ambitions—is one in which religious violence and the tendencies taken to precede it (e.g., absolutism, intoler-ance, literalism) are characterized as perverse expressions of otherwise pacific faiths or alternatively as manifestations of as-yet-undisciplined belief systems that must somehow be reshaped. It is taken for fact that the greatest threat confronting the civilized world is religiously motivated terrorism, and thus it is assumed that experts on the phenomenon will be able to contribute not only to its amelioration but also to the moral and legal tasks of assigning responsibility and directing pun-ishment when it occurs—a service many of them are all too willing to provide. They strike a populist chord within a largely religious populace, smartly distancing themselves from their "secularist" counterparts while offering assurances that it is not religion that is to blame but only the actions of an unenlightened minority lacking in either will or capacity to free their beliefs from the bonds of uncritical acquiescence (or what Kant once famously referred to as "self-incurred tutelage"). And while their solutions are often as convoluted as their explanatory models, these academics, policy analysts, and journalists are able to reach consensus on the view that if some believers, particularly those identified with Islam, are to be rec-onciled to the modern world, they will need to be remade and reformed in accor-dance with the latter's values—which, far from entailing a disavowal of violence, more often involves a reconfiguration of the precise reasons for which one ought to be willing to suffer and inflict suffering and even to die and kill.[53]

Thus Mark Juergensmeyer, whose highly influential book I mentioned above, concludes his study with five "scenarios for peace," that is, five possible ways in which the "war with religious terrorists" might come to an end. These scenarios are (1) destroy terrorism with sheer force ("In order for the destructive strategy to work, a secular government must be willing to declare total war against religious terrorism and wage it for many years"); (2) "terrify terrorists" with the threat of violent legal reprisals or imprisonment; (3) terrorism, in some vaguely apocalyptic manner, "wins"; (4) by "supporting moderate leadership within the communities," religion is henceforth "taken out of politics and retired to the moral and meta-physical planes"; and finally, (5) permit "religious values and expressions of faith" into the public and political spheres. While he does not rule out the potential effi-cacy of the first two, and hopes that the third will not come to pass, it is the remain-ing two scenarios—both played out on what he calls "the battlefield of ideas"—that for him hold the greatest appeal.[54] Despite his acknowledgment of the unlikelihood of being able to depoliticize Islamic teachings from without, he offers examples of liberal Muslim intellectuals (such as Hassan Hanafi and Abdolkarim Soroush) who, with Western moral and material support, have the potential to bring about a reformation from within. For in addition to arguing that interpretations of scripture "are relative and change over time," these reformists "advocate an unmediated form of religion that is both personal and public."[55] What makes them especially attractive to Juergensmeyer and other liberal analysts is that "like socially responsible Protestants," they "see a prophetic role for religion in the public arena. This is a form of social activism that eschews political power in favor of moral suasion, and it has transformed the idea of struggle into a contestation of ideas rather than opposing political sides."[56] It is not that Juergensmeyer judges all Islamic sensibilities to be inherently incompatible with modern political culture—indeed, his final scenario goes so far as to gesture toward the possibility of "healing politics with religion."[57] He merely asserts that if some believers are to be recognized by and have their voices heard in liberal democracies, they will need to "enter the public arena in undogmatic and unobtrusive ways."[58] Hence Juergensmeyer, like many of the other experts cited here, urges that along with fighting religious terrorism through the deployment of more conventional means (i.e., "the judicious use of state violence"), the US government ought to simultaneously pursue a strategy of locating and bolstering indigenous Muslim "renovators" (to use Mark Lilla's term) with whose help a religiosity more commensurate with liberal democratic values might begin to be cultivated.

What has all this to do with secularism? A recent article by Saba Mahmood may help to bring some of these issues together.[59] It has become something of a commonplace to assert that the doctrine of secularism—so far as it recognized the ultimate irresolvability of theological debates, discovered a political ethic altogether free of religious attachments, and constitutionally mandated state neutrality with regard to specific religious truths—emerged as the political solution to Europe's bloody religious conflicts and in doing so established the principles of toleration and freedom of conscience in their place. Mahmood, however, demonstrates the inadequacies of such accounts and proposes in their place a conception of secularism more consistent with the aims and effects of its realization in the modern state. Taking as her focus current US efforts to reform the sensibilities of Muslims deemed dangerously inclined toward fundamentalist interpretations of Islam—a venture commenced under the aegis of the National Security Council's "Muslim World Outreach" and uncannily resembling the strategy advocated by Juergensmeyer—Mahmood suggests that such projects be seen not as an abrogation of secular principles but as their reasonable extension.[60] In so arguing, Mahmood perceptively draws our attention to the *disciplinary* or *civilizing* impetus internal to secularism, one that resides less in the separation of religious from political institutions, or in the displacement of religion from the public domain, than in "the kind of subjectivity a secular culture authorizes, the practices it redeems as truly (versus superficially) spiritual, and the particular relationship to history it prescribes."[61] Mahmood's interrogation shows that far from providing for the peaceful coexistence of a multiplicity of identities and beliefs, secularism rather insists on the production of "a particular kind of religious subject who is compatible with the rationality and exercise of liberal political rule."[62] In other words, to reiterate a point I have been making throughout this chapter, we might say that liberal secularity—or at least that brand of liberal secularity currently being exported to the ends of the earth—is premised not simply on the *toleration* of difference but on the power of a strong state to enforce this principle and to ensure that religion will henceforth assume a modulated form. Of course, there is a way in which the very category of religious violence already presupposes this solution, for it was born out of a period, much like our own, in which the perceived threat to a collective way of life was precisely what sustained it and in which the reconstitution of religion's place and meaning within civil society was taken to be a critical precondition for the survival of both.

So when a respected scholar like Mark Juergensmeyer writes of the different mechanisms by which "the war against terrorism might come to an end" and advocates not only the careful use of state violence but also a strategy of reshaping Islam from within, there seems to be a strikingly familiar logic at work. To be sure, secularism takes on myriad configurations, and they do not all insinuate a common telos; likewise, the subjects it produces and the relationship to "religion" it enjoins will vary across time and space.[63] But amid the geopolitical-ideological terrain in which we currently find ourselves—the terrain in which the discourse I have enumerated finds its mandate and intelligibility—secularism is ineluctably bound up with sovereign power, and together they constitute a politics of religion-making. Violence figures prominently in this arrangement: both as that which might at any time erupt among certain forms of religious life and as that which the secular state inflicts in order to forestall such threats and to better facilitate its various modes of subjectivation and accumulation. One is transgressive, inhumane, gratuitous; the other, necessary and salvific, administered on behalf of universal humanity and in accordance with "a secular calculus of social utility and a secular dream of happiness."[64]

I have suggested that the category and contemporary renderings of religious violence ought to be seen as coextensive with a particular modality of liberal political rule. Whether the authors whose work I have critically assessed are self-consciously invested in this vision of liberal secularity and the predatory procedures it currently sustains is, it seems to me, inconsequential for the argument I have been making (though we would no doubt be naive to dismiss such a possibility). Instead, what I have been exploring is the prospect that between a specific object of discourse (religious violence) and a specific kind of political formation (secularism) there appear a number of disquieting correspondences. These include not only an array of shared diagnoses as to where the roots of religious aggression lie—a lack of critical distance between divine text and lived experience, an overemphasis on received authority, a lack of individualism on the part of believers, a traditional culture of martyrdom, and so forth. They also include a concept of religion within which can be discerned both a terrifying figure of the premodern past and an enlightened believer perfectly at home in this world. And in the complex of attitudes and emotions, antipathies and fears, that constitute life in a modern nation-state, in the possibilities thereby enabled and foreclosed, it is the latter figure that is rendered normative and whose attributes are fostered; the former that must be transfigured or made extinct. "Religious violence" assists in carrying such projects forward.

■ NOTES

Earlier versions of this essay were presented at Hofstra University and as part of the 2007 American Anthropological Association panel "Liberal Tradition, Ways of Life, and Difference," in Washington, D.C. I am grateful to Talal Asad, Daniel Colucciello Barber, Jake Kosek, Saba Mahmood, and Michael Nijhawan for their generous feedback and criticisms.

1. The well-known theorist and historian of religion Bruce Lincoln succinctly captures this view: "It is tempting, in the face of such horror, to regard the authors of these deeds as evil incarnate: persons bereft of reason, decency, or human compassion. Their motives, however—as revealed by the instructions that guided their final days—were intensely and profoundly religious. We need to take this fact seriously, uncomfortable though it be, since it can tell us important things about the events of the 11th, the broader conflict of which those events are a part, and also the nature of religion." Note, however, that it is not just *any* religion that is to blame: "Rather, these men embraced an extremely militant reformulation of maximalist currents within Islam.... It was their religion that persuaded Mohamed Atta and eighteen others that the carnage they perpetrated was not just an ethical act, *but a sacred duty.*" Bruce Lincoln, *Holy Terrors: Thinking about Religion after September 11* (Chicago: University of Chicago Press, 2003), 16 (emphasis added).

2. See, for example, Richard King, "The Association of 'Religion' with Violence: Reflections on a Modern Trope," in *Religion and Violence in South Asia: Theory and Practice*, ed. John Hinnells and Richard King (London: Routledge, 2005), 226–57.

3. See William T. Cavanaugh, *Theopolitical Imagination: Discovering the Liturgy as a Political Act in an Age of Global Consumerism* (Edinburgh: T&T Clark, 2002); William T. Cavanaugh, "The Violence of 'Religion': Examining a Prevalent Myth," *Kellogg Institute for International Studies Working Papers* 310 (2004), 1–41, http://nd.edu/~kellogg/publications/workingpapers/WPS/310.pdf; William T. Cavanaugh, *The Myth of Religious Violence: Secular Ideology and the Roots of Modern Conflict* (New York: Oxford University Press, 2009).

4. Cavanaugh, "Violence of 'Religion,' " 28. Lincoln's *Holy Terrors* is one book beleaguered by such difficulties (although Cavanaugh does not cite it). Despite beginning his book by criticizing past efforts to define religion, Lincoln proceeds to do just that, suggesting that while earlier attempts were problematic (inasmuch as they relied, for instance, on concepts derived from Protestantism), these "hardly render futile all efforts at definition...particularly when one understands these as provisional attempts to clarify one's thought, not to capture the innate essence of things." Innate essence or not, he nevertheless provides what he calls a more "proper definition" of religion, one that is "polythetic and flexible" and includes a minimum of four domains: (1) discourse, (2) practice, (3) community, and (4) institution. But, as Cavanaugh might ask, would not each of these features also be found in what are thought to be secular domains of modern life? Perhaps preempting such questions, Lincoln's definition becomes circular and self-referential. What makes practices and communities "religious" is their reliance on religious discourse, which Lincoln defines as "a discourse whose concerns transcend the human, temporal, and contingent, and that claims for itself a similarly transcendent status." Lincoln, *Holy Terrors*, 2–5. Yet it seems that many kinds of discourse—especially those aspiring to universal applicability, much like Lincoln's definition of religion—would easily fulfill these criteria, leaving one to question the status of the remaining domains.

5. "On the surface," Cavanaugh writes, "the myth of religious violence establishes a dichotomy between our peace-loving secular reasonableness and their irrational religious fanaticism. Under the surface lies an absolute 'religious' devotion to the American vision of a hegemonic liberalism that underwrites the necessity of using violence to impose this

vision on the Muslim other. Thus, we must bomb them into the higher rationality" ("Violence of 'Religion,'" 34–35).

6. See Talal Asad, *Formations of the Secular: Christianity, Islam, Modernity* (Stanford, CA: Stanford University Press, 2003); Talal Asad, "Trying to Understand French Secularism," in *Political Theologies: Public Religions in a Post-Secular World*, ed. Hent de Vries and Lawrence Sullivan (New York: Fordham University Press, 2006), 494–526; Partha Chatterjee, "Secularism and Tolerance," in *Secularism and Its Critics*, ed. Rajeev Bhargava (New Delhi: Oxford University Press, 1998), 345–79; Saba Mahmood, "Secularism, Hermeneutics, and Empire: The Politics of Islamic Reformation," *Public Culture* 18, no. 2 (2006); 323–47; Winifred Sullivan, *The Impossibility of Religious Freedom* (Princeton, NJ: Princeton University Press, 2005); Charles Taylor, "Modes of Secularism," in *Secularism and Its Critics*, ed. Rajeev Bhargava (New Delhi: Oxford University Press, 1998), 31–53; Charles Taylor, *A Secular Age* (Cambridge, MA: Harvard University Press, 2007).

7. It is this conceptualization of secularism—which I do not mean to suggest is the *only* possible conceptualization—that seems most elusive to those who for various reasons seek to posit particular political formations (or themselves) as essentially nonsecular. Thus the secularity William Connolly opposes his own pluralistic vision to is premised on a rather restricted notion of the concept, one rooted more in the transcendental reason of the liberal Enlightenment—to which thinkers like Rawls and Habermas are heir—and less in the way secularism has actually manifested itself coextensively with the dictates of liberal democratic market states. In the latter, secularism is geared toward neither the banishment of religion from the public sphere nor, in a more philosophical register, the proscription of religious or metaphysical modes of argumentation but, rather, toward the construction of distinctive modalities of religious subjectivity and belonging—above all, in Connolly's world, those that assent to and embody a range of commitments and sensibilities (tolerance, awareness of finitude, introspection). This line of secularism has always opposed itself to Europe's more radical ideologies, but such oppositions (and concomitant prescriptions) in no way render it less "secular"—which is what I aim to demonstrate below by contrasting what I take to be two differential ways in which religious violence has been theorized. See, for instance, William Connolly, *Why I Am Not a Secularist* (Minneapolis: University of Minnesota Press, 1999).

8. Michel Foucault, "The Subject and Power," *Critical Inquiry* 8, no. 4 (Summer, 1982), 783.

9. Alasdair MacIntyre puts it as thus: "Any conception of the human good according to which, for example, it is the duty of government to educate the members of the community morally, so that they come to live out that conception of the good, may up to a point be held as a private theory by individuals or groups, but any serious attempt to embody it in public life will be proscribed. And this qualification of course entails not only that liberal individualism does indeed have its own broad conception of the good, *which it is engaged in imposing politically, legally, socially, and culturally wherever it has the power to do so,* but also that in so doing its toleration of rival conceptions of the good in the public arena is severely limited" (*Whose Justice? Which Rationality?* [Notre Dame: University of Notre Dame Press, 1988], 336 (emphasis added).

10. For critical analyses of such reactions to the cartoon incident, see Talal Asad, "Reflections on Blasphemy and Secular Criticism," in *Religion: Beyond a Concept*, ed. Hent de Vries (New York: Fordham University Press, 2008), 580–609; Webb Keane, "Freedom and Blasphemy: On Indonesian Press Bans and Danish Cartoons," *Public Culture* 21, no. 1 (2009): 47–76; Brian Goldstone, "Violence and the Profane: 'Islamism,' Liberal Democracy, and the Limits of Secular Discipline," *Anthropological Quarterly* 80, no. 1 (2007): 207–307.

11. Slavoj Žižek, "Defenders of the Faith," the *New York Times*, March 12, 2006, 4.12.

12. See Slavoj Žižek, *The Fragile Absolute: Or, Why Is the Christian Legacy Worth Fighting For?* (London: Verso Books, 2001).

13. Mark Juergensmeyer, *Terror in the Mind of God: The Global Rise of Religious Violence* (Berkeley: University of California Press, 2001).

14. Ibid., 6.

15. "[When] scarcity is encoded in the Bible as a principle of Oneness (one land, one people, one nation) and in monotheistic thinking (one Deity), it becomes a demand of exclusive allegiance that threatens with the violence of exclusion" (Regina Schwartz, *The Curse of Cain: The Violent Legacy of Monotheism* [Chicago: University of Chicago Press, 1997], xi).

16. Ibid., 12. Schwartz supports this claim by suggesting, drawing on the work of Peter Alter, that we look to nineteenth-century German pietism—and not, as is often believed, to the French Revolution—for the origins of modern nationalism. In her view, this alternative history helps to "show how and why the following assertion holds: 'in nationalism, the religious is secularized, and the national sanctified'" (ibid., 13). For a challenge to the idea that nationalism is merely a form of secularized religious belief, see Asad, *Formations of the Secular*, 187–94; and, in something of a different register, Hans Blumenberg, *The Legitimacy of the Modern Age* (Cambridge, MA: MIT Press, 1985).

17. Hector Avalos, *Fighting Words: The Origins of Religious Violence* (New York: Prometheus Press, 2005), 18. Avalos, a Harvard-trained philologist and professor of religious studies, elaborates: "In fact, even so-called pacifistic religions often approve of violence in subtle ways. I saw that 'peace' itself was simply the name for the set of conditions favorable to a proponent group rather than some absolute rejection of violence. Other times, 'peace' was simply an intermediary state in which pacifism was maintained for political and self-interest rather than for any systematic opposition to all violence."

18. Ibid., 20, 29.

19. Anthropologist James Faubion's otherwise subtle commentary ends up reinforcing similar assumptions. "That the logic of religious violence is different from the logic of either social or political violence is worth underscoring," he writes, leading him to conclude that if nonviolent clerics are to have any success in curbing it, "they will first have to face squarely *how deep the connection is between the religious imagination and violence.*" James D. Faubion, "Religion, Violence, and the Vitalistic Economy," *Anthropological Quarterly* 76, no. 1 (2003): 82–84 (emphasis added). For a more "scientific" study that advances a similar position, see James K. Wellman and Kyoko Tokuno, "Is Religious Violence Inevitable?" *Journal for the Scientific Study of Religion* 43, no. 3 (2004): 291–96.

20. One reason for paying attention to this perspective is that it seems to command a great deal more authority at the nexus of popular opinion and policy making—at least in the United States, whose population is, according to innumerable polls, largely "theistic" and where positions such as Žižek's are unlikely to gain mainstream purchase. Of course, such a realization must be brought to bear on any discussion of secularism in the United States, for a nation never to have elected a president who did not openly believe in God and where civil religion has long overlapped with the dominant political imaginary is also bound to require a notion of secularism not restricted to, say, the ideological structure of French *laïcité*.

21. See especially Sullivan, *Impossibility of Religious Freedom*; and Mahmood, "Secularism, Hermeneutics, and Empire."

22. Hent de Vries, *Religion and Violence: Philosophical Perspectives from Kant to Derrida* (Baltimore: Johns Hopkins University Press, 2002), 212, 1. De Vries opens his impressive *Religion and Violence* with the claim that violence "finds its prime model—its source, force, and counterforce—in key elements of the tradition called the religious. It can be seen as the very element of religion. No violence without (some) religion; no religion without (some)

violence." It remains unclear to me, however, what de Vries means by "the tradition called the religious" or why violence should be seen as intrinsic to it.

23. Talal Asad writes: "Anything that can be used to counter attempted subversions of the state—any cruelty or deception—acquires justification as a political technique. In 'a state of exception,' liberal democracies defend 'the rule of law' not only by issuing administrative orders to eliminate public disorder but also by extrajudicial means of secret violence (the inflicting of pain and death), so long as that contradiction doesn't cause a public scandal" ("Trying to Understand French Secularism," 508).

24. Charles Kimball, *When Religion Becomes Evil: Five Warning Signs* (San Francisco: HarperCollins, 2002), 7. Later Kimball explains: "As human institutions, all religions are subject to corruption. The major religions that have stood the test of time have done so through an ongoing process of growth and reform, a process that continually connects people of faith—Jews, Hindus, Muslims, Buddhists, Christians, and others—with the life-sustaining truths at the heart of their religion. The religions differ in many ways, of course, but they converge in teaching both an orientation toward God or the transcendent and compassionate, constructive relationships with others in the world" (ibid., 39).

25. Lloyd Steffen, *Holy War, Just War: Exploring the Moral Meaning of Religious Violence* (London: Rowman and Littlefield, 2007), 49.

26. Ibid., 126. The category of evil has certainly received ample attention in recent scholarship, particularly as regards America's war against terrorism. Here I simply point to its widespread use not only by Bush and his supporters on the Religious Right but among self-proclaimed secular academics and public intellectuals as well. Thus even a sophisticated thinker such as Jonathan Lear has refuted the suggestion (promulgated by "shallow-minded relativists") that "evil is simply the term that each side gives to the other." Instead he argues, utilizing his background in psychoanalytic theory, that inasmuch as the terrorists were driven by envy—a notion that adequately encompasses Lear's concept of evil—the "reasons they give us and the reasons they give themselves aren't necessarily what is motivating them." "In this war," he concludes, "we need to understand the concrete movements of *irrational* thought: not to understand its reasons but to learn how to deal with unreason." Jonathan Lear, "The Remains of the Day," *University of Chicago Magazine* 94, no. 2 (2001), http://magazine.uchicago.edu/0112/features/remains-3.html. Terry Eagleton is undoubtedly right to observe that such pronouncements function to "foreclose the possibility of historical explanation." He writes: "In the disparagement of rational analysis which it suggests, it reflects something of the fundamentalism it confronts. Explanation is thought to be exculpation. Reasons become excuses.... Like the sublime, [evil] lies beyond all rational figuration." It is interesting to note, however, that while Eagleton is adept at questioning the analytical purchase of the term *evil*, he is unable (or unwilling) to scrutinize the ways in which "fundamentalism"—here glossed as "the disparagement of rational analysis"—is deployed with similar effects. Terry Eagleton, *Holy Terror* (Oxford: Oxford University Press, 2005), 116.

27. Two notable examples in this regard are Scott Appleby, *The Ambivalence of the Sacred: Religion, Violence, and Reconciliation* (New York: Rowman and Littlefield, 1999); and Charles Selengut, *Sacred Fury: Understanding Religious Violence* (New York: AltaMira Press, 2003).

28. Andrew Sullivan, "This *Is* a Religious War," the *New York Times Magazine*, October 7, 2001, 44.

29. Jessica Stern, billed by her publisher as "the foremost US expert on terrorism," concludes her influential book with a set of policy recommendations centered around explaining why the Islamic world is "particularly vulnerable to terrorism." A political realist, Stern argues that "democratization is not necessarily the best way to fight Islamic extremism," the

implication being that "finding a way out of this vicious cycle while still maintaining US interests" may require the United States to support regimes that are able to keep extremists in line. Jessica Stern, *Terror in the Name of God: Why Religious Militants Kill* (New York: HarperCollins, 2003), 287–88.

30. Sullivan, "This *Is* a Religious War," 48.

31. In a popular article entitled "The Great Separation," Mark Lilla remarks: "We must somehow find a way to accept the fact that, given the immigration policies Western nations have pursued over the last half-century, they are now hosts to millions of Muslims who have great difficulty fitting into societies that do not recognize any political claims based on their divine revelation. Like Orthodox Jewish law, the Muslim Shariah is meant to cover the whole of life, not some arbitrarily demarcated private sphere, *and its legal system has few theological resources for establishing the independence of politics from detailed divine commands*" (the *New York Times Magazine*, August 19, 2007, 50 [emphasis added]).

32. Susan Buck-Morss, *Thinking Past Terror: Islamism and Critical Theory on the Left* (London: Verso Books, 2003), 5.

33. Talal Asad, *Genealogies of Religion: Discipline and Reasons of Power in Christianity and Islam* (Baltimore: Johns Hopkins University Press, 1993), 199. Incidentally, there is a growing tendency on the Left to argue similarly with regard to global Pentecostalism. One example is Mike Davis's much-cited essay "Planet of Slums," which presents African and Latin American Pentecostalism as little more than a "song of the dispossessed," a "religion of the informal periphery" that "admirably refuses the inhuman destiny of the third world city" (*New Left Review* 26 [March–April 2004]: 33–34).

34. Buck-Morss, *Thinking Past Terror*, 43.

35. Ibid., 49. Earlier, she argues: "As a discourse of political opposition, Islam is capable of playing the role that 'reason' does in the Western discourse of the Frankfurt School.... Just as in Western critical theory the great defenders of reason are those who criticize the rationalization of society in reason's name, so today's progressive Muslims are able to use Islam as an immanent, critical criterion against its own practice, with similar effect" (ibid., 47).

36. Martha Nussbaum, *The Clash Within: Democracy, Religious Violence, and India's Future* (Cambridge, MA: Harvard University Press, 2007), 332.

37. In his recent reflections on suicide bombing, Talal Asad demonstrates how this condition of unrecognizability, when carried into the terrain of a war on terrorism, may well necessitate symbolic interpretation when people feel that they can no longer take the ordinary behavior of their neighbors as unproblematic. Not only government officials, then, but civilians as well are encouraged to engage in a private hermeneutics that "presupposes that what appears on the surface is not the truth and seeks to control what lies beneath. *Through interpretation, it converts absences into signs*." Talal Asad, *On Suicide Bombing* (New York: Columbia University Press, 2007), 31 (emphasis added).

38. Nussbaum, *Clash Within*, 1. It should be noted that in Nussbaum's telling it is the Hindu Right—and not political Islam—that comes to stand for such civilizational differences. My point, however, is that in trying to unsettle one kind of prejudice (say, the equation of all Muslims with violent extremism), the basic structure that provided its rationale goes largely unquestioned.

39. One particularly well-regarded example is Kwame Anthony Appiah, *Cosmopolitanism: Ethics in a World of Strangers* (New York: W. W. Norton, 2007).

40. Wendy Brown, *Regulating Aversion: Tolerance in the Age of Identity and Empire* (Princeton, NJ: Princeton University Press, 2006), 182. Tolerance therefore emerges as that which characterizes an enlightened and peace-loving people and as that attribute that must be inculcated in those who presently lack it. To a liberal sensibility, as Wendy Brown has shown, intolerance cannot be abided and therefore marks certain subjects as particularly

intolerable, as beyond the pale of civilization. If such subjects are what "civilization cannot tolerate," she writes, "then tolerance and civilization not only entail one another but mutually define what is outside of both and together constitute a strand in an emerging transnational governmentality. To be uncivilized is to be intolerable is to be a barbarian.... That which is inside civilization is tolerable *and* tolerant; that which is outside is neither."

41. Veena Das and Deborah Poole, "The State and Its Margins: Comparative Ethnographies," in *Anthropology in the Margins of the State*, ed. Veena Das and Deborah Poole (Santa Fe: School of American Research Press, 2004), 7. Similarly, the "mythologeme" of a smooth passage from the state of nature to the social contract, with the violence of the former definitively excluded from the sociality produced by the latter, is discarded in Giorgio Agamben's retheorization of sovereignty. He argues that "far from being a prejuridical condition that is indifferent to the law of the city, the Hobbesian state of nature is the exception and the threshold that constitutes and dwells within it." In this scenario "sovereignty presents itself... as a state of indistinction between nature and culture, between violence and law, and this very indistinction constitutes specifically sovereign violence." Giorgio Agamben, *Homo Sacer: Sovereign Power and Bare Life* (Stanford, CA: Stanford University Press, 1998), 106, 35.

42. Carl Schmitt, *The Concept of the Political* (Chicago: University of Chicago Press, 1996), 46–47. Needless to say, it was according to this rationale that German Jews, even those fully assimilated into the nation, could as domestic enemies—or those who "in a specially intense way, [were] existentially something different and alien" (ibid., 27)—be denied access to those rights granted normal citizens. A number of observers have noted that the treatment of Muslims in Western countries in the wake of September 11, 2001—indefinite detainments without charge or trial, harassments in everyday life, blatant intimidations in the mainstream press, policies of racist profiling—bear similarities to the prewar actions taken toward European Jews.

43. On "fear" as a political category and its uses in current discourse, see Elizabeth Anker, "The Only Thing We Have to Fear," *Theory and Event* 8, no. 3 (2005), http://muse.jhu.edu/journals/theory_and_event/v008/8.3anker.html.

44. Thus Emmanuel Kant writes in a footnote to his *Perpetual Peace*: "It is usually accepted that a man may not take hostile steps against any one, unless the latter has already injured him by act. This is quite accurate, if both are citizens of a law-governed state. For, in becoming a member of this community, each gives the other the security he demands against injury, by means of the supreme authority exercising control over both of them. *The individual, however, (or nation) who remains in a mere state of nature deprives me of this security and does me injury by mere proximity. There is perhaps no active molestation (*facto), *but there is a state of lawlessness (*status injustus) *which, by its very existence, offers a continual menace to me*" (*Perpetual Peace* [New York: Cosimo Press, 2005], 56–57n3 (emphasis added).

45. Richard Tuck, *The Rights of War and Peace: Political Thought and the International Order from Grotius to Kant* (Oxford: Oxford University Press, 1999), 8. Richard Tuck asserts that unlike political liberalism's "original position," which for Rawls named nothing more than a purely hypothetical situation, the state of nature in the writings of nearly all social contractarians (including Kant) was meant to signal an empirical and ever-present historical possibility. The thinkers in this tradition, Tuck writes, "were prepared to give actual examples of the state of nature, something which would have been ridiculous had they genuinely believed in its purely heuristic character." Tuck's argument belies Agamben's suggestion that for Hobbes the state of nature was not a real historical epoch but, rather, "a principle internal to the State revealed in the moment in which the State is considered 'as if it were dissolved'" (*Homo Sacer*, 36). On the empirical status of the state of nature, with particular reference to the Americas, see also Das and Poole, "State and Its Margins," 8–9.

46. Sullivan, "This *Is* a Religious War," 50. Elucidating the relation between religious violence and the concretization of state power, Reinhart Koselleck points out that "from the second half of the sixteenth century onwards, a problem developed with a virulence which overreached the resources of the traditional order: the need to find a solution to the intolerant, fiercely embattled and mutually persecuting Churches or religion-bound fractions of the old estates, a solution that would circumvent, settle, or smother the conflict. How to make peace? On the greater part of the Continent this epoch-making question found its historic answer in the Absolutist State" (*Critique and Crisis: Enlightenment and the Pathogenesis of Modern Society* [Cambridge, MA: MIT Press, 1988], 17). William T. Cavanaugh argues that this canonical story, so crucial for apologists of the modern nation-state, is premised on a historiographical mistake and therefore constitutes the central *mythos* of political philosophy. He suggests that post-Reformation conflicts did not "necessitate the birth of the modern State; they were in fact themselves the birthpangs of the State"—from which it follows that far from "saving" us from mortal violence, the state was rather able to regulate and direct violence in novel ways. Cavanaugh, *Theopolitical Imagination*, 56.

47. Lincoln, *Holy Terrors*, 61 (emphasis added). Likewise the late philosopher Judith Shklar writes: "Liberalism…was born out of the cruelties of the religious civil wars, which forever rendered the claims of Christian charity a rebuke to all religious institutions and parties. If the faith was to survive at all, it would do so privately. The alternative then set, and still before us, is not one between classical virtue and liberal self-indulgence, but between cruel military and moral repression and violence, and a self-restraining tolerance that fences in the powerful to protect the freedom and safety of every citizen" (Judith Shklar, *Ordinary Vices* [Cambridge, MA: Harvard University Press, 1984], 5).

48. Asad, *Genealogies of Religion*, 207.

49. John Rawls, *Political Liberalism* (New York: Columbia University Press, 1996), xxviii.

50. Romand Coles, *Beyond Gated Politics: Reflections for the Possibility of Democracy* (Minneapolis: University of Minnesota Press, 2005), 9.

51. Here I refer to claims such as Sullivan's that the doctrine of toleration "was an attempt to answer the eternal human question of how to pursue the goal of religious salvation for ourselves and others and yet also maintain civil peace. What the [American] founders and Locke were saying was that the ultimate claims of religion should simply not be allowed to interfere with political and religious freedom. They did this to preserve peace above all—but also to *preserve true religion itself*" (Sullivan, "This *Is* a Religious War," 53).

52. Incidentally, Rawls's later work exhibits a strikingly different attitude toward the use of religious argumentation in public debate, one closer to the perspective I am exploring here. Those democratic theorists (such as William Connolly and Jeffrey Stout) who wish to posit a more "generous" democratic ethos by distancing themselves from "secularists" like Rawls, Rorty, and Habermas need to account for the fact that even for these liberal thinkers, at least in their later work, religious reasoning is not in itself deemed threatening to public debate; rather, only *particular kinds of comprehensive doctrines are to be guarded against.* Thus in his "The Idea of Public Reason Revisited," Rawls would write: "Central to the idea of public reason is that it neither criticizes nor attacks any comprehensive doctrine, religious or nonreligious, *except insofar as that doctrine is incompatible with the essentials of public reason and a democratic polity.* The basic requirement is that a reasonable doctrine accepts a constitutional democratic regime and its companion idea of legitimate law" (in John Rawls, *The Law of Peoples* [Cambridge: Harvard University Press, 1999], 132 [emphasis added]).

53. "Secularism has to do with particular structures of freedom and sensibilities within the differentiated modern nation-state. It has to do with conceptualizing and dealing with

sufferings that appear to negate or discourage those freedoms and sensibilities—and therefore it has to do with agency directed at eliminating sufferings that conflict with them. In that sense secular agency is confronted with having to change *a particular distribution of pain*, and while in that capacity it tries to curb the inhuman excesses of what it identifies as 'religion,' it allows other cruelties that can be justified by a secular calculus of social utility and a secular dream of happiness. It replaces patterns of premodern pain and punishment with those that are peculiarly its own" (Asad, "Trying to Understand French Secularism," 508; [emphasis in original]).

54. Juergensmeyer, *Terror in the Mind of God*, 234–37.

55. Ibid., 235.

56. Ibid., 235–36.

57. Ibid., 238.

58. Ibid., 240. As Juergensmeyer puts it in the book's concluding paragraph: "Religion gives spirit to public life and provides a beacon of moral order. At the same time it needs the temper of rationality and fair play that Enlightenment values give to civil society. Thus religious violence cannot end until some accommodation can be forged between the two— some assertion of moderation in religion's passion, and some acknowledgement of religion in elevating the spiritual and moral values of public life. In a curious way, then, the cure for religious violence may ultimately lie in a renewed appreciation for religion itself" (ibid., 243).

59. Mahmood, "Secularism, Hermeneutics, and Empire."

60. Although Mahmood appears to be replacing one normative understanding of secularism with another, I believe that her article is better read in the way she describes it: namely, as an examination of "the particular conception of secularism that underlies the current consensus that Islam needs to be reformed—that its secularization is a necessary step in bringing 'democracy' to the Muslim world—and the strategic means by which this programmatic vision is being instituted today" (ibid., 323).

61. Ibid., 328. For insightful accounts of the specific ways in which such authorizations of "truly spiritual" religiosities have taken shape, see the contributions by Kerry Mitchell and Rosemary R. Hicks to the current volume.

62. Mahmood, "Secularism, Hermeneutics, and Empire," 344.

63. In his recent consideration of French *laïcité*, Talal Asad suggests that "no actually existing secularism should be denied its claim to secularity just because it doesn't correspond to some utopian model. Varieties of remembered religious history, of perceived political threat and opportunity, define the sensibilities underpinning secular citizenship and national belonging in a modern state. The sensibilities are not always secure, they are rarely free of contradictions, and they are sometimes fragile. *But they make for qualitatively different forms of secularism*" ("Trying to Understand French Secularism," 507 (emphasis in original).

64. Ibid., 508.

6 The Politics of Spirituality: Liberalizing the Definition of Religion

Kerry A. Mitchell

This essay arises as a response to a question posed in the call for papers for the "Politics of Religion-Making" conference: "What are strategies with which the institutionalized study of religion (academe) responds to the theoretical deconstruction of the concepts through which it is legitimized?"[1] As part of a conference already geared toward collective self-reflection on the part of scholars of religion, this question adds a further, second-order level of self-reflection, for it already presupposes one level of self-reflection in the "theoretical deconstruction" that it invokes as a given. Given this self-reflection performed by theoretical deconstruction, the question asks, how do scholars reflect on that self-reflection? By way of answer, one may begin by inquiring into the significance of the doubling of self-reflexivity that the question assumes, a doubling that is intensified through the call for further reflection, that is, the call for reflection upon the strategies of self-reflection applied toward the self-reflective operation of theoretical deconstruction.

Biologists Humberto Maturana and Francisco Varela, on the one hand, and their sociological interlocutor Niklas Luhmann, on the other, have recognized the involution of reflexivity as a defining feature of life. Maturana and Varela placed self-reflexivity at the center of their concept of "autopoiesis," which explains the self-reproduction/self-organization of biological systems.[2] Luhmann applied this concept to the self-maintenance of social systems as they differentiate themselves with respect to their environments.[3] The complexity of these theories is too great for detailed rehearsal in this forum. I invoke these figures in order to suggest that the question concerns the life of the academic study of religion as an institution, that is, its strategies for self-organization and self-reproduction. In other words, the question calls for an explanation of the self-interested nature of the study of religion.

An inquiry into such self-interest requires a locale, for this is precisely what self-interest organizes: a place, a center with a periphery, a standard by which to judge near and far. I have chosen the study of American religion for this locale and more specifically the study of "spirituality" as opposed to "religion." One may be familiar with the shift in popular American usage that has distinguished these two terms as seen in the expression "I'm spiritual, but I'm not religious." This phrase and its associated sentiments arise out of a criticism of the category of religion. From the perspective of those who recognize the distinction, religion refers to organizations and doctrines, to particular groups and the beliefs of their members.

Spirituality, on the other hand, is said to be more individual and personal, focusing on feeling and experience rather than adherence to particular dogma.[4]

This popular theoretical deconstruction, one that gives rise to spirituality as a distinct category, calls for an expansion of or supplement to the category of religion that would include phenomena beyond the boundaries of religious institutions traditionally understood. And indeed, several scholars have responded to this call by attempting to theorize this distinctive mode of religiosity. In the following I will show how that theorization has been informed by a particular kind of self-interest on the part of scholars. Specifically, I will discuss how the theorization of "spirituality" has been heavily informed by the discourse of liberalism, even to the point of celebrating this politico-intellectual tradition.[5] Specifically, I argue, the way that many scholars have used the interpretive categories of "self" and "freedom" reproduces rather than illuminates the discourse that governs spirituality as a social phenomenon.

In response to the accusation of liberal bias, scholars could respond by saying, "So what?" Only when it is blind does bias become a shortcoming. Scholars could simply note and affirm their liberal bent and move on. This ignores, however, fundamental problems that have to do not with objectivity but with analysis itself. The scholarly assertion that the freedom to shape one's religiosity is a fundamental and distinctive feature of spirituality as a religious mode ignores the fact that freedom, in itself, is not an analytical category. As an analytical category, freedom marks the cessation of analysis, an assertion that an event or state is, in some respect, unconditioned. The assertion of freedom may valorize spirituality, especially within the discourse of liberalism, but it does so at the cost of removing spirituality from more substantive analysis. A further obscurity arises in the concept of "the self." Conceived as a doctrine or affirmation that helps to constitute spirituality, a focus on "the self" leaves much in darkness, particularly the social aspect of spirituality. How does the category of "self" lead one to an understanding of the networks of relations within which spirituality takes shape? One may note that the analytical efforts of scholars have not managed to dispel the criticism that spirituality itself is an all-too-nebulous category.[6]

In outlining alternative approaches to the study of spirituality, I do not propose to simply abandon the concepts of freedom and the self. These concepts find wide popularity outside of scholarly usage and therefore stand as features of social life to be analyzed in all their characteristics, including their obscurantism. Rather, I propose ways to give these concepts clearer definition with respect to a social context. Here I take two figures as guides: Michel Foucault and Niklas Luhmann. In his recently translated *The Hermeneutics of the Subject*, Foucault set out a definition of spirituality as "the search, practice, and experience through which the subject carries out the necessary transformations on himself in order to have access to the truth." Foucault delivered the lectures from which this quotation is drawn while he was developing his notion of the "care of the self." Moving away from the thrust of his earlier work, but still retaining an eye for operations of power, Foucault placed spirituality within a network of practices that restricted as much as expressed the freedom that could lead to self-discovery. Those practices could include, Foucault continued, "purifications, ascetic exercises, renunciations, conversions of looking, modifications of existence, etc., which are, not for knowledge but for the subject, for the subject's very being, the price to be paid for access to the truth."[7] In this passage Foucault recognized a spiritual existence as one governed by a play of will and its restriction. While highlighting self and subjectivity, Foucault nevertheless left room for the exercise of power within spirituality. Such powerful practices do not stand external to the spiritual self. Rather, they constitute it.

Luhmann's work offers guidance with a similar bent. In his study of the social construction of intimacy in eighteenth-century Europe, he wrote of the development of "incommunicability." He argued that this concept governs the code of romantic love and its mandate that relationships manifest spontaneity, passion, and individuality. This insistence that love arise as an expression of one's self, Luhmann contended, is guaranteed by prohibitions: what can be clearly articulated in an objective manner will not be recognized as a legitimate foundation for a relationship. Prospective lovers must make their plans appear as outgrowths of the natural flow of events, their feelings must exceed the bounds of social propriety, and they must refuse to let their speech stand as an adequate expression of the bond they hope to cultivate. Only through such prohibitions and restrictions can a "self" that is "free" of social conventions become plausible as a source of intimacy.[8]

Taken together, a focus on power and incommunicability offers ways to conceptualize freedom and self so as to place spirituality within social networks and operations. Such a focus avoids the metaphysical positivism that informs liberal discourse on these concepts. By addressing the labor of the negative in the construction of free individuals in search of spiritual truth, the concepts of power and incommunicability provide analytical pathways that, with respect to spirituality, offer great promise.

To lay out these pathways, it will be useful to flesh out the liberal discourse as it has come to dominate thinking about spirituality. I do this in two sections: one dealing with the historiography of spirituality and the other dealing with treatments of spirituality's core features in the present. In the first section I show how, within liberal readings of spirituality, a focus on freedom and the self accompanied a tendency toward celebration rather than analysis. In the second section I suggest how a focus on power and incommunicability can lead to a more nuanced appreciation of spirituality's key features and their social construction.

■ SPIRITUALITY: A LIBERAL HISTORY

In discussing the historiography of spirituality, I limit my analysis to the works of three influential authors: Robert Wuthnow, Wade Clark Roof, and Leigh Schmidt, with particular focus on Schmidt. These scholarly analyses of the origins and development of spirituality, I contend, mirror the object of study: both are characterized by an inward turn toward the individual and consciousness, and both are characterized by a celebratory mode of discourse. As for explaining such a tendency, perhaps the effort to empathize with and appeal to a "spiritual" reading audience played a role. And of course the individual proclivities of the authors cannot be excluded. But such causal explanations are speculative. Instead I stress simply that the liberal bias of this scholarship leads toward reproduction of spiritual discourse rather than explication of it.

In his 1988 study, *The Restructuring of American Religion*, Wuthnow detailed the historical decline of denominationalism as the central organizing principle of American religion.[9] Highlighting the dramatic increase in participation in higher education, particularly in the 1960s, Wuthnow saw the emergence of a "new class" and with it a revolution in cultural attitudes. Citing public opinion surveys, Wuthnow documented stark increases in expressions of tolerance for African Americans, homosexuals, and Jews; a greater willingness to accept women in positions of influence outside the home; and an increased concern for civil liberties.[10] Moreover, he saw a trend toward disaffiliation with respect to religious organizations during this time period. In this way he argued that the social and cultural shifts of the 1960s saw the "growing liberalization of American culture."[11] This trend, he noted, had of course provoked a countermovement. Thus the major trajectory of his argument follows the decline of denominationalism and the rise of a liberal/conservative split as the central organizing feature of American religiosity. But this new structure came with a tilt toward one side of the divide. The entire terrain of American religiosity, Wuthnow claimed, had shifted left during the 1960s. To be sure, Wuthnow was critical of the naïveté that this liberalism could entail, particularly with respect to its fostering of an individualism that relied on the "legitimating myths" of freedom and technology under the guiding hand of the state.[12] Nevertheless, his thesis of the ascendancy of liberalism prepared the ground for a more celebratory study of religious individualism that would later fall more firmly under the term *spirituality*.

Here the work of Wade Clark Roof stands out. In *A Generation of Seekers*, published in 1993, Roof set out to detail the more liberal and individualistic religiosity that Wuthnow laid out as a large-scale trend. Like Wuthnow, Roof saw the 1960s as a watershed moment for American religiosity and for American culture more broadly. Roof claimed that the baby boomers had embarked on their own kind of religious journey, one more individualized, open, and dynamic than that which could be captured by the entrenched religious institutions in which they had been raised. The baby boom generation had moved, in Roof's eyes, to the vanguard of religious evolution, evincing a sensibility that was more self-reflective and adaptable than what had come before. With this movement, Roof did not trumpet an appreciation for liberalism. Rather, following Wuthnow but without the caveats, Roof took the shift toward liberalism as a given, as the new reality of the American religious terrain that now needed to be explored and detailed.

In describing what this new kind of religiosity looked like, Roof's title, *A Generation of Seekers*, emphasizes exploration. First and foremost, this new religiosity placed a premium on movement, on openness to new possibilities. In this way, Roof claimed, the boomers not only reflect the influence of the 1960s. Rather, this new kind of religiosity, this "spirituality," as he called it, redeemed the 1960s that had been tainted with the aura of failure. "The 1960s," Roof wrote, "were an era of expanding horizons. Opportunities opened up for people growing up then that were far greater than anything their parents had known—career options, changing gender roles, new family types, choice of lifestyles."[13] Noting the disillusionment that followed during the next two decades, Roof went on to describe the spirituality of the boomers of the 1990s: "They are still exploring; but they are exploring in new, and, we think, more profound ways.... They move freely in and out, across religious boundaries; many combine elements from various traditions to create their own personal, tailor-made meaning systems. Choice, so much a part of life for this generation, now expresses itself in dynamic and fluid religious styles."[14] Thus the promise of the 1960s, the excitement and optimism that had accompanied the expansion of horizons, had acquired a new field of application in the 1990s. Rather than—and here one must assume what Roof left implicit—the promise of a fully enlightened political and social order, the promise of the 1990s had taken on a "more profound" character in the realization of the freedom to pursue one's individual spiritual path.

Roof connected this concern for self with a broader social orientation, and—without dwelling on the term—with liberalism, through the notion of freedom. Writing of the cultural developments of the 1960s, he noted how "freedom of choice had invaded the more private, intimate realms of sexuality and family, producing an immense variety of acceptable alternatives."[15] He suggested that the concern for freedom extended into the value of tolerance, a concern for the freedom for others. In similar fashion, the rising affluence of the boomer generation led to a concern to extend such affluence beyond the individual. Rather than focusing on individual career success and the accumulation of material goods as their parents had, Roof argued that boomers "were predisposed to post-material values, to pursuing greater equality, peace, environmental protection, and quality-of-life, far more so than the generation before them."[16] Thus the freedom-loving individuality of the boomers, Roof claimed, was accompanied by an enlightened social outlook. In this way, Roof implicitly portrayed the concern for freedom and postmaterial values, expressed religiously in an individualized spirituality unencumbered by the baggage of institutions and tradition, as the flowering of liberalism.

While remaining somewhat in the background of both the celebrations and the criticisms of spirituality as put forward by Wuthnow and Roof,[17] liberalism takes center stage for Leigh Schmidt's historical treatment, *Restless Souls*.[18] In this treatment of the roots of contemporary American spirituality, Schmidt rejected the historical grounding of spirituality in the 1960s put forward by both Wuthnow and Roof. Such a focus, he suggested, put too much emphasis on novelty and disregarded the way that spirituality formed "a historically shaped tradition of its own."[19] That tradition, Schmidt continued, finds its ground in the nineteenth century with the "rise and flourishing ... of religious liberalism in all its variety and occasional eccentricity."[20] By locating spirituality in this tradition, Schmidt hoped to debunk the standard criticisms of spirituality that portrayed it as both superficial and faddish. Schmidt placed contemporary American spirituality, neither the invention of "rambling boomers" nor the watering down of Protestant or Enlightenment sensibilities, within a lineage with specific characters: "Transcendentalists, romantic Unitarians, Reform Jews, progressive Quakers, devout disciples of Emerson and Whitman, Spiritualists, questing psychologists, New Thought optimists, Vedantists, and Theosophists, among sundry other wayfarers."[21] Schmidt contended that this group, while diverse, displays a core of common traits that finds reflection in the twenty-first century. Here Schmidt pointed to an appreciation for meditative, solitary, and even mystical encounter with the transcendent; a tendency to locate that transcendence in immanence, that is, within the individual and/or the world, with a consequent universalism that sees all religious paths as expressions of a common human nature; and a dual and tension-filled commitment to social justice and personal creativity.[22]

Before engaging Schmidt's particular conclusions about nineteenth-century religious liberalism, consider his motivations for writing this history in the way that he did. In his introduction to *Restless Souls*, Schmidt took a relatively measured tone in evaluating the liberalism he was about to explore. He wrote that the figures he would treat had "charted a path—at least, so they imagined—away from the old 'religions of authority' into the new 'religions of the spirit.' "[23] By portraying this distinction as a perhaps imagined one, Schmidt established the potential for critical distance in his analysis of liberalism. One might anticipate an evaluation of this claim to have escaped authority through a liberal spirituality, an analysis of how this liberation from authority is produced imaginatively, with a consequent treatment of the powers that have shaped such imagination. One could see a signal of such a possibility in the words he used to describe his approach: "contextual, even handed"; "poised between criticism and celebration"; "fair minded"; and informed with "judiciousness."[24] Indeed, while one might recognize in Schmidt's introduction an appreciation for liberalism as a tradition, his self-presentation made clear that he intended to write from a position of some distance and reserve.

In the body of his work, however, it becomes clear that Schmidt had a particular interest in defending a liberal spirituality. Consider the kind of criticism he brought to the theme of universalism among religious liberals. Treating this theme through the phrase "sympathy of religions," he wrote: "They built their identity on cosmopolitan openness, but did breadth come at the expense of depth? Religious universalism could be thin and placeless; it could disorient as much as reorient lost pilgrims. Cultivating the sympathy of religions made for a restive, not restful posture; a fluid and relational precept, it supported the new flux and flow of modern religious identities. It was the métier of all those aspiring, audacious souls who declared themselves free to explore the piety of the world."[25] Schmidt here iterated the charge that a spirituality of the world left individuals without any grounding in actual community. But he quickly transformed that evocation of placelessness into a celebration of modernity. These religious liberals were at first "disorient[ed]," "lost," and "restive." But without comment or explanation, Schmidt turned from this characterization ridden with anxiety to one much more positive in tone. The sympathy of religions now "supported" these restless souls whose identity was not so much lost and placeless as it was flowing and changing (there is a circular logic at work here, for one would think that this religious cosmopolitanism would contribute to the fragmentation and complexity of identity that it is here supposed to ameliorate). And such support was not passive. Rather, this cosmopolitanism was the "métier" of religious liberals, an expression of expertise or proficiency. The difficulties such cosmopolitanism might present show that those who dwelled in it were "aspiring, audacious." Here Schmidt added overtones of American independence. These daring and proficient masters of the flow of modern identity have "declared themselves free to explore the piety of the world." The declaration of freedom indicates a right not only to self-determination but to cultural imperialism. Immediately prior to the passage cited above, Schmidt described how these religious liberals "ransacked other cultures for spiritual treasures; it was always a fine line between creative appropriation and naked thievery."[26] Despite this caveat, however, by the end of the paragraph Schmidt was content to place liberals on the sunnier side of that line: not thieves but explorers. And Schmidt's conclusion to the chapter on religious universalism is unambiguous: "In decisive and enduring ways, these romantic souls confronted religious narrowness and bigotry with a positive vision of a cosmopolitan spirituality, the piety of the world."[27]

Schmidt's treatment of the theme of freedom is equally illustrative of his celebration of a liberal perspective. Again the rhetorical frame suggests a critical distance, while the content belies a clear preference for one of the options under consideration. Schmidt wrote:

"The struggle at the heart of liberal spirituality…was over the firmness and fragility of religious identity in the modern world. Was being a Christian something that remained neatly bounded by authority, tradition, and liturgy—by unreserved affirmation of the Nicene Creed or the Westminster Confession, by the Bible's utter sufficiency or the pope's infallibility, by the sacraments or strict Sabbath observance? Or were religious identities much more fluid and unbounded than orthodoxies of whatever kind imagined?"[28] Given Schmidt's word choice, one must find his invocation of a "struggle" within religious liberalism as disingenuous. Schmidt described the option for a "firm" religious identity as one that is "neatly" bound by "unreserved" affirmations, the Bible's "utter" sufficiency, and "strict" Sabbath observance. Against this kind of religious identity, Schmidt posed one more flexible than that provided by "orthodoxies of whatever kind imagined." But he had just imagined such orthodoxy, and it was not one of "whatever kind." This kind of firm religious identity was coded with absolutism though his qualifiers. Can one really imagine that liberal spirituality would struggle with a choice presented in this way?

A few pages later in the same chapter on freedom, Schmidt displayed a similar bias in presenting the critical spirit within liberalism. Describing Sarah Farmer's establishment in 1894 of Greenacre, a conference center devoted to religious pluralism, Schmidt wrote:

All she required of participants was a commitment to spiritual openness and respectful engagement rather than sectarian rivalry and judgmental exclusion. That meant, first and foremost, a sincere attentiveness to the presentation of alien perspectives. Invidious comparisons were to be a matter of private reflection, not public pronouncement; points of agreement were to be conscientiously privileged over marks of difference. As Farmer summarily explained her principles, "The spirit of criticism will be absolutely laid down—if it comes in it will be gently laid aside; each will contribute his best and listen sympathetically to those who present different ideals. The comparison will be made by the audience, not by the teachers." Finding a way to cut through religious hatred and intolerance was her grandest ideal, and Farmer pursued that dream with both impossible optimism and splendid dedication.[29]

One should note that Schmidt's discussion of Farmer's prescriptions is much more strongly worded than, and in many respects qualitatively distinct from, the evidence that he cited through direct quotation. Reading Schmidt's words as a paraphrase of the quotation, one finds a series of rhetorical distortions. In table 6.1 I present Schmidt's argument and evidence in parallel.

Note how Schmidt's words mirror the Farmer citation clause by clause, with one outlier on the part of Schmidt. The parallels, however, involve a significant recasting of, indeed, an apology for, what might otherwise appear as (liberal) authoritarianism on the part of Farmer. To begin with Farmer, note the unambiguous construction: criticism was to be "absolutely" excluded from the discussions held at Greenacre. Schmidt rephrased this imperative prohibition on the part of Farmer, however, in terms of a voluntary commitment on the part of the participants, a commitment to "openness" and "respectful engagement." Why criticism could not be open and respectful is not clear. Moreover, the "spirit of criticism" becomes, in Schmidt's paraphrase, an expression of "sectarian rivalry" and "judgmental exclusion." Here Schmidt did not entertain the possibility that Farmer's prohibition of criticism constitutes "judgmental exclusion," and the phrase is instead projected onto the participants at Greenacre. Passing over the second, innocuous parallel, note how Farmer's blanket prohibition of comparison on the part of Greenacre's teachers becomes, in Schmidt's paraphrase, an exclusion only of "invidious," that is, odious, offensive comparison, a qualification absent in the Farmer citation. Through these interpolations Schmidt cast Farmer's assertion of authority as an expression of communal consensus with respect to values of tolerance and respect. In this way Schmidt justified Farmer's exclusion of a critical spirit, even at the most basic level of comparison, in the name of combating "religious hatred and intolerance." Finally, Schmidt's summation of Farmer's rules of order is particularly odd. It is unclear what is "impossible" about her optimism in thinking that religious liberals would accede to such restrictions, an impossibility belied by Schmidt's laudatory apology itself.

By now Schmidt's predispositions with regard to liberalism should be clear. But before moving on, I turn to his conclusion to explore the stakes that might have

TABLE 6.1. *Leigh Schmidt's paraphrase of Sarah Farmer*

Leigh Schmidt (*Restless Souls*, 2005)	Sarah Farmer (Greenacre, 1894)
All she required of participants was a commitment to spiritual openness and respectful engagement rather than sectarian rivalry and judgmental exclusion.	The spirit of criticism will be absolutely laid down—if it comes in, it will be gently laid aside.
That meant, first and foremost, a sincere attentiveness to the presentation of alien perspectives.	Each will contribute his best and listen sympathetically to those who present different ideals.
Invidious comparisons were to be a matter of private reflection, not public pronouncement;	The comparison will be made by the audience, not by the teachers.
Points of agreement were to be conscientiously privileged over marks of difference.	

driven Schmidt to portray his subject matter in the way that he did. In the final paragraph of *Restless Souls*, and employing the evangelical "we", Schmidt wrote: "So, if we really want to do something about narcissism and selfishness, about loose religious and civic connections, about the intolerant narrowness of fundamentalist orthodoxies, about the hubris of empire, we need to work with what got us here—a robust liberal tradition with strong religious elements. At its best that tradition has effectively joined mystical openness and social justice, spiritual seeking and political emancipation, globalism and localism, universality and variety.... [Religious liberalism] offers a prospect—not of the finished work of salvation, but of the incomplete labor of democratic freedom and cosmopolitan progressivism."[30] Schmidt here invoked a practical aim: his analysis is meant to help spiritual liberals "do something" about a variety of ills ranging from the levels of individual psychology, to social cohesion, to the threats of religious particularism, and to political imperialism. Indeed, the subjects of his work bear quite a burden by the end: they are pillars of "democratic freedom" and a progressivism that could extend beyond America's borders. His assertion that nineteenth-century religious liberalism and contemporary spirituality form a tradition may have been offered in the hopes that, through recognition of their collective heritage, spiritual liberals could gain strength and resolve in the struggles that Schmidt has laid out for them. With such high stakes in play, one may understand why Schmidt represented liberalism in a most positive light.

Within the larger context of liberal studies of spirituality, Schmidt provided something of a reversal. While he celebrated the individuality and freedom that he saw in his object of study, he also highlighted the fact that these traits stem from a tradition. He thus made explicit what remained largely implicit in earlier work. For such honesty his work is to be commended, for it also makes the theoretical problems of such celebration much clearer.

■ THEORIZING SPIRITUALITY: POWER AND INCOMMUNICABILITY

Earlier I mentioned the social import of the obscurity engendered by the concepts of freedom and self. Indeed, I would propose that for all the theoretical problems posed by a focus on freedom and self, the strength of the liberal tradition may rely on the vagueness and misdirection that these concepts entail. In what follows I will lay out in greater detail some of the theoretical limitations of such categories, as well as their social productivity. Here the analysis of subjectivity put forward by Luhmann provides a useful starting point, particularly in the way that it challenges the concept of the self as an interpretive focus.

In the English preface to his opus magnum, *Social Systems*, Luhmann argued for the impossibility of subjectivity as a sociological concept. The problem, Luhmann argued, lies in the singularity of the subject. Inherent in the logic of subjectivity is the idea that the subject constitutes all objects that appear for it. In this way one cannot have a plurality of subjects. As Luhmann wrote, "Because every subject conceives of itself as the condition for the constitution of all the others, those others could be subjects, but not real, so to speak, *subjective* subjects. From the perspective of each subject, every other one possesses merely a derivative, con-stituted, constructed existence."[31] Luhmann discussed the attempt to theorize a plurality of (subjective) subjects under the heading "intersubjectivity," a concept he found most rigorously expressed in the phenomenology of Edmund Husserl. Here Luhmann reached his foundational rejection of the subjectivist tradition in social theory: "Husserl, in his famous 'Fifth Cartesian Meditation,' made it impos-sible to deny the problem of 'intersubjectivity' any longer. His answer, that the social is an 'intermonadological community,' is theoretically so weak that it can be read as an expression of embarrassment, indeed as an admission of defeat. There can be no 'intersubjectivity' on the basis of the subject."[32] From Luhmann's per-spective, Husserl's understanding of society as a community of monads, a group-ing of subjects each of whom recognizes all the others as fundamentally "derivative," simply repeats the foundational logic of subjectivity without solving the problem it poses for social theory. Specifically, Luhmann suggests that if one's primary conceptual tool is a singularity, that is, the monad, one will never be able to explain the organization of plurality, that is, social order.

Luhmann's critique does much to outline the problems in using "the self" or "subjectivization" as interpretive categories that could illuminate a social phenomenon. Just as useful, moreover, is his explanation of why the subject has come into such wide usage despite its impossibility. Speaking historically, Luhmann contended that the opacity of the subject does not simply constitute a failure of intellectual diligence on the part of scholarship. Rather, this opacity arose as a necessary consequence of the historical advent of modernity. The conception of the subject, Luhmann wrote, "began its career at the historical moment when modern European society discovered that it could no longer describe itself in the old categories of a stratified society, its essential forms and essential hierarchy, but could not yet say what was the case instead."[33] This inability to describe society gave rise to a correspondingly opaque conception of the "parts" of society: sub-jects. The opacity of the subject with respect to its environment, that is, other sub-jects, arose as a necessary reflection of the lack of a unified self-description of (European) society. Thus Luhmann wrote that "the hidden nonconstructability of 'intersubjectivity' is the theoretical counterpart of the indescribability of society."[34] The opaque subject thus functioned as a "stopgap concept" to deal with a transi-tional period in modern European history, and in this way the concept of the sub-ject could be justified in its limitations.

Luhmann's thesis that the conceptual limitations of subjectivity perform a social function serves to illuminate a foundational issue in the study of spirituality. Specifically, this thesis encourages scholars to recognize the nebulous character of spirituality as a primary datum and not an analytical shortcoming. The difficulty in defining spirituality may be "intentional," which is not to suggest a conscious desire to deceive or conceal but, rather, that the conceptual opacity of spirituality may reflect certain forms of social organization in which this phenomenon arises. Put simply, if spirituality grows out of a particularly complex and fluid social nexus, one should expect its shape to retain some of the fluidity of the environ-ment toward which it is to apply and for which it is to serve as a guide. By way of contrast, it should come as no surprise that those who grow up in a stable community made up of the same members, who maintain the same occupation for the majority of their life span, whose lives will unfold within a fairly limited range of reasonably anticipated possibilities, should find a place in a relatively fixed and objective social form that might be called a "religion." But what of those whose neighbors and associates change every few years, whose career paths twist and turn, whose plans and intentions are repeatedly met with surprise, disappointment, and radical reorientation? Would one expect their religiosity, or whatever gives them a sense of meaning and identity, to maintain a fixity and objectivity so alien to the rest of their lives?

Obviously, stasis and change cannot be neatly attributed to religion and spirituality, respectively. The freedom and fluidity of spirituality and the ossification and restriction of religion are caricatures, stereotypes, a polar opposition across a single spectrum. But with the increasing complexity of contemporary society one would expect new symbol systems by way of reflection. Seeking the same kind of conceptual clarity for spirituality as one might find for a religion with roots in a radically different (and simpler) form of social organization is simply to argue with the object of analysis. Scholarship would be better served by an attempt to understand precisely how the indeterminacy of spirituality, and of its operative categories of self and freedom, functions in the maintenance of social order.

How might such reflections inform an understanding of freedom and the self within the context of spirituality? Here an example might be helpful. Stef Aupers and Dick Houtman, following the work of Paul Heelas, asserted a "binding doctrine in the spiritual milieu: the belief that in the deeper layers of the self, one finds a true, authentic, and sacred kernel, 'unpolluted' by culture, history or society, which informs evaluation of what is good, true, and meaningful. Such evaluation, it is held, cannot be made by relying on external authorities or experts, but only by listening to one's 'inner voice.' "[35] Aupers and Houtman illustrated the social effects of such a doctrine through their own research and quote an informant, Chantal, working for a company called MCR. She related an incident where she described herself to a consultant:

> It was an inspiring visit and suddenly he looked at me intrusive and said "I hear your story. It sounds perfect, looking at it from the outside, but where are you?" In other words: "The story is not yours. It is the standard 'format' of the company you are presenting, but where is your passion? What makes you Chantal instead of Miss MCR?" I thought "... I have no answer to this question and I have to do something with that."[36]

Aupers and Houtman saw this experience as the trigger for a process of socialization, and they identified the origin of this process as a feeling of "alienation" with respect to a social role. But as they themselves noted, Chantal did not simply encounter her situation as unsatisfying; she spoke with a consultant who pushed her to reevaluate her personal narrative.[37] I would stress that the effectiveness of his communication arose from his invocation of incommunicability. He proclaimed her narrative "perfect," but he nevertheless refused to recognize it as authentic. Through the invocation of an inside perspective that would yield a "you," the consultant did not propose a doctrine of the self to fill the space his rejection created. Rather, he erected a barrier to communication and demanded that the barrier be crossed. Rather than a belief in the self, such a call stimulates individualization: not a commonly shared belief but an operation of differentiation. What, precisely, are the conditions that allow such a refusal and shape Chantal's inability to overcome it? I do not reject Aupers and Houtman's assertion of a commonly shared "doctrine," but that is just one side of the coin. The other side is a set of socially constructed prohibitions and limitations through which an "inner voice" becomes plausible as a source of meaning and identity. Those prohibitions can be strategically invoked and applied at particular places and times. Through a focus on what cannot be said or understood, what is not allowed as legitimate communication, scholars of spirituality might open windows onto a variety of communicative strategies through which this kind of religiosity perpetuates itself.[38]

I do not know whether scholars could identify a "code" of spirituality along the lines of Luhmann's proposal of a code of intimacy in eighteenth-century romance novels, discussed earlier in this essay. The comparison would be interesting: demands for spontaneity, passion, excess, and instability would surely differ for spiritual versus romantic intimacy. But such comparisons aside, I would point out that a focus on commonly held doctrines might be a relatively thin approach to understanding spirituality as a system of communication. In contrast, studying the variety of impossibilities, or at least communicative difficulties, entailed by the discourse of spirituality might illuminate some of the dynamism of spirituality as a form of religious individualism. The focus thus turns to practices rather than contents of consciousness, the latter of which are for spirituality necessarily individualized and relentlessly plural.

If a doctrine of the self can be illuminated by operations of incommunicability, likewise the assertion of liberty might be better understood through an analysis of power. Here, of course, one need not remain with Luhmann for theoretical inspiration, although his treatment of incommunicability as a practice leads in this direction.[39] Nor need one accept his rejection of subjectivity as a useful sociological concept. As long as one avoids a conception of the subject as a monadic entity, subjectivity may still prove useful for social analysis. I described earlier how Foucault refocused his theoretical lens on the "self" rather than the more disembodied network of operations he had earlier described through the notion of power/knowledge. How might such a perspective illuminate the practice of spirituality in the contexts discussed above?

To give only one example, consider once more Schmidt's discussion of the prescriptions offered by Sarah Farmer with respect to Greenacre. Through the lens of the late Foucault, one could view Farmer's assertion of authority not as a reflection of values whether liberal or otherwise but, rather, as a regulation of practice that was formative for liberal subjectivity. Here the renunciation of criticism was considered as the price to be paid for access to the truth of the "piety of the world." Rather than representing such renunciation as an exercise of freedom, where participants voluntarily open themselves to the difference of others and thereby accept the freedom of those others to be different, a Foucauldian lens would ask how the structures of authority at Greenacre created the channels through which its participants came to knowledge of themselves and of the world they inhabited. Such an

analysis could include freedom within it, that is, it could investigate how the practices of spirituality could result in a sense of an unfettered and free individuality
despite, or even as a result of, the operation of communal structures of authority.
Such a perspective would thus focus on social technologies and could create a
genealogy of those technologies that would relate them to other realms of
society.[40]

Drawing on Foucauldian sensibilities, Jeremy Carette and Richard King have
pointed out how the individualism of spirituality belies an operation of power, one
in which corporations prey on those who consider themselves "free" in their con-
sumeristic approach to spiritual development. Carette and King thus framed spirituality as a religious manifestation of neoliberal ideology where a market mentality
substitutes for critical perspective in the construction of meaning and identity. In
this way they argue that an individualized spirituality loses the potential for critical refashioning of the social order.[41] Taking a nonessentialist approach toward
subjectivity, such reflections on power illuminate the social construction of spirituality even in its supposed bases in liberty and self-realization.

As is often the case with such analyses of "soft" power, Carette and King have
come under fire for their criticisms. John Drane rebuked the authors for their
alleged suggestion of a "Machiavellian plot on the part of business people" to
market spirituality, and he instead points to "individual therapists" as the primary
culprits.[42] But such a complaint arises from an essentialist understanding that
ignores the subtleties of the kind of power that Carette and King criticize. To return
to Foucault, one may recall his injunction that "the idea that there is either located
at—or emanating from—a given point something which is a 'power' seems to me
to be based on a misguided analysis.... In reality power means relations, a more-
or-less organized, hierarchical, co-ordinating cluster of relations."[43] Thus the blam-
ing of particular entities for the exploitation of spirituality misses the systemic,
transubstantial nature of corporate power. Corporations exercise their power
through their organization of individuals. Individual authors and practitioners
who participate in this system become corporate agents through their cooperation. Rather than identifying villains and conquering them, Carette and King call
for a critical perspective on the nature of cooperative action, a perspective that a
radically individualized spirituality has trouble conceptualizing.

✷ ✷ ✷

Taken together, these analyses of scholarship on spirituality suggest that the
conceptual limitations of the liberal perspective on spirituality are no accident.
The power of the liberal tradition lies largely in the way it shapes theory, the models
of explanation through which the world, including the liberal tradition itself, is to
be understood. But if the blind spots created by a liberal reading of spirituality are
unavoidable, scholarship may do better than to shed light on this darkness through
alternative paradigms. Rather, an analysis of the blind spots as blind spots may
provide a richer understanding. Here the works of Luhmann, Foucault, and ultimately Husserl suggest the continuing promise of a phenomenological approach
to the study of religion. One may recall that in Husserl's phenomenology, the halo

of indeterminacy surrounding every object of intention does not signal a short-coming of subjectivity but a feature of the world as world, an indispensable aspect of the nature of "things," and a logically necessary condition of every phenomenon as such. Luhmann and Foucault took the phenomenological postulate that the "unknown" is an integral feature of reality and worked it into their social analyses. They showed how prohibitions, restrictions, renunciations, and silences provide the formative conditions for codes, discourses, doctrines, and beliefs. In this way their works are particularly useful for treating the more obscure aspects of spirituality precisely because they take obscurity seriously: that is, as a feature of the logic of the world and not the illogic of the analyst.

In sum, scholarship has rich theoretical resources for studying religious individualism in a way that does not reinscribe its fundamental obscurities by way of celebration. And there is much self-interest in investigating incommunicability as an aspect of shared belief, power in relationship to liberty. The central doctrine of liberalism is relatively straightforward, articulable, and unenlightening: individuals should be free as long as that freedom does not interfere with the freedom of others. What cannot be said or understood within the discourse of liberalism, on the other hand, plays a more subtly powerful role than any collective affirmation. The place of liberty within liberalism is relatively well defined, if tautologically vacuous (to be sure, liberalism promotes and depends upon liberty—but what that means is difficult to pinpoint within the discourse itself). The question of power dynamics within liberalism is a much richer and more interesting field of inquiry.

■ NOTES

1. See http://www.hofstra.edu/pdf/Cul_RelReg.pdf.

2. Humberto Maturana and Francisco Varela, *Autopoiesis and Cognition: The Realization of the Living* (Boston: D. Reidel, 1980).

3. Niklas Luhmann, *Social Systems* (Stanford, CA: Stanford University Press, 1985).

4. See Wade Clark Roof, *A Generation of Seekers* (San Francisco: Harper, 1993), 67–68, 76–79, 119–48; Wade Clark Roof, *Spiritual Marketplace: Baby Boomers and the Remaking of American Religion* (Princeton, NJ: Princeton University Press, 1999), 33–35, 173–79; Brian Zinnbauer Kenneth Pargament, Brenda Cole, Mark Rye, Eric Butter, Timothy Belavich, Kathleen Hipp, Allie Scott, Jill Kadar "Religion and Spirituality: Unfuzzying the Fuzzy," *Journal for the Scientific Study of Religion* 36 (1997): 549–64; Bron Taylor, "Earth and Nature-Based Spirituality: Part I," *Religion* 31 (2001): 175–93.

5. This liberal mode of religious studies scholarship also operates beyond the study of spirituality. In their chapters in this volume, Rosemary R. Hicks describes how the academic understanding of Sufism has been decisively informed by liberal democratic political thought, while Brian Goldstone lays out the liberal and secularist underpinnings of the concept of religious violence. For an alternative to the liberal historiography of spirituality, see Catherine L. Albanese, "Introduction," in *American Spiritualities: A Reader* (Bloomington: Indiana University Press, 2001), 1–15. Further divergences from the liberal tradition are discussed toward the end of this essay.

6. Steven J. Sutcliffe, "Rethinking 'New Age' as a Popular Religious *Habitus*: A Review Essay on *The Spiritual Revolution*," *Method and Theory in the Study of Religion* 18 (2006): 307–8.

7. See Michel Foucault, *The Hermeneutics of the Subject: Lectures at the College de France, 1981–1982* (2001; New York: Picador, 2005), 15.

8. Niklas Luhmann, *Love as Passion: The Codification of Intimacy* (Stanford: University of California Press, 1986).

9. Robert Wuthnow, *The Restructuring of American Religion: Society and Faith since World War Two* (Princeton, NJ: Princeton University Press, 1988).

10. Ibid., 153–64.

11. Ibid., 157.

12. Ibid., 241–96.

13. Roof, *A Generation of Seekers*, 4.

14. Ibid.

15. Ibid., 48.

16. Ibid., 59.

17. In terms of critical approaches toward spirituality, note that Wuthnow's later work, *After Heaven*, questions the embrace of seeker spirituality described by Roof in the roughly contemporaneous *Spiritual Marketplace*. See Robert Wuthnow, *After Heaven: Spirituality in America since the 1950s* (Berkeley: University of California Press, 1998); and Roof, *Spiritual Marketplace*. But even here one can see clear limits to Wuthnow's critique. *After Heaven* offered scant mention of the state that Wuthnow had identified as a pervasive and subterranean influence on the revolution in American religiosity he had described earlier in *The Restructuring of American Religion*. Further, Wuthnow's later criticism of the freedom of spiritual seeking has nothing to do with the legitimation of political order. The problem of this idea of freedom of choice, Wuthnow suggested, concerns individuals in themselves: they lack "the social support they need" and are not edified in terms of virtue (*After Heaven*, 16). In important respects, therefore, Wuthnow's *After Heaven* is missing the critical voice that he had applied toward liberalism in his earlier work.

18. Leigh Schmidt, *Restless Souls: The Making of American Spirituality* (San Francisco: Harper San Francisco, 2005).

19. Ibid., 2.

20. Ibid., 6.

21. Ibid., 2, 7.

22. Ibid., 12.

23. Ibid., 7.

24. Ibid., 11, 22–23.

25. Ibid., 138–39.

26. Ibid., 138.

27. Ibid., 140.

28. Ibid., 184.

29. Ibid., 193–94.

30. Ibid., 289–90.

31. Luhmann, *Social Systems*, xl (original emphasis).

32. Ibid., xli.

33. Ibid., xl.

34. Ibid.

35. Stef Aupers and Dick Houtman, "Beyond the Spiritual Supermarket: The Social and Public Significance of New Age Spirituality," *Journal of Contemporary Religion* 21, no. 2 (2006): 204.

36. Ibid., 206–7.

37. Ibid., 208.

38. For further discussion along these lines, see my work on the production of spirituality in national parks: Kerry A. Mitchell, "Managing Spirituality: Public Religion and National Parks," *International Journal for the Study of Religion, Nature and Culture* 1 (2007): 431–49.

39. Note the self-presentation of the Rockefeller Foundation as discussed in Hicks's essay. Its professed lack of specific plans for resolving international problems may be seen as just such an instance of powerful incommunicability. Such refusal to affirm a particular agenda legitimates the political, for instance, liberal democratic, aspect of the foundation's funding aims: support of "creative work" that "[cut] across cultural boundaries."

40. In another example of the application of Foucauldian sensibilities in this arena, Brian Goldstone describes elsewhere in this volume how the discourse of "religious violence" implies a secularist model of subjectivity that naturalizes a liberal political and moral stance with respect to conflict.

41. Jeremy Carette and Richard King, *Selling Spirituality: The Silent Takeover of Religion* (London: Routledge, 2004).

42. Drane, "Selling Spirituality: The Silent Takeover of Religion," *Evangelical Quarterly* 78, no. 2 (2006): 183.

43. Michel Foucault, "The Confessions of the Flesh," in *Power/Knowledge: Selected Interviews and Other Writings, 1972–1977,* ed. Colin Gordon, trans. Colin Gordon, Leo Marshall, John Mepham, and Kate Soper (New York: Pantheon Books, 1980), 198, quoted in Allan Megill, *Prophets of Extremity: Nietzsche, Heidegger, Foucault, Derrida* (Berkeley: University of California Press, 1985), 248–49.

7 Comparative Religion and the Cold War Transformation of Indo-Persian "Mysticism" into Liberal Islamic Modernity

Rosemary R. Hicks

In 1906, American spiritualist W. J. Colville placed himself in the lineage of comparative religionists Max Müller and Harvard's James Freeman Clarke and urged northeastern audiences to distinguish between "Mohammedans" of different kinds. "It is a great mistake to suppose that the devotees of any system are *all* narrow-minded or bigoted," Colville contended and proceeded to identify the most reasonable devotees. While "Sunnees" were the most inflexible, held fast to rigid interpretations of the Qur'an, and tended to be Arab, Turkish, or Tartar (the Muslims seemingly most threatening to American interests over the nation's short history), the mystical "Sheeah" of Persia were more enlightened and "elastic in their interpretations." Finally, estimation—especially that of Persian Shi'a, was the was the *most* modern and liberal Mohammedanism and thus a source of universal religious truth.[1] Colville was not the first American to tie Persian Sufism to cosmopolitan sensibilities, nor was he the last. His Transcendentalist and Protestant predecessors (including Ralph Waldo Emerson and William James) had likewise contrasted Indian and Persian traditions favorably against the "hot and rigid monotheism of the Arab mind."[2] A century later, features on Pakistan and Iran in the *New York Times* and *National Geographic* indicated that, while largely unsure of the differences between Sunni and Shi'i traditions, Americans increasingly saw Indo-Persian Sufisms as the most moderate and liberal forms of Islam and antidotes to (generally Arab) radicalism.[3] Such seemingly similar constructions must prompt one to ask: Are these racial and religious distinctions continuous? Further (and be the answer yes, no, or something in between), what were the intellectual frameworks and institutional networks through which these liberalisms and mysticisms took shape?

Several scholars mistakenly situate Americans' growing interests in mysticism in the 1960s. Huston Smith, a best-selling author of books on world religions, credits Iranian expatriate Seyyed Hossein Nasr with spreading knowledge of Sufism in the 1960s and after.[4] Nasr's importance for American cultural history cannot be overstated, as I detail below. In fact, just days after Iranian President Mahmoud Ahmadinejad's contested appearances at the United Nations and Columbia University in 2007, National Public Radio aired its tenth program on Sufism in one year and invited Nasr to speak about the twelfth-century Persian Sufi (and best-selling poet in America), Jallaladin Rumi.[5] For over fifty years,

Nasr had endeavored to educate Americans about Sufism, Shi'ism, and Persian philosophy. During that interview, Nasr again promoted the universal aspects of all religions as outlined in his recent book, *The Garden of Truth: The Vision and Promise of Sufism, Islam's Mystical Tradition* (2007). Like Huston Smith, Wade Clark Roof attributed American interest in cosmopolitan mysticism to demographic changes in the 1960s that sparked a "spiritual marketplace" for Eastern traditions and fostered multicultural and pluralist sensibilities.[6] Exploring Americans' earlier interests in the East, Leigh Eric Schmidt described how liberal Gilded Age and Progressive Era New Englanders saw Eastern mysticisms as a source of ethical universals and attempted to foster a cosmopolitan "sympathy of religions" to facilitate civic cohesion and economic expansion. Schmidt traced idealist philosophies of mysticism through the Transcendentalists, William James, and Huston Smith's 1960s Harvard experiments with Timothy Leary and LSD.[7] However, while Schmidt and Roof thus help explain Americans' growing sympathies to the notion of "liberal" mysticism, neither account for the political dynamics and racial constructs through which Americans fit Islamic practices into this form. Nor do they discuss how critics of phenomenological and idealist approaches like Nasr's also came to see mystical ideals as essential to creating a modern world community.

In what follows, I examine the intertwined production of popular culture and politics as they took shape in Cold War debates over the racial and cultural character of modern Islam; in particular, I reveal how mysticism was increasingly conflated with moderation. In the years after World War II, Muslim and non-Muslim academics retooled colonial and Orientalist categories while defining a "liberal Islam" suitable for the modern world. Their programs, established in connection with growing US involvement in South Asia and the Middle East, helped reinforce Persian and South Asian Sufisms as the Islam of liberal modernity in different ways. Most important here, they did so both for the liberal idealists discussed in earlier genealogies of mysticism in America *and* for their philosophical materialist and secular modernist critics. Like Kerry Mitchell and Brian Goldstone (both in this volume) and several of the scholars they engage, I draw out the entangled assumptions about liberalism and religion evident in nineteenth- and twentieth-century texts. I also utilize interviews and archival records in order to nuance these close readings, trace how racial and religious categories were implemented and altered in various projects, and chart the networks through which the contours of liberal Islamic mysticism took shape. In doing so, I follow Webb Keane, who takes modernity—as articulated in Protestant expansion—to be "a term of self-description in a narrative of moral progress," and Talal Asad, who reveals modernization to be both a political project and an economic one.[8] In contrast to Keane, however, I focus on thinkers who found modernization to be simultaneously moral *and* destructive (or "dystopian") and in the conclusion to this chapter turn to issues Asad did not discuss in his essay on the theorist whom I found at the nexus of these networks: Wilfred Cantwell Smith.

Wilfred Cantwell Smith (1916–2000) came to see secularism as destabilizing Islamic modernization and a specific kind of Sufism as essential to fostering a just global society. Most know the eminent Canadian scholar for his 1960s theories about Persian cultural traditions and the world-historical development of religious faith. I illuminate here how he and his Muslim and non-Muslim colleagues—including

Indo-Pakistani scholar Fazlur Rahman (1919–88), Nasr (b. 1933), and European émigrés H. A. R. Gibb (1895–1971) and Annemarie Schimmel (1922–2003)—debated the nature of mysticism at the McGill Institutes of Islamic Studies and at Harvard University. In so doing, they defined *some* practices as modern, others as pre- or antimodern, and still others as timeless and perennial. Their deliberations were rooted in older Orientalist traditions, inflected by postwar developments in the social sciences and field of comparative religions, solidified in writings and academic programs, and contributed to various ideas about the identities and strategic interests of "West" and "East." Scholars somewhat indebted to Smith's 1963 *The Meaning and End of Religion* have since examined how religion and mysticism *became* modern categories in the hands of colonialists, imperialists, missionaries, academics, and liberal pluralists of the nineteenth and twentieth centuries.[9] However, like H. Smith, Roof, and Schmidt, they have overlooked the Cold War dynamics through which "reformed mysticism" became salient in relation to American concerns about secularism, modernity, communism, and Islam.

Before examining some of the institutions in which these intellectuals dismantled and reassembled ideas about mysticism, liberalism, modernity, and Islam, I must note that not every scholar involved in Cold War programs supported US interests exclusively or agreed that secularism was synonymous with economic and political modernization. Rather, some caught up in the promise of modernizing Muslim-majority countries understood reformed mysticism to be the antidote to modern crises of secular nationalism, economic imperialism, godless communism, and world war. In the postwar wake of fascism and face of communist atheism, W. C. Smith and his colleagues found rational, revitalized, and liberal Islam to be the only hope for Islamic republics. Therefore, Smith concluded in 1957, it was also essential to creating a modern world community. Smith recruited scholars to his programs whom he hoped could produce authentic Islamic liberalism in the new Islamic Republic of Pakistan and the overly secularized nation of Iran while countering the insufficiently liberal attitudes of Arab Muslims and designs of both capitalist and communist neo-imperial regimes. He and most of his colleagues excoriated "otherworldly" idealist tendencies and, by crosscutting some Protestant Orientalist categories with others, redefined authentic Islamic mysticism as the socially engaged and ethically liberal practice of a rational ideal.

■ RIGID RELIGION VERSUS ENGAGED MYSTICISM: THE RACE OF MODERNITY AND CULTURE OF REASON

Ideas about mysticism often figured centrally in eighteenth- through twentieth-century models of reason and world-historical progress. Many of these, in turn, derived from colonial contexts. Academics, imperial administrators, and missionaries frequently cited "superstitious" Sufi practices as their proof that Muslims were irrational, apolitical, and otherworldly or argued that rigidly inflexible and illogical Semites required the help of colonial caretakers. Even while emphasizing Muslims' ostensibly weak deliberative and administrative capacities, British officials in South Asia attempted to annex the economic and political power of international Sufi networks.[10] Meanwhile, French officials in North Africa found Sufi practitioners to be less otherworldly and more prepared to battle colonial armies than they had expected.[11] Some mapped European Christian debates about mysticism onto colonial contexts and consequently viewed mystical orientations as more creative and less dogmatic than other forms of religiosity,[12] while others simply sought to exploit intra-Muslim tensions exacerbated by the different imperial situations. The officials and Orientalists who considered "Soofism" to be less concerned with Islamic law and distant from Arab dogmatism often also viewed "mystics" as potential sympathizers with projects against other Muslim sources of power.[13] Simultaneously, they and others blamed "otherworldly" individualist mysticism for the ostensible decline of Islamic civilization. In the context of such post-Enlightenment rationalist discourses, some Muslim and non-Muslim intellectuals deployed anti-Sufi narratives against popular piety and "superstitious" practices and cited Sufism as the reason for the end of Islamic eminence. As the twentieth century unfolded, others— including those discussed here—stressed the rational or suprarational observances of "reformed" (philosophical, not emotional and superstitious) Sufi traditions. They did so partly in attempts to deflect the criticisms of secular modernizers and newly independent Muslim governments that regarded Sufis as a potential challenge to state power.[14] Wilfred Cantwell Smith grappled with these multiple narratives during his undergraduate years in Oriental studies at the University of Toronto and his graduate work at Cambridge and formulated his first synthesis of them during his dissertation research in Lahore.[15]

Smith's early understandings of mysticism, reason, and race derived in part from the work of idealist Orientalists who created binaries that separated ostensibly rigid, dogmatic, Semitic traditions from exotic Indo-Persian mystical wisdom. However, Smith had adopted socialism during his undergraduate years with Social Gospel activists in Toronto and during his graduate work in England. Thus, his understandings also derived to a large extent from materialist philosophers' claims that ideals (particularly religious ones) were nothing more than the "mystification of reason" and misunderstanding of material reality. These materialists likewise utilized binaries created to facilitate colonial projects in their models of how reason progressively liberated humans from religion and other ideals. Although Smith initially rejected what he saw as ahistorical religious idealisms, his models of racial mind-sets and civilizational development increasingly reflected both idealist and materialist sources. This was in part because, like other advocates of social Christianity, Smith left a small space for transcendence. In fact, John Macmurray, the influential Christian socialist and antiwar philosopher of "personalism," was one of Smith's most enduring influences. Macmurray asserted that modern world community should be based in Jesus's teachings about the kingdom of heaven, which "can be expressed in such a way as to exhibit the main theoretical conceptions of Communism." These include "the unity of theory and practice," or ideals and action, and the anti-individualist, interpersonal nature of humanity.[16]

Macmurray's thoughts on idealist mysticism, world-historical development, and global community aired on BBC radio throughout the 1930s. In a segment entitled "The Roots of Our Culture" (published in *Freedom in the Modern World*, 1932), he combined materialist critiques and German biblical criticism to explain why Europe had failed to realize freedom yet went to war in its name. Modern crises emerged out of culture, he contended, and modern community out of true religion: "Three old civilizations have been mixed together to form the culture of which we are the heirs—the Hebrew, the Greek, and the Roman, a religious, an artistic, and an organizing, administrative, or scientific civilization. These three streams of old experience have never really fused. Indeed the main problem of European civilization hitherto has arisen from the strain that their antagonisms have set up, and from the effort, never successful, to unite them in a single culture."[17] Overcoming these clashes required a messianic, but not overly mystical, solution.

For Macmurray, "Hebrew Christianity," a Christianity that remained faithful to Jesus' Jewish origins instead of eliding them, synthesized these three elements. Crucially, though, he argued that Western European "pseudo-Christianity" was more Roman than Greek or Hebrew. Under the illusion of freedom, the bureaucratic and materialist culture of "pseudo-Christianity" in Western Europe encouraged capitalist expansion, oppressed the European poor, and fueled violent imperialism abroad.[18] Consequently, "faith," the authentic *activity* of real religion, had been distorted, Macmurray argued, and made "the history of our civilization [into] a struggle *against* Christianity."[19] Instead of creating an interpersonal world community, Europe had cultivated world war.

As to whether real religion—i.e., authentic Hebrew-Christian faith—would overcome the antihumanist fascism of Mussolini, the excesses of Soviet Communism (what he saw as the Eastern expression of Greek humanism), or Hitler's "mystical" frenzy of nationalism, Macmurray admitted that he did not know. What he did know was that the immanent and ethical practice represented in the historical life of Jesus opposed otherworldly mysticism and promoted global community. "Mystics" who withdrew from the world to consider transcendent reality performed a necessary task, he allowed, but erred in prioritizing contemplation over communion.[20] As he later elaborated in *The Clue to History* (published in 1938, the year W. C. Smith arrived in England), such mystical withdrawal without return valued individual religious experience as an end in itself rather than as one movement in a larger life of transformative action. In 1939, Smith took this perspective to Lahore and to the intertwined projects of modernization and liberation he saw unfolding in the Subcontinent.

■ FROM ENGLAND TO SOUTH ASIA: ANGLOS AND INDIANS
   AND THE SIGNIFICANCE OF THE "WEST"

Sheila McDonough, Smith's first doctoral student at McGill, chronicled how the young scholar had traveled to India with hopes that World War II would end British imperialism. Like many Cambridge students animated by clashes between socialism and fascism occurring across Europe and its colonies, Smith supported the socialist independence movement of fellow Cambridge alumnus Jawaharlal Nehru. He conducted dissertation research while teaching "Islamic history" for the

Canadian Overseas Mission Council at Foreman Christian College in Lahore and while working to foster Hindu–Muslim dialogue and prevent political fragmentation. In keeping with Macmurray, Smith viewed organized religion as divisive and in need of reform. Like Marx, he insisted on reading religious identity (especially in India) as a product of class dynamics rather than inherent racial essences or mindsets. Like his Social Gospel colleagues, Smith saw the revolution as God's plan unfolding in history, and like his mentor, Nehru (the Congress Party president who minimized philosopher and activist Muhammad Iqbal's fears for Muslim safety in a majority-Hindu independent India), Smith believed democracy to be essential to antifascist freedom and socialist independence. At that time, McDonough argues, this was Smith's "orthodoxy."[21]

Though McDonough does not discuss Smith's understandings of mysticism, his perspective from Lahore (Iqbal's home until his death in 1938) likewise demonstrates the influences she mentioned. Regarding rationality, religion, and progressive liberation, Smith argued in his work from that time, *Modern Islam in India: A Social Analysis*: "To save his personality from meagerness and to develop it with ampler freedom to create, man needs the activity of science, and the freedom offered by social science rather than the contemplation of the metaphysician. The scientific activity might well be guided by some dynamic morality, such as that which Iqbal construed religion to be in his more progressive ventures. But that is to ascribe to religion a far different aim from his present one of the traffic with mystic ultimates."[22] In his prognosis of the imminent end of imperialism and the entry of independent India into the modern world community, Smith criticized the "aggressive mystic frenzy," "idealistic zeal," "mystic irrationalism," "mystic idealism" and "mystic pacifism" of Iqbal and other proponents of Muslim statehood.[23] After the war, Smith's understanding of mysticism changed radically.

When Smith returned to North America, he learned of Nazi–Communist collaboration in Germany, of the actions of Stalinist forces in Spain, and (from his brother, Arnold, then the Canadian ambassador to the Soviet Union) of the gulag and Siberian camps. Despite Cambridge's rejection of his Marxist dissertation, Smith published it in 1946 and retained a crucial relationship with one of his British dissertation advisers, H. A. R. Gibb. Gibb was then at Oxford but emigrated to America in 1956. In 1946, Smith also enrolled at Princeton, home to the first center for modern studies of the Near East. There he studied under another eminent Arabist, Phillip K. Hitti, and earned a master's degree in 1947 and doctorate in 1948. While at Princeton, Smith watched the British Empire begin to crumble: Indian independence in 1947 and the creation of Pakistan were followed by the reconfiguration of Palestine in 1948. Meanwhile, Smith witnessed influential American theologians in nearby Manhattan recant their Marxism, stress that social justice required liberty and democratic order, and join Rockefeller-funded programs to develop new models for international relations.[24] In 1949, Smith traveled to several countries on a Rockefeller Foundation grant meant to afford text-based Orientalists "direct acquaintance with contemporary thought and movements."[25] The destruction Smith witnessed upon his return to Lahore affected him deeply, as did the fact that Indian nationals rejected his Marxist analysis and banned his book. These experiences convinced Smith to involve Muslims in all future attempts at academic and social reform and to publish a partial retraction of *Modern Islam in India*.[26]

In 1949, Smith was appointed Birks Professor of Comparative Religion at McGill. In his 1950 inaugural address, Smith asserted that Islamic modernization required more idealism than he had imagined, which meant letting some mystics in. Moreover, Muhammad Iqbal's antisocialism then resonated with Smith, as well as with his American funders. Whereas he had previously decried idealism, before the end of the decade Smith argued that philosophy and "Sufism" (a term he used interchangeably with *mysticism*) were two potential sources of modern reform. As he later put it, the "intellectualism of the former and the humanism of the latter could provide important bases for reinterpretation."[27] According to McDonough, Smith's attempts to wrest modern meaning from between authentic universal faith and cultural traditions resulted in his turning to Iqbal anew. After Smith recruited her to McGill in 1953, the two spent years discussing Iqbal, his Persian and Urdu verses, and his theories of social change (the subjects of McDonough's dissertation). Iqbal held that Islamic reform facilitated social justice. "When Smith had turned away from Marxist thought and back to Iqbal," McDonough argued, "he had done so explicitly because he had come to realize that persons needed to be rooted in something bigger than themselves, a sense of goodness and justice as transcendent values."[28] Over the next decade, and partly following Iqbal's world-historical perspective and prescriptions for Islamic reform, Smith sought to establish programs for liberalizing ostensibly static Islamic law by infusing it with the creative impulses of Eastern mysticism. Although Iqbal had ultimately denounced Western influences, Smith and those he recruited to McGill believed that liberal education would equip Muslim intellectuals to produce indigenous reform.

■ LIBERALISM AND RELIGION: BETWEEN AMERICAN INSTITUTIONS AND INTERNATIONAL MODERNIZATION

During and after World War II, US foundations poured billions of dollars into developing area studies and cultural studies programs at universities around the world and into fostering societies suitable for cooperation with democracy and capitalism. Many of the academics first to teach Islam, Near Eastern, and Middle Eastern studies in the United States had trained in Europe and migrated to these foundation-financed institutes after World War II. Others settled in religious studies departments or divinity schools that were likewise primarily at private universities such as Harvard, Yale, Columbia, and Princeton and financed by the Ford, Carnegie, and Rockefeller foundations. Smith and Gibb were of a "generation of Orientalists" sympathetic to Islam and advocated Arab-friendly approaches to modernization.[29] Though neither were US citizens, both helped to shape US political and public opinion. Moreover, unlike Gibb (who often held that race determined culture and mindset—especially among Arabs), Smith did so while seeking to counter the effects of some US policies abroad.

In the early 1950s, foundation boards expanded their activities while simultaneously deflecting accusations of communist sympathies.[30] The 1953 *Rockefeller Foundation Annual Report*, for example, was submitted late, as Presidents Raymond Fosdick and Chester Barnard had been called before the Cox and Reece congressional committees of 1952 and 1953. In that report, incoming president Dean Rusk defended the organization's attempts to build a "world community" (somewhat subversive language in the era of McCarthy). Although the foundation granted funds to the United Nations and Brookings Institution, Rusk contended, it had no position "on such questions as World Government, Atlantic Union, the role of the United Nations, international trade policies, regulation of armaments, security alliances, and so forth... [but] has provided support for studies or for creative work in such fields as international economics, international law, comparative government, history, creative arts and the so called "area studies," i.e., studies which cut across cultural boundaries and establish a bridge of information and understanding despite differences in language, race, creed, or cultural tradition."[31] Despite Rusk's apolitical and almost humanitarian framing, the former assistant secretary of state for Far Eastern affairs under Truman had enduring concerns about "the totalitarian challenge to personal liberty and intellectual freedom [that] survived World War II in virulent form."[32] Moreover, he saw studies of Islam and Muslim-majority countries (particularly those with communist nationalist movements) as pivotal to Cold War modernization efforts.

In 1951, the Rockefeller Foundation granted Smith $214,800 to found the first North American center for studying modern Islam: the Institute of Islamic Studies at McGill University in Montreal.[33] According to Smith's assistant director, Smith had immediately and single-handedly proposed the institute to the university upon arriving at McGill, secured funding from the Rockefeller and Ford foundations, and began finding scholars to fill it.[34] While searching for scholars, Smith turned not to the Princeton center where he had trained (also financed by the Rockefeller Foundation) but to his earlier intellectual network. In the early 1950s, Gibb introduced Smith to the first Pakistani minister of education, Fazlur Rahman. Rahman had completed his dissertation on Islamic philosophy at Oxford. Not long after, Gibb left Oxford for Harvard, and Smith recruited Rahman to McGill.

Gibb accepted a post as director of the newly inaugurated Middle East Institute at Harvard the same year in which the Rockefeller Foundation broke all previous funding records. The foundation afforded Harvard's program its largest single disbursement of 1956 ($205,000) after trustees had decided to expand their efforts in Latin America, Asia, the Middle East, and Africa.[35] The year just prior, the foundation gave Smith's institute its largest single grant ever in the humanities—over half a million dollars—with the provision that income from the endowment be used to maintain the structure that made McGill unique: Muslim representation among the faculty and students.[36] Gibb and Smith collaborated on various Rockefeller- and Ford-funded projects in the 1950s and 1960s. In addition to introducing Smith and Rahman, Gibb later introduced Smith to one of his Harvard advisees: Seyyed Hossein Nasr. During and after their years at McGill, Rahman and Nasr presented specific (often contrasting) Indo-Persian Sufi traditions as the most authentic practices of Islam under modern conditions. Further, they made these traditions central to educational programs implemented in Pakistan and Iran, Harvard and Chicago, and elsewhere. Though disagreeing on multiple issues, Rahman and Nasr were like Smith in that both viewed Iqbal's reformism as instructive but incomplete. Iqbal's commentaries on how Islamic law, mysticism, and modernization fit between East and West, Persia and Arabia, and Sunni and Shi'i traditions animated their discussions for decades. Before detailing their disputes over mysticism and modernity, we must first understand Smith's vision for involving these well-connected scholars in the process of liberalizing Islam.

■ POSTSOCIALIST PROGRESS, ANTISECULAR CRITIQUE, AND SUFI-INSPIRED LIBERALISM IN THE MIDDLE EAST

Most Cold War modernizers working in government and private institutes viewed "traditional" religions as impeding economic privatization and political progress. They insisted on separating religion from politics and economics under ostensibly secular systems of democracy and capitalism.[37] Secular leaders and intellectuals in Muslim nations seemed to be pivotal business partners and promising allies for campaigns against the Soviet Union. However, not all leaders in newly independent nations were convinced that capitalism best fit Islamic practice and/or their national interests. Upon seizing power in a military coup, Gamal Abdel Nasser pursued socialism in Egypt, and communist factions had long been active in Iranian nationalist movements. Iranian Prime Minister Mohamad Mosaddeq's 1951 nationalization of the British–Iranian oil industry and Nasser's 1952 coup had underlined the possibility that the Middle East might go red. Following these events, Operation Ajax (the 1953 British–American overthrow of Mosaddeq and installation of the American-friendly shah) seemed proof that modernists could birth a secular and capitalist Middle East.

In his 1950 inaugural address as the chair of comparative religion at McGill, Smith detailed a different perspective on postwar "scientific" studies of religion than that of secular modernizers. The science of religion was a failure if not "useful to the religions in enabling them to function better," he argued. "Modernity" was the stage of development in which humans became capable of self-consciously directing religious evolution, and "only religions so liberated can, so far as I can sense, serve men who have entered into the heritage of modern knowledge."[38] Sufism could facilitate Islamic liberation, Smith maintained, by infusing orthodox *sharia* with liberal leanings. Like other postwar Orientalists immersed in the academic reorganization of methods among the social sciences, religious studies, and area studies, Smith attempted to connect the "big tradition" evident in Islamic texts to diverse local practices. He also sought to navigate between two dominant methods in the "science of religions": what he saw as the insufficiently historical phenomenology of scholars such as Mircea Eliade and Rudolph Otto and the overly secular historical sociology of Émile Durkheim and Max Weber. Meanwhile, Smith hoped to help Muslims reform Islam, achieve equitable independence, and avoid new imperial threats. In juggling these various commitments, he reworked Protestant Orientalist distinctions between "rigid" religion (embodied in static laws and institutions) and revitalized individual faith. Mapping this model onto Islam, Smith argued that "the distinction between external, formal authority and internal appreciation corresponds by and large to the dichotomy in historical development between Sunni and Sufi. It is true that the greatest Muslims have been Sufis.... Nonetheless, it is the law which has kept Islamic society together."[39]

This perspective constituted Smith's new point of departure, which he installed in programs at McGill and on which he elaborated in his writings. Smith revised and expanded his 1946 analysis with the help of specialists on Turkey (Niyazi Berkes), the Arab world (Gibb, then at Harvard, and not Hitti, whom Smith described in 1957 as an apologetic Arab nationalist), and South Asia (Rahman.) To this he added his Princeton dissertation detailing the insufficient modernization of orthodoxy at Cairo's Al-Azhar University and his 1951 retraction. In the resulting *Islam in Modern History*, Smith argued that modern conditions required a modern "world community."[40] Instead of a "social analysis" condemning mystical idealism, Smith contended that such endeavors required a greater measure of transcendence. Significantly, although he never again mentioned Macmurray, he also never abandoned his personalist understandings of religion or the racial and cultural models with which he charted historical development.

In working out his new approach, Smith sought a transformative source of religious commonality that did not create ahistorical phenomenological categories or reduce religion to mere reaction. During this time, he reaffirmed his faith in liberalism, the processes of history, and the practice of personalist faith. Smith explained that political independence allowed Muslims to assume responsibility for their own spiritual and social evolution. "The economic, political, social, cultural, and spiritual development on which [Muslim countries] are now embarked constitutes a history that is Islamic history in a renewed, full sense," he argued.[41] Muslim leaders *did* face the lasting impediments of imperialism and new challenges from an increasingly international capitalist economy. Nevertheless, their primary task in "catch[ing] up with 'lost centuries'" was ideological, not economic, and involved ensuring that religiosity evolved in ways conducive to individual and social reform: "The task might seem less major for those who wish to dichotomize life, keeping their ideals and their daily living in water-tight compartments. But it is not slight for a religion whose genius it is to apply its moral imperatives to day-to-day living, to wed the ultimate meaning of life to the society in which one participates, to seek justice in the midst of machines."[42]

For Smith, this genius for seeking justice must be wedded to humanist impulses and proper theological education, thus producing a socioreligious liberalism not found in the "cumulative traditions" of orthodoxies and institutions. "Westernizing secularists" threatened personal faith—the universal source of social transformation—by not recognizing that, unlike Western Christianity, Islam was not likely to be secular. Thus, secularists were little different from Christian missionaries, he contended, and ignored "basic moral problems" that secularism could not address. Responding to his colleagues who wanted Muslims to abandon Islam or to "relegate it to an unobtrusive corner of their living, and build their societies as liberal humanists," Smith asserted that "liberalism and humanism in the Muslim world, if they are to flourish at all, may perhaps be Islamic liberalism and Islamic humanism; or that in any case, some basis must be found for matters of this weight."[43]

As to the nature of liberalism, Smith never viewed it as conservatism's opposite. Rather, as he explained in 1946, "liberalism" had a deeper meaning that structured conservatism, as well, and "is permanently valid." This more universal principle was "the objective valuation of freedom, particularly in the individual human spirit."[44] At that time, Smith saw economically induced "reactionary" traditionalism, not secularism, as threatening Islamic evolution. However, the violence and disillusionment of Partition challenged Smith's hopes for creating a just and thriving Islamic state, as did the 1953 Pakistani street riots in which thousands of religious minorities were murdered when the new government failed to intervene. In his 1957 book, Smith maintained that Islamic liberalism could bring social justice. This time, he argued that conflicts involving ethnic, nationalist, and religious identities were not rooted in economics but in changing and *changeable* beliefs—a perspective that echoed Macmurray and one he later underlined in his 1963 opus, *The Meaning and End of Religion*: "In so far as such doctrines are correlative of such matters as Apartheid policy in South Africa or the 1947 Panjab massacres, they will, one might humbly suggest, *simply have to be modified*." Moreover, Smith reiterated what he began to argue in 1950: that the solution to fundamentally modern questions—"how to turn our nascent world society into a world community, on a group level; and on a personal level, how to find meaning in modern life"—was a religious one.[45]

In the late 1950s, Fazlur Rahman moved to McGill. Smith had previously described Rahman's work on Islamic education in Pakistan as "an effective illustration of a typical and true modern liberalism whose structure is fully Islamic."[46] At McGill, Rahman similarly sought to guide evolving Islamic thought and practice toward historical fulfillment. Iqbal, McDonough argues, had wanted to chronicle the intellectual history of the Qur'an, Sufism, and Islamic law within the context of world religious history and to "show how Muslim legal thinking had developed in the context of particular social, economic and political contexts." Rahman, she maintains, also tried to fulfill some of these intentions in his book *Islamic Methodology in History*.[47] Smith relied on Rahman's 1955 analysis to demonstrate that liberal modernization was legitimately Islamic and shared Iqbal's and Rahman's optimism about the role of properly reformed Muslim intellectuals in the future of the faith.[48] Perhaps most significantly, in my reading, Smith and Rahman also borrowed Iqbal's critique of unreformed mysticism.

During his own efforts to effect reform in India, Iqbal had argued that nationalism, atheistic socialism, and "the *medieval* technique of mysticism" were ineffective responses to the crises of modernity. In terms that resonated with Smith after Partition, Iqbal had contended that "religion, which in its higher manifestation is neither dogma, nor priesthood, nor ritual, can alone *ethically* prepare the modern man for the burden of great responsibility which the advancement of modern science necessarily involves. . . . It is only by a fresh vision of his origin and future, his when and whither, that man will eventually triumph over a society motivated by an inhuman competition and a civilization which has lost its spiritual unity by its inner conflict of religious and political values."[49]

Smith still viewed Sufis as mostly stressing "the individual rather than society, the eternal rather than the historical," and as generally avoiding "investments in political processes." During the decline of Islamic civilization, he argued, socially engaged and philosophically sophisticated Sufis had devolved into superstitiously irrational practices (something Iqbal had asserted and Rahman echoed in 1970; significantly, though subscribing to the "decline" thesis, they did not cite Sufis as the cause of it).[50] Further, Smith still regarded Iqbal as the perplexing "Sufi who attacked Sufism, and perhaps the liberal who attacked liberalism," and Rahman likewise blamed Iqbal for the failure of Indian modernization.[51] Nevertheless, both agreed with Iqbal that dynamic, engaged mysticism and modern education would enable shari'a reform.

■ MODERNIZING THE "MYSTIC" AND "MIDDLE" EASTS: INDO-PERSIAN CREATIVITY, RIGID ARAB RELIGION

According to Smith, modern Islamic liberalism could indigenously develop any-where. Nevertheless, after studying debates at Al-Azhar and witnessing the 1956 Suez Canal crisis, he did not think it likely to emerge among Arabs. This Semitic–Aryan distinction proved crucial to uniting various elites (including Nasr) around the pivot of engaged mysticism and antisecular critique. Though partial to Persian and South Asian Sufisms, Smith never used the word *Aryan*. Rocked by the horrors of Nazism, he had condemned Hitler and fascism in 1946 and argued against ethnic or religious communalism in favor of socialist struggle. Yet, like Macmurray and the philologists with whom he conducted his undergraduate and graduate studies, Smith attributed Muslim–Christian differences to their separate origins in Palestinian and Greco-Roman cultures. He further argued that Greek thought, while instrumental in inculcating liberalism and humanitarianism in Christians, had little impact on Islam. Smith warned against growing antirationalist and anti-Sufi movements, ones he viewed as rooted in Arab reactions to imperialism and (citing Rahman) in Wahhabism. These movements were tragic, he wrote, in that "every major Islamic reformer of the modern age showed deep Sufi influence."

Smith also conjectured about the move of Islamic authority away from Arab lands to South Asia, where, he believed, he saw the emergence of an indigenous Islamic liberalism that was not enslaved to law and tradition.[52] For Smith, South Asian liber-alism came not from the "medieval mysticism" Iqbal described as "otherworldly" but from a dynamic, rational, reformed practice Rahman called "neo-Sufism." These assumptions influenced which partners Smith deemed appropriate for moderniza-tion projects, structured his attempts to move studies of modern Islam away from the Middle East and toward South Asia,[53] and conditioned the political and cultural history through which Indo-Persian Sufisms began to dominate some Americans' understandings of Islamic modernism and, later, Islamic "moderation."

Smith and Rahman reworked older Orientalist categories in their reformist and modernizing efforts at McGill. Neither saw esoteric Indo-Persian Shi'i traditions as orthodox, no matter their appeal to American progressives or Pakistani bourgeois. Middle-class liberals who invested in such otherworldly mysticism forsook rigid formalism, they acknowledged, but in the 1953 Pakistani uprisings had no conceptual and practical framework to restrain them from performing horrific violence. Meanwhile, observant Muslims adapted Islamic law, but without the creative vision necessary for effecting true self-conscious reform.[54] For them, this imbalance explained Maulana Maududi's Pakistani Jama'ati Islaami movement, which the two found similar to the Muslim Brotherhood "among the Arabs."[55] Although not otherworldly, such uninspired scholars and lay leaders made Islam into a social and political system of absolute answers to modern questions instead of viewing it as "a faith in which God provides mankind anew each morning the riches whereby it may answer them."[56] Rahman further elaborated on the insufficient efforts of previous Indian modernists. Early reformers had been "adaptive, not creative," while second-generation modernists were too Westernizing and thus "drove Modernism in terms of modern social-moral values into the lap of conservative *anti-liberalism*." Citing Gibb and Smith, Rahman explained the "enigma" of how Iqbal's modernist intentions, activism, and anticolonialism had produced a conservative apologetics. Though "intellectually a Modernist," Iqbal was "ethically a revivalist" who condemned Westernism in such strong terms that he left no room for reformation. If "the ethos of Pakistan is to survive, let alone prosper and bear fruit, the term 'Islamic Republic' must be given a real content," Rahman asserted, "or else be swallowed up in all sorts of extremes—Revivalism, Communism, etc.— it is impossible to predict which of them may be successful."[57] The solution for both scholars: a rational and activist Sufism that produced the liberal impulses necessary to reforming Islamic law.[58]

While Smith and Rahman discussed the future of Islamic modernism in Pakistan, Nasr abandoned his hopes for secular modern progress in Iran. Raised partly in McCarthy's America and disillusioned by his studies at MIT and Harvard, Nasr found solace in a private Boston library in the 1950s. There he encountered English-, French-, and German-language works on antimodern Traditionalism and Perennialism (loosely: a neo-Platonic philosophy according to which all religions express one primordial truth). Initially interested in neo-Vedantic theosophy, Nasr also discovered early twentieth-century Europeans' writings on Indo-Persian traditions and Islamic mysticism. As Nasr recounts, he had thus "been guided by the grace of Heaven to the eternal *sophia* of which Islamic wisdom is one of the most universal and vital embodiments."[59] Despite his proclaimed antimodernism, Nasr became part of Smith's modernizing network. These interlinking politics of mysticism and modernization illuminate how contemporary, and sometimes contradictory, notions of "moderate" liberal mysticism came to characterize US policy and popular culture.

■ MODERNIZED MYSTICISM AND POLITICAL POWER: EDUCATION REFORM IN NORTH AMERICA, PAKISTAN, AND IRAN

In the tenth year of the McGill Institute of Islamic Studies, Smith detailed its "unique" and "fundamental significance" as the "very special endeavour to train a cadre of new students in Islamics who have learned to integrate with their awareness of their religious tradition the new conception of intellectual inquiry…the novel notion that true knowledge of Islam lies in the future, not in the past. The dynamic consequence of this idea will, we believe, ramify through the Muslim world for the next fifty years."[60]

Working with various university faculty, administrators, ambassadors, and heads of state, McGill colleagues recruited Muslim scholars to ensure such transformations. An early experiment was the Rockefeller-funded Group on Pakistan Studies, which met for the first time at McGill in October 1956.[61] Those assembled regarded Islamic education as the primary front of development and had thus invited Ishtiaq Husain Qureshi, the second Pakistani minister of education, who

was then at Columbia University, to attend. The group unanimously elected Smith
to chair the meetings. However, finding that his approach did not match the
US-dominated interests of other representatives, Smith resigned after the first
one.[62] Soon thereafter, Smith and his colleagues began working directly with
Muslim heads of state. In 1961, Smith sent a letter to Pakistani president General
Ayub Khan and urged him to support transforming the Colombo Plan for
Cooperative Economic and Social Development from "a one-way street of
'assistance' and...imbalanced programme merely of technology" into "a true collaboration between peoples in both technical and in more profoundly human
affairs."[63] Not long after, Smith allowed Fazlur Rahman and Isma'il al-Faruqi leave
from McGill so as to develop a "daughter" institution in Pakistan with Qureshi. In
the meantime, he turned his attention to Iran.

During his years at McGill, Smith became interested in Iqbal's thoughts on
Persian civilization and Zoroaster's and Mani's influences on humankind's
global religious history. Although most romantic idealists and Orientalists considered India a spiritual paradise throughout the nineteenth and twentieth centuries, the identity of Persia/Iran was ambiguous. During the twentieth century,
it was construed as both Indo-European and Islamic, part of the Mystic East
and the rigid Middle East. Ernst Renan had rendered philological distinctions
between rational "Aryan" or "Indo-European" sociolinguistic groups and the
less creative "Semitic mind" of dogmatic Palestinians a science. For him, as for
Goethe, Persian Sufism was an "Aryan Islam" that exemplified a simultaneously
aesthetic and rational ideal. Renan's colleagues, Max Müller and Robertson
Smith, attempted to establish links between the Indo and European sides of
Aryanism against the foil of Semitic rigidity.[64] These scholars later influenced
Iqbal, who had undertaken graduate work at Cambridge under the direction of
Thomas Arnold (a student of Robertson Smith, follower of Max Müller, and
mentor to H. A. R. Gibb), as well as under E. Browne and R. A. Nicholson, who
viewed Persian Sufism as a primary factor in Islamic cultural advancement.
Iqbal subsequently moved to Munich, where he wrote a dissertation entitled
"The Development of Metaphysics in Persia."[65] Though enamored of German
philosophy, Goethe's poetry, romantic idealizations of Eastern spirituality, and
world-historical models, Iqbal reversed his opinions about the value of both
Persian mysticism and Western influences upon his return to politically fraught
India. For his part, Smith published his research on Persian traditions, Islam,
and the world history of religion (which he juxtaposed to personalist faith) in
1963. Smith did not mention Macmurray or Iqbal by name in that treatise but
did refer his readers to his 1957 discussion of Indo-Persian Sufi creativity and
rigid Arab apologetics. Meanwhile, he sought opportunities to extend McGill's
educational and modernizing influence in the progressively secularizing nation
of Iran.

In 1958, when Smith was en route from the International Islamic Colloquium
in Lahore, Tehran University hosted him as a visiting lecturer. Nasr had earned his
doctorate from Harvard that year and had just joined the faculty at Tehran
University (where his father, onetime Iranian minister of education, had been dean
of the Faculty of Humanities) when Smith arrived. The two then met many times

in India and Pakistan over the years and shared their skepticisms of secular technological rationalism. In the meantime, Nasr began attending meetings on Shi'i philosophy involving French Islamicist Henry Corbin and the noted Iranian philosopher and religious leader Sayyid Muhammad Husayn Tabataba'i, whose works further transformed Nasr's ideas. Nasr incorporated Corbin's analysis of Shi'ism into his larger model of how a perennially emerging universal truth united the world's various religious traditions. At a 1961 meeting of the World Congress of Orientalism, Nasr recounted, Smith had been extremely interested in these attempts to "revive later Islamic philosophy" and in Nasr's "view of other religions. We had debates and discussions all the time about what you call, in a sense, a theology of world religions."[66]

In 1962 Nasr delivered a series of lectures as the first visiting professor at Harvard's Center for the Study of World Religions (then, on Smith's suggestion, directed by former McGill professor of divinity Robert Slater).[67] Nasr visited Smith in Montreal that year and there met Japanese scholar Toshihiko Izutsu, with whom he later utilized Corbin's work to explicate the mystical wisdom of Ibn 'Arabi and his Persian commentator, Mulla Sadra. According to one Harvard scholar of medieval Arabic and Islamic political thought, Corbin's "reorientaliz[ing]" thought convinced "a whole generation of Iranian intellectuals" that Persian culture supplied unrefined Arab Islam with wisdom, mysticism, and spirituality.[68] For his part, Smith appreciated Nasr's antisecularist, antisocialist, shari'a-observant perspective, if not the extent of his idealism. Additionally, while seeking to reform Islamic education in Iran, Nasr maintained close connections with the Pakistani Philosophical Congress and several figures in the Ministry of Education (including Rahman and al-Faruqi).[69] Between 1958 and 1978, Nasr traveled to Pakistan over twenty times and delivered the celebrated Iqbal Lecture there in 1966—just two years after Smith had spoken in the same capacity.[70] Neither Smith nor Rahman shared Nasr's professed Traditionalism or antimodernism. Nevertheless, they likely read Nasr's commitments to Sufism and shari'a, Islamic revivification, and educational reform as precisely the kind of modern engaged mysticism needed to combat secularism and reactionary apologetics. This was especially likely in that Iqbal's University of Munich doctoral dissertation had been the first academic treatise to combine European Enlightenment philosophy, Persian Sufi traditions, and Islamic metaphysics for western audiences, and Nasr's *Three Muslim Sages* (which grew out of his 1962 Harvard lectures) was the second.

Although some relationships among these intellectuals solidified during the tumult of the 1960s, others changed. In 1964, Smith assumed directorship of the Harvard Center and left the directorial duties at McGill to Charles Adams. Nasr returned to Harvard soon after for a second appointment as a visiting professor, whereupon Smith held an honorary banquet and introduced him to Huston Smith. In the 1950s, W. C. Smith considered Huston Smith's approach to be closest to his own.[71] Thereafter, however, Nasr converted the latter to the Traditionalist mysticism and Perennialist perspective with which W. C. Smith disagreed. Nasr also deepened his connections with McGill scholars in the 1960s and 1970s, as both McGill and Harvard added faculty specializing in Persian and South Asian traditions. During the violent opposition to Khan's administration in Pakistan, Rahman returned to the United States and soon thereafter took a position at the University of Chicago, where he worked on Ford-funded projects and advised the US State Department.[72] Meanwhile, Hermann Landolt joined the McGill faculty in 1964 following his studies with Henry Corbin at the Sorbonne and, along with Nasr and Izutsu (whose philological work informed Smith's notion of Islamic "faith"), helped to found the Tehran branch of the McGill Institute in 1969.[73] Not long after, Nasr and Corbin established the Imperial Iranian Academy of Philosophy under the patronage of the Pahlavi empress. The imperial government had chartered the Iranian Academy to construct a *pre-Islamic* nationalist history. Nevertheless, as evident in the volume from McGill's jointly funded Canadian–Iranian conference, *Iranian Civilization and Culture: Essays in Honour of the 2,500th Anniversary of the Founding of the Persian Empire,*[74] Nasr and others devoted their work to Shi'ism, Sufism, and theosophy.

During the 1970s, Nasr's connections to the Iranian government intensified. One scholar described this relationship as "regime religiosity," wherein the monarchy quieted claims to a pre-Islamic heritage so as to combat the influence of Ayatollah Khomeini.[75] For their part, Nasr and his McGill colleagues endeavored to convince the monarchy and secular nationalists that Islam was authentically Persian. Nasr later served as director of the Iranian Academy, working alongside Corbin and Izutsu, and incorporated Corbin's analyses of Iranian Shi'ism into his 1972 *Sufi Essays* and 1975 English translation of Tabataba'i's *Shi'ite Islam.*[76] In contrast to Khomeini's supporters— many of whom were small business owners alienated by the shah's support of American corporations—Nasr, Corbin, Izutsu, and Landolt further argued that Persian Islam was specifically mystical. Simultaneously, Nasr sought to prove that Shi'ism was the source of both Islamic orthodoxy and authentic mysticism.

Nasr published his translation of and commentary on *Shi'ite Islam* at a pivotal moment when few Americans (academic, political, or otherwise) knew much about Shi'ism. By framing rational mysticism *as* Eastern and as specifically Shi'i, Nasr and his colleagues participated in defining the nature of Oriental spirituality, of authentic Islam, and of the character of the Iranian state. In so doing, they challenged modernizers' attempts to associate Persian traditions with rigid Arab religion and simultaneously contested nationalist efforts to build a state around secularism or mythologized pre-Islamic Zoroastrianism. By 1977, Nasr was serving as the Empress Farah's private secretary. He was in London on related business when the revolution began. The only prominent student of Tabataba'i to leave Iran during that time, Nasr has not returned. His published works during the 1970s proved invaluable for secular modernizers and other figures attempting to understand Shi'i traditions and Iran, and his popular and academic writings since then— though less political—remain important for reinforcing the image of Indo-Persian mysticism as moderate Islam.

■ EXPERIMENTS ALTERED: REVOLUTIONARY MYSTICISM
AND THE ROADS NOT TAKEN

Following the revolution, several analysts attempted to explain why modernization failed in Iran's pro-business, non-Arab environment. In 1980, historian
Richard Bulliet reviewed several of these works in an essay intended for the *New
York Review of Books* and argued that most overemphasized the influence of
Ayatollah Khomeini and/or the shah. Further, by insisting that modernity did away
with religion, secular modernists created the problem of explaining its return, he
noted, and thus read Iranian movements as "crypto-Communism" or simple
nationalism. Bulliet contended that religion had never gone anywhere. Rather,
many Iranian Muslims had sought to create a more "creatively modern" and "creatively humane" state than that of the secular shah. One such pivotal figure ignored
by 1980s political analysts, he argued, was sociologist 'Ali Shari'ati (1933–77). The
editor who commissioned Bulliet's essay returned it unpublished. All who read the
piece, he explained, found simply "baffling" Bulliet's idea that Iranian Muslims
might attempt to be creatively modern or humane.[77]

Shari'ati and Nasr were colleagues in Iran, and Bulliet was one of the first, but
not the last, to note the former's significance. In a memorial lecture published
nearly fifty years after Smith's *Islam in Modern History*, Francis Robinson pointed
to Shari'ati as the kind of reformer Smith had sought in 1957. For Smith, Shari'ati,
and Iqbal, Robinson argued, Islam was modern, liberal, and fundamentally
concerned with "social justice."[78] Shari'ati had turned to Sufism after working in
Paris with Louis Massignon, Corbin's predecessor and another sympathetic
Orientalist.[79] His and Nasr's works framed Persian mysticism as authentic universal
religion and formed part of a centuries-long "dialogic interaction" among South
Asian, European, Arab, and North American nations through which Iranian
national identity was contested.[80] However, in contrast to Shari'ati, whose work in
Paris with anti-imperialist "third world intellectuals" and antiestablishment Iranian
reformers garnered him prison time in Tehran, Nasr found monarchy to be an
ideal form of governance and maintained that elite practices of mysticism upheld
the true human economy.[81] The same year that Shari'ati returned to Iran, Smith left
McGill for Harvard and left the institute to Adams. After the shah closed the
Hosseini-ye Ershad (where Nasr and Shari'ati once taught together), Shari'ati lost
his institutional affiliation, while Nasr held positions as vice-chancellor at Tehran
University and as director of the Imperial Academy.

Shari'ati's specifically modernist and anti-imperialist perspective, as expressed in
his lecture "Mysticism, Equality, and Freedom," seems in many ways closer to those
of early McGill scholars than does Nasr's perspective.[82] Nevertheless, Nasr's individualist Traditionalism and institutional connections better fit some modernists'
models of Islamic reformation than did Shari'ati's modern liberal (but anticapitalist)
mysticism. Such reversals demonstrate that ideas about religiosity are interconnected
with changing assumptions about modernity, politics, and economics, revealing the
inherent instability of these categories. Nasr's "antimodern" educational reforms
rarely focused on matters crucial to Smith and Rahman personal liberty and economic

distribution. In contrast, Shari'ati addressed precisely those issues. Further, Nasr held that the pious practices of an elite group could render an entire community ethical. This kind of social division of labor stood in stark contrast to the transformative interpersonal practice Smith envisioned. Just as Shari'ati started to emphasize the interdependence of "mysticism, [socialist] equality, and freedom," however, Smith traded his historical materialism and revolutionary politics for a revolutionary personalism premised on faith. At Harvard, Smith again sought to establish that engaged Indo-Persian Sufisms were authentic and liberatory *practices* of Islam. However, the specialists he invited to assist with this project ultimately focused less than Smith did on social transformation, and more on transcendent ideals.

■ (NEO)LIBERAL MYSTICISM IN NORTH AMERICA: ISLAM IN THE AGE OF AQUARIUS

During his years in the United States, Smith continued to pursue Iqbal's and Macmurray's strategies of transforming society by transforming individual faith, though sometimes with unanticipated consequences. The 1958 National Defense Education Act funded studies of religion and politics in the Middle East and South Asia and facilitated the growing popularity of Indo-Persian mysticisms. Shortly thereafter, changes in immigration legislation allowed thousands of Muslims from previously barred "Asiatic" countries (including South Asia and the Middle East) entrance to the United States. In subsequent years, studies of Islamic thought moved away from the political and economic concerns of social sciences and area studies networks to the religious studies programs largely led by American scholar-practitioners and focused on traditions most attractive to the 1970s seeker generation.[83] While still largely critical of such philosophical idealism and phenomenological approaches to religious studies, Smith continued his occasional collaborations with Nasr and his colleagues—particularly those familiar with Muhammad Iqbal.

In 1965, Smith invited Annemarie Schimmel (author of *Gabriel's Wing: A Study into the Religious Ideas of Sir Muhammad Iqbal*) to join the Harvard faculty.[84] Nasr, Schimmel's friend and colleague, recommended that Smith transform an endowment earmarked for translating Indo-Pakistani Islamic poetry into a permanent position for her. According to Nasr, Smith agreed and arranged with the Harvard president and relevant academic deans to bring Schimmel to the United States for one semester each year. Although Schimmel initially declined Smith's invitation, she eventually accepted the position as Harvard's first chair of Indo-Muslim culture and after 1970 alternated between Cambridge and Lahore. At Harvard, Schimmel continued to write on Islam in South Asia, translate works of poetry, and use Protestant-inflected categories of mysticism in her analyses. In 1975, Schimmel published what became her most famous book: *Mystical Dimensions of Islam*.[85] Later, she noted the work of Smith, Iqbal, Nasr, and Corbin in her coedited volume on the contribution of "Abrahamic" religions to a world beset by secular modernism.[86]

As during his earlier sojourn in the United States, Smith reformulated his commitments to liberalism in the 1960s. He continued to critique communism but by 1963 had mainly relegated liberal commentary to his footnotes. Like Reinhold

Niebuhr, Smith was increasingly critical of US foreign policy and had chided Eisenhower's secretary of defense, John Foster Dulles. Niebuhr had viewed Dulles as hijacking American anticommunist liberalism and transforming it into a "holy war." Smith agreed but specifically blamed Dulles's inflammatory foreign policy on his Calvinist lack of appreciation for human freedom.[87] In 1973, Smith moved to Canada to begin a program in comparative religions at Dalhousie University. When he returned to Harvard in 1978, the academic and popular studies of Sufism there involved less social commentary and more connections to "the New Age." Nasr and Schimmel worked somewhat separately from Smith, who was then at the Center for World Religions.[88] Both elaborated on the works of Corbin and Sufi Perennialist Frithjof Schuon and served with other Traditionalist scholars on the editorial board of Fons Vitae, a publishing house dedicated to disseminating works on idealist philosophy, Sufism, and the essential commonality of all religions. During that time, Schimmel also wrote the preface for an American edition of Schuon's *Understanding Islam*, in which she compared Schuon's work with "the beautiful lines of the Indo-Muslim poet philosopher, Muhammad Iqbal."[89]

After the revolution, Nasr and Smith saw each other frequently at conferences and other events but never again met privately. Recalling what he described as their last personal meeting in early 1978, before events in Iran brought questions about Shi'i traditions into American popular awareness, Nasr described Smith as "very quiet and very pensive about what was going to happen as growing segments of the population resisted the Shah's regime." When asked about Smith's view of Shari'ati, Nasr then recounted that he had later visited Smith again at home in autumn 1978. Though "the Iranian Revolution was fully ablaze [and] the name of Shari'ati was being discussed so much, he never talked to me about him," Nasr maintained. Nasr acknowledged that Smith was attracted to his work because it dealt with Sufism but also suggested that the two rarely discussed Iqbal due to his own critical view of "modernist Islamic so-called reformers." In any case, Nasr and Smith's differences were obvious by then.

Nasr did not divulge the contents of their discussions about Iran but described his primary disagreements with the elder scholar as rooted in "the *process* whereby you could reassert the reality of Islamic thought in a contemporary setting." According to Nasr, "He thought in terms of some form of modernization. I thought in terms of revitalization, which is something quite different." This difference became increasingly clear as Nasr's views—including his opinions of Iqbal—developed through his work with Corbin and Schuon. Nasr asserted that Iqbal "was not really an *Islamic* philosopher." Rather, he was "deeply influenced by nineteenth-century and twentieth-century European philosophy, by Nietzsche and by neo-Hegelianism, and by things like that. Now, I stand at the other side. I'm totally opposed to these kinds of philosophies. I think they miss out on what is fundamental in philosophy, which is a vision of *reality* in its traditional sense. And I myself feel I belong to the Islamic philosophical tradition, which is a continuous tradition.... But Iqbal's greatest contribution, I think, to Islam was his poetry inspired by Sufism." Later, Nasr asserted that Smith viewed him, in stark contrast to Iqbal, as "a young philosopher, who was deeply Islamic, never missed a prayer, at the same time knew more about Kant and Hegel than he did, and who was a sort of living example of Islamic thought. That's what he had been looking for all the time. And so although I opposed many of his theses about Iqbal, that didn't really matter to him."

Nasr is likely right in his impressions, given that Smith initially saw him as a rational mystic engaged in educational reform, and as combining the philosophical humanism of the West with Islam. Over time, however, and as Nasr increasingly described Sufi, Shi'i, and Sunni Islam as rooted in the same eternal essence detailed by Islamic philosophers and neo-Platonists, those connections could not hold. In contrast to Smith and Rahman's evolved neo-Sufism, Nasr elucidated the ways in which Persian Shi'i mysticism was the ultimate phenomenological expression of primordial religious truth. Huston Smith later defended Nasr's approach against the criticism of their older mentor and others who, he argued, misunderstood Nasr's "unity of religions" as denying history: "[Nasr] is told that he should shift away from claims to universality so as to take more seriously the social, interactive dimension of the lived religious or philosophical metaphor. In Wilfred Cantwell Smith's wording of this criticism, 'the historian must stand guard against a vitiation of man's *actual* religious living by enthusiasts for emaciating abstractions.'"[90]

Unlike Nasr, but like Macmurray, W. C. Smith was wary of combining idealist abstractions with American liberal projects. On December 11, 1979 (a month into the hostage crisis and the same year that Smith served as the president of the Middle East Studies Association), he commented on the situation for the *New York Times*: "When the Shah's regime came to power, it started off by being a liberal, progressive, modern sort and the West supported it. But it gradually shifted to becoming autocratic, tyrannical, oppressive. And the Western liberal world, most particularly the countries that supported the Shah and trained his Savak, taught them how to torture their own people and so on. The young students of Khomeini sense that the Western liberals are the people who backed those who crush us."[91] While Smith criticized such American enterprises, Nasr developed closer connections to American liberal and neoliberal networks. In 1984, at the request of friends at the American Enterprise Institute, Nasr wrote the preface to *A Muslim's Reflection on Democratic Capitalism* (Muhammad Abdul-Rauf's 1979 response to Michael Novak's *The Spirit of Democratic Capitalism*). Therein, he argued that Islam supported capitalism, not socialist nationalism or state limits on personal wealth.[92]

* * *

The idealizations of Indo-Persian Sufisms as modern and moderate Islam discussed here were rooted in both idealist and materialist philosophies of race, culture, and religion. They were structured into strategic programs and attained an aura of factuality as Americans pursued political and economic interests in the wake of Partition, during continuing turmoil in Palestine, and after the Iranian Revolution. In the process of these developments, the natures of Pakistan, Iran, Shi'ism, and modern Islam were caught between changing images of the rigid "Middle" and enlightened "Mystic" Easts. Meanwhile the economic and political aspects of these designations receded from view. Such idealizations maintain their sway in the United States, as the picture of a Pakistani dervish and provocative title on the December 2008 cover of *Smithsonian* magazine, among other things, attest. "The Sufi Question," it reads: "Can the joyous Muslim movement counter the forces of radical extremism?"

Some American Sufis concerned about domestic and foreign policies under the "War on Terror" hesitate to contest these problematic generalizations and the U.S. strategies built in light of them for fear of being labeled political— a term some reserve for their "fundamentalist" opponents.[93] These dynamics derive not simply from reactions to September 11th or from a renewed 1960s counterculture, but from the Cold War politics charted above and the colonial framings on which they rested.

A few scholars *have* questioned narratives of engaged liberal mysticism. "With the greatest respect," R. S. O'Fahey and Bernd Radtke recently offered, "one cannot but wonder whether Fazlur Rahman, as a Muslim with modernist views of his own, found what he sought in neo-Sufism, a 'rational mysticism' suitable for the eighteenth century and beyond."[94] They challenged the evidence for universal neo-Sufism against narratives derived from French colonial encounters in North Africa but failed to notice how Rahman, Schimmel, and Smith created various models of liberal engaged mysticism to make sense of British colonial categories, of materialist philosophical debates, and of their work in South Asia and understandings of Iqbal. Moreover, O'Fahey and Radtke failed to recognize the analytic position that, despite their different geographical foci, they and Rahman shared: defining Islamic traditions in terms of "liberation."

At the turn of the new millennium, Smith and others (including Adams and Nasr) contributed to a memorial volume for Toshihiko Izutsu. In his piece, Smith again attempted to account for what happened in Iran. Modernization and liberalism had not failed, he contended; Westernization had. Smith cited Western imperialism and reactionary traditionalist "resurgence" (like the Arab apologetics he described in 1957) as the enemy of authentic Islamic liberalism. Moreover, he again decried the "Western secular liberalism" of the shah, who had allied himself with US policies and later become a "brutal dictator." Significantly, in closing, Smith denied that popular narratives about Islamic fundamentalism and Islamic fascism made sense. Echoing Macmurray, Smith declared that "fascism was something that *we* did . . . we in the West."[95]

■ CONCLUSION: LIBERALISMS, MYSTICISMS,
AND THE THEATER OF COMPARATIVE RELIGION

Following the publication of his 1963 opus, *The Meaning and End of Religion*, W. C. Smith became better known as the scholar to first challenge the universality of "religion." Many of Smith's colleagues saw him as an anti-Orientalist avant la lettre, and multiple aspects of Smith's anti-essentialist work remain important to religious studies and Islamic studies. Still, Smith's later work on world theology reconstituted the idealist cultural frameworks he had used in earlier attempts to modernize Islam—ones that derived from political claims to rational modernity mapped onto geographic space. Although McDonough argues that Smith abandoned notions of historical progress when he abandoned Marxism, Smith's enduring commitment to world-historical "process" (something Iqbal shared) seems to contradict this.[96] Like Niebuhr, the "realist" critic of idealism and US foreign policy, Smith was chastened by his experiences with American modernizers and used the words *liberalism* and *modernization* cautiously in the 1960s and after. Nevertheless, Smith continued to narrate the process of history and unfolding of liberal personalist ethics in terms of racial-cultural traits: Semitic rigidity, Indo-Persian flexibility, and the dialectical synthesis of both. Thus, his and Nasr's different approaches converged in their projects to establish rational Indo-Persian mysticism as an ideal practice of Islam. These intersections helped to fix the ostensible natures of Indians, Persians, and Arabs against the standard of a West that both agreed was (for better or worse) modern and liberal.

In a 2001 essay, Talal Asad examined Smith's 1963 analysis and some of his underlying assumptions. He attributed Smith's static understanding of Islamic law and failure to account for the reciprocal relationship between practice and faith to Smith's "missionary perspective" (a combination of his "methodological individualism" and pietistic reading). Notably, Asad still finds that Smith's antiessentialism and recognition of human interdependence make the text "indispensable reading for any student of comparative religion."[97] Without attending to Smith's materialist background and philosophy of ethics, however, Asad misses how Smith's efforts to cultivate human interdependence worldwide originated from and intensified his hope to cultivate antisecular liberal personalism. For Smith, as for Macmurray before him, individualism is antithetical to personalism: a transformative practice of faith that requires intertwining separate subjectivities in a way that renders absolute autonomy— and otherworldly mysticism—impossible. Perhaps more important, though, Asad finds Smith to be inattentive to secularism, which partly functions to "define 'religions' in the plural as a species of (non-rational) belief." Asad maintains that "religious" persons may share some of the fundamental assumptions of secularism: namely, that the scientific method produces overlapping confirmations about the nature of the world and that "the knowledge gained from these disciplines together support an enlightened morality."[98] Though Smith rejected secularist goals, such secularist assumptions did structure his methods for modernizing and moderating otherworldly Sufis and illiberal Arabs and/or creating a "world community" that involved Islam.

Over the course of his career, W. C. Smith increasingly challenged the notion that empirical research was empty of metaphysical presuppositions and even argued that "Westernizing secularists" had turned out to be idealists. Moreover, he counted himself among transcendental idealists toward the end of his life, largely to oppose secularism, atheist humanism, and scientific objectivity—all of which he saw as equally idealist metaphysical positions.[99] Eventually, Smith also decided that mystics were perennially most adept at the visionary task of imagining world community.[100] It was perhaps for this reason that Jacques Waardenburg credited him, in addition to Corbin and Massignon, with "open[ing] up dimensions of mystical experience, Gnostic spirituality, and *personalistic* faith in Islam."[101]

Asad's insistence that scholars must investigate "the construction of specific historical narratives" on which generalizations are made is critical for religious studies. Perhaps more salient for Smith's 1963 and 1957 works and those of his colleagues, though, is Asad's earlier essay, "The Idea of an Anthropology of Islam."[102] In this work, Asad also argues against particular narrative tropes—specifically those that portray ideology as socially deterministic and dramatize the differences between Islamic practices in narratives about "big" (centralized law) and "little" (local Sufi) traditions. As another scholar implied, the mental gymnastics involved in creating rational, reformed mysticism in modernist terms are necessary only within the modernist, Protestant, Orientalist logic from which tropes of individualist, "other-worldly" mysticism derived.[103]

I conclude by suggesting that, in addition to investigating narratives about religion, scholars might also investigate dramatized narratives about liberalisms and mysticisms. While some contemporary academics argue that the category of mysticism has been dismantled in the academy, others echo twentieth-century philosophers who feared that mysticism can cause an illiberal and anti-ethical slide toward fascism.[104] Smith and some of his colleagues shared such fears, which is why several of them emphasized ethics and avoided mysticism—except for a modern, rationalized model of reform. In the Cold War intersection of multinational strategic interests and Orientalist knowledges discussed here, various (often conflicting) liberalisms and mysticisms materialized. Whatever else they might also be, liberalism, mysticism, and modernity were and are among a host of flexible categories enshrined, altered, and rendered real in various academic, political, and economic projects. Not only did the concepts discussed here emerge through specific contextual developments, they came—through contested political deployments—to form philosophical categories, racial frameworks, and strategic assumptions on which later projects were built. Far from constituting objective facts on which to base policy or general elements of an amorphous social imaginary, these contingent constructs continue to change the warp and woof of global engagements and the building *and* crossing of boundaries in specific and unpredictable ways.

■ NOTES

Thanks go to Shazia Ahmad and Salwa Ferahian for assistance with archives at McGill University and to Marcia Hermansen, Hossein Kamaly, and the *Secularism and Religion-Making* editors for many helpful comments. I owe Amir Hussain special thanks for his assistance with the Wilfred Cantwell Smith papers and for sharing his memories of Smith. Any flaws within are most certainly my own.

1. W. J. Colville, *Universal-Spiritualism: Spirit Communion in All Ages among All Nations* (New York: R. F. Fenno and Co., 1906), 206. My thanks go to Erika Dyson for this reference. Timothy Marr examines pre-twentieth-century depictions of Islam in *The Cultural Roots of American Islamicism* (New York: Cambridge University Press, 2006).

2. William James, *The Varieties of Religious Experience* (Scotts Valley, CA: IAP Press, 2009), 232–33.

3. Jane Perlez, "A Journey to and from the Heart of Radical Islam in Britain," the *New York Times*, June 2, 2007; Waleed Ziad, "In Pakistan, Islam Needs Democracy," the *New York Times*, February 16, 2008; Kira Salak, "Iran: Travels Hostile Territory," *National Geographic Adventure*, August 2007; Don Belt, "Struggle for the Soul of Pakistan," *National Geographic*, September 2007.

4. Huston Smith, "Nasr's Defense of the Perennial Philosophy," in *The Philosophy of Seyyed Hossein Nasr*, ed. Lewis E. Hahn, Randall E. Auxier, and Lucian W. Stone (Chicago: Open Court, 2001), 3–85.

5. *Morning Edition*, National Public Radio, September 28, 2007.

6. Wade Clark Roof, *Spiritual Marketplace: Baby Boomers and the Remaking of American Religion* (Princeton, NJ: Princeton University Press, 1999), 189, 139.

7. Leigh Eric Schmidt, "Cosmopolitan Piety: Sympathy, Comparative Religions, and Nineteenth-Century Liberalism," in *Practicing Protestants: Histories of Christian Life in America, 1630–1965* Laurie F. Maffly, Leigh E. Schmidt, and Mark Valerie (Baltimore: Johns Hopkins University Press, 2006), 200; and (on Timothy Leary) Leigh E. Schmidt, *Restless Souls: The Making of American Spirituality* (San Francisco: HarperSanFrancisco, 2005), 251–54. For comparative religionists' fascinations with the "Mystic East" of India, Richard King provides an unparalleled analysis in *Orientalism and Religion: Post-Colonial Theory, India, and "the Mystic East"* (London: Routledge, 1999). On the influence of this kind of Orientalist Transcendentalism in America, see Leigh Eric Schmidt, "The Making of Modern 'Mysticism,'" *Journal of the American Academy of Religion* 71, no. 2 (2003): 273–302.

8. Webb Keane, *Christian Moderns: Freedom and Fetish in the Mission Encounter* (Berkeley: University of California Press, 2007), 201; Talal Asad, *Formations of the Secular: Christianity, Islam, Modernity* (Stanford, CA: Stanford University Press, 2003).

9. Most important here are Talal Asad, *Genealogies of Religion: Discipline and Reasons of Power in Christianity and Religion* (Baltimore: Johns Hopkins University Press, 1993); Asad, *Formations of the Secular*; Omid Safi, "Bargaining with *Baraka*: Persian Sufism, 'Mysticism,' and Pre-modern Politics," *Muslim World* 90 (Fall 2000): 259–87; Schmidt, "Making of Modern 'Mysticism'"; Tomoko Masuzawa, *The Invention of World Religions, or, How European Universalism Was Preserved in the Language of Pluralism* (Chicago: University of Chicago Press, 2005); King, *Orientalism and Religion*; and Keane, *Christian Moderns*.

10. Robert Rozehnal, "*Faqir* or Faker? The Pakpattan Tragedy and the Politics of Sufism in Pakistan," *Religion* 36 (2006): 34–35.

11. See Carl Ernst, "Between Orientalism and Fundamentalism: Problematizing the Teaching of Sufism," in *Teaching Islam*, ed. Brannon M. Wheeler (New York: Oxford University Press, 2003), 108–23.

12. Safi, "Bargaining with *Baraka*."

13. See Carl Ernst, *The Shambhala Guide to Sufism* (Boston: Shambhala Publications, 1997), 1–18.

14. Elizabeth Sirriyeh, *Sufis and Anti-Sufis: The Defence, Re-Thinking, and Rejection of Sufism in the Modern World* (Richmond, Surrey: Curzon, 1999).

15. Information on W. C. Smith's life (with the exception of his views on mysticism) is drawn from Willard Oxtoby, ed., *Religious Diversity: Essays by Wilfred Cantwell Smith* (New York: Harper and Row, 1976); Sheila McDonough, "Wilfred Cantwell Smith in Lahore 1940–1951," *Studies in Contemporary Islam* 3, no. 1 (2001): 55–81; William Graham, "The Scholar's Scholar," *Harvard Divinity Bulletin* 29, no. 2 (2000): 6–7; and Kenneth Cracknell, "Introductory Essay," in *Wilfred Cantwell Smith: A Reader*, ed. Kenneth Cracknell (New York: Oxford Oneworld, 2002), 1–26.

16. John Macmurray, *Creative Society: A Study of the Relation of Christianity to Communism* (New York: Eddy and Page, 1936), 56.

17. John Macmurray, *Freedom in the Modern World: Broadcast Talks on Modern Problems* (London: Faber and Faber, 1932), 70–71.

18. Ibid., 77–105.

19. Ibid., 62 (emphasis added).

20. See also Amy Limpitlaw, "Macmurray's Understanding of Mysticism," in *John Macmurray: Critical Perspectives*, ed. David Fergusson and Nigel Dower (New York: Peter Lang, 2002), 252–61.

21. McDonough, "Wilfred Cantwell Smith in Lahore," 55–64.

22. Wilfred Cantwell Smith, *Modern Islam in India: A Social Analysis* (1946; New York: Russell and Russell, 1972), 164.

23. Ibid., 182, 325, 279, and 247, respectively.

24. For Cold War–era theologians, see Gary Dorrien, *Soul in Society: The Making and Renewal of Social Christianity* (Philadelphia: Fortress Press, 1995).

25. The Rockefeller Foundation, *The Rockefeller Foundation Annual Report 1952* (New York: Rockefeller Foundation, 2003), 293.

26. Sheila McDonough, *The Flame of Sinai: Hope and Vision in Iqbal* (Lahore: Iqbal Academy Pakistan, 2002), ii; Charles Adams, "The Development of Islamic Studies in Canada," in *The Muslim Community in North America*, ed. Baha Abu-Laban, Regula B. Qureshi, and Earle H. Waugh (Alberta: University of Alberta Press, 1983), 187.

27. Wilfred Cantwell Smith, *Islam in Modern History* (Princeton, NJ: Princeton University Press, 1957), 58.

28. McDonough, *The Flame of Sinai*, 228.

29. Peter Johnson and Judith Tucker, "Middle East Studies Networks in the United States," *MERIP Reports* 38 (1975): 10.

30. For the Cold War history of foundation grants, 1958 National Educational Defense Appropriations funding, and the role of these grants in changing Orientalist paradigms and institutes into those focused on "area studies," see Timothy Mitchell, "The Middle East in the Past and Future of Social Science," in *The Politics of Knowledge: Area Studies and the Disciplines*, ed. David Szanton (Berkeley: University of California Press, 2004), 74–118.

31. The Rockefeller Foundation, *The Rockefeller Foundation Annual Report 1953* (New York: Rockefeller Foundation, 2003), 30.

32. Ibid., 35.

33. The Rockefeller Foundation, *The Rockefeller Foundation Annual Report 1951* (New York: Rockefeller Foundation, 2003), 81, 396–97.

34. Adams, "Development of Islamic Studies in Canada."

35. The Rockefeller Foundation, *The Rockefeller Foundation Annual Report 1956* (New York: Rockefeller Foundation, 2003), 3.

36. The Rockefeller Foundation, *The Rockefeller Foundation Annual Report 1955* (New York: Rockefeller Foundation, 2003), 149–57; and Rockefeller Foundation, *Annual Report 1951*, 79–81.

37. On the specifically Protestant underpinnings of American secularism, see Janet R. Jackobsen and Ann Pellegrini, "Introduction: Times like These," in *Secularisms* (Durham, NC: Duke University Press, 2008), 1–38.

38. Wilfred Cantwell Smith, "The Comparative Study of Religion: Reflections on the Possibility and Purpose of a Religious Science," in *McGill University, Faculty of Divinity, Inaugural Lectures* (Montreal: McGill University, 1950), 48.

39. Ibid., 57.

40. Smith, *Islam in Modern History*, vii.

41. Ibid., 300.

42. Ibid.

43. Ibid., 302–3.

44. Smith, *Modern Islam in India*, 378.

45. Wilfred Cantwell Smith, *The Meaning and End of Religion* (1963; Minneapolis: Fortress Press, 1991), 319–20n4 (emphasis added) and 8, respectively.

46. Wilfred Cantwell Smith, "*New Education in the Making in Pakistan: Its Ideology and Basic Problems* by Fazlur Rahman," *Pacific Affairs* 27, no. 1 (March 1954): 84.

47. McDonough, *Flame of Sinai*, 214–15.

48. Specifically, Smith cited Fazlur Rahman, "Internal Religious Developments in the Present Century Islam," *Cahiers d'histoire mondiale/Journal of World History* 2 (1955): 870–71.

49. Muhammad Iqbal and Saeed Sheik, ed., *The Reconstruction of Religious Thought in Islam* (1930; Lahore: Institute of Islamic Culture, 1986), 188–89 (emphasis added).

50. Smith, *Islam in Modern History*, 37; Fazlur Rahman, "Revival and Reform in Islam," in *The Cambridge History of Islam: The Further Islamic Lands, Islamic Society, and Civilization*, vol. 2, ed. P. M. Holt, Ann K. S. Lambton, and Bernard Lewis (Cambridge: Cambridge University Press, 1970), 632–56.

51. Smith, *Islam in Modern History*, 63n44; and Fazlur Rahman, "Muslim Modernism in the Indo-Pakistan Sub-Continent," *Bulletin of the School of Oriental and African Studies: University of London* 213 (1958): 82–99.

52. Smith, *Islam in Modern History*, 303n2, 55–59, and 293, respectively.

53. Graham, "Scholar's Scholar," 6.

54. Smith, *Islam in Modern History*, 235–45; Rahman, "Muslim Modernism in the Indo-Pakistan Sub-Continent," 86–92.

55. Smith, *Islam in Modern History*, 235.

56. Ibid., 235–45.

57. Rahman, "Muslim Modernism in the Indo-Pakistan Sub-Continent," 85–87, 95, and 98, respectively (emphasis added).

58. Smith, *Islam in Modern History*, 244–45; Rahman, "Muslim Modernism in the Indo-Pakistan Sub-Continent," 86.

59. Seyyed Hossein Nasr, "Intellectual Autobiography," in *The Philosophy of Seyyed Hossein Nasr*, ed. Lewis E. Hahn, Randall E Auxier, and Lucian W. Stone (Chicago: Open Court, 2001), 4. These Traditionalists included Rene Guenon, Frithjof Schuon, Martin Lings, and Titus Burckhardt.

60. McGill University Archives, Institute of Islamic Studies, 1947–, Director's Records 1947–1973, RG 84, "Annual Report, 1961–1962," 1.

61. Maureen Patterson chronicles expanding Pakistan and South Asian studies in "Context for Development of Pakistan Studies in North America: Pre-Partition Interest in Proposed Pakistan Area of South Asia," *Pakistan Studies News: Newsletter of the American Institute of Pakistan Studies* 6, no. 1 (Spring 2002): 1–3; and in "Pakistan Studies in North America: 1947–1989," *Pakistan Studies News: Newsletter of the American Institute of Pakistan Studies* 6, no. 11 (Fall 2003): 8–10.

62. McGill University Archives, Institute of Islamic Studies, 1947–, Director's Records 1947–1973, RG 84, "Conference on Pakistan Studies, McGill University, November 1 and 2, 1955"; Institute of Islamic Studies, 1947–, Director's Records 1947–1973, RG 84, "Letter of Wilfred Cantwell Smith to Dr. Stanley Maron, December 1, 1955"; and Institute of Islamic Studies, 1947–, Director's Records 1947–1973, RG 84, "Memorandum: Group on Pakistan Studies, May 17, 1956."

63. McGill University Archives, Institute of Islamic Studies, 1947–, Director's Records 1947–1973, RG 84, "Letter of Wilfred Cantwell Smith to President Ayub Khan, February 21, 1961." Smith described how he was encouraged by Khan's address to the Pakistan Philosophic Congress regarding religion, philosophy, and "the 'serious imbalance' between modern man's technological prowess and moral and spiritual neglect."

64. See Edward Said, *Orientalism* (New York: Vintage Books, 1979); Masuzawa, *Invention of World Religions*; and Gil Anidjar, *Semites: Race, Religion, Literature* (Stanford, CA: Stanford University Press, 2008).

65. McDonough, Flame of Sinai, iii, 9–12 and 33–62. See also Leonard Lewisohn, "An Introduction to the History of Modern Persian Sufism, part II: A Socio-Cultural Profile of Sufism from the Dhahabī Revival to the Present Day," *Bulletin of the School of Oriental and African Studies* 62, no. 1 (1999): 56.

66. Unless otherwise noted, Nasr's comments derive from a personal interview by the author on May 1, 2008.

67. John B. Carman and Kathryn Dodgson, *Community and Colloquy: The Center for the Study of World Religions, 1958–2003* (Cambridge, MA: President and Fellows of Harvard College, 2006), 11–17.

68. Muhsin Mahdi, "The Study of Islam, Orientalism, and America," in *Mapping Islamic Studies: Genealogy, Continuity and Change*, ed. Azim Nanji (Berlin: Mouton de Gruyter, 1997), 170–71. Some of the differences among these figures are charted in Mona Abaza, "A Note on Henry Corbin and Seyyed Hossein Nasr: Affinities and Differences," *Muslim World* 90, no. 1 (2000): 91–107.

69. For more on Isma'il al-Faruqis work and his relationship to scholars at McGill and Harvard, see Rosemary R. Hicks, *Creating an 'Abrahamic America' and Moderating Islam: Cold War Political Economy and Cosmopolitan Sufis in New York after 2001*" (New York: Doctoral DIssertation for Columbia University, 2010).

70. Nasr, "Intellectual Autobiography," 57.

71. Huston Smith was of no relation to Wilfred Cantwell Smith. See Wilfred Cantwell Smith, "Comparative Religion: Whither—and Why?" in *The History of Religions: Essays in Methodology*, ed. Mircea Eliade and Joseph Kitagawa (Chicago: University of Chicago Press, 1959), 31–58. Nasr counts Huston Smith among his closest collaborators and friends and as a "fellow wayfarer in the American academic world" ("Intellectual Autobiography," 62).

72. For Rahman's work in Karachi and return to the United States, see Earle H. Waugh, "Beyond Scylla and Kharybdis: Fazlur Rahman and Islamic Identity," and Donald L. Berry, "Fazlur Rahman: A Life in Review," in *The Shaping of an American Islamic Discourse: A Memorial to Fazlur Rahman*, ed. Earle H. Waugh and Frederick M. Denny (Atlanta: Scholars Press, 1998), 15–36 and 37–48.

73. Smith, *Meaning and End of Religion*, 296n93.

74. Charles J. Adams, ed., *Iranian Civilization and Culture: Essays in Honour of the 2,500th Anniversary of the Founding of the Persian Empire* (Montreal: McGill University Institute of Islamic Studies, 1972).

75. Matthjis Van den Bos, *Mystic Regimes: Sufism and the State in Iran, from the Late Qajar Era to the Islamic Republic* (Leiden, Netherlands: Brill, 2002), 112–14.

76. Hamid Algar, "'Allama Sayyid Muhammad Husayn Tabataba'i: Philosopher, Exegete, and Gnostic," *Journal of Islamic Studies* 17, no. 3 (2006): 326–51.

77. Letter from editor Robert Silvers to Richard Bulliet, dated March 28, 1980. My thanks to Richard Bulliet for access to this material.

78. Francis Robinson, "Other Worldly and This Worldly Islam and the Islamic Revival. A Memorial Lecture for Wilfred Cantwell Smith. Delivered at the Royal Asiatic Society on 10 April, 2003," *Journal of the Royal Asiatic Society* 3, no. 14.1 (2004): 47–58.

79. See Mehrzad Boroujerdi, *Iranian Intellectuals and the West: The Tormented Triumph of Nativism* (Syracuse, NY: Syracuse University Press, 1996).

80. Mohamad Tavakoli-Targhi, *Refashioning Iran: Orientalism, Occidentalism, and Historiography* (New York: Palgrave, 2001), 135.

81. Seyyed Hossein Nasr, "Sufism and the Perennity of the Mystical Quest," in *Sufi Essays*, ed. Seyyed Hossein Nasr (Albany: State University of New York Press, 1972), 27.

82. Compare 'Ali Shari'ati's "Mysticism, Equality, and Freedom," in *Marxism and Other Western Fallacies: An Islamic Critique*, ed. Hamid Algar and trans. R. Campbell (Berkeley:

Mizan Press, 1980), 97–122, with Nasr's, "Sufism and the Perennity of the Mystical Quest" and Seyyed Hossein Nasr, "Shi"ism and Sufism: Their Relationship in Essence and History" (both in *Sufi Essays*, ed. Seyyed Hossein Nasr [Albany: State University of New York Press, 1972], 25–42 and 104–22, respectively.)

83. On the dominance of Sufism in American religious studies departments, see Marcia Hermansen, "The Academic Study of Sufism at American Universities," *American Journal of Islamic Social Sciences* 24, no. 3 (2007): 23–45.

84. Annemarie Schimmel's *Gabriel's Wing: A Study into the Religious Ideals of Sir Muhammad Iqbal* (Leiden, Netherlands: E. J. Brill, 1963).

85. Annemarie Schimmel, *Mystical Dimensions of Islam* (Chapel Hill: University of North Carolina Press, 1975). On Schimmel's use of Protestant-derived categories, see Safi, "Bargaining with *Baraka.*"

86. See Annemarie Schimmel and Falaturi Abdoldjavad, eds., *We Believe in One God: The Experience of God in Christianity and Islam* (London: Burns and Oates, 1979).

87. Smith, *Meaning and End of Religion*, 278n31.

88. This history is according to Richard Frye, a historian of Iran who was also instrumental in securing Schimmel's appointment at Harvard through the Durrani Fund and who thought that Schimmel and Nasr (and Smith, at times) erred in seeing religion as the primary focus, if not cause, of all else (personal communications, May 22 and 25, 2007, and June 3, 2007).

89. Annemarie Schimmel, foreword to Frithjof Schuon, *Understanding Islam* (Bloomington, IN: World Wisdom Books, 1998), v.

90. Huston Smith, "Nasr's Defense of the Perennial Philosophy," 157n16 (emphasis added).

91. Wilfred Cantwell Smith, in "The Explosion in the Moslem World: A Roundtable on Islam," the *New York Times*, December 11, 1979.

92. Seyyed Hossein Nasr, foreword to Muhammad Abdul-Rauf, *A Muslim's Reflections on Democratic Capitalism* (Washington, DC: American Enterprise Institute, 1984), vii–viii.

93. See Ron Geaves, "Who Defines Moderate Islam 'Post'–September 11?" in *Islam and the West, Post 9/11*, ed. Ron Geaves, Theodore Gabriel, Yvonne Haddad, and Jane Idelman Smith (Burlington, VT: Ashgate, 2004), 62–76. On Feisal Abdul Rauf and the ASMA Society (American Sufi Muslim Association-turned-American Society for Muslim Advancement), see Hicks, *Creating an "Abrahamic" America and Moderating Islam.*"

94. R. S. O'Fahey and Bernd Radtke, "Neo-Sufism Reconsidered," in *Islam: Critical Concepts in Sociology*, ed. Bryan S. Turner (New York: Routledge, 2003), 77n8.

95. Wilfred Cantwell Smith, "Islamic Resurgence," in *Consciousness and Reality: Studies in Memory of Toshihiko Izutsu*, ed. Sayyid Jalal al-Din Ashtiyani, Hideichi Matsubara, Takashi Iwami, and Akiro Matsumoto (Boston: Brill, 2000), 8, 14, and 15 (emphasis added), respectively.

96. Ibid., 3.

97. Talal Asad, "Reading a Modern Classic: W. C. Smith's 'The Meaning and End of Religion,'" *History of Religions* 40, no. 3 (2001): 206 and 222, respectively.

98. Ibid., 221.

99. See Smith, in Cracknell, *Wilfred Cantwell Smith*, 75.

100. Wilfred Cantwell Smith, *Towards a World Theology: Faith and the Comparative History of Religion* (Philadelphia: Westminster Press, 1981).

101. Jacques Waardenburg, "Islamic Studies and the History of Religions: An Evaluation," in *Mapping Islamic Studies: Genealogy, Continuity and Change*, ed. Azim Nanji (Berlin: Mouton de Gruyter, 1997), 202 (emphasis added).

102. Asad, "Reading a Modern Classic," 201; Talal Asad, "The Idea of an Anthropology of Islam" (Washington, DC: Georgetown Center for Contemporary Arab Studies, 1986).

103. Safi, "Bargaining with *Baraka*."

104. See, for example, Schmidt, "The Making of Modern 'Mysticism,'" 273–74; and Steven Wasserstrom, who argues that studies of mysticism dominate the history of religions due to the influence of Massignon, Corbin, Schimmel, and Nasr. Wasserstrom, *Religion after Religion: Gershom Scholem, Mircea Eliade, and Henry Corbin at Eranos* (Princeton, NJ: Princeton University Press, 1999), 240.

8 Apache Revelation: Making Indigenous Religion in the Legal Sphere

Greg Johnson

■ RELIGION-MAKING AND INDIGENOUS TRADITIONS

How is Apache revelation "made" in contemporary legal settings? Why would Apache representatives argue for the religious significance of numerous objects while simultaneously denying that the objects are sacred under the law? What does this process reveal about religious discourse in settings fraught with ambiguity and real-world consequences? I address these questions in what follows, but first I will briefly address religion-making in the context of indigenous traditions in general terms.

On the basis of my ongoing research in American Indian and Hawaiian contexts, I am persuaded that religion-making is a promising analytical rubric for the study of indigenous traditions and religious claims, though it skirts rather close to several pitfalls. These, however, are avoidable so long as we take care to be clear about what we mean by religion-making and, in the process, distance our claims from the missteps of "invention of tradition" discourse that has come under fire from critics for its unmasking pretensions, on the one hand, and its implicit but telling reinstatement of authenticity, on the other.[1] While serious scholarship cannot—indeed, should not—always avoid the former criticism, it must work diligently to stave off the latter. If we allow discourses of authenticity and their proxies to enter our parlance, we recapitulate the errors of previous scholars of religion who have obscured from view the very objects of our study through celebration of them.[2] To this end, religion-making holds out promise so long as it is not imagined to be contrastive with the study of unmade religion. There is no doubt that some religious phenomena are more seamlessly made than others, but this observation is a call to a thoroughgoing religion-making analysis, not a claim that some forms of religion stand outside of such processes.

Other cautions are in order. We should be skeptical of the sense of agency suggested by religion-making. To insist that religions are made is not to ascribe full intentionality or potency to their makers. Structural forces—not the least of which are oppositional or factional—and unintended consequences "make" religion as much as acting subjects do. That said, we should be cautious about letting the pendulum swing too far in the other direction such that we begin to regard agency as a romantic fiction. Indeed, I will argue for a fairly agency-strong view of religion-making in my analysis of Apache claims.

Additionally, I am of the view that "modernity" should not be regarded as a necessary condition through and against which analysis by way of religion-making becomes useful. For all that colonialism, nation-state formation, capitalism, secularism, and related forces have undeniably shaped our world and the ways religious claims receive articulation, I side with those who do not see the modern predicament as instating a categorically different context for identity formation, cultural representation, and religion-making.[3] I am not suggesting that scholars cease to problematize and conceptualize the stakes and consequences of modernity but only that we pull back from separating out human experience in ways that demark before and after. Processes of cultural borrowing, adapting, reification, othering, and other characteristics of "hot" societies have shaped native traditions prior to modernity's discovery of them.[4] Moreover, a number of scholars have illustrated how modernity has been indigenized in a range of ways across the globe.[5] Thus, while modernity remains a useful category and a historical reality, it should be conceptualized not only as a force that indigenous peoples must react against but also as a resource they craft to their own interests and ends. In this capacity, modernity is usefully conceptualized as encompassing apparently secular venues—like courtrooms—*and* explicitly religious forms of speech that are announced in them. Indigenous peoples, I would suggest, do not stop being themselves or step out of time when they enter such spaces and announce provocative words within them. Rather, they make do with the cultural and political materials at hand, sometimes with rather surprising results.

Another way to frame a discussion of religion-making with reference to indigenous traditions is to differentiate between two related but distinct senses of religion-making. The first, which undergirds my initial comments above, is one drawn from the contributions of social constructivist insights to the study of religion.[6] While some anthropologists have long been comfortable and productive working with antiessentialist assumptions about culture and its products, scholars of religion—and especially of nondominant traditions—have largely been reluctant to embrace such moves, wishing instead for an analytical approach that is neither essentialist nor reductionist.[7] Waiting for this theoretical Godot has resulted in lost time and missed opportunities. I am of the mind that this impasse is not likely to be resolved and therefore scholars of indigenous religions should carry forth, especially because the contemporary moment is at once rich, volatile, and understudied.

If one proceeds down the constructivist path in order to ask how religion is made, one soon encounters a second, more specific sense of religion-making. This sense of the term has been articulated in particularly powerful ways by Talal Asad and others working at the intersection of secular liberalism and contemporary Islam.[8] Here an incisive launching point for analysis is to argue that secular liberalism—by way of its publics, policies, and institutions—is not neutral with regard to religion but, rather, configures and channels possible expressions of religion, banishing some, taming others, and celebrating a select few (those that happen to model and mirror liberal ideals). This line of analysis has fairly shaken the study of religion but by and large has not had commensurate impact on the subfield of religion and indigenous traditions. Some anthropologists, however, have been engaged in analysis along these lines with tremendously productive results.[9] I share their willingness to explore contemporary indigenous traditions from this perspective and am particularly convinced that the study of legal arenas is made far richer—if far more complex—by means of such analysis.

That said, the context of repatriation law presents a particular set of analytical challenges and opportunities that cannot be fully engaged or discerned if viewed only from an Asadian perspective on religion-making. The relevant laws—while emerging from secular nation-state apparatuses and predilections—mark a deliberate attempt on the part of legislators to engage and provide redress to nondominant communities, in part through taking seriously nonliberal modes of evidence deemed appropriate to them, including religious speech. Exciting and often perplexing responses have erupted from the side of native communities in the process of engaging this interstitial legal space at the edges of US constitutional jurisprudence. Given this emergent configuration of legal categories and indigenous voices, I am persuaded that repatriation discourse should not be read as yet another instance of defaced or disarmed religion. Nor should religious utterances in this context—or any context—be regarded as simple iterations of "tradition" that demand nothing from the scholar beyond mere reporting. Instead, I argue that what we begin to see here is how native people carry forward and expand their traditions through their encounters with secular liberalism and two of its central categories, religion and law. I would also suggest that a good deal of tradition is made in the process, even if the results are not always recognizable to some audiences. My point is that embracing a narrow sense of religion-making vis-à-vis secular liberalism should not be accompanied by losing sight of the perspectives enabled by a more broadly construed social constructivist position. Ideally, scholars should look through both frames. At a minimum, such a bi-focal religion-making analysis guards against the prospect of subtly reembedded forms of religious protectionism and its analytical concomitants.

I press this point because I am struck that the two aforementioned approaches are sometimes imagined and engaged as being at odds, especially with regard to the politics of scholarly analysis. Indeed, it has been somewhat of an awakening for me to realize that the constructivist positions I find so productive are in fact themselves the subject of considerable scrutiny by a number of contemporary theorists. Whether based in critiques of "reading" meaning out of ritual practices, concerns about non-insiders critiquing traditions, or challenges to subordination-resistance models of analysis, the Asadian tradition applies fairly direct pressure to the operative premises of constructivist religion scholars such as J. Z. Smith and Bruce Lincoln. The pressure I refer to is quite apparent across the academy, even in this volume. Insofar as the study of religion is itself politically "made" and contested, it behooves scholars of religion to be as self-conscious of our disciplinary struggles as we are attentive to the traditions we study.[10] If nothing else, we might note that the boundary-marking practices and authorizing discourses are often strikingly similar in both cases.

My interest in this context is to reassert the relevance of constructivism. While it is not fashionable in the current theoretical climate, I would insist that constructivism remains radical as a means to study religion. This is for two primary and related reasons: (1) its approach to analyzing traditions is thoroughgoing—nothing is shielded or exempt from potentially destabilizing questions; (2) it is an analytical stance that affirms the role of external analysts and their penchant for probing deeply, even when soft tissues and raw nerves are encountered. These analytical points are crucial for those of us who regard religions as being made and enlivened by moments of struggle, the outlines of which can go unexplored by less incisive modes of scholarship. I emphasize these points because I worry that, in the name of theoretical sophistication, some scholars of religion-making occasionally trade against the most productive and hard-won analytical principles of a discipline that has only recently found its nontheological footing. Thus, in a modest rebalancing effort, in the case that follows I foreground constructivist elements of my analysis. If Asadian insights have helped to focus my questions, the bluntness of a constructivist approach has enabled me to ask them.

■ APACHE REVELATION

In the midst of a recent and heated repatriation dispute, a White Mountain Apache representative was pressed to provide more information to substantiate Apache religious claims regarding a number of rare cultural objects. He responded thus: "I go back to what one of our elders said, What more documentation is there after Revelation? What more documentation is needed to understand the first chapter of Genesis on how the earth was created?"[11] At the same meeting Apache representatives also invoked the Ten Commandments, Leviticus, and, interestingly enough, a variety of negative references to Mormonism, to which I will turn focused attention below. Why this appeal to Judeo-Christian sources and images at a moment when explicitly Apache evidence was requested? How might scholars of religion begin to make sense of such claims?

First, it is clear enough that the Apache speakers were quite aware of their audience's background, predilections, and religious sympathies. Choosing thus to speak in the discourse of the audience potentially makes political and cultural sense in a variety of ways I will unpack below. There is also, of course, a potent point about religious authority being made, which I will also explore. To launch this discussion, however, I want to begin with a more radical claim: appealing to Revelation and Genesis is a classically Apache way to speak. My point here is not historical, though many Apaches are Christians. My point pertains to form: to invoke Revelation and Genesis in this way is to engage a venerable Apache tradition—it is to speak metaphorically.[12] This assertion enables a comparative theoretical observation: namely, metaphor is the formal vehicle of tradition writ large—it is that trope that enables likeness to be coaxed out of difference, continuity out of rupture, and just as miraculously, political sympathy—here from nonnatives—out of historical antipathy.

The context in which Apache representatives likened Apache revelation to Genesis, Leviticus, the Ten Commandments, and the Book of Revelation was two federal repatriation meetings, one in the course of a dispute with the Denver Art Museum in 2002 and one in the course of a dispute with the Chicago Field Museum in 2006. Both disputes concerned the fate of cultural objects, including numerous Gaan masks and other ritual objects, which I describe below.

We will return to the 2002 meeting below, but first I focus upon the 2006 dispute because it remains unsettled and the questions it raises are at the explosive intersection of religious freedom claims and property law. Specifically, the Apache insist that the objects, held by the museum since 1903, should be returned to them as "cultural patrimony," a category that hinges upon the putative inalienability of the objects. The museum has rejected this proposal vehemently. Interestingly, the museum has offered to repatriate the objects as "sacred objects," a legal category that does not presuppose inalienability. The museum has been willing to relinquish these specific objects but is not willing to budge on the question of property rights on principle. The museum insists that it has clear title to the objects and that all such objects—that is, those purportedly collected in good faith by way of a chronicled transaction—should be similarly regarded as museum property. The Apache representatives insist that the objects are and were communal property that could never have been alienated in good faith, evidence of the sale notwithstanding. They have launched a broad argument regarding all such sales: given the realities of colonial history, all transactions of this time must be regarded as coerced and the product of asymmetrical power relationships. It is in this context that the museum staged forceful resistance, which included evidence presented by lawyers and multiple examples drawn from scholarly literature. Responding, the Apache mounted a vigorous campaign, bringing a number of elders to the meeting, speaking about the objects as conduits of medicine and healing for the community.

Most relevant for our purposes, they spoke of the objects in terms of revelation. Interestingly, however, revelation as they invoked it signaled not the opening up of speech with reference to the future but a closing off of this very possibility. To achieve this goal, they spoke in a variety of compelling religious idioms to articulate their revelation and in so doing demonstrated much about how religion is made. When analyzing their claims what we do not learn is very much about the content of their revelations, whether Apache or Christian (whatever that distinction might mean today). What we do learn is how some Apache representatives make various categories, devices, and rhetorics of religion work for them. And judging from a federal committee's reaction, the Apache can be very persuasive.[13]

The persuasive power of the Apache claims, I will argue, is principally located at the level of form. This form has two central features: (1) joint authorship by speakers who are situated across social divides, such that nondominant speakers enlist dominant representatives, tropes, and habits of mind to make their claims; (2) this dynamic is enabled and managed by code-switching between radically different kinds of claims, which I will characterize as majority-inclusive and minority-specific claims.[14] The former point is best unpacked with reference to the non-Indian amplifications of Apaches claims, which I will only touch upon.[15] The latter point concerning two kinds of rhetoric is what concerns us here, particularly the role of majority-inclusive claims. Such claims rely upon arguments based in metonymy—"we are (a part of) you"—and arguments based in metaphor—"we are (somewhat) like you." Some arguments, including those invoking Revelation, mobilize both tropes simultaneously.

■ THE LAW

The Native American Graves Protection and Repatriation Act (NAGPRA) is a law designed to foster communication and compromise toward the end of returning certain categories of human remains and cultural items to Native Americans, Native Alaskans, and Native Hawaiians.[16] It has functioned in this spirit many times, enabling museums to consult with native representatives and regain thereby historically strained integrity. For their part, native peoples have engaged the law in a variety of creative and forceful ways in the process of asserting claims upon ancient human and cultural remains in the broader enterprise of articulating their contemporary identities. However, the law has not always functioned smoothly. The conflicts the law seeks to address are historically complex in a variety of ways, and the statute itself is hardly a gem of clarity and exactness. It is to be expected, then, that passions will flare, that sides will become entrenched and reactionary, with the result that the law sometimes catalyzes reification of the very antagonisms it seeks to remedy. This is particularly the case when far-reaching issues of precedent are at stake. The *Apache vs. Field Museum* dispute is one such instance of this, with each party backing away from conversation to adopt maximalist rhetorics— the museum's drawn from discourses of empirical evidence and property rights; the Apaches', from nonfalsifiable religious claims announced in a range of keys.[17] By means of its very definitions, the law established conditions for such crises of criteria. That is, the evidentiary parameters of NAGPRA include both modalities of evidence—hard science and religious claims—and the law declares that these apples and oranges shall be weighed equally, with a simple preponderance of evidence (51 percent) tipping the balance one way or the other.

In recognition of potential impasses and pitfalls that might emerge by way of this evidentiary predicament, legislators drafted into the law a requirement that a Review Committee be established to hear and mediate disputes in the effort of resolving disputes prior to them ending up in court.[18] Upon hearing disputes, the committee renders non–legally binding advisory opinions that may be admitted as evidence in legal proceedings. Thus far most disputants have appeared willing to engage in the review process, though some have made it clear that they consider such review to be preliminary at best; a few have expressed contempt for the process, and several judges who have heard NAGPRA disputes appear to regard the committee's role in similar terms. In the end, such differences not only are about the role of the committee but are more broadly and seriously about the constitutionality of the law itself. The predicament it faces has not been lost on the committee. Indeed, the very dispute we are considering has been an occasion for repeated metareflection for the committee, which has posed such tough questions to itself as "What is fact?" and "How do we find one?"[19]

INSTITUTIONS AND OBJECTS

It is useful to reflect for a moment about the parties and objects in the dispute at hand so as to not rush to judgment about them, morally or analytically. Institutional and corporate identities are every bit as complicated as individual ones. Museums and tribes, like people, have internal struggles, change attitudes over time (indeed, can hold apparently contradictory attitudes at one time), and learn to speak in a range of ways to a range of audiences. Depending where one looks, for example, one can find descriptions of the Field Museum over the last century that depict it as the epitome of a colonial enterprise—"a jackal operation" in the words of one critic[20]—and, quite in another regard, as pathbreaking and progressive. In August 2007, for example, the Field Museum established a significant international precedent by voluntarily repatriating a variety of Maori remains.[21] But in the case at hand, we want to note, the museum is firmly resisting repatriation of Apache objects at a time when a number of other museums and institutions have acceded to similar requests.[22] For their part, the White Mountain Apache of Arizona must be appreciated for their political savoir faire.[23] While indisputably "traditional" in terms of a thriving language community, a robust ritual life, and a range of subsistence practices, they are power brokers who know how to get things done— like protect putatively sacred peaks from development and manage vast tracts of real estate.[24] It is instructive to consider how vocal they have been in preventing the development of one ski area while promoting their own.[25] I am not marking them out for criticism; rather, I wish to call attention to the full range of expertise and interests that makes them who they are—a point I will reframe with reference to their religious claims shortly.

As for the objects, such items as Gaan (Mountain Spirit) masks, which were and are worn by Crown Dancers in a range of ceremonies dedicated principally to life passages and healing, have long been represented in the anthropological record in religious terms.[26] In a manner instructive with regard to representational circulation, this textual sedimentation of Apache religion becomes, on the one hand, a resource for Apache claims in the present and, alternatively, a standard against which Apache claims are measured.[27] My point here is—whatever one makes of such claims—to note that anthropological sources do in fact support a link between these objects and Apache religious lives. For example, this literature suggests that in ceremonial settings many Apaches have historically regarded the Crown Dancers as the Gaan themselves, much in the way Hopis are said to regard Kachina Dancers as Kachina spirits in ritual contexts.[28] Furthermore, central to the dispute at hand is the long-documented practice of retiring Gaan masks from use after ritual performances, which has been reflected in anthropological literature and in Apache claims as evidence for the sacredness of the objects.[29] Related to their central ritual function, the Gaan figure prominently in Apache mythology, particularly with reference to stories about health and the proper order of society.[30] In such myths one sees a direct correlation between the presence of the Gaan and a generally positive state of social affairs and, conversely, the absence of the Gaan and social disorder.[31] Moreover, it is clear that the Gaan and Gaan masks have taken on a heightened metonymic function in recent years. According to anthropologist Richard Perry, who argues that contemporary emphases upon female puberty rituals function to reassert Apache identity, "it may be significant in this vein that the *gaan*, who play a central role in the ceremony and have potent meaning for the Apache in their own right, have now become a tribal logo, appearing on signs, stationary, and other such 'presentations of self' to the outside."[32] Thus, when the Apache struggle over the place of Gaan masks, their sentiments, ambitions, and arguments must be read in this broader frame—their concerns about the Gaan masks are finally about their identity writ large.[33]

■ FIGHTING WORDS

The context within and against which Apache claims took shape was the museum's position, which was outlined with stark rhetoric. Announcing a claim that is as analytically interesting as it is provocative, the museum's attorney declared, "The evidence provided by the Tribe that these items could not be sold is limited to current assertions."[34] The attorney discerned a crucial feature of the kinds of claims we are considering—their radically presentist quality. However, for our analytical purposes his insight is undercut by the implicit status of authenticity that his argument relies upon. In any event, he then turned to broader legal issues, suggesting that the tribe's request "could have very troubling implications. In fact, we believe that the Tribe is trying to erode the standards set forth in NAGPRA in order to materially change the balance of several critical tenets of property law." Having thus pronounced what amounts to a carefully framed challenge to the Review Committee, he stated the museum's baseline regard for Apache tradition in stark terms: "[The Review Committee's finding] would support the erroneous contention that simple assertions of opinion and contemporary evidence of practices and beliefs is enough to overcome clear and objective evidence from the time of collection.... We believe this kind of action would undermine the overt structure as well as the spirit, purpose and intent of NAGPRA."[35]

How did the Apache respond? Forcefully, with the Word of God. Vincent Randall, a White Mountain tribal elder, began the Apache rejoinder with two paradigmatic exempla, both drawn from Judeo-Christian contexts. Indeed, one might say that he appealed to the dominant religio-discursive tradition in a remarkably efficient and elegant manner, invoking the Ten Commandments at the outset and the Book of Revelation in closing. Discussion of the Ten Commandments and Revelation enabled Randall to establish conceptual parameters for conceiving of religious vitality as inseparable from the making of society (as with the commandments) and potential dissolution of it (as the apocalyptic imagery of John attests). For these reasons among others, his presentation deserves attention for the ways it speaks to the articulation and reception of religious themes in the legal sphere, particularly with reference to the dynamic ways by which even the most tired religious images can be brought to life in moments of political struggle.

Randall's presentation was not about the Ten Commandments or the Book of Revelation in a simple or direct sense. Nonetheless, Randall and the other Apache representatives established themselves as adept managers of the rhetorical possibilities opened up by such references. Consider, for example, how Randall's closing words served notice of the power of the Apaches' conviction and of their ability to speak across cultural worlds in compelling ways. Facing the committee, he intoned, "You have spiritual words, you have a Bible, and the last book in your Bible is Revelation. Are there any other books after Revelation? We have come today before you with our revelation, there is no more documentation."[36] In this way, dominant religious tropes were invoked to establish a template for engaged reception of nondominant religio-political assertions. If the audience could be made to see the objects as something like the Ten Commandments (things no one can be said to own), and if they could regard the claims of Apache elders as having something like the status of revelation, and if the Apache could persuade the committee that their preferred shape of society—right down to the proper boundaries of the family unit—is not so alien, however differently arrived at, then the Apaches could begin to hope that their culture-specific claims might find a modicum of receptivity.[37]

Having framed the basics of the dispute and the Apaches' position, let us delve deeper into their arguments. Doing so entails considering a precursor to the Field Museum conflict. This dispute, which played out in 2002, was between a coalition of Apache tribes and the Denver Art Museum. Similar issues and objects were at stake, though with some interesting twists. I am principally interested in the ways the Denver Art Museum dispute may be read as a kind of rhetorical testing ground for the Apache. Four years later some of their lines of argumentation were dropped, while others were retained and even amplified. For the purposes of the present analysis, I focus on Apache claims vis-à-vis Mormonism because these are particularly suggestive in terms of this volume's attention to religion-making.

Unlike their 2006 arguments concerning cultural patrimony, in 2002 Apache representatives argued that the Gaan and other objects held by the Denver Art Museum are sacred.[38] However, the transcript of that dispute records something I have observed with regularity in repatriation history: comparatively little testimony is advanced regarding the objects per se. Instead, the transcript reveals detailed accounts of colonial history, current crises, and considerable discourse devoted to constructing the authority of the group and its representatives. This last element is what interests me most here: throughout the implementation history of NAGPRA, groups have frequently approached this task in apparently exogenous terms, through majority-inclusive discourse.[39] That is, discussions about citizenship, military service, and broad appeals to the universal sacrality of the dead figure centrally—as do fairly stark appeals to Jewish and Christian tropes and texts, as we have already seen. Why do they move in this direction as opposed to giving highly detailed, culturally specific information? Beyond what I have already suggested, what work does this discourse perform?

Consider their words. Vincent Randall was the lead spokesperson in this dispute, as he also was in the Field Museum context. He opened by asserting that the Denver Art Museum had set up a detour, "and we are here today for you to straighten that detour out, that we get back on the road that we're supposed to be walking with the Almighty."[40] *Almighty*, of course, would light up specific registers for North American audiences. The subsequent pages of his testimony show that reference to the Almighty was not a passing appeal but an introduction to a building argument: "Just as much as the Book of Leviticus is the law of the Israelites, so are these items also used with regulations of how—not only how it is created from being spirit filled to how it is used and how it is returned to give it the respect and honor that it should be given. In that sense, it's not in the realm of the arts. The symbols that are painted on these things are not for art form. They are representative of the instructions that are given by these special people that were given this knowledge."[41]

Randall then segued into a reference to Revelation similar to his invocation of it in the Field Museum dispute, but with a twist: "In talking about this situation one of our elders gave an example that was very clear. In the book that—the way of life in Christian world is that book from Genesis to Revelation. There's nothing else after Revelation, not unless you're a Mormon and the books that were found in New York or wherever. But the basis is that's it. There's nothing else beyond that. In that sense, what was used, after it is used there's nothing else."[42] One can regard this reference to Mormonism as a rather incidental side comment, but I suggest a different reading. He continued, providing context for the claims introduced at the opening of this chapter:

> And this is not the first time that any regulatory part of the government has always keep telling us, we want more documentation. I go back to what one of our elders said, what more documentation is there after Revelation? What more documentation is needed to understand the first chapter of Genesis on how the earth was created? We have many churches today because they interpret those things, but they are going to pay for it one of these days because they're adding onto those books and other things.... Now we don't want to do that. We're a people that have been given these things, and this is as much as we can tell.[43]

After his own presentation, Randall translated the testimony of an elder who spoke in Apache: "And he said that these masks should be returned to us and put away properly because the next time there will be another set used for that time for that purpose. And when that is finished, then that's it. That's over. Just as much as he said the Bible is the Bible, there's nothing more after that. There's no more written word after that."[44]

A clear theme emerges here: extending tradition beyond its authorized boundaries is to court moral decay. But why, specifically, the distancing from Mormon revelation? The content of the tradition signals a start, for native peoples are assigned a rather prominent if contested role therein. Geography matters here too—the Arizona Apache live within a Mormon-influenced space; many of their own have converted to the tradition, so internal and external borders are being patrolled through this discourse. Recent history might be a factor as well, for in recent years fundamentalist Mormons have come under intense media scrutiny, and Apaches might want to distance themselves from this for obvious reasons.[45] These issues are significant, but I will suggest a different answer.

In the context of the Apaches' immediate discursive needs, Mormon revelation represents bad form. *Continued* revelation is the pitfall pinpointed by the Apache. As developed in their rhetoric, this represents a tear in the fabric of transcendent authority. Thus the Apache, I propose, wish to distance themselves from the Latter-Day Saints for much the same reason many scholars have long avoided them. Joseph Smith had the good fortune to operate in a modern world in which his ideas could circulate quickly and freely; by the same token, one can see in his archived words, proclamations, and prophecies the plain mark of the all-too-human, of something made. For scholars this confronts us with a Kierkegaardian chasm of sorts. Either we back away from the edge and look for *real* religion elsewhere, as many have done, or we jump the chasm and, doing so, must thereby regard other religious discourses and practices in terms of the lesson afforded by the made quality of Mormonism. As for the Apache representatives, they have responded to the Review Committee that to speak about the objects any more than they have would be tantamount to bastardizing their own tradition through unauthorized expansion of it, much in the way they suggest that Joseph Smith did to Christianity. In a fascinating manner, Apache authority is here announced and constituted by means of their rhetorical distancing from it—that is, these contemporary Apache representatives construct the authority of tradition by insisting that its integrity stands above and beyond them.

With reference to authority and tradition, here I would like briefly to consider the Apaches' minority-specific claims. If the foregoing quotations suggest that Apaches sometimes appeal to exogenous sources to construct claims to authority, now I will sketch the outlines of their endogenous claims. These claims are notable because they assert cultural specificity without advancing much content to this end. As with majority-inclusive rhetoric, these claims announce authority formally, though to different ends insofar as concern here is to delimit possible speakers rather than to open up possible audiences. Only certain people, with certain language, who communicate with certain spirits enjoy the capacity to speak authoritatively about the objects in question. This is an oppositional and markedly defensive rhetoric. This defensive mode takes on particular significance in light of the Field Museum's dismissal of Apache claims as mere opinion.

At the Denver meeting, Randall had this to say:

> It seems to me that the greater society on the outside does not consider our experts at all. The Ph.D.s and so forth, and which I do not question, but that is your world, but we also have a world that where we have our own Ph.D.s, and these Ph.D.s are 24/7 learning experience from the time they are born....When you earn your Ph.D., you learn that, your trade and your things from a teacher, a human being. These people get direct instructions from the Almighty, whether you call him God. We call him (Native American language), which means Ruler of Our Life, and those are the direct teachings that are brought to them. So weigh your factors on who you're educated by.[46]

This theme extends to language, Apache being transparent and accurate, English being the language of error and obfuscation: "It flabbergasts me that you don't understand your own language....Our language is so complex, so complex that what we say is what we mean. And we have a high demand upon accuracy of our language and our thoughts that we have to tell it—when we're told something to retell it we have to retell it exactly the way we heard it. And I say that that's the reason why we never had lawyers and your society is full of lawyers today because you don't understand your own language."[47] Contrastively, Apache is a language of purity, having preverbal origins: "Our people spoke to each other long, long ago, just by looking at each other. Just by their eyes they made decisions. That is no longer there, and people say it's because some of us do not respect these things anymore that has gone away."[48]

To enact this difference, the Apache did something simple but dramatic in both disputes. They called forward elders to testify in Apache, with Randall and others translating. Speaking in Apache was a profoundly efficient way for the Apache to authenticate their perspective by tapping into a well-established economy of exotic purchasing power. Beyond this, their style of communicating and translating created the palpable sense of a transparent language that enables direct communication of and with truth. For example, Randall asked an elder, "What is your name?" He responded, "Levi Dehose." Randall queried, "What do you know?" He responded, "It is a living thing because it comes from an almighty God."[49] In this answer we see a powerful double utterance of authorization, a speaking forth of majority-inclusive imagery by specifically Apache means. Other forms of authority construction included claims to instruction by animals like hummingbirds, holding up Apache law over and against NAGPRA, and implied secrecy and secret ritual authority.[50]

■ MAKING UP OR MAKING DO?

The two primary kinds of claims I have addressed—expansive and restrictive rhetorics—share a notable feature: a marked absence of content. This is not uncommon in repatriation contexts. One response is to suggest that the tribes do not know enough about their traditions to offer more. Perhaps that is the case some of the time. Alternatively, issues of secrecy and secretism may explain aspects of this situation.[51] But we should consider the effectiveness of the native representatives' presentations. The majority of the time the Review Committee has sided with claimants despite the paucity of specific evidence. What explains this success? There is a scandal brewing here, I think. Namely, native representatives know more about how the category "religion" works than many scholars of religion. When they face bleary-eyed committees and courts, native representatives realize that no amount of detail (i.e., content) is likely to persuade such audiences of the religious quality of something. They see that speaking religiously will. It is through form, not content, that they make religion work.[52] And this form is consistent whether the claims are universalistic or relativistic: it announces nonfalsifiable claims to authority.[53] Expressed in majority-inclusive terms, such form creates analogical and metaphorical spaces and opens previously unsympathetic ears such that referents from the dominant society become vehicles to communicate their authority and gravitas; announced in a relativistic key, such form wards off potential challenges and, of course, emphasizes exclusivity of knowledge. "Religion" is made either way and doubly so in their conjunction.

To test my assertion that the Apache representatives understand "religion" better than many scholars of religion—and certainly better than most legislators—consider again the basic structure of their principal claim. Randall and others insisted that the Gaan and related objects are *not* sacred objects as defined by the statute. They did so, I am arguing, not to undermine the religiousness of the objects but to reinstate precisely this aspect of them. Under NAGPRA, as we have noted, "sacred objects" may be private property and thus subject to alienation. This formulation runs afoul of a classic constructivist position. I am making reference to Durkheim's famous distinction between private and communal property, which he made on the basis of widespread linkages of the former to the realm of the profane and the latter to the sacred, particularly in relationship to alienability—the sacred is that which is withdrawn from circulation. This, argues J. Z. Smith, is crucial to the topography of the sacred. Summarizing Durkheim he writes, "The sacred is power that is in common; the profane is that which is individual (here expressed as private property)."[54] While there is no doubt that the Apache wish to acquire the disputed objects and to set a pivotal precedent, the Apaches' claim that the objects are "cultural patrimony" (i.e., inalienable) fit well with classic constructivist accounts of the sacred such as, for example, that of Durkheim. In other words, Apache claims upon their objects may be analytically regarded as "sacred"— employing discourse that locates authority and ownership as standing above and beyond individuals—even while their legal argument required denial of this because of limitations of the definition of the sacred in the law.

This last point brings me back to a distinction I raised early in this chapter, as two different modes of analysis enabled me to see diverse aspects of Apache engagements with religious language. I distinguished between religion-making in the following two senses: (1) with reference to social constructivism as an analytical position that assumes that all religion is human and therefore "made" and (2) as a critique of secular liberalism and its effects on religion. While appreciating the fact that scholars in these respective camps stand in somewhat different relationships to the academic enterprise and its Enlightenment roots, I asserted that the study of religion is best served by a perspective informed by both. As I understand their relationship, the latter sharpens the questions and impact of the former by specifying certain domains and discourses—those that are often taken to be neutral with regard to religion (e.g., aesthetics, education, and law)—and shows how influential and fraught these can be in the shaping and disciplining of religious discourse and subjects. Repaying this favor, social constructivist insights help remind us that the aim of scholarship is neither to reinstate the putative authenticity of the traditions we study nor to yearn after what these might have been prior to their engagement with the modern West. In the case of Apache revelation, my analysis was initially inspired by a constructivist curiosity about the words I heard the Apache utter in repatriation meetings. Sharpening my questions along the lines of the more narrow sense of religion-making helped me to see that the Apaches' words revealed a variety of historically sedimented engagements with institutions and publics shaped by modern, secular governance. Had my story ended there, however, it would have been incomplete. Pulling back to reframe my findings in broader, constructivist terms helped me to see the formal and comparative issues at stake in how Apache people "make" religion, even if their legally framed claims disavowed the sacred quality of the objects.

■ NOTES

I would like to thank Russell McCutcheon, Ruth Mas, Glenn Penny, Kathy Fine-Dare, and the editors of this volume for their comments on earlier drafts of this chapter.

1. Regarding the invention of tradition debates, see Eric Hobsbawm and Terrence Ranger, eds., *The Invention of Tradition* (Cambridge: Cambridge University Press, 1983); Roger Keesing, "Creating the Past: Custom and Identity in the Contemporary Pacific," *Contemporary Pacific* 1 (1989): 19–42.

2. Bruce Lincoln, "Theses on Method," *Method and Theory in the Study of Religion* 8 (1996): 225–27.

3. Marshall Sahlins, "Goodbye to *Triste Tropes*: Ethnography in the Context of Modern World History," *Journal of Modern History* 65 (1993): 1–25.

4. Robert Brightman, "Culture and Culture Theory in Native North America," in *New Perspectives on Native North America*, ed. Sergei Kan and Pauline Strong (Lincoln: University of Nebraska Press, 2006), 351–94; Peter Nabokov, *A Forest of Time: American Indian Ways of History* (New York: Cambridge University Press, 2002).

5. Jonathan Friedman, *Cultural Identity and Global Process* (London: Sage Publications, 1994); James Clifford, "Varieties of Indigenous Experience: Diasporas, Homelands, Sovereignties," in *Indigenous Experience Today*, ed. Marisol de la Cadena and Orin Starn (Oxford: Berg Publishers, 2007), 197–224.

6. Examples of this literature include, Bruce Lincoln, *Discourse and the Construction of Society: Comparative Studies of Myth, Ritual, and Classification* (New York: Oxford University Press, 1989); Jonathan Z. Smith, *Relating Religion: Essays in the Study of Religion* (Chicago: University of Chicago Press, 2004).

7. Exceptions to this tendency include Sam Gill, *Mother Earth: An American Story* (Chicago: University of Chicago Press, 1987); Paul Johnson, *Secrets, Gossip, and Gods: The Transformation of Brazilian Candomble* (Oxford: Oxford University Press, 2002); Tisa Wenger, *We Have a Religion: The 1920s Pueblo Indian Dance Controversy and American Religious Freedom* (Chapel Hill: University of North Carolina Press, 2009).

8. See, for instance, Talal Asad, *Genealogies of Religion: Discipline and Reasons of Power in Christianity and Islam* (Baltimore: Johns Hopkins University Press, 1993); Talal Asad, *Formations of the Secular: Christianity, Islam, Modernity* (Stanford, CA: Stanford University Press, 2003); Saba Mahmood, *Politics of Piety: The Islamic Revival and the Feminist Subject* (Princeton, NJ: Princeton University Press, 2005).

9. Elizabeth Povinelli, *The Cunning of Recognition: Indigenous Alterities and the Making of Australian Multiculturalism* (Durham, NC: Duke University Press, 2002); Ronald Niezen, *The Origins of Indigenism: Human Rights and the Politics of Identity* (Berkeley and Los Angeles: University of California Press, 2003).

10. Bridging the two modes of religion-making analysis, in some respects, is recent scholarship that explores historical and ideological formations around the category "religion" and the institutional trajectories of the study of religion. See, for instance, Tomoko Masuzawa, *The Invention of World Religions: Or How European Universalism Was Preserved in the Language of Pluralism* (Chicago: University of Chicago Press, 2005).

11. Native American Graves Protection and Repatriation Act (NAGPRA) Review Committee, *Official Transcript of the Twenty-Third Meeting of the NAGPRA Review Committee* (Tulsa, OK: National Park Service, May 31–June, 2002), 16.

12. Consider the Apache idea—paradoxical at first glance—that the most traditional manner of speaking Apache is to say something entirely new. This claim has been persuasively argued by Keith Basso, a linguistic anthropologist. Apache metaphor, writes Basso, functions principally through imagining and expressing novel semantic categories as a means to address accidental lexical gaps in their language. I wish to extend his insight to the ways Apaches speak English and invoke Western religious idioms to address political and pragmatic gaps in novel contexts such as legal disputes. See Keith Basso, *Western Apache Language and Culture: Essays in Linguistic Anthropology* (Tucson: University of Arizona Press, 1990).

13. In the case at hand and in a previous dispute (discussed below), the NAGPRA Review Committee has announced findings that align with the Apaches' position. See *Federal Register* 72, no. 25 (February 7, 2007): 5738–40.

14. I have elaborated upon this distinction elsewhere. See Greg Johnson, *Sacred Claims: Repatriation and Living Tradition* (Charlottesville: University of Virginia Press, 2007).

15. For an indication of this process and to see how manifestly persuasive the Apaches' claims were in their immediate context, see the reactions of Review Committee members. The Review Committee unanimously supported the Apache and, more tellingly, rearticulated Apache claims in the process. Reporting their findings, committee members serially added historical information and moral gravitas to the Apache presentation, some doing so with remarkably detailed presentations. See NAGPRA Review Committee, *Official Transcript of the Thirty-Third Meeting of the NAGPRA Review Committee, vol.* 2 (Denver, CO: National Park Service, November 3–4, 2006), 34–110.

16. NAGPRA has generated considerable commentary from a variety of perspectives. See, for instance, Kathleen Fine-Dare, *Grave Injustice: The American Indian Repatriation Movement* (Lincoln: University of Nebraska Press, 2002); Tim McKeown and Sherry Hutt, "In the Smaller Scope of Conscience: The Native American Graves Protection and Repatriation Act Twelve Years After," *UCLA Journal of Environmental Law and Policy* 21, no. 2 (2003): 153–213.

17. On maximalist and minimalist discourse, see Bruce Lincoln, *Holy Terrors: Thinking about Religion after September* 11 (Chicago: University of Chicago Press, 2003).

18. According to the law, the Review Committee is to be constituted by seven members, "3 of whom shall be appointed by the Secretary from nominations submitted by Indian tribes, Native Hawaiian organizations, and traditional Native American religious leaders with at least 2 of such persons being traditional Indian religious leaders; 3 of whom shall be appointed by the Secretary from nominations submitted by national museum organizations and scientific organizations; and 1 who shall be appointed by the Secretary from a list of persons developed and consented to by all of the [other] members" (Public Law 101-601, sec. 8).

19. Consider this brief aside by committee member Dan Monroe: "I don't want to debate you about philosophy at this point and what is and isn't a fact, except to make the point that in my view within the context of both the statute and the regulation and this particular case as it stands goes considerably beyond, in fact, looking at, quote and unquote, 'facts.'" See NAGPRA Review Committee, *Official Transcript of the Thirty-Second Meeting of the NAGPRA Review Committee* (Juneau, AK: National Park Service, May 30–31, 2006), 10.

20. Steven Conn, *Museums and American Intellectual Life, 1876–1926* (Chicago: University of Chicago Press, 1998), 99.

21. Ray Lilley, "Museum Returns Tattooed Head to New Zealand," Associated Press, September 11, 2007, http://www.msnbc.msn.com/id/20697034/.

22. For example, the University of Michigan (see http://www.lsa.umich.edu/%20umma/ nagpra/faq), the University of Pennsylvania (see http://www.museum.upenn.edu//%20 new/exhibits/nagpra/whitemountain.shtml), and the Southwest Museum of the American Indian (see http://www.cr.nps.gov/nagpra/fed_notices/nagpradir/nir0359.html) have repatriated similar objects.

23. For a discussion of Apache influence in Southwest repatriation politics, see John Welch and T. J. Ferguson, "Putting *Patria* Back into Repatriation: Cultural Affiliation Assessment of White Mountain Apache Tribal Lands," *Journal of Social Archaeology* 7, no. 2 (2007): 171–98.

24. See, for instance, Ingo Schroder, "Performing Resistance: The Dramatization of Western Apache Nativism, 1880s–1990s," *Acta Americana* 8, no. 2 (2000): 23–36.

25. This dispute concerns development of a ski area on national forest land in the San Francisco Peaks and use of treated sewage water for snowmaking. See Ninth Circuit Court of Appeals, *Navajo Nation* (2007).

26. John Bourke, "Notes upon the Religion of the Apache Indians," *Folklore* 2, no. 4 (1891): 419–54; Albert Reagan, "Notes on the Indians of the Fort Apache Region,"

Anthropological Papers of the Museum of Natural History 31 (1930): 281–345; Keith Basso, *Western Apache Witchcraft* (Tucson: University of Arizona Press, 1969); Alan Ferg, *Western Apache Material Culture* (Tucson: University of Arizona Press, 1987); Charlotte Heth, ed., *Native American Dance: Ceremonies and Social Traditions* (Washington, DC: National Museum of the American Indian and Starwood Publishing, 1992).

27. On such apparent paradoxes in the mimesis of culture, see, for instance, James Clifford, *The Predicament of Culture: Twentieth-Century Ethnography, Literature and Art* (Cambridge, MA: Harvard University Press, 1988); Michael Brown, *Who Owns Native Culture?* (Cambridge, MA: Harvard University Press, 2003).

28. Grenville Goodwin, "White Mountain Apache Religion," *American Anthropologist* 40 (1938): 24–37; cf. Edwin Loeb, "A Note on Two Far-Travelled Kachinas," *Journal of American Folklore* 56, no. 221 (1943): 192–99.

29. Goodwin, "White Mountain Apache Religion"; Heth, *Native American Dance*, 75.

30. Goddard Pliny, *Myths and Tales from the San Carlos Apache*, Anthropological Papers of the American Museum of Natural History 24, no. 1 (New York: American Museum of Natural History, 1918); Grenville Goodwin, *Myths and Tales of the White Mountain Apache* (New York: J. J. Augustin, 1939).

31. Grenville Goodwin, *The Social Organization of the Western Apache* (Chicago: University of Chicago Press, 1942), 64.

32. Richard Perry, *Apache Reservation: Indigenous Peoples and the American State* (Austin: University of Texas Press, 1993), 179.

33. What is not clear based on conflicting testimony is the degree to which the masks and other objects were considered inalienable by Apaches at the time of their acquisition by the museum. Also unclear is information regarding the material conditions in Apache country during the time of the objects' transfer. Apache claimants have argued that times were so bad that even the most cherished and powerful objects were sold in hopes of feeding one's family. See NAGPRA Review Committee, *Official Transcript of the Thirty-Third Meeting of the NAGPRA Review Committee, vol.* 1 (Denver, CO: National Park Service, November 3–4, 2006), 26–27. As I have noted, the museum has responded that no such devastating conditions prevailed and that the objects were acquired aboveboard with full consent (ibid., 42–45). Curious about the rather large gap between these claims, I consulted the relevant literature and found that the evidence cuts both ways. In short, I found examples of rather quotidian objects, like water dippers, commanding rather high and fiercely negotiated prices, as well as evidence of considerable wealth among some Apache, which was often displayed in lavish ritual performances. See, for instance, Thomas Mails, *The People Called Apache* (Englewood Cliffs, NJ: Prentice Hall, 1974), 47–68; and Reagan, "Notes on the Indians of the Fort Apache Region," 310. I also found plenty to suggest that other Apache lived in an entirely more desperate way and that these people frequently expressed anxiety and fear regarding transactions that involved selling ritual objects. See Mails, *People Called Apache*, 166–69; and Reagan, "Notes on the Indians of the Fort Apache Region," 302–4.

34. NAGPRA Review Committee, *Official Transcript of the Thirty-Third Meeting, vol.* 1, 52.

35. Ibid., 56.

36. Ibid., 36.

37. On legal contexts, taxonomic structures, and metaphor, see Smith, *Relating Religion*; and from the perspective of critical legal studies, see Peter Fitzpatrick, *The Mythology of Modern Law* (New York: Routledge, 1992). Another recent work of significance here is Winnifred Sullivan, *The Impossibility of Religious Freedom* (Princeton, NJ: Princeton University Press, 2005). While I follow Sullivan's argument concerning the impossibility of

religious freedom, my attention here is less to outcomes or even conditions of possibility for certain outcomes and more to the discursive spaces opened up in legal contexts that may be put to a variety of purposes.

38. NAGPRA Review Committee, *Official Transcript of the Twenty-Third Meeting*, 12.

39. Greg Johnson, "Narrative Remains: Articulating Indian Identities in the Repatriation Context," *Comparative Studies in Society and History* 47, no. 3 (2005): 480–506.

40. NAGPRA Review Committee, *Official Transcript of the Twenty-Third Meeting*, 12.

41. Ibid., 13.

42. Ibid., 14.

43. Ibid., 16.

44. Ibid., 20.

45. See, for instance, John Krakauer, *Under the Banner of Heaven: A Story of Violent Faith* (New York: Doubleday, 2003).

46. NAGPRA Review Committee, *Official Transcript of the Thirty-Third Meeting, vol.* 1, 20–21.

47. Ibid., 103.

48. NAGPRA Review Committee, *Official Transcript of the Twenty-Third Meeting*, 13. A related discussion regarding the truth content of oral tradition and legal discourse erupted between Terry Knight of the Ute Mountain Ute Tribe and members of the Review Committee at the thirty-seventh meeting of the committee. NAGPRA Review Committee, *Official Transcript of the Thirty-Seventh Meeting of the NAGPRA Review Committee* (Green Bay, WI: National Park Service, May 14–15, 2008).

49. NAGPRA Review Committee, *Official Transcript of the Thirty-Third Meeting, vol.* 1, 23–24.

50. NAGPRA Review Committee, Official Transcript of the Twenty-Third Meeting, 10; NAGPRA Review Committee, Official Transcript of the Thirty-Third Meeting, vol. 1, 103, 25.

51. On secretism, see Johnson, *Secrets, Gossip, and Gods*.

52. For a provocative analysis of religious form in relationship to and codependency with the secular, see Russell McCutcheon, "'They Licked the Platter Clean': On the Co-Dependency of the Religious and the Secular," *Method and Theory in the Study of Religion* 19 (2007): 173–99.

53. Lincoln, *Holy Terrors*, 5–8.

54. Smith, *Relating Religion*, 107.

9 Making Religion through Secularist Legal Discourse: The Case of Turkish Alevism

Markus Dressler

Previously rather silent and marginalized in public discourse, the Alevis of Turkey embarked since the late 1980s on a revival and reconceptualization of their traditions, publicly asserting their difference from the Sunni Muslim majority. They began to build organizations and networks and to campaign for official recognition of Alevism (Turk.: *Alevilik*). Until that time considered pretty much secularized and assimilated in Turkish society, they now took recourse to discourses of identity and religion, increasingly conceptualizing Alevi difference in terms of belief and practice, history, philosophy, and theology.[1] The still ongoing reframing of Alevism follows implicitly the grammar of a (world-)religion discourse that neatly separates between religious and secular spaces and practices.[2] In this essay I inquire into the ways in which the recent reconceptualization of Alevism in religious terms relates to the laicist discourse on religion in Turkey. The particular aim is to specify the role of secular law and legal discourse on the subordination of Alevi identity and practice, as well as its active differentiation from and/or empowerment vis-à-vis Sunni Islam.[3]

The larger aim of this essay is to contribute to our understanding of the role of specific "knowledge regimes of secularism" in processes of religion-making.[4] Largely following the work of Talal Asad, I understand secularism not only as defining itself against religion but as being itself deeply implicated in the making of religion within the context of the nation-state. Following a discussion of the contributions of the legal perspective for an analysis of laicism and its impact on the Alevi question, this chapter will provide an overview of the particularities of Turkish secularization and the institutionalization of Turkish laicism with particular focus on the Alevi issue. In order to work out how laicist and Islamic discourses interact in the negotiation of the legitimacy of Alevism as a religious practice and identity, I will then analyze a number of specific judicial contestations. A major thrust is put on the way in which assertive secularism (such as Turkish laicism) is less interested in dividing the religious from the secular and more concerned with distinguishing between legitimate and illegitimate forms of religion in line with nationalist, state-centered interests. The final analysis will discuss the ways in which Turkish laicism molds public discourses on religion and reflect on recent shifts in the internal balance of power between competing interpretations of secularism in Turkey.

■ SECULARISM, LAICISM, AND THE LEGAL PERSPECTIVE

> The nation-state requires clearly demarcated spaces that it can classify
> and regulate: religion, education, health, leisure, work, income, justice,
> and war. The space that religion may properly occupy in society has to
> be continually redefined by the law because the reproduction of
> secular life within and beyond the nation-state continually affects the
> discursive clarity of that space.
> —Talal Asad, *Formations of the Secular. Christianity, Islam, Modernity*

In the broadest sense I use the term *secularism* for political projects that are actively involved in differentiating between religious and secular spaces, symbols, bodies, and practices—independent of whether this is done in the name of religious, agnostic, or atheist agendas. These politics of secularism have, as the above quote by Asad underlines, been closely entangled with the formation and maintenance of the modern nation-state.

For the Turkish variety of secularism I use the term *laicism*. The vernacular term *laiklik* is derived from the French *laïcité*, with which it shares some basic characteristics. Historical differences between the French and Turkish cases (which are not relevant for my purpose since the aim is not a systematic comparison) notwithstanding, some of the traits of laïcité, as recently described by Olivier Roy, can directly be applied to the Turkish case and show points of convergence between the French and Turkish knowledge regimes of secularism. As for the organization of political space, laïcité endorses not only the primacy of the political over the religious, as is common in Western forms of secularism, but also the control of religion in the public.[5] Both French and Turkish laicist discourses are rhetorically directed against a previous, now othered, political order, in which religion had a central role in the organization of the state and public life. Reminiscent of Turkish Kemalist sentiments, Roy argues that laïcité as a legal and political principle would touch "the heart of French identity," and thus a perceived crisis of laïcité would be regarded as a crisis of the national self.[6] He further characterizes laïcité as a principle that reifies itself through processes of negation rather than affirmation: "The defense of *laïcité* is more than ever the defense of an identity that has difficulty defining itself positively because…it is largely based on myths, including the myths of consensus."[7] In this manner, the discourse of laïcité would be employed to distract from social and economic problems by transforming them into a debate about ideas. This has a paradoxical side effect: "Far from condoning off religion, militant *laïcité* constantly brings it back to the center of the debate and makes it the explanation for social disorders."[8] It is especially this element of French laïcité, which is also part of Turkish *laiklik*, that I am interested in, namely, the work of laicist discourse toward the normalization of particular notions of religion and the secular or, in other words, how laicism disciplines the religious by subordinating it to a modernist/secularist framework.

The legal perspective serves several purposes in this investigation. First, it sheds light on the historical particularities of the Turkish form of secularism. Turkish laicism is both historically and semantically connected to Turkish nationalism.

With roots going back to the late Ottoman Empire, they became guiding principles in the formative years of the Turkish Republic, when they were established as core of the state ideology of Kemalism. They have been honored by the constitution since 1937 and are heedfully guarded by the Kemalist establishment.[9] In broadest terms, the Kemalist modernization project, named after Kemal Atatürk, the first president of the Turkish Republic (founded in 1923), can be described as a civilizationist project initially dedicated to securing Turkish political independence and a refashioning of the newly imagined Turkish nation in distinctively "Western" style.[10] As such it is an authoritarian project that uses law as a major tool for the implementation and legitimation of a homogenizing modernism. I am interested in the place ascribed to religion within this context: How is religion molded within the political and legal power dynamics that constitute the discourse of Turkish laicism, the original and primary goal of which was to control religion and to limit its role in politics and the public sphere? And how and to what extent, viewed from the opposite angle, do Islamic discourse in Turkey, in general, and categories borrowed from the Islamic legal tradition, in particular, inform the grammar of Turkish laicism?

Second, the perspective on law provides new insights into the formation of the Alevis as national subjects within Turkish modernity. In the formative years of the Turkish Republic, Alevis were not able to develop a public voice. With the exception of a temporary period of political activism in the name of a distinct Alevi identity in the 1960s,[11] it was not until the late 1980s that Alevis began to demand their right to cultural and religious self-determination. Since then, however, they have begun to challenge—though hardly ever explicitly—the laicist order, which does not recognize an Alevi identity separate from Sunni Islam.[12] One arena where this conflict is fought out is the court. In both Turkish courts and since recently also the European Court of Human Rights, Alevis sue the Turkish state in the name of religious freedom.

What is distinctive about the role of law in the process of the Alevi re-formation is its terminological specificity and normalizing effect. I argue that having been subject to authoritarian laws and regulations preventing their recognition as a socioreligious community different from Sunni Islam, Alevis have learned to use the language of religion, in Turkey strongly shaped by the grammar of Turkish laicism, to turn it against the latter's coercive aspects. Selectively taking recourse to the language of a more liberal and pluralist secularism, they have begun to subvert the dominant interpretation of Turkish secularism, which insists on the hegemony of the state in defining religion and legitimate religious practices in public.[13]

In this way, third, the perspective on law through the lens of the Alevi debate provides an interesting view on the rivalry between conflicting trajectories of Turkish secularism, the opposite poles of which may roughly be characterized as authoritarian laicism (emphasizing state control of religion) on the one side and liberal secularism (emphasizing religious freedom) on the other. Recent developments seem to indicate a shift toward a more liberal interpretation largely parallel to the gradual move towards a neoliberal economic order that Turkey has experienced since the 1980s. However, the supporters of an authoritarian, state-centered laicism are not willing to concede defeat easily. Consequently, the tensions between liberal and Kemalist interpretations of laicism, both of which are closely connected to particular political and socioeconomic interests, continue to function as important ideological markers in Turkish politics.

■ THE WORK OF TURKISH LAICISM TOWARD THE RELIGIOUS OTHERING OF THE ALEVIS

Despite the efforts of many Turkish nationalist Alevis to paint the formation of the Turkish Republic in line with the Kemalist master narrative as a story of liberation of Alevism from centuries of oppression under Ottoman rule, empirical data tell a more sober story. The "Alevi Question" of Turkey historically emerged in the context of Turkish nation-building. Since it had become a political force to reckon with in the last decade of the Ottoman Empire, Turkish nationalism operated for the most part in tandem with Islam. Until the beginning of the Turkish Republic the ideal of Islamic unity—which hardly differentiated between national and religious ideas, sentiments, and practices—functioned as primary model for the nation as a moral and social community and was part of the rhetoric of Turkish nationalism.[14] Within this context Alevi difference posed a problem that needed to be explained and rationalized, or minimized. From the beginning of the republic onwards, the state pursued a double strategy with regard to Alevi difference, at times ignoring it and at times encouraging Alevi assimilation into Sunni Islam. Following the defeat of the Ottomans in World War I, Alevis were not protected by the Lausanne Peace Treaty, which only specified guaranties for the "non-Muslim minorities"; their socioreligious institutions were not recognized by the new Turkish state. Within the language of Turkish nationalism the term *minority* (*azınlık*) is reserved for non-Muslims, understood to be outside of the Turkish Muslim nation. Since in principal considered Muslims and Turks, the Alevis could not make claims for minority rights but were considered a legitimate part of the Muslim Turkish nation. In other words, nonrecognition of their socio-religious and ethno-cultural difference has been the price they had to pay for being integrated into the national project.

The discourse of Turkish laicism is dominated by the principles of separation of religion and politics and control and administration of religion by the state. While the former justifies repression of religious activism in politics, the latter secures the superiority of the state over religious institutions. This superiority is embodied in the Directorate for Religious Affairs (DRA).[15] The DRA is the sole institution authorized to represent Islam in the Turkish Republic and therefore Alevis are, to the extent that they are considered Muslims, under its suzerainty. It is important to understand the role of the DRA within the structure of Turkish laicism. Located *within* the state organization, the DRA represents theological authority combined with secular-political legitimacy. The laicist Turkish state thus formally divides and brings together within its structure theological and secular authorities. This inclusion and thus containment of theological authority within the state apparatus is one of the particularities of Turkish laicism.

The privatization of religion has been a key feature of secularist projects worldwide, which were both predicting and claiming for the public to be a space

untainted by religious claims.[16] Demanding privatization as a must for the establishment of secularity, the Turkish laicist discourse is organized by private–public
distinctions correlated with ideas about legitimate and illegitimate religion. Turkish
secularism from this perspective is less about policing the boundaries between
religious and secular spheres and more about asserting state hegemony over the
definition and signification of what are legitimate practices in the public sphere.[17]
As for Islam, it is the task of the DRA to define, represent, organize, and regulate its
public forms, and thusly the DRA embodies the normalizing, executive side of
Turkish secularism. Religious activities outside the oversight of the state are still
perceived as a threat by the Kemalist public. In the logic of Turkish laicism, "religious" Alevi spaces and activities located outside the DRA are illegitimate.

In the last two decades, Alevis increasingly challenged the politics of Turkish
secularism—in most cases, however, without directly criticizing laicist Kemalism.
Alevis accuse the DRA of trying to assimilate them into mainstream Sunnism and
of therefore violating the constitutional principle of equality and nondiscrimina-
tion based on religion.[18] They claim that they would be discriminated against by
the state since the type of Islam sponsored by the DRA would one-sidedly represent Sunni Islam; the DRA employees would be almost exclusively Sunni and in its
activities, such as its publications and sponsored events, the organization of religious education, the interpretation of Islamic law, policies regarding places of
worship, and the organization of religious holidays, follow the Sunni and disregard
the Alevi tradition.

The Alevi politics of the DRA provide us with a window into the inner workings of state-sponsored laicism and particularly the laicist state's concept of religion and Islam. To explore the grammar of this politics I will analyze an interview
with Ali Bardakoğlu, then president of the DRA, in which he comprehensively
explained the DRA's position on the Alevis and defended its religious neutrality.
According to Bardakoğlu, the religion concept of the DRA would "take as its basis
a general definition of religion that includes the beliefs and rituals of all groups
subordinated to and within Islam."[19] In line with the impartiality requirement
specified in the Turkish Constitution, the DRA would keep equal distance to all
Muslim subgroups, a stance that allowed it to serve the nation in a unifying manner.
Likewise, if the DRA were to sponsor a particular subgroup of Islam such as the
Alevis, this action would compromise its impartiality. The DRA could only support
practices accepted by all Muslims—practices to which Bardakoğlu refers as "the
common share of Islam." While the DRA would not oppose any practices conducted by a particular Muslim group in addition to this "common share," it would
be against its legally defined mandate to actively support such particularism.[20]

One of the most contested issues between Alevis and the Turkish state concerns
the status of the Alevi *cemevis*, literally "houses of community," in which Alevis
celebrate their main ritual, the *ayın-i cem* (ceremony of community). Alevis claim
that *cemevis* are places of worship and should as such receive the same recognition
as the houses of worship of other religions.[21] Since *cem* is considered a religious
term in the language of Turkish laicism, and since it used to be established practice
not to allow religious practices and spaces outside the oversight of the DRA, Alevis
themselves, in order to prevent direct confrontation with the state, until recently

tended to present the *cemevis* as cultural and not religious spaces. In his response to the increasing Alevi demand for recognition of the cemevi as place of worship Bardakoğlu again draws on the common share argument: "We can't be against the Alevi *cemevi*s, their traditional cultures, their supplications, their *cem* rituals—they are valuable, too. However, I do not think that it would contribute to the unity... of our society if we were to include them—that is these particularities beyond the common share [of Islam]—into the legal structure and make them part of the Directorate's services."[22]

Differentiating between the "traditional cultures" of Alevism and the "common share" of Islam and asserting the supremacy of the latter, Bardakoğlu combines culturalist with theological arguments. He explains that the cemevi could not be considered a place of worship, since the only Islamic place of worship would be the mosque, independent of whichever Islamic subgroup someone belongs to. Further, the rituals and supplications performed in the *cem* ceremonies could not be considered an equivalent to the Islamic ritual prayer, as would be apparent from both scientific examination and historical experience.[23] In this context it would be the task of the DRA to strive for "always providing objective and comprehensive knowledge on religion, and on Islam," and to advocate the "scientific and authentic interpretation of Islam": "The forms of worship of Islam, the core of Islamic belief, and the core of Islamic ethics are very clear. This matter is so clear that it can't be discussed; it is clear from the sources as well as from the tradition. However, in geographies and cultures where this is not sufficient, or not seen as sufficient, different additional religious motives and understandings have always continued to exist."[24]

■ THE BINARY RELIGION CONCEPT OF TURKISH LAICISM

Abundant claims to science, reason, and objectivity are characteristic of the DRA's self-legitimation within the parameters of a laicist discourse that contains a strong dose of skepticism against established religion. The rhetoric of the DRA provides a window into the concept of religion dominant in Turkish public discourse. This concept rests on a culturalist argument that is constructed around a set of binaries emblematic for the language and thought of secular modernism (table 9.1). It shows also how the Islam represented by the DRA is anchored within the Sunni tradition, with its particular taxonomies and truth claims.

TABLE 9.1. *The Binary Religion Concept of the Directorate for Religious Affairs*

Characteristics of Laicist Religion	Characteristics of "Cultural" Pseudo-religion
science/reason	ignorance/superstition
objectivity	subjectivity
center	periphery
history	contingency
authenticity/uniqueness	patchwork syncretism ("illicit innovations")
universality	locality
orthodoxy	heterodoxy
▶ religion	▶ culture

The implicit distinction between religion and culture on which Bardakoğlu draws in his positioning of Alevism, and which echoes discourses of religious revivalism, serves to divide the unchanging, objective essentials of "true" religion from contingent "additions" referred to the realm of the cultural, the local, the contingent—in sum, the inauthentic/"heterodox." To strengthen the argument and hide its normalizing underpinnings, it is presented in the language of science and avoids openly theological statements. Declaring the Islamic mainstream the legitimate "orthodoxy" as empirically reflected in history and founded in Islamic sciences, Bardakoğlu claims total objectivity for his organization's interpretation of Islam (which counts as the state's official understanding of Islam). Covered in the mantle of scientific impartiality, this move enables the DRA to defend Sunni mainstream practice as the norm of and for Islam in Turkey.[25]

At this point it is helpful to take a step back and reflect on the logic and work of binary constructions within the discourse of religion. Asad discusses the role of binaries such as belief/knowledge, reason/imagination, symbol/allegory, and sacred/profane as constitutive of secular discourse.[26] These binaries play an important part in the discursive constitution of the religious in dialogue with its dialectical other, the secular. As Russell McCutcheon has pointed out, the function of binary pairs is "to mark a discursive boundary of a structure that manages the various items that constitute actual historical existence."[27] In other words, binary concepts are, beyond being heuristic tools, a means of world ordering, that is, "devices that we use and argue over while making a world that suits our differing purposes."[28] McCutcheon's reflections are helpful in disentangling heuristic from political motivations behind the formation, legitimation, and maintenance of binary concepts. They invite us to sharpen our understanding of the normalizing perceptions and judgments that form the subtext to the construction and maintenance of particular binaries such as religion/secular and religion/culture. From this perspective, the affinity of binary pairs to the semantics of modernist discourses on religion, in particular the world-ordering machinery of secularism, becomes apparent.

■ CONTESTING RELIGION IN THE COURT ROOM

In recent years, there have been steps toward a gradual recognition of Alevism. Since 1998, certain Alevi foundations and associations receive money annually from various state ministries—minimal sums if compared to the budget of the DRA but nevertheless reflecting a certain recognition by the state that the Alevis are a sociopolitical reality that needs to be addressed. Mostly, however, the gradual increase of recognition of Alevism is achieved through the negotiation of concrete conflicts of interests. Courtrooms have become a major arena for Alevi contestations of the hegemonic nationalist-laicist discourse. The following intertwined issues dominate the legal debate: (1) the question of Alevi representation within the state system of religious administration, that is, the DRA, and the related question of receiving material support by the state; (2) the issue of representation of Alevism by the state, most fiercely contested in the context of mandatory religious school education and the presentation of Alevism in textbooks; (3) the question of who has the authority to signify Alevism, that is, the right to identify the meanings of Alevi symbols and practices; and (4) the question of the relationship of Alevism to Islam. In particular this last issue, which looms in the background of all the previous ones, puts light on how negotiations of Alevi representation, identity, and legitimacy are theologically framed. Since it touches on the hegemony of the laicist discourse to authoritatively define the religious, this issue is the most unsettling for the laicists. It shows how the logic of Turkish laicism needs to constantly produce religious others in order to justify and maintain its privileged position in the public sphere and how it is extremely reluctant to allow public negotiation of the meanings of religion/Islam. As stated earlier, the DRA is interested in drawing a sharp line between religion and culture, associating Alevi practices and spaces with the latter.[29] However, Alevis challenge the hierarchical and centralized definition of Islam by the state.

Din or Mezhep? The Religious Semantics of Turkish Laicism

On February 13, 2002, the Second Instance Civil Court in Ankara banned a newly founded Alevi umbrella organization, the Cultural Association of the Union of Alevi and Bektashi Organizations (CAAB), on charges of threatening the national unity of the country, that is, separatism—more precisely, cultural and religious separatism. As state attorney Fuat Samancı reasoned in his official comment on the ban, "The word *Alevi* is a religious term. The foundation of an association that focuses on Alevism under this term would destroy the indivisible unity of the state's nation and country."[30]

The court decision was based on the Turkish Constitution (articles 14 and 24) and the code of law on associations (article 5). These articles criminalize separatism based on religion (*din*) or a religious subgroup (*mezhep*), as well as activities in the name of a distinct religion or religious subgroup. The respective laws not only show the homogenizing ambition of Turkish laicism, and its connection to a nationalist reading of history that establishes Turkish identity by putting emphasis on its victimization through inner and outside foes, but also reveal roots in a distinctively Islamic approach to religion as reflected in the use of terminology from the Islamic legal tradition such as *din* and *mezhep*.

It appeared to be evident for the court that the CAAB was a religious organization and therefore had to be forbidden. Thus, the ruling, albeit negative for the CAAB, actually strengthened a particular position within Alevism, namely, the understanding of Alevism as a religious formation. The irony of this was made blatant in the Alevi organization's appeal, in which it rejected the religious category imposed on it by the court and declared that Alevism would be neither a religion nor a religious subgroup. In October 2002, the Second Chamber of the Supreme Court of Appeals annulled the ban of the CAAB in a close three-to-two vote. In their legal comment, the judges of the majority vote explained that the association could not be banned as long as it would not actually engage in activities of a religion or religious subgroup.[31] They further explained that they could find no evidence for subversive or separatist aims in the association's statutes. Interestingly, the commentary makes no statement as to whether Alevism could be regarded as a religious subgroup, an argument on which the initial ban of the CAAB was based. The commentary does, in fact, not mention the terms *Alevi* and *Alevism* at all; throughout, it refers only to "the association" and the question as to whether it would conflict with Turkish law and constitution. Thus, it circumvents the issue of the religious dimension of Alevism that had been the basis for the initial ban of the CAAB. While the judges of the majority vote refrained from defining Alevism, Alevism was called a mezhep in the commentary of the two judges who opposed the appeal. The commentary of the latter explicitly states that, as the statute of the association under question would indicate, the association would be committed to activities on behalf of the mezhep Alevism—thus violating the Turkish law on associations.[32]

Four months later, Attorney General Fahri Kasırga filed an appeal against the Supreme Court of Appeals' decision. He argued, following the DRA's standard position toward the Alevis, that the state had to maintain equal distance toward all Islamic subgroups and, therefore, organizations in the name of the Sunni or of the Alevi mezhep could not be allowed: "When associations that are based on religious difference are freely founded and their activities allowed, then naturally members of the other religious subgroups [*mezhep ve cemaat*]—such as the Naqshibandi-Aczimendi-Mecusi and so forth—, who also want to benefit from this right, will create associations in their respective names; such a restructuring will gradually take on the mission of [reopening] the [Sufi] lodges and convents and thus reach dimensions which would endanger the laicist order."[33] However, the court rejected the appeal and thus affirmed the right of the Alevis to open organizations in their own name. Once more circumventing the issue of the religious character of Alevism, which had been the basis for the attorney general's reiterated fear for the laicist order, the Supreme Court of Appeals referred to Alevism as "cultural variation" (*kültür çeşitliliği*) and declared that the CAAB should not be forbidden as long as it would not in practice endanger the public order—thus again putting emphasis on action as opposed to form in line with the court ruling that had initially defended the legality of the CAAB.[34]

Until recently, barely any of the hundreds of regional and transregional Alevi associations throughout Turkey operated under names considered "religious" by the laicist discourse. Those that did usually had to face legal consequences often leading to their prohibition.[35] In order to prevent this from happening, most Alevi associations restrained themselves from using the name "Alevi," which was considered an illegitimate "religious" designation if used by formally organized groups, but referred to themselves in recognition of the hegemonic terminological convention as "cultural" organizations. The practice of locating Alevism in the realm of culture is, a concession to the reigning religion discourse and, is in line with the culturalist arguments brought forward against the Alevis by the DRA, as discussed above. The CAAB, however, challenged this practice, and its judicial success was hailed by Alevi activists as a political breakthrough in their struggle for recognition. For Alevis, the achieved right to name their organization was perceived as a step toward religious self-determination with strong symbolic significance. Alevi attorney and activist Ali Yıldırım, president of the Istanbul branch of the Alevi Hacı Bektaş Veli Cultural Foundation, proudly stressed that "for the first time Alevis have founded an association with their own name. In the [CAAB's] regula-tions were not only terms like *cem* and *cemevleri*, but also terms like *Alevism, Bektashism, Alevi teaching,* and *Alevi philosophy*" (emphasis added).[36] Yet it has to be noted that while the CAAB was allowed to name itself ("Alevi"), the prerogative to sig-nify this label (as "cultural" or "religious") still remained in the hands of the laicist court.

The intricate legal maneuvering around the legality of the CAAB makes clear how careful Alevis until recently still had to be when articulating their identity in a manner that challenged terminological conventions sanctioned by laicism. In recent years, they gradually dared being more confrontational, and they are now more often openly challenging the state by emphasizing their religious difference from Sunni Islam. The successful appeal of the CAAB is an example of judicially gained steps toward a recognition of Alevism.[37] The debate on the legality of the CAAB also shows the theological dimension of laicist discourse and how this discourse is not static but evolving through subtle, though constant, negotiation. Changing political contexts certainly contributed to the seemingly contradictory approaches by state institutions vis-à-vis the Alevi question in the recent past. Since the emergence of political Islam as a serious force in Turkish politics in the 1990s, Kemalist secularists periodically align with Alevis, who are promoted as laicist/secular Muslims and thus a natural buffer against "reactionary Islam" (*irtica*). In 1998, the year in which Alevis were for the first time granted some money from the state's budget, Kemalist elites were, in the aftermath of the military-sponsored political and judicial crackdown against the Islamist Welfare Party in 1997, on high alert vis-à-vis the Islamist movement. In early 2002, at the time when the CAAB was initially prohibited, the Islamist threat seemed to be contained. At the time of the CAAB's successful appeal, however, the conserva-tive Justice and Development Party (AKP)—regarded by Kemalists as Islamist and a threat to the Kemalist legacy—had become the dominant political force in Turkish politics. In addition, the pressure by the EU on Turkey to improve the status of minorities, the Alevis included, had increased.[38]

While I do not think that the process of Alevi recognition can be explained by these political contexts alone, they certainly impact on the debate on Alevism. Recent years have seen both remarkable political stability (with the AKP having won two strong consecutive majorities in the general elections of 2002 and 2007) and attempts from Kemalist and ultranationalist forces to undermine that stability. For the Alevis, the political developments have been rather ambivalent. On the one side, there are strong Alevi voices that perceive the AKP as deeply rooted in an Islamist worldview that is regarded as traditionally intolerant of Alevism. On the other hand, it is unde-niable that the current AKP regime has gone much further than any previous government in holding out prospects of a formal recognition of the Alevi community and reduction of institutional discrimination. Crucially, however, in doing so the government reaffirmed Islam as framework for the "Alevi Opening", as the move has been labelled by the press. In late 2007, the government pushed for a new debate over the question of Alevi recognition, promising back then among other things that it would consider recognizing *cemevis* as places of worship.[39] Regular workshops bet-ween Alevi organizations and government representatives discussing Alevi claims were organized in 2009 and 2010. While the government made parallel to these workshops certain symbolic gestures of recognition (*cemevis* were recognized as legal Alevi meeting places, but explicitly not as places of worship; schoolbooks were modernized adding more and non-pejorative information on Alevism and related communities), this recognition itself at the same time cemented the subordination of Alevism under an Islamic reference system.[40]

The Law as Tool for the Advancement of Religious Freedom

While Alevi organizations previously, as, for example, in the debate about the legality of the CAAB, tended to get sued by state attorneys in the name of laicism, Alevi activists have in recent years become more proactive themselves. Reflecting an important shift within the power balances of secularist discourse in Turkey, it is now mostly Alevis who draw on the law to challenge particular state practices. Invoking more liberal notions of secularism, they initiate law suits both on the national level as well as at the European Court of Human Rights (hereafter: ECHR) in order to advance their cause. An example is the following case of the state-loyal, Turkish nationalist (Alevi) CEM Foundation, which in June 2005 submitted a petition to the Office of the Prime Minister, complaining that the state administration would undermine the Alevis' rights of religious freedom and thus violate the Turkish Constitution as well as Turkish and international law.[41] In particular, the CEM Foundation demanded that the cemevi should be recognized as a place of worship and public service, that the Alevis should receive a share of the DRA's budget, that a certain amount of the positions of the DRA's staff should be reserved for Alevis, and that Alevism as topic should be integrated into the mandatory religious education at public schools.[42]

In the negative response received two months later, the Prime Ministry rejected the foundation's petition, reasoning that Alevis would be part of Islam—implying that since the state's services for Muslims would also be for Alevis, the latter would not need special treatment.[43]

Characteristic for the laicist discourse is the implicit link between the political argument (which connects the distinction between private and public with notions of illegitimate and legitimate religion, respectively) and the theological argument (defining Alevism as a subgroup of Islam). Through their role as organizers and supervisors of Islam, the laicist state institutions signify meanings of Islam, in our example qua positioning Alevism towards their notion of normative Islam. This we see also in the next instance of the discussed legal battle. The CEM Foundation filed a law suit against the Prime Ministry at an Ankara Court, which, however, rejected the Alevi claims, reasoning that the claimants would not have been able to show that Alevis would in fact be discriminated in their freedom of religious expression or that they would be forced to follow a different creed. Further, Turkish law and constitution would not allow for the recognition of places of worship other than the mosque, and neither would it be possible for the state to employ civil servants for the conduct of Alevi rituals or to pay for services that deal with Alevi ritual. As a matter of fact, the state's neutrality in matters of religion would serve all religious denominations since it would prevent some orientations from being privileged in comparison to others. Put differently, positive discrimination of Alevism by the state would need to be rejected in the name of neutrality. Nevertheless, the court confirmed the religious nature of Alevism: "There is no doubt on the matter that Alevism is a serious, coherent religious belief and an interpretation of Islam which is embraced by a large amount of people."[44] In the logic of Turkish laicism it is precisely this confirmation of Alevism as "an interpretation of Islam" that allows the different organs of the Turkish state to reject what appears from the view of a unitarian state-Islam as privileged treatment. This laicism does not tolerate religious plurality in the public sphere since such plurality is perceived as a threat to the ideal of a religio-national unity, which, by implication, has a strong Sunni coloring.

In another recent case, the 5th Chamber of the Istanbul First Instance Administrative Court ruled in November 2006 in favor of Alevi parent Ali Kenanoğlu, who had in 2005 filed for his son's exemption from the mandatory classes in Religious Culture and Ethics, which start at fourth grade. Kenanoğlu, vice-president of the Alevi Bektashi Federation, maintained in his complaint that his son would receive a religious education that was "against the will of his parents and in contradiction with their religious and philosophical beliefs."[45] The state was represented by the Istanbul City Directorate for National Education. The directorate argued that the plaintiff would not be registered as belonging to a religion other than Islam and that therefore the child would need to attend the mandatory religion classes.[46] In addition, the courses on "Religious Culture and Ethics" would, contrary to the plaintiff's allegations, not be based on Sunnism: "The course does not take as its basis the teachings of a particular religious orientation [mezhep], but the fundamental values of Islam."[47] Again, the "common share" argument is evoked in order to justify the state's claim to represent the supposedly impartial and all-encompassing kernel of Islam. Put forward from an essentialist position, the argument cannot acknowledge that it is this hegemonic position itself that sets the normative standards by which it then judges itself as well as others. However, the court took the side of the plaintiff and ruled that the child should, considering the basic right of religious freedom, be exempted from religious education and that this would be independent of the child's religious affiliation.

The Governor of Istanbul filed a first appeal against the decision with the State Council. In its ruling, the 8th Chamber of the State Council heavily referenced a recent decision by the ECHR, in which the necessity of an impartial and pluralistic presentation of religion in accordance with the European Convention on Human Rights was emphasized (see below).[48] By criticizing the current curricula of the Religious Culture and Ethics courses as religiously biased and not pluralistic enough, the State Council indirectly not only affirmed the Alevis' religious difference but demanded their equal treatment in the name of religious freedom. Following the judgment, Alevis requested the government to apply the ruling, that is, to make the Religious Culture and Ethics classes voluntary. But the government refused to comply with these demands and a policy change in the near future seems rather unlikely (May 2011).[49]

Alevism at the European Court of Human Rights

The presented court negotiations point to a change in legal discourse reflecting a more sympathetic approach towards Alevi claims of recognition, as well as to a shift in the power balance between different patterns of meanings of Turkish lai-cism, among which religious freedom has begun to weigh more heavily. Whether judicial contestations will eventually lead the legislative and executive bodies of the state to establish more pluralistic religion policies and endorse full religious freedom for Alevis and other nonrecognized groups remains to be seen and depends on a variety of national and transnational political factors. Alevis have by now brought up several cases against Turkey with the ECHR by means of which they exert, especially within the context of Turkey's ongoing membership negotia-tions with the EU, additional pressure on Turkey to ameliorate their situation.[50]

As the above-mentioned State Council decision in favor of Alevi complaints against the mandatory religious education in schools indicates, decisions of the ECHR can play an important role in inner-Turkish judicial contestations. The State Council had made explicit references to a case at the ECHR court where an Alevi claimant had argued against the Sunni bias of the Religious Culture and Ethics classes, which would infringe on the religious freedom rights of non-Sunni stu-dents. Drawing on the European Convention on Human Rights, the ECHR had ruled, in October 2007, in favor of the Alevi claimant.[51] The claim forced the jury of the ECHR to determine whether Turkey's mandatory Religious Culture and Ethics classes would be biased toward Sunnism and violate the religious convic-tions of Alevi students. In order to make this judgment, the court was forced to engage in a theological discussion insofar as it had to assess the relationship of Alevism to Sunni Islam. Representing the claimant, advocate Kazım Genç, president of the Alevi Pir Sultan Abdal Cultural Association, implicitly rejecting the Turkish state's "common share" argument, declared at the court hearing that "Alevism is both in regards of its teachings/philosophy as well as in regards of its religious practices totally different from Islam, and an entity for itself."[52] Its own investigation, however, led the ECHR to a different definition of Alevism, situating it broadly in the Islamic tradition: "Alevism originated in central Asia but devel-oped largely in Turkey. Two important Sufis had a considerable impact on the emergence of this religious movement: Hoca Ahmet Yesevi (12th century) and Haci Bektaşi Veli (14th century). This belief system, which has deep roots in Turkish society and history, is generally considered as one of the branches of Islam, influenced in particular by Sufism and by certain pre-Islamic beliefs. Its religious practices differ from those of the Sunni schools of law in certain aspects such as prayer, fasting and pilgrimage."[53]

It is worth mentioning that this definition largely corresponds with the approach of the French historian of religion and expert on Alevism Irène Mélikoff (1917–2009), who had participated in the hearing as adviser to the claimants. While the extent to that her influence on the court decision and its wording cannot be assessed, the fact that the court choose a definition of Alevism strongly shaped by the mainstream academic account as represented by Mélikoff's work is remark-able.[54] Doing so, the court has in its definition of Alevism privileged a scholarly narrative as opposed to Sunni and Alevi narratives, respectively. In fact, this is an excellent example of how secular authorities participate in the production of knowledge about religion, in this case the question of the religious history and nature of Alevism. Within the knowledge regime of secularism, secular authorities have a privileged position in defining the religious—a definition on which their own status as secular authorities depends. In this sense, religion-making is a distinctively secularist matter.

■ TURKISH LAICISM REVISITED

The classical leitmotif of Kemalist laicism is the separation of religion and politics, reflected in the secular legitimation and organization of political rule and ensured by a system of control of religion by the state in order to secure its subordination in the public. This dominant leitmotif is, however, increasingly challenged by a second leitmotif, which gained weight in recent years: the leitmotif of religious freedom, from which some even derive the idea of protection of religion by the state.[55] The tension between these two leitmotifs, which is a tension between negative and positive freedoms, is obvious, and public debate reflects increased awareness in this regard. The general trend, as reflected in the discussed court negotiations, seems to be toward a gradual modification of Turkish laicism in the direction of a more liberal secularism.[56]

The conflict between authoritarian laicism on the one side and a more liberal secularism on the other is complex and comprises entangled issues of political ideology and cultural hegemony, as well as economic and political privileges.[57] Viewed from the outside, Kemalist laicism in its Jacobean variety appears caught in a self-created tragic circle. By criminalizing religious practices and languages it holds as dangerous for the Turkish nation-state project, it renders contestations of religious identities a matter of daily debate and thus contributes to their reification. Criminalizing the very name "Alevi" by associating religious separatism with it and by connecting the question of state recognition of Alevism with theological debates about its origins and essence encourages the framing of Alevism in religious terms and maintains its contested character in public debate. In this debate the question of Alevism's religious quality is projected through the kaleidoscope of the fractured political sphere of Turkey, thus producing readings of Alevism through particular political prisms. Vernacular Alevi discourses are obviously part of this dynamic.

The comparison with Germany, where a considerable Alevi minority (roughly half a million people of Alevi descent) has participated in, if not spearheaded, the Alevi revival, brings to the forefront the power of the discursive framework of state institutions and public opinion when it comes to the articulation of religious difference. In Germany, Alevis can gain certain privileges upon obtaining official recognition as a religious community by the state. The adoption of a rhetoric of identity based on notions of religious difference as pushed for by Alevi representatives in Germany reflects an adjustment to the German discourse of identity politics, wherein religion is cast as a legitimate ground for state recognition as a distinct community.[58] When Alevis in Germany struggle for recognition as a "Corporation of Public Law" and try to establish religious education in public schools, both pursuits force them to specify the religious contours of Alevism.[59] Thus, while the religio-political discourse of Turkey discourages Alevis from pursuing a politics of representation that relies on language and symbols associated by the laicist knowledge regime with religion, and is more favorable to representation of Alevism in terms of culture and folklore, in Germany identity politics privilege religious difference over other rhetorics of group difference. Also, there is much less sociocultural and political pressure on Alevis in Germany to position themselves vis-à-vis Islam. In Germany, Sunni Islam is not in a privileged position in comparison to other interpretations of Islam, and Islam as such is not necessarily the standard against which Alevism is measured. Therefore it is rather unproblematic for Alevis in Germany (at least as far as the state and the "German" public are concerned) to go in their self-representation beyond the boundaries of Islamic discourse.[60] For those Alevis (and this is certainly the majority) who prefer to remain within an Islamic frame of reference, anti-Muslim prejudice in Germany allows them to present themselves as a kind of "alternative Islam," that is, secular, tolerant, in short: "modern."[61] To sum up, in Germany Alevis can take advantage of a discourse that privileges religious over cultural rhetorics of difference, and enunciations of Alevi identity are not, as in the Turkish case, confined by the semantics and language conventions of Islam and Turkish nationalism.[62]

■ CONCLUSION

Turkish laicists are, not unlike their French cousins, at tremendous unease with the idea of a public sphere allowing for a civically and politically active role of religion. What is at stake in the discussed legal contestations is, on one level, the hegemony to define the language and the rules of conduct in the Turkish public sphere. When Alevis are allowed to self-identify using "religious" language, then the hegemony of state-administered laicist discourse and practice, understood as depending on its exclusive right to define the scope and legitimate roles of religion in the public, is under threat. While the knowledge regime of Turkish laicism therefore discourages the framing of group identities (other than those of the officially recognized religions) in religious terms, at the same time religious language registers in the public discourse as a powerful though divisive tool for identity claims. This reflects the enormous tension between the Kemalist knowledge regime of laicism and traditional worldviews shared by more conservative parts of society. In the public debate on the legitimacy of the Alevis' religious difference this tension plays out as ambivalence in regard to how Turkish secularism ought to be, that is, in relation to its Jacobean and more pluralist leitmotifs, respectively.

The Alevi case points to the peculiar role of legal discourse in the normalization of religion.[63] Perceived through the lenses of the secularization paradigm, the differentiation of modern life into distinguishable spheres of values and interests requires institutions that regulate conflicts around the boundaries between these spheres. From this perspective, positive law itself a product of the modern differentiation process, plays also an important role in the mediation of such conflicts. Independent of whether one adheres to or rejects the differentiation thesis, weighing religious against secular claims while sorting out the criteria for legitimate and illegitimate claims with regard to religion (and indirectly also the secular), legal discourse partakes in the demarcation and reification of the thusly juxtaposed spheres of secular and religious authority. In short, legal discourse plays an important role in the objectification of religio-secular realities. Indeed, I would suggest that there is a connection between the formal rejection of religious claims as valid evidentiary parameters in Turkish courtrooms and the concomitant prevalence of—even if not recognized as such—religious tropes in laicist discourse. It is part of the internal logic of secularism to create religious others. When religious arguments are formally denied legitimacy in legal and/or public discourse, as in the Turkish case, they nevertheless enter this discourse indirectly through the othering semantics of secularism. The religion-productive work of secularism shows itself also when it normalizes distinctions between secular and religious spaces and practices. By making the public subscribe to the religious–secular binary, it renders (religio-)secularism—of whatever variety—a paradigmatic way of making sense of the world. As I tried to show, Turkish laicist legal discourse is particularly religion-productive since it is fixated on defending the domains of the laicist public and thus constantly erects boundaries against illicit forms of religion. One should not, however, understand this religion-productive effect of secularist discourse as a monocausal force through which "religion" per se comes into being. I do not mean to postulate secularist discourse as a necessary precondition for religion. I simply aim to point to the mutual reaffirmation of secularist and religionist discourses, which operate both within the semantics of the modern nation-state, committed to its postulate of creating a homogeneous, morally bound, and controllable citizenry.

Turkish laicism confines the domain of religion positively by exclusive definitions, as reflected in the religion concept normalized by the DRA, and negatively qua prohibition of certain terms and practices (as, for example, in the case of the Alevi *cemevi*). In either way, it is in the name of laicism that religious significations are both challenged and reified. As explained, this should not be seen as paradoxical since it is part of the dualist logic of religion discourse as it has—through post-Christian political concepts, as well as colonial and postcolonial governmental practices and hegemonies—moved beyond its original "Western" loci and successfully globalized itself.[64] In countries such as Turkey, where the reigning institutions still hold sacred the promises of modernism, postsecular sensitivities have a difficult stand, and therefore the hegemonic interpretation of matters of faith as well as faith-related practice will, at least in the near future, remain under the influence of the dichotomist religio-secular way of understanding, objectifying, and compartmentalizing the world.

To conclude, I argue that the recent religionization of Alevism is strongly shaped by and evolving in dialogue with the grammar of Turkish laicism. We can see that clearly in the legal debates on the nature of Alevism in the courts, where the legitimacy of Alevism is negotiated through religious categories that are molded by laicist discourse. Not only is the legal arena understood as a thoroughly secular place, but law has historically been and still understands itself as a major agent of secularization. As within the broader religio-political discourse, so in the legal arena, too, recognition of Alevism appears currently only possible within an Islamic framework, which permeates the grammar and semantics of Turkish laicism. Within the laicist public sphere of Turkey, Alevis are forced to position themselves theologically within an Islamic system of reference: Is

Alevism a mezhep, that is, a legitimate Islamic subgroup/legal tradition? Or is it, rather, a *din* (religion) in its own right? The reformulation of Alevism is not negotiated in a neutral space, but the mode of its negotiation is shaped by the unequal power relations of the Turkish public sphere. It is not that terms such as *mezhep* and *din* would be alien to the Alevi tradition; but in the Turkish public sphere their particular meanings are coined by mainstream Islamic understandings, while the primary right to interpret them is in the hands of the laicist institutions, who are authorized to define and regulate religion. What the Turkish case therefore shows is how the grammars and languages of religion and secularism are intertwined, forming a religio-secular continuum in which their semantic similarity is constituted by the very difference they each claim in relation to the other.[65]

■ NOTES

1. The Alevi revival has attracted much scholarly attention. See, for example, Krisztina Kehl-Bodrogi, "Die 'Wiederfindung' des Alevitums in der Türkei. Geschichtsmythos und kollektive Identität," *Orient* 34 (1993): 267–82; Karin Vorhoff, " 'Let's Reclaim Our History and Culture!'—Imagining Alevi Community in Contemporary Turkey," *Welt des Islams* 38 (1998): 220–52; Markus Dressler, *Die alevitische Religion. Traditionslinien und Neubestimmungen*, Abhandlungen zur Kunde des Morgenlandes, no. 53, 4 (Würzburg: Ergon, 2002). For the German diaspora situation, see Martin Sökefeld, *Struggling for Recognition: The Alevi Movement in Germany and in Transnational Space* (Oxford: Berghahn Books, 2008).

2. See Markus Dressler, "Religio-secular Metamorphoses: The Re-making of Turkish Alevism," *Journal of the American Academy of Religion* 76, no. 2 (2008): 280–311.

3. The Alevis of Turkey, two-thirds of whom speak Turkish and roughly one-third of whom speak Kurdish dialects, and who are not to be confused with the Arab ʿAlawīs (Nusayris), make for roughly 10 to 15 percent of Turkey's population. They insist on their difference from Sunni Islam, manifested historically in their social and political marginalization within Ottoman and Turkish societies and their ritual and social practices, as well as in a worldview strongly shaped by Twelver Shiite mythology, Islamic mysticism, pre-Islamic Turkish traditions, and, more recently, modern humanistic ideals. For a concise account of Alevi history, beliefs, and practices and the modern transformations of the Alevi tradition, see Markus Dressler, "Alevīs," in *Encyclopaedia of Islam*, 3rd ed., ed. Gudrun Krämer, Denis Matringe, John Nawas (Leiden: Brill, 2008), 93–121.

4. José Casanova, "Immigration and the New Religious Pluralism: A EU/US Comparison," paper presented at "The New Religious Pluralism and Democracy," Georgetown University, April 21–22, 2005, 7, http://www.ipri.pt/eventos/pdf/Paper_Casanova.pdf (accessed March 6, 2010).

5. Olivier Roy, *Secularism Confronts Islam* (New York: Columbia University Press, 2007), 26.

6. Ibid., 16. I would like to emphasize that it is not my aim to endorse any functionalist notion of secularism/laicism as it shines through in Roy's text.

7. Ibid., 31.

8. Ibid., 32.

9. By "Kemalist establishment" I refer to those secular elites, who have until the early 2000s largely dominated the political sphere (with particular strongholds in the educational system, the judiciary, and the army), and have, due to their socio-economic position, been able to lead relatively comfortable secular lives, but see their privileges and

lifestyles under threat by the socio-economic transformations of the last years and the growing political and economic power of conservative segments of society. Esra Özyürek, *Nostalgia for the Modern. State Secularism and Everyday Politics in Turkey*, (Durham: Duke University Press, 2006); E. Fuat Keyman, "Assertive Secularism in Crisis: Modernity, Democracy, and Islam in Turkey," in *Comparative Secularisms in a Global Age*, ed. Elizabeth Shakman Hurd and Linell Cady (Hampshire: Palgrave, 2010), 143–58.

10. See Alev Çınar, *Modernity, Islam, and Secularism in Turkey. Bodies, Places, and Time* (Minneapolis: University of Minneapolis Press, 2005); Nilüfer Göle, *The Forbidden Modern: Civilization and Veiling* (Ann Arbor: University of Michigan Press, 1997).

11. See Elise Massicard, "Alevism in the 1960s: Social Change and Mobilization," in *Alevis and Alevism. Transformed Identities*, ed. Hege Irene Markussen (Istanbul: Isis Press, 2005), 109–35.

12. In the view of hegemonic Turkish laicism, recognition of inner-Islamic difference can only be recognized in the private sphere.

13. For a discussion of the private–public distinction as an organizing principle of Turkish laicism, and the ways in which this distinction impacts on the Alevi struggle for recognition, see Markus Dressler, "Public/Private Distinctions, the Alevi Question, and the Headscarf. Turkish Secularism Revisited," in *Comparative Secularisms in a Global Age*, ed. Elizabeth Shakman Hurd and Linell Cady (Hampshire: Palgrave, 2010), 121–42.

14. See A. Holly Shissler, *Between Two Empires: Ahmet Ağaoğlu and the New Turkey* (London: I.B.Tauris, 2003).

15. A massive state bureaucracy, the budget of which is larger than that of many government ministries, the DRA is responsible, among other things, for Islamic education, mosque construction and maintenance, provision of legal opinions (*fatwas*), and the pilgrimage to Mecca. See İştar Gözaydın. "A Religious Administration to Secure Secularism: The Presidency of Religious Affairs of the Republic of Turkey," *Marburg Journal of Religion* 11, no. 1 (June 2006), http://www.uni-marburg.de/fb03/ivk/mjr/pdfs/2006/articles/goezaydin2006.pdf (accessed March 6, 2010).

16. For a description and critique of the privatization thesis, see José Casanova, *Public Religions in the Modern World* (Chicago: University of Chicago Press, 1994).

17. See Dressler, "Public/Private Distinctions, the Alevi Question, and the Headscarf."

18. Legally, it is the DRA's responsibility to equally serve all Muslims of Turkey; §10 of the Turkish Constitution stipulates that "in front of the law everybody is equal without discrimination based on language, race, color, sexuality, political thought, philosophical conviction, religion, religious subgroup or similar reasons.... All state organs and administration units are obliged to proceed in all of their operations in line with the principle of equality in front of the law." In line with this egalitarian principle, §136 of the constitution specifies that the DRA should "execute its duties, which are specified by special regulation, refraining from any kind of political opinions or considerations, and dedicated to nationalist solidarity and integration in line with the principle of laicism" (*Türkiye Cumhuriyeti Anayasası*, http://www.tbmm.gov.tr/develop/owa/anayasa.madde?p1=1&p2=1. [accessed October 16, 2009]). The respective "special regulation" defines the duties of the DRA as to "organize the affairs relating to the beliefs, principles of worship and ethics of the Islamic religion, to enlighten society on the topic of religion, and to administer places of worship" ("Diyanet İşleri Başkanlığının Kuruluş ve Görevleri Hakkında Kanun," *Yeni Hukuki Net.*, Kanun 633, §1. http://www.hukuki.net/kanun/633.15.text.asp. [accessed January 20, 2011]). All translations here and throughout are mine.

19. Ahmet Kerim Gültekin and Yüksel Işık, "Diyanet İşleri Başkanı Prof. Dr. Ali Bardakoğlu'yla Söyleşi," *Kırkbudak* 3 (2005): 5.

20. Ibid., passim.

21. In this line, Alevi member of parliament Ali Rıza Gülçiçek (former president of the influential European Federation of Alevi Communities) introduced in November 2006 a bill into parliament which requested to Parliament granting *cemevis* as houses of worship the same status as mosques, churches, and synagogues. Such a status would not only would be of symbolic significance but comes along with services (such as free electricity and water) from the municipality. The bill was rejected. Necdet Saraç, "Cemevi Yine Yok Sayıldı", November 24, 2006 http://www.birgun.net/writer_2006_index.php?category_code=1187090418&news_co de=1164384439&year=2006&month=11&day=24 (accessed April 30, 2011).

22. Gültekin and Işık, "Diyanet İşleri Başkanı," 6.

23. Ibid., 6–8.

24. Ibid., 5, 13.

25. Comparable to the DRA, the Department of Language and Culture in India similarly bases its authority on secular/rational/theological/scientific/historical claims and functions as a disciplining apparatus that defines the parameters of religious practice in the public. See the contribution by Mark Elmore in this volume.

26. Talal Asad, *Formations of the Secular: Christianity, Islam, Modernity* (Stanford: Stanford University Press, 2003), 23.

27. Russell T. McCutcheon, "'They Licked the Platter Clean': On the Co-dependency of the Religious and the Secular," *Method and Theory in the Study of Religion* 19 (2007): 190.

28. Ibid., 184.

29. It is important to remember in this discussion that official assessments of the legitimately religious have material implications insofar as the state supports only those formations of Islam that comply with its definitions.

30. Hatice Yaşar, "Meğer Aleviler de Yokmuş," *Radikal*, February 15, 2002, http://www.radikal.com.tr/haber.php?haberno=29341 (accessed March 6, 2010).

31. What actually constituted a "religious" activity was, however, not specified.

32. Alevi Bektaşi Federasyonu, "Yargıtay'dan ABKB'ye Onay…!" http://www.alevifederasyonu.com/index.php?option=com_content&task=view&id=247&Itemid=261 (accessed March 6, 2010).

33. Adnan Keskin, "'Alevi İsmi Sakıncalı,'" *Radikal*, May 7, 2003, http://www.radikal.com.tr/haber.php?haberno=74420 (accessed February 22, 2007). Naqshibandi, Aczimendi, and Mecusi are Islamic communities perceived in the laicist discourse as actively undermining the Kemalist order.

34. Adnan Keskin, "Alevi-Bektaşi Derneği'ne Onay," *Radikal*, May 25, 2003, http://www.radikal.com.tr/haber.php?haberno=76229 (accessed September 14, 2007). It has to be noted that the ruling was influenced by a liberalization of the Legal Code for Associations in the context of adopting EU legal standards, to which the judges made explicit references.

35. Ali Yıldırım, "İçişleri Bakanlığından geri Adım: 'Cem, Cemevleri, Dernekler Yasasına Aykırı Değil,'" http://www.alevifederasyonu.com/index.php?option=com_content&task=view&id=241&Itemid=261 (accessed October 17, 2009). Only once before had an Alevi association been granted the right to found an association bearing an Alevi name. The Alevi Bektaşi Education and Culture Foundation won a legal battle to this extent already in 2000. See Şehriban Şahin, "The Alevi Movement. Transformation from Secret Oral to Public Written Culture in National and Transnational Social Spaces" (Ph.D. diss., New School for Social Research, 2001), 108.

36. Yıldırım, "İçişleri Bakanlığından".

37. Already in October 2001 the Supreme Court of Appeals had ruled that associations using the words *cem* or *cemevi* in their regulations should not be sued anymore, as had

previously been judicial practice. Yıldırım, "İçişleri Bakanlığından." However, exceptions of Alevi-friendly municipalities notwithstanding, Alevis still often fight uphill battles against local municipalities to get the construction of *cemevis* approved (Commission of the European Communities, *Turkey Progress Report.*, November 9, 2010. http://ec.europa.eu/ enlargement/pdf/key_documents/2010/package/tr_rapport_2010_en. [accessed January 20, 2011]).

38. See the annual reports (since 1998) on Turkey's progress toward accession released by the Commission of the European Communities (Brussels), accessible online.

39. Yüksel Işık, "AKP Aleviliği Keşfediyor," *Radikal İki*, November 25, 2007.

40. See Kose, Talha "The AKP and the 'Alevi Opening': Understanding the Dynamics of the Rapprochement". *Insight Turkey* 12. no.2 (April 2010): 143–64. Drawing explicitly on the principle of laicism, the recommendations in the final report on the workshop, presented by the government in March 2011, were limited to mainly symbolic gestures and thusly continued this politics of subordination/assimilation.

41. *Aleviyol*, "Alevilerin Davacı, Başbakanlığın Davalı Olduğu Duruşmalar Başlıyor", June 19, 2007, (accessed September 9, 2007).

42. Erdal Şafak,"Alevi Talepleri," *Sabah*, June 22, 2005, http://www.sabah.com.tr/Yazarlar/ safak/2005/06/22/Alevi_talepleri (accessed April 30, 2011).

43. "Başbakanlık: Alevilik İslam'ın Alt Kimliği," *Radikal*, June 21, 2007, http://www. radikal.com.tr/haber.php?haberno=224742 (accessed April 30, 2011).

44. "Alevilerin İbadethane Talebine Mahkemeden Ret," *Star*, January 12, 2008, http:// www.stargazete.com/guncel/alevilerin-ibadethane-talebine-mahkemeden-ret-82364.htm (accessed March 7, 2010).

45. "Din Dersine 'Dur,'" *Radikal*, November 24, 2006, http://www.radikal.com.tr/haber. php?haberno=205484 (accessed March 7, 2008). The Alevi Bektashi Federation is the largest Alevi umbrella organization in Turkey, claiming to represent roughly four hundred thousand Alevis through its member associations.

46. In Turkey, Christianity and Judaism are the only officially recognized religion categories other than Islam.

47. Behzat Miser, "Mahkeme Zorunlu Din Dersini Seçmeli Yaptı," *Radikal*, November 25, 2006, http://www.radikal.com.tr/haber.php?haberno=205567 (accessed March 7, 2008).

48. The judgment also made references to the principles of religious freedom and equality written in the Turkish Constitution. In its current form, the curricula of the Religious Culture and Ethics courses would not fulfill these principles. "Danıştay: Bu Müfredatla Din Dersi Zorunlu Olamaz," *Radikal*, March 4, 2008, http://www.radikal.com.tr/ haber.php?haberno=249211 (accessed March 7, 2010).

49. Umay Aktaş Salman, "Çelik: Sorun Yok, Aynen Devam," *Radikal*, March 5, 2008.

50. It is mostly leftist and state-critical Alevi groups that try to get support from European institutions (Martin Sökefeld, "Alevis in Germany and the Politics of Recognition," *New Perspectives on Turkey* 28–29 [2003]: 153). The more conservative groups, such as the CEM Foundation are afraid of the negative image in the nationalist discourse that such an appeal to European institutions can lead to, and they therefore prefer Turkish institutions as addressees for their complaints.

51. Belma Akçura, "Aleviler Haklı," *Milliyet*, August 29, 2007, http://www.milliyet.com. tr/2007/08/29/guncel/axgun02.html (accessed March 7, 2010).

52. "Tarihi Hata: AİHM'de 'Alevilik, Ayrı bir Dindir' Görüşü Savunulmuş!" *Alevi Yolu*, November 13, 2006, http://www.tumgazeteler.com/?a=1795769&cache=1 (accessed January 20, 2011). This dissociation of Alevism from Islam has led to severe criticism from many Alevis. The president of a local Alevi association in Elazığ, for example, threatened to

sue for damages those Alevi representatives who denied that Alevism is part of the Islamic tradition (Enser Alatürk, "Alevîleri İslam Dışı Gösterenlere Dava Açacağız," *Zaman*, November 24, 2006). For a more detailed discussion of Alevi attempts to situate Alevism outside of Islam, see Markus Dressler, "The Modern Dede: Changing Parameters for Religious Authorities in Contemporary Turkish Alevism," in *Speaking for Islam. Religious Authorities in Muslim Societies*, ed. Gudrun Krämer and Sabine Schmidtke (Leiden: Brill, 2006), 285–90.

53. Council of Europe, European Court of Human Rights, *Case of Hasan and Eylem Zengin v. Turkey*, 1448/04, *Judgment*, Strasbourg (October 9, 2007), 2.

54. For her most comprehensive monograph on Alevism, see Irène Mélikoff, *Hadji Bektach. Un mythe et ses avatars. Genése et évolution du soufisme populaire en Turquie* (Leiden: Brill, 1998). Mélikoff situates Alevism squarely within a Turkish-Islamic framework. For a critique of her approach, see Markus Dressler, "Irène Mélikoff's Legacy: Some Remarks on Methodology." *Türk Kültürü ve Hacı Bektaş Veli Araştırma Dergisi* 52, no. 3 (2009): 13–20. Online available: http://www.hbektasveli.gazi.edu.tr/dergi_dosyalar/52-3.pdf.

55. For a discussion of these different dimensions of the *laiklik* principle as negotiated in the Turkish public, see Dressler, *Die alevitische Religion*, 146–54.

56. Seufert discusses the current AKP government, and its intellectual environment's interest in softening the definition of Turkish secularism and loosening the state's grip on religion. See Günter Seufert, "Religion: Nation-Building Instrument of the State or Factor of Civil Society? The AKP between State- and Society-Oriented Religious Politics," in *Turkey beyond Nationalism?*, ed. Hans-Lukas Kieser (London: I. B. Tauris, 2006), 129–43.

57. See Markus Dressler, "On Turkish Laicism," *Immanent Frame. Secularism, Religion, and the Public Sphere*, July 30, 2008, http://www.ssrc.org/blogs/immanent_frame/2008/07/30/on-turkish-laicism/ (accessed March 7, 2010).

58. Initially, Alevis in Germany used to draw more on notions of culture and kinship than on religion. For insightful accounts of this transformation, see Krisztina Kehl-Bodrogi, *Von der Kultur zur Religion. Alevitische Identitätspolitik in Deutschland*, Max Planck Institute for Social Anthropology Working Papers, no. 84 (Halle: Max Planck Institute for Social Anthropology, 2006); Martin Sökefeld, "Difficult Identifications: The Debate on Alevism and Islam in Germany," in *Islam and Muslims in Germany*, ed. Ala Al-Hamarneh and Jörn Thielmann (Leiden: Brill, 2008), 267–97.

59. Recognition as Corporation of Public Law would grant them certain privileges and considerable autonomy in the organization of their internal affairs. In order to offer confessional education at public schools, they have to obtain the status of a "religious community" (*Religionsgemeinschaft*) in a legal sense. This requires a certain coherence of religious dogma and the existence of an institutional body that could authoritatively define the teachings of the community, supervise the development of curricula, and represent the community vis-à-vis the state. Ursula Spuler-Stegemann, *Muslime in Deutschland. Informationen und Klärungen* (Freiburg: Herder Spectrum, 2002), 229–32 and 247–54.

60. See Dressler, "Modern Dede," 285–87. On the work of "religion" in Germany cf. the chapter by Michael Nijhawan in this volume.

61. Sökefeld, "Alevis in Germany and the Politics of Recognition," 145–48.

62. Cf. the chapter in this volume by Arvind Mandair, who, in his discussion of the problems faced by Sikh men who wear the turban in France and the United States, makes similar observations on the way in which locally hegemonic discourses on religion and culture impact on the interpretation of religious/cultural practices.

63. Cf. the contribution by Greg Johnson in this volume.

64. See the contributions of Richard King and Arvind Mandair, as well as the introduction to this volume.

65. Markus Dressler, "The Religio-Secular Continuum. Reflections on the Religious Dimensions of Turkish Secularism". Winnifred Fallers Sullivan, Mateo Taussig-Rubbo, and Robert A. Yelle (eds.), *Law and Religion after Secular Liberalism*, Stanford University Press 2011, 221–41.

10 Bloody Boundaries: Animal Sacrifice and the Labor of Religion

Mark Elmore

▪ OF GOATS AND GODS

The deity's (*devatā*) matted locks shook wildly atop its chariot. The men carrying it struggled to keep it from falling to the ground, and the deity's medium (*gūr*) fell into a violent trance. His head jerked backward, and his hat (*ṭopi*) fell to the ground, announcing the *devatā*'s arrival. Violently possessed, the medium launched into an abuse-laden jeremiad. "You have neglected your duty. You have failed to fulfill your promise, and now you will be punished," he screeched. The target of this abuse was Rita, a middle-aged woman standing in her doorway with a stainless steel plate heaped with flowers, sweets, and 10-rupee notes.[1] She was stunned. Perplexed, she protested: "But I have remembered you every morning and evening. Daily, I give thanks for your miracle [*pratyakṣa*]." To the *devatā*, her pleas were vapid excuses for unjustifiable behavior; they only increased his anger. A year before, the deity performed a series of interventions that brought financial prosperity to the home. Both parties agreed on this fact, but they disagreed about the payment. Always hungry, the deity demanded a large feast of sacrificial goats, but the woman thought that her constant attention and prayers would be more pleasing. The deity was not pleased; he was hungry.

▪ THE PROBLEM

This dispute between Rita and her family deity is part of a robust debate over the legitimacy of animal sacrifice in the northwest Indian state of Himachal Pradesh, a debate occurring in local and transregional publics. It consumes the bureaucrats of several government ministries and is a common discussion topic over chai and chillum alike. It divides parents and their children, deities and their patrons, in addition to government officials and their constituents. This essay argues that debate over the legitimacy of animal sacrifice is dependent on what I call the labor of religion.

In the past, steep mountain passes and violent rivers separated the region from the fertile plains of the Punjab and the high deserts or Western Tibet, but the strength of these natural barriers is crumbling. Expanding transportation and communication networks now reach once-remote villages. The intrepid curiosity of global capitalism transforms rivers and mountains into unrealized profit, and concerns over being properly modern or properly Hindu are more influential than ever. Measured according to global development standards, the changes are impressive. Since 1985, the state gross domestic product has grown at an annual rate of more than 7 percent, attaining average annual growth rates of 8.8 percent from 1985 to 1990. As of 2001, 100 percent of villages in the state were electrified. The literacy rate had reached 77.13 percent from 31.96 percent in 1971. Infant mortality rates have dropped dramatically, and the number of health clinics and hospitals has exploded.[2] Yet improvements in the underlying conditions of life fail to capture the heady mix of fear and exuberance that has accompanied these radical changes. Beneath the bullish statistics and the self-congratulatory governmental press releases lies a complex mix of anxieties that generate new spheres of concern, or problematics, where there was once only the unreflective reflex of common sense.[3] Under the precipitating conditions of this anxiety, ritual practices like goat sacrifice have become a space where Himachalis struggle to define themselves, their gods, and their histories.

When Himachalis argue about the legitimacy of sacrifice—blood over fruit or interior versus exterior—their arguments are not simply about the most efficacious forms of ritual practice. They are defining themselves as individuals and members of a community. Taking that premise seriously, this essay does not seek to substantiate the claims of one position against another, marshaling historical data or appealing to abstractions like "rights" or "cruelty" to adjudicate whether or not animal sacrifice is legitimate. It seeks to understand the regimes of truth that underwrite Himachali self-understanding and the unintended effects of shifts in these regimes of truth.[4] Paying attention to these dynamics, as opposed to arbitrating a debate, pushing an agenda, or cataloging the accomplishments of modernization, the essay shows how debates such as that between Rita and her family deity are both produced by and productive of new and competing definitions of religion. In so doing, it provides some insight into the *effects* of rethinking and reorganizing life in relation to contemporary conceptions of religion.[5]

I refer to this dynamic reconfiguration of life as the "labor of religion," by which I mean the structuring force exerted by emergent (and disputed) conceptions of religion's meaning, function, and goals as well as the efforts of specific actors to define and delimit the scope of religion.[6] The genitive ambiguity in the phrase "labor of religion" captures the complexity of this dynamic. It suggests an irresolvable dialectic relying on both the conscious labor of particular actors to define religion and the conceptual labor that exceeds the control of any individual. In this respect, the labor of religion is not unlike the labor of the state as discussed in contemporary political science. In his classic study of state and society relations, Timothy Mitchell addresses a paradox at the heart of political science: while the field is devoted to the study and explanation of the state, no one has been able to define the state precisely. While scholars have long recognized this problem, whether as a function of nominalism or conceptual precision, Mitchell's innovation lies in his reorientation of the question. Traditionally, disagreement turned on whether scholars defined the state in narrow terms or whether they understood the boundaries between state and society as more porous. Rather than engaging in such polemics, Mitchell shifts the problem from one of "conceptual precision" (of precisely defining the state) to "the detailed political process through which *the uncertain yet powerful distinction* between state and society is produced."[7] He suggests that theorists turn away from concerns about the precise boundaries of the state and toward the formation of these boundaries *and their effects*. This essay extends the spirit of Mitchell's analysis to the category of religion by arguing that much of religion's contemporary power resides in this definitional ambiguity. This ambiguity—between the urge to define and the insufficiency of any definition—is the engine of religion's labor.[8]

In the discussion that follows, I track religion's labor through a series of ethnographic vignettes. In the first story, we travel to a small isolated village where we meet a man who discovers a new ability to remake ritual practices in line with his reformist definition of religion. This story illustrates how a growing vernacular literature on local traditions and the experts who research and write such literature are reshaping the daily practices of villagers across the state. The individuals who marshal this literature have become the new arbiters of cultural authenticity; increasingly, they are the people who decide what is and is not permitted in temples and festivals across the state rather than the temple presidents or even the deity's medium (*gūr*). In short, the story explores the epistemological labor of religion. In the second vignette, we trace the growth of a dispute that develops from a small debate between temple officiants into a volatile national debate. Among other things, this story shows how broad national discussions of religion can provide catalysts for escalating and transforming local debates. In this story, the viral character of the national debate on religion quickly infects a local debate reshaping motives, goals, and daily actions in line with translocal norms. Here we explore the politics of religion's labor. In the last section, we track the historical labor of religion to better understand how the actions of persuasive individuals (example one) and larger translocal discourses (example two) have affected the performance and understanding of one particular festival in the Kullu Valley over the past century.

■ REDEFINING AUTHORITY IN PUJARLI

The road to Pujarli was long and dangerous.[9] The late monsoon rains had transformed the road's fine dust into a surface slicker than oiled ice. We were traveling to a distant village located in one of Himachal Pradesh's most remote valleys.[10] Several local historians encouraged us to attend a reestablishment ceremony (*pratiṣṭā*) that would be "more authentic than any we had ever seen." Although estimates varied, they expected several hundred animal sacrifices.

Wet, muddy, and cold, we finally arrived at a tiny cluster of houses and the end of the road. We were ecstatic to be off the motorcycle as we began searching for a place to stay, but our difficulties were just beginning. Normally when we reached settlements this far from the normal circuits traveled by pilgrims and tourists, villagers greeted us with great enthusiasm, offering chai, roti, and a dry place to sleep, but the people we met at the end of the road were less than hospitable. There were no offers of chai, water, or even a place to sit outside of the rain. A colleague (a regional development officer in the Department of Language and Culture) who lives in Shimla had given us the name of a local contact and informed him that we would be visiting, but as we searched for our contact the villagers' distrust of us grew ever stronger. We spent the next couple of hours explaining why we were visiting the village and why we could be trusted. It was not that they were skeptical of a foreigner. They thought that we were working for the government, suspecting we had arrived to collect back taxes or to solicit bribes. The bags of strange electronics did not help.

Finally, after expressing our own distrust of state officials and sharing some detailed information about the histories of local deities, we were introduced to Ashok Sharma, who, we were informed, was a great historian of the valley. If anyone could help us, he was our man. Ashok invited us to stay in his home for the night, and after a warm dinner of lentils and roti, we sat in his study discussing our work. Despite what we had heard on the street, Ashok was primarily a botanist and conservation biologist interested in the medicinal properties of local plants. In connection with that work, he had done some research with villages nearby collecting stories about healing and herbal practices. Somewhat perplexed, I asked him why his neighbors thought he was a historian of theological culture (*devīdevatā saṇskṛti*). Eager to appear modern and scientific, Ashok explained that he did not believe in the power of local deities but that he considered himself a very religious man. He was a member of the Radhasoami reform movement, which advocates vegetarianism and meditation practices designed to unify the soul with universal sonic energies (*suratsabdhayoga*).[11] Intrigued by this disjunction, I asked him what he thought of some of the most influential contemporary historians of Himachal, including one man who is a Member of the Legislative Assembly (MLA) for a nearby valley. He confessed that he had read none of their work.

Early the next morning my assistant and I woke and began our ascent to the village, alleged to be less than an hour away. About three hours and two thousand vertical feet later, the village was nowhere in sight. Yet we stumbled onto something equally interesting. We came to an opening in the valley. Verdant terraces were etched into the valley walls, and snowcapped peaks loomed in the distance. It was strange to see such extensive terraced agriculture at this elevation (near thirteen hundred feet), and I began wondering if there was a large village nearby that had been omitted from governmental maps (common in areas like this that border China). However, approaching the fields, I realized that they did not contain corn, rice, or wheat. They were fields of marijuana. We had arrived at harvest time, and the plants were fully mature. Though marijuana plants are common in this region, they are normally wild or cultivated only in small patches. Farmers tended these fields meticulously. They were well irrigated, and all the male plants had been removed to inhibit pollination and encourage the females to develop the large buds that produce the strongest hash. Working in the fields, grandmothers and children alike were busy cutting, stacking, and rubbing the plants.[12] Strangely, broken stalks and rotting plants littered several of the fields. The plants were lying haphazardly as if cut by an absentminded demiurge with scissor hands. On further inspection, I noticed a pattern in the destruction. The terraces were divided into sections, each of which (I assume) was managed by a different family or farmer; each of these plots had at least one destroyed area. Perplexed, I approached some nearby farmers in search of an explanation.

"What happened here?" I asked.

"Only one week ago, the government arrived. They cut our plants and left them to waste. They told us we would be fined or imprisoned if we did not destroy the fields immediately," said a young man in the group.

"Do you think that people will stop growing the plants [*caras*] now?" I asked.

"Of course not [*bilkul nahīṃ*]," he chuckled. "Look around. What can the government do out here? They have no power," he said, returning to his work.

In many ways, I had come to the limits of state control. Here there are no roads, schools, or tourists (domestic or otherwise). The government can do little more than chop a few plants. But a debate at the festival among the participants would soon evaporate my heady feeling of arriving at the edge of modern governance.

We arrived in the village late that afternoon just as the reestablishment festival was beginning. Festivals such as this are rare, and villagers had invited guests from throughout the region, luring them with the promise of meat (*prasād*) and all-night dancing (*natī*). Accompanied by two other local deities, the primary god approached the village from the valley below, returning from a three-day tour of nearby temples. The men snaked their way up the steep slopes playing brass horns, carrying the deities, and smoking cigarettes. As they entered the village, the head of one of the wealthier families sacrificed a goat and threw it over the procession as a welcoming gift.

Quickly, the festival atmosphere turned from giddy and expectant to tense and conflicted.[13] Not everyone in the crowd welcomed the gift. Even though this sort of offering is common, there were people in the crowd who thought that the rite was inappropriate, and the disagreement precipitated a much larger debate about the remainder of the festival. The festival had not been performed for sixty years, and the only people who had seen it were too young to remember the details and too old now to be helpful.[14] Disputants argued over most of the festival's rites, but the greatest disagreements centered on when to fire the guns, when to offer goats, and when and where to offer the pig. No one knew of a textual source for the rite. Temple managers could not remember any customary practice, and the pronouncements from the deities themselves (through their mediums) were conflicting. Though all these people had opinions and arguments, there was no single person/entity invested with the authority to make a binding decision. Normally in this region, the deity's medium or a government official (the local MLA) would settle the dispute, but the villagers seated around me all agreed that the medium and the MLA were biased. Neither understood the "authentic" or "true" practice; they sought only to strengthen their own positions. After hours of intense arguments, with darkness settling on the village, Ashok arrived with some of his relatives to attend the festival. Finding no one to arbitrate these disputes, the disputants agreed that Ashok was the only person who could decide how they should proceed. Disputants considered his expertise objective, and everyone agreed that he was a pious man unstained by the local and governmental interests that had been driving the debate all afternoon.[15] In the end, Ashok struck a compromise. He decided that villagers could offer no sacrifices until it was dark but the shooting could proceed beforehand. He would allow the pig sacrifice, but festival participants could not watch.[16]

This dispute and its resolution evidence the development of new methods for deciphering truth from falsehood and new forms of expertise. All available historical evidence (oral histories, colonial records, textual fragments, and other archival sources) suggests that in previous centuries authority was located in local deities and their functionaries; the expertise for deciphering truth from falsehood developed in relation to these deities. In the decades that followed Indian independence, land reforms redistributed temple property to peasants, robbing the temples of their economic base and forcing the government to assume greater control of temple management and festival organization. This shift in power has produced a deep resentment between local temple communities and state government. For many the fight over cultural heritage is between the government and local officials. Yet this story highlights how the labor of religion often proceeds more powerfully beneath the surface tensions. The authority that once resided in local temples and which the state government seeks to manage can sometimes escape the control of both.

The outcome of this debate evidences a shift to the purported objectivity of vernacular ethnohistory and a new class of experts who create and employ it.[17] Villagers accepted Ashok's decision as authoritative, not because of his connection to the village, the deity, or governmental mandates but because of his presumed expertise in Himachal's theoculture (devīdevatā saṇskṛti).[18] Sometimes the labor of religion does not proceed through the "educational" efforts of cultural revolutionaries or the dictums of government. Sometimes it slips through the cracks produced by competing regimes of truth. While confusion over Ashok's vocation provided an opportunity to resolve this particular debate, when local disputes become translocal media events, their resolution cannot be so quickly or clearly achieved, as the following story so clearly demonstrates.

■ RELIGION'S LABOR AND MEDIA AMPLIFICATION

The prevalence of animal sacrifice at many popular tourist sites across the region has become a flash point for drawing the lines between religion and state. Governmental administrators have passed laws prohibiting animal sacrifice, and reformers draw on long traditions of substitution from Sanskrit literature to legitimate the offering of intentions in place of live animals. These efforts have met a wide array of resistance.[19] Not surprisingly, many villagers resist understanding their family deities as mental abstractions, but the same individuals who legislated and now "enforce" these public prohibitions—politicians, police officers, and district administrators—have also inhibited the eradication of animal sacrifice. While advocating the elimination of animal sacrifice in legal codes and administrative policies, many continue to offer sacrifices in their own homes, at night, and as we will see, in times of crisis. This is not because they are morally corrupt or ignorant, as their critics assert.[20] It is because these moments of exception dissolve the boundaries that otherwise limit theistic agency to a social function (binding Himachali identity) or a psychological resource. Seen in this light, animal sacrifice is problematic not because it violates a timeless prohibition on violence or because it cracks the sheen of neo-Hinduism; the problem lies with incommensurable conceptions of the limit, location, and function of religion.[21] Innumerable daily interactions evidence this irreconcilability, from the performance of domestic rites to state policy. Here we examine one recent, well-publicized incident that remains a touchstone for both sides of the debate.

Since the late 1990s, the *Amar Ujālā*, a Hindi-language daily, has reshaped the landscape of North Indian journalism.[22] Its aggressive approach to marketing, distribution, and local news coverage has helped it become the most widely read news daily in the Himalayas. Its success in Himachal results primarily from its intimacy with local markets. In contrast with other daily newspapers based in Delhi, Lucknow, or Chandigarh, the *Amar Ujālā* has correspondents in even the remotest of villages who can transmit stories and images instantly using the region's rudimentary communication networks. However, the lack of locally trained journalists has forced *Amar Ujālā* to recruit reporters from other regions of India. Like Western-trained anthropologists, these visitors sometimes misunderstand the events they report.

Tejpal Negi is an exceptional writer and inquisitive researcher who rose quickly to local prominence after moving from the neighboring state of Uttaranchal to the remote region of Rampur Bushahar. From the moment he arrived, Negi focused on local issues, giving representation to people the state government had long ignored. In the process, he became a popular public figure trusted by villagers across the region. However, in the fall of 2001, he gravely overestimated his influence and popular sentiment.

Drought was ravaging the region. The apple trees, which are the region's financial lifeblood, were emaciated. In a region where crop failure quickly becomes famine, water is everything. This is evidenced as much by the popularity of the region's numerous snake gods (*nāg devatās*) who control the weather as it is by the weather predictions that dominate daily chitchat. The drought threatened to destroy even the most productive of fields. Meteorologists were predicting no rain, and the mediums of most snake deities said that they were powerless.

In the years before the drought, Bhīmākālī's temple, in Sarahan village, had become the center of a pilgrimage tourism circuit. Its photogenic location near the snowcapped ranges of Kinnaur and Western Tibet and its classical cedar and granite architecture secured its place among the state's most marketable tourism destinations. In accordance with legislation drafted in 1984 designed to eradicate temple corruption and better manage large temples, Bhīmākālī came under the control of the Department of Language and Culture in October 1986.[23] This department is the primary governmental force behind religious modernization and the consolidation of regional difference in the Western Himalayas; it has worked to reform both the financial and ritual practices of the state's most prominent temples and funded a robust community of scholars and writers in the service of the state.[24] In response to complaints by tourists and powerful government ministers, department officials met with the chief minister, whose family has controlled the Bhīmākālī temple for at least five hundred years, to ban animal sacrifice within the temple complex.

This decision was unprecedented, and it violently shook the temple's conceptual and practical foundations. Adjacent to the main temple, which may be as old as the seventh or eighth century, is a large sloping well said to be the home of one of the most vicious deities in the region, Lankara vīr.[25] Although detailed records of this temple are scanty,[26] contemporary oral narratives and colonial documents identify it as a site of human sacrifice through the early nineteenth century.[27] While the British abolished human sacrifice at the temple,[28] animal sacrifice remained common until the Department of Language and Culture assumed control. The later ban enraged Bhīmākālī's villagers. They protested to local officials but were powerless against the seduction of tourism revenue. Divided by the demands of government and those of Bhīmākālī, villagers were forced to continue their sacrifices outside the temple and in their homes. One local farmer explained the problem: "The local people think that animal sacrifice must be performed. Now that here [in the temple] sacrifice is prohibited, they go outside. They go to the hills and do the sacrifice.... They ask the goddess to bring rain. They are farmers. How can farmers be successful [*suphal*, fertile, profitable] without rain? How will they fill the bellies of their families if they are not successful? For this reason, they continue to do sacrifice outside the temple." Yet common villagers are not the only people who continue performing these sacrifices. Birbadra Singh, the current heir to the region's royal family and the state's chief minister when this dispute occurred, continued to perform these sacrifices. While Singh's understanding of the meaning and cause of the drought is unknown, for most of Sarahan's villagers the drought proved that the goddess was unhappy that sacrifices were not being offered in her temple compound.

When the drought finally broke late in 2001, the rain was understood as a gift from the goddess. Elated at their good fortune and angry with the government, villagers planned a large festival to thank the goddess's kindness. Villagers organized the festival without the oversight of the temple committee to limit exposure to the authorities, but word spread quickly. On the appointed day, hundreds of villagers—including temple officials and local state administrators—arrived with goats, rams, lambs, chickens, pigs, and buffalo. The animals were slaughtered, and people feasted all day on the meat. Through her medium, the goddess expressed her satisfaction. Many others, however, were less than satisfied.

The next day Tejpal Negi published an article in the *Amar Ujāla* with the deceptively simple title "Animal Sacrifice outside of Bhīmākālī Temple."[29] Though Negi continues to claim impartiality, the article is a strongly worded criticism of animal sacrifice and those performing it. The article spares no one. After chronicling the different animals sacrificed and the conditions of the sacrifice, he recounts what he considers to be the cruelest (*sabse krur*) sacrifice, a water buffalo. The buffalo was mutilated and chased for a kilometer before villagers shot it three times. Shocked by such behavior, the author suggests complicity between the villagers and government officials, insinuating that the state effectively sanctioned the activities. He argues that they knew of the sacrifices and did nothing to stop them. Imagining himself as a lone rational voice, he closes by confessing his astonishment that "no one raised their voice against [*khilāph*] this barbaric [*barbar*] incident."[30]

Negi's article highlights a gap between the official policies and the actual practices of state ministers and bureaucrats, including the chief minister, who both tolerate and perform these sacrifices. Its readers did not miss the indictment. Maneka Gandhi, who was educated in Himachal before her marriage to former prime minister Sanjay Gandhi, sent a personal letter to the Himachal Pradesh

government condemning their inaction and holding them responsible for the incident.[31] Invested as it was with the incalculable aura of the Nehruvian dynasty and
the political power of her parliamentary seat, the state officials could not ignore
her petition. Response to the letter was swift. From the state offices, blame shifted
to local police officials in Sarahan who translated Gandhi's condemnation into
baton bruises for those who participated in the rite. Yet many of Sarahan's villagers
remained unapologetic for continuing the rites of their ancestors, and the anger
Negi had incited returned to him magnified by the national circuit it had traversed.
The villagers demanded a public apology. The police threatened to beat him and
the government threatened to expel him. The problem was not the sacrifices but
the article that publicized them. Despite these considerable threats, Negi remains
unapologetic.

Implicit in Negi's writing, villagers' actions, and the responses they elicited are
competing theories of ritual efficacy. For the villagers performing this sacrifice, the
blood offering is integral to their relationship with Bhīmākālī, sustaining relations
of mutual care—the deity provides for the people, and they provide for her. These
deities are not unknowable concepts beyond human understanding or representation. They are unassailably real with desires and needs not unlike those of humans.
Villagers often compare their special capacities and specific needs to those of children, naughty adolescents, government ministers, or wise old women,[32] and all too
aware of the frequency of drought, disease, floods, and famines most dread the
goddess's less than gentle reminders of their obligations. Simply put, blood offerings are ends in themselves. They are pragmatic, material transactions, and one
cannot substitute a goat with thought or intention . As one villager told me, substituting intentions in place of goats would be like repaying a loan with smiles.

Negi's position, fast becoming hegemonic in the region, relies on a very different logic of ritual efficacy. These discourses reject the logic of materiality on which
animal sacrifice relies. For Negi and others like him, these offerings are barbaric
and pernicious delusions. As he told me on several occasions, the offering of meat
to the deity is nothing more than a strategy to assuage guilt and legitimate inhumane practices. "Who eats the meat?" he would ask me: "It is not the god. People
eat the meat." For him, communication between deities and people occurs between minds and spirits; their success or intensity is effected by intention (saṅkalp),
not coarse substances like blood or money. In this context, material exchanges are
superfluous, only intentions matter. As long as one's intentions are pure, he told
me, the deity will be pleased—offering internal devotion in good faith is more
effective than offering meat without good intentions.[33]

Yet formulations such as this substituting emotion or cognition for action and
matter are literally incomprehensible to villagers like the president (pradhān) of
the Jākh temple in the Pabbar River Valley. In response to a question about substituting prayers for animal sacrifices, he responded confused and slightly agitated,
"But how will Jākh eat? Like the villagers at this festival [an annual spring rite], he
is hungry. If we do not feed him, he will be angry. Have you not heard the stories
of his anger?" I had heard such stories; and they were nothing short of terrifying.
Only a few days before, one villager explained a recent "natural disaster" as a product of Jākh's anger. Every few years as the heavy monsoon clouds crash against the

steep Himalayan foothills, pushed by warmer air on the plains and constrained by the mountains, the clouds are forced to rise quickly, and as the temperature drops the clouds literally burst, dropping as much as twenty inches of rain in an hour. In 1999, a cloudburst in a village just below the temple ripped a new steel bridge from its moorings and erased most signs of human habitation in the lower part of the valley. The burst took everything: state-built roads and bridges, innocent children, the fields of wealthy landholders; and for those lucky enough to survive it was a miraculous proof (*pratyasksa*) of his power and the consequences of ritual inattention.

These competing formulations of ritual efficacy and their attendant consequences highlight another aspect of the labor of religion. For Jākh's *pradhān*, the question of religion simply does not arise. There is only the deity, his demands, and his blessings. Questions about whether a particular rite is or is not religious simply do not arise. He is not concerned with adherence to orthodox standards or about the limits of what is or is not properly Hindu or an acceptable component of Himachal's theoculture (devīdevatā saṇskṛti). Yet for Negi and the cluster of critics who coalesced around him, the legitimacy of these rites was always a question to be determined in relation to religion. Negi and most critics of animal sacrifice in the region do not reject the existence and operation of gods; they are not atheists. Rather, they reject the idea that gods are like people—subject to hunger, anger, and bribes. For them, God is beyond the capriciousness of daily life.[34] Droughts and cloudbursts are meteorological events produced by storms, geography, and the laws of nature; they are not evidence of the machinations of any deities. Accordingly, deities cannot be influenced by blood sacrifices or 500-rupee notes. Faith is the only offering appropriate to divinity.

These antithetical approaches to the logics of ritual highlight one of the most powerful effects of religion's labor in contemporary Himachal. Increasingly, Himachalis are coming to understand interactions with their local deities and the festivals that punctuate the year's rhythm in relation to religion, and as they do this the incredibly diverse modes of interacting with local gods are being flattened and superseded by the seductive simplicity of faith (*viśvās*). The rapid expansion of faith as the central concept used to frame the region's polytheism, to understand its ritual transactions, and to distinguish the region from other parts of South Asia began appearing in the years following India's independence from colonial rule.[35] Its growth parallels two concurrent developments: the growth of vernacular ethnomedia and the increasing autonomy of the region within India's federalist system. These connections are not accidental, as it is in the writings and political efforts of the region's first chief minister, Y. S. Parmar, that faith really gains currency. These developments have become so pervasive that it is now common to hear villagers explaining the power and effectiveness of all ritual in terms of faith. When I asked villagers to explain how a deity was able to expel a demon, to cure a child's ailment, or to produce very fertile fields, by far the most common response was, "Yah to viśvās kī bat hain" (literally, "It's a faith thing").[36] This oft-repeated formula draws on a powerful ambiguity. For some, the phrase meant that their faith was literally the agent producing the desired result. For others it meant that the rite's efficient cause was beyond the discriminating capacities of the human mind.

In the face of God's sovereignty, faith is our only recourse. The growth of faith within Himachali discourses has had an enormous effect on *pratyakṣa* everything from ritual reform to self-transformation. Yet nowhere are these changes more apparent, and arguably more powerful, than in the reproduction of Himachali identity both as a personal ideal and as a normative state-authored agenda. As the final section will show, it is the equation of faith and religion that facilitates the rewriting of these festival symbols of regional unity. Here we see not so much, as Durkheim would have it, that "religion is eminently social" but that in Himachal the historical labor of religion creates a new object that becomes symbolic of the social.

■ DURKHEIM HISTORICIZED, OR, HOW RELIGION'S LABOR PRODUCES SYMBOLS

The most famous festival in contemporary Himachal Pradesh is Kullu Daśaharā. It is one of the few regional events that warrants national media coverage on an annual basis, and people come from across the country to participate in a festival that some believe has its origin in the time of the *Mahābhārata*. Yet the current national status of the festival is a very recent phenomenon. Before the 1970s, the festival was a local festival for local people. An early account of this ritual in 1871 by Colonel Harcourt, one of the region's most important early colonial administrators, describes the festival as a weeklong event that drew seventy or eighty deities from the Kullu Valley to the town of Kullu to pay their respects—and their debts—to the valley's most important deity.[37] Harcourt understands the festival as a periodic display of royal power organized to consolidate the kingdom. As such, it was an opportunity for the king to reassert allegiance in a region riven with political, linguistic, and theistic difference and, not coincidentally, for the British to perform and maintain their relations with the king. As Harcourt explains it, the festival renews tenuous social bonds, the mediums of local deities predict the blessings and difficulties of the coming year, and villagers receive guidance or repay debts. All of these transactions are sealed with the offering of animal sacrifices. In the decades following Harcourt's description numerous travelers, administrators, and local writers described the festival, but neither the specific ritual activities nor the meanings ascribed to them differ significantly from Harcourt's original description. It is therefore all the more revealing when both the contents and the meaning of the festival began changing in the years following Indian independence. The dissolution of remaining royal power, a series of socialist land reform measures, and the absence of a unified governing administration in the period from 1947 through the late 1960s led to the near dissolution of the festival. Stripped of their land revenues, temple authorities could not afford to send deities and their attendants to the festival. The royal family had neither the money nor the inclination to finance their travels. In these years, only the people from the immediate area visited the famous Kullu *maidan*. The festival's quick slide into memory was prevented only after the emerging state government recognized the importance of regional theoculture in the fight for independent state status. Growing governmental awareness of the importance of fairs and festivals in the fight to attain statehood emerged as a by-product of the collection effort surrounding the production of the 1961 census.

In 1961 the Indian national census began publishing supplements to its statistical data on the "Fairs and Festivals" of each state. In some states, administrators treated these publications as distractions, and the ensuing publications were quickly forgotten, but in Himachal Pradesh the project became integral to the struggle for state independence. Researchers, writers, and photographers were employed throughout the state to collect and present an authoritative archive of the region's innumerable fairs and festivals. The resultant publication is a hodgepodge of personal memoir, thoughtful reconstructive summaries, undigested lists, modernist fantasy, and nationalist polemic. Despite the volume's uneven quality and clarity, it was effectively the first attempt by Himachalis to formulate a canon of the region's cultural practices, fast becoming an index for assessing both authenticity and innovation. The details of its reports were used to formulate most of the state's basic policies on festival management. The detailed descriptions of rituals, processions, and practices have been copied and repeated by scholars, journalists, and advertisers. Despite the volume's authoritative status and the consistent repetition of the festivals detailed therein, many contemporary festivals differ in one significant detail from those described in the 1961 volume. They eliminate or hide animal sacrifice.

In the 1961 volume, animal sacrifice appears like many of the other details of the described rituals. Writers exhibit no need to problematize the ritual, to explain it, to criticize it, to lament it, or to celebrate it as a unique facet of local ritual practice. Perhaps most marked in this volume are the numerous color photographs of the ritual in all of its various stages. The volume includes photographs of goats being paraded to their slaughter, of action shots moments before final decapitation, and even of the blood offered to the deity. For these authors and the editorial board that compiled the volume animal sacrifice was simply one component of local ritual practice that needed to be represented as much as the deities' origin stories, descriptions of local dances, or the timing and attendance of the festival. The ritual had not yet come to signify anything other than itself.

Like the production of all canons, the 1961 volume makes possible the condensation of disparate materials into a unified authoritative whole—a condensation that facilitates the metonymic traffic between the specific and the general, between specific fairs and festivals and what would come to be called Himachal's theoculture. Each fair or festival thus becomes a symbol of the category with which it is now associated. Transformed into symbols, they assume their place in the standing reserve of the state.[38] Now the daily and periodic interactions between villagers and their deities mean something other than what they do.[39]

Where the rites represented in the 1961 volume characterize most interactions with deities as pragmatic transactions aimed at securing a desired result (rain, the alleviation of suffering, general prosperity, immortality, etc.), it is now much more common to understand an offering as a sign of devotion or a festival as a cultural performance.[40] It now becomes possible for the first time to see a local deity or the rite more generally as a symbol (*pratik*) of natural, psychological, or social forces.[41]

On October 11, 1978, *Girirāj*, a state-run newspaper, announced the culmination of religion's labor in Kullu: "After the formation of Viśāl Himachal [the complete state of Himachal, 1971] there has been a refinement of the form of Kullu Daśaharā.... This festival is now understood as an international festival.... This festival has really now been made into a symbol of the mutual citizenship and refined unity of the state."[42] How has the festival been "refined"? In recognition of the strategic importance of Kullu Daśaharā and similar festivals, the new state government expanded its support for the Department of Language and Culture, vowing to support the travel of deities and their delegations to the festival. Providing the festival's financing, made a series of important changes to the traditional festival. The central fivefold sacrifice that had disturbed orthodox Hindus and sensitive travelers like Penelope Chetwode for generations was removed.[43] The government department assumed control of much of the festival's organization, its timing, and its financing. It shifted its timing to follow immediately in the wake of national festivals celebrating Rama's victory over Ravana. Finally, it began promoting the festival as part of its tourism development strategy. In the wake of these changes, the festival quickly became a spectacle of regional unity.

While the festival now attracts hundreds of deities, most have become little more than bystanders. Festival participants no longer need deities to predict the future, to heal children, or to resolve disputes. The mediums who once spoke the will of god have become one more amusement among the festival sideshows. Villagers and visitors no longer need to offer goats and pigs to their gods. They need only arrive to enjoy the cultural unity. Now that, as another *Girirāj* article announces, the festival is a "Symbol of Ancient Culture" they need only bear witness to the evidence of Himachal's ancient religion (devīdevatā saṇskṛti). To argue that this symbolization has only recently become possible is not to argue that rituals were meaningless in the past or that rites did not perform a social function. The difference now is that the second-order work of connecting the rite to a larger abstract has become integral to the rite itself. Now when one attends the festival in Kullu, one is participating in the best example of Himachal's devīdevatā saṇskṛti. The vast majority of people who now attend the festival do not go to ask the deity a question or to heal their child. They go to participate in Himachali religion. Here religion's labor proceeds by stripping local practices of their specificity and redefining the logic and target of the festival. Ironically, in order to become an exemplar of Himachal's unique religion, the festival was transformed into a state-organized gathering indistinguishable from the innumerable others in Madhya Pradesh or Tamil Nadu.

■ THE END ALWAYS COMES TOO SOON

Employing a dynamic and historicized understanding of the labor of religion, this essay argues that much of the recent clamoring over "public religion" and the definition of religion is misplaced.[44] Debates about the disappearance or reappearance of religion employ unreflective conceptions of religion. They commonly assume that religion is transparent (everyone knows religion when they see it) and problematize its place within modern nation-states as a simple question of correctly locating boundaries.[45] This essay starts from another position. It assumes not only that the boundaries separating religion and its others are historically conditioned and ever unstable but, more fundamentally, that they develop in relation to particular regimes of truth and horizons of intelligibility. The negotiation of these boundaries in relation to changing regimes of truth constitutes the labor of religion. Seen in this light, the work of the historian of religion is not simply to show that religion assumes different forms in different places and times but to explore the dynamic process within which religion becomes legible and through which it becomes an object to be saved, eradicated, or ignored. The problem of religion for us is not one of conceptual precision, of distilling religion's essence in order to insulate it from its detractors or to banish it from secular modernity. Rather, the problem I examine is one of identifying the regimes of truth, their strategic operation, and the politics (and thus the styles of individual and communal formation and regulation) they legitimate. This is not a metaphysical or ontological project but, rather, a project we might call, following Ian Hacking, the historical ontology of religion.[46]

I hope by now it is clear that this analysis is not an exercise designed to bolster the foundations of multiculturalism. The debate over animal sacrifice and its ensuing constructions of religion, identity, history, and governance are not interesting because they differ from a particular normative fiction about Euro-American enlightened secularism. The debate is interesting because when read in the manner I suggest above, it unsettles the foundations on which discussions of secularism, modernity, and European hegemony depend. Tracing the boundary formations of religion and its others as performances rather than prescriptions, in a place that is literally "off the map," I hope to gain some distance from the regimes of truth we assume in our rejection *or* embrace of secularism. Such an approach, I believe, offers a clue into the puzzle that is "modern religion."

■ NOTES

1. I have changed the names in this essay to protect the people who so generously shared their lives with me.

2. Himachal Pradesh Planning Department, http://hpplanning.nic.in/.

3. Michel Foucault, James D. Faubion, and Robert Hurley, *Power* (New York: New Press, 2000).

4. Michel Foucault and Colin Gordon, *Power/Knowledge: Selected Interviews and Other Writings, 1972–1977*, 1st American ed. (New York: Pantheon Books, 1980), 107–33.

5. For broader discussions of this idea, see Talal Asad, *Genealogies of Religion: Discipline and Reasons of Power in Christianity and Islam* (Baltimore: Johns Hopkins University Press, 1993); Russell T. McCutcheon, *Manufacturing Religion: The Discourse on Sui Generis Religion and the Politics of Nostalgia* (New York: Oxford University Press, 1997).

6. To be clear, when I use the phrase "labor of religion," I am referring exclusively to the discursive machinations of religion. I do not attribute any metaphysical agency to the concept or its purported objects. Additionally, the primary term that I am translating as "religion" here is not the more customary *dharma*. This word is more commonly used throughout the Subcontinent to designate the English word *religion*; however, in Himachal the word is not used to discuss what happens in temples and between villagers and their local deities. For this, the primary expression is *devīdevatā saṇskṛti*, literally "god-goddess culture."

7. Timothy Mitchell, "Society, Economy, and State Effect," in *State/Culture: State-Formation after the Cultural Turn*, ed. George Steinmetz (Ithaca: Cornell University Press, 1999), 78 (emphasis added).

8. On the failure of all such definitions, see the influential analysis of Talal Asad in *Genealogies of Religion*.

9. Because of the potentially sensitive nature of this story, I have changed the village's name. Pujarli is the name of many villages in the Western Himalayas.

10. The "we" in this story refers to my longtime assistant and me.

11. Lawrence A. Babb, *Redemptive Encounters: Three Modern Styles in the Hindu Tradition* (Berkeley: University of California Press, 1986); Mark Juergensmeyer, *Radhasoami Reality: The Logic of a Modern Faith* (Princeton, NJ: Princeton University Press, 1991).

12. Villagers believe that children's hands are best for producing the hash. The resin in the plants adheres more easily to their soft skin.

13. Skeptical readers may reasonably ask whether villagers staged the debate for a curious ethnographer. To my defense, I can only say that no one ever asked my opinion. No one explained their rationale afterward, and never, during the debate, did anyone even seem to notice me as I mingled among other visitors. Moreover, the only people who might have been interested in my reaction had already spent many days with me at nearby festivals enjoying goat stew.

14. Actually, the number of years is unknown. People who had seen the rite, all in their seventies and eighties, disagreed on when it was held, giving estimates of anywhere from forty years ago to one hundred years ago.

15. For an interesting look at the production of experts and its role in the transformation of society, see Timothy Mitchell, *Rule of Experts: Egypt, Techno-Politics, Modernity* (Berkeley: University of California Press, 2002).

16. I witnessed similar forms of arbitration on a number of occasions while traveling or working with local ethnohistorians and government ministers tasked with managing Himachal's "cultural traditions."

17. In many ways, this shift is structurally similar to that which accompanied the development of the social scientific study of religion. See, for example, Louis K. Dupré, *The Enlightenment and the Intellectual Foundations of Modern Culture* (New Haven, CT: Yale University Press, 2004), chaps. 6–9; Tomoko Masuzawa, *In Search of Dreamtime: The Quest for the Origin of Religion* (Chicago: University of Chicago Press, 1993).

18. In other publications I explore the explosion of vernacular literature (in such publications as *Somasī, Himprastha, Girirāj*, and innumerable pamphlets and short books) written by local farmers and pharmacists as well as government officials and professionally trained historians. See my dissertation (currently being revised for publication): Mark Elmore, "States of Religion: Postcolonialism, Power, and the Formation of Himachal Pradesh" (Ph.D. diss., University of California, Santa Barbara, 2005).

19. On this form of "counterculture," see Michel Foucault, Michel Senellart, and Arnold Ira Davidson, *Security, Territory, Population: Lectures at the Collège De France, 1977–1978* (New York: Palgrave Macmillan, 2007), Lecture 8.

20. On these criticisms, see the editorial pages of *Amar Ujālā* and *The Tribune* (Chandigarh).

21. On the long history of such attempts and failures, see Wilhelm Halbfass, *Tradition and Reflection: Explorations in Indian Thought* (Delhi: Sri Satguru Publications, 1992).

22. See http://www.amarujala.com.

23. Management of the temple was assumed on October 6, 1986. "Schedule 1: Temples Administered under Srno Hindu Public Religious Institutions of Charitable Endowments Act, 1984," ed. Department of Language and Culture, Internal Publication Shimla, India.

24. Currently, twenty-two temples come under the direct control of the state government according to the provision of the Hindu Public Religious Institutions of Charitable Endowments Act, 1984. Ibid.

25. Informants, particularly at this temple, often asserted that this deity was actually a form of the ubiquitous, if underappreciated, Bhairav.

26. The Nepalese burned most of the records in the early nineteenth century as they retreated in defeat. The current patriarch of the region's royal family, Birbadra Singh, controls the remainder.

27. R. H. Deuster and Himachal Academy of Arts, Culture and Languages, *Kanawar*, Rare Book Publication 1 (Shimla, India: H. P. Academy of Arts, Culture, and Languages, 1996).

28. Padam Dev Singh facilitated many of these reforms.

29. Tejpal Negi, "Bhīmākālī Maṇdir Ke Bāhar Paśuoṃ Ki Bali," *Amar Ujālā*, November 7, 2001.

30. Ibid.

31. Maneka Gandhi married into the Nehruvian dynasty. Since the death of her husband, Sanjay Gandhi, in 1980, Maneka Gandhi has become a powerful political force in her own right. She has been a member of the Lok Sabha since 1989.

32. For examples, see, Molu Ram Thakur, *Myths, Rituals, and Beliefs in Himachal Pradesh* (New Delhi: Indus Pub. Co., 1997). During my fieldwork, I collected the origin stories of more than five hundred deities, which amply document this assertion. I hope to make many of them available online in the near future.

33. See Martin Luther, *Preface to the Letter of St. Paul to the Romans* (Grand Rapids: Christian Classics Ethereal Library), http://www.netLibrary.com/%20urlapi.asp?action=su mmary&v=1&bookid=2009153.

34. Importantly, when Negi discusses these issues he uses the singular *bhagavan* rather than the specific name of an individual god or the collective name "gods and goddesses" (*devīdevatā*).

35. The interventions of Y. S. Parmar were critical in this regard. Also, see the extracts collected in the 1961 census describing the fairs and festivals of Himachal. These extracts come from administrators all across the state and give us a good idea of the way that English-speaking state officials conceived their traditions. India, Office of the Registrar General, Ram Chandra Pal Singh, and India, Superintendent of Census Operations Himachal Pradesh, *Himachal Pradesh: Fairs and Festivals* (Delhi: Manager of Publications, 1967).

36. There was a strong correspondence between those who offered such formulations and the rejection of animal sacrifice.

37. A. F. P. Harcourt, *The Himalayan Districts of Kooloo, Lahoul and Spiti* (Delhi: Vivek Publishing House, 1972[1871]).

38. Martin Heidegger, *The Question Concerning Technology and Other Essays*, trans. William Lovitt (New York: Harper and Row, 1977).

39. The most common Hindi word used for rituals in Himachal is *rītī-rivāj*, which McGregor glosses as "manners, customs, ways; observances." It is also commonly referred to simply as *rivāj*, which means "1. Currency, usual occurrence 2. Custom, practice." R. S. McGregor, *The Oxford Hindi–English Dictionary* (New Delhi: Oxford University Press, 1993), 865–66.

40. The most interesting evidence for this transformation comes from the annals of the region's vernacular authors as preserved in *Somasī, Girirāj*, and *Himprastha*.

41. The change is not only a product of modernity or colonialism; it has happened at other times in South Asia. One of the most interesting of these cases is the semanticization of ritual that occurred in Kashmir with the formulation of high Hindu Tantra in the adept

hands of Abhinavagupta. See Alexis Sanderson, "Purity and Power among the Brahmans of Kashmir," in *The Category of the Person*, ed. S. Collins and S. Lukes M. Carrithers (Cambridge: Oxford University Press, 1985) 190–216; Alexis Sanderson, "Meaning in Tantric Ritual," in *Essais Sur Le Rituel, Iii*, ed. Anne-Marie Blondeau and Kristopher Schipper (Louvain: Peeters, 1995), 15–96.

42. "Bhāvātmak Ekatā Kā Pratīk Kullū Daśaharā," *Girirāj*, October 11, 1978.

43. Penelope Chetwode, *Kulu: The End of the Habitable World* (New Delhi: Times Books International, 1989).

44. See, for example, Mark Lilla, *The Stillborn God: Religion, Politics, and the Modern West* (New York: Knopf, 2007); Timothy Fitzgerald, *The Ideology of Religious Studies* (New York: Oxford University Press, 2000).

45. For examples of this trend within South Asian studies, see Ashis Nandy, "The Politics of Secularism and the Recovery of Religious Tolerance," in *Secularism and Its Critics*, ed. Rajeev Bhargava (Delhi: Oxford University Press, 1998), 321–344; T. N. Madan, "Secularism in Its Place," in *Secularism and Its Critics*, ed. Rajeev Bhargava (Delhi: Oxford University Press, 1998), 297–320.

46. Ian Hacking, *Historical Ontology* (Cambridge, MA: Harvard University Press, 2002).

11 Religion-Making and Its Failures: Turning Monasteries into Schools and Buddhism into a Religion in Colonial Burma

Alicia Turner

> If anything can be done to encourage the monks to take a greater
> interest in secular education, which they might easily do without
> interference with their religious duties, Burma will possess a system of
> vernacular education such as exists no where else in the East.
> —*Report on Public Instruction in Burma for the Year* 1912–13

The historical project of religion-making became a central technology of colonial power. It served to contain the diversity of ritual, cosmological, and supernatural discourses Europeans encountered in a regimented and bounded category of religion. In this way, the colonial production of religion was as much about transforming the potentially dangerous ways in which these discourses operated in the world as it was training colonial subjects in the conceptual boundaries that regimented modern life. However, religion as an ordering technology of colonialism did not always succeed, even in those places where the discourses it sought to constrain seemed the most familiar. Local religious discourses rarely were easily translated into the new universals of religious and secular. The hegemonic status that the category of religion obtained has served to obscure those historical moments when the efforts to make local discourses respond to the category of religion failed. Attention to these failures offers an opportunity to investigate the depth of the challenges religion-making posed through the insights of those who resisted it on the ground.

Colonial Buddhist Burma is a particularly fruitful place to look at the expectations of the category of religion, not only because Buddhism was central to the construction of the concept of world religions in European discourse but also because Buddhism was perceived by many at the time as a particularly modern religion, free from superstition and ritual and based on ethics and ancient textual doctrines.[1] Buddhism was supposed, in this view, to require the least transformation to be a fully modern religion, because it had preserved the truest essentials of a religion with the fewest of corrupting accretions. This meant that Europeans were more prone to see their expectations of religion in Buddhism and were bewildered when Buddhist practice defied their expectations.

As Arvind Mandair argues elsewhere in this volume, the colonial education system, and in particular the institution of the Anglo-vernacular school, was a key instrument of religion-making in British India. Recent studies, particularly the work of Gauri Viswanathan, have demonstrated the ways in which colonial education served to shape Indian elites in the categories of colonial modernity.[2] Burma, as part of British India until 1935, was not exempted from this history, and it was through an offshoot of the colonial education system—hybrid Buddhist Anglo-vernacular schools—that religion-making would eventually most impact the Burmese elite. However, colonial officials in Burma, a province on the periphery of the British Indian empire, argued that the projects developed on the Subcontinent were not always the most appropriate for the Burmese context. As education policies were adapted to Burma, a project that sought to engage local institutions directly and reform the conceptual landscape with a bounded concept of religion failed in its attempt to shape Burmese thought and action.

The impulse to create a colonial education system came from outside Burma in directives from superiors in the Indian colonial administration. Although prior to 1860 there were a small number of missionary and government schools in the province, local administrators had not emphasized education in part because the Buddhist monasteries, supplemented by small lay-run house schools, produced what colonial officials perceived as high levels of literacy. When the requirement for a colonial education system was imposed in the 1860s, colonial officials chose to engage the monasteries and shape them into a near-universal system of primary education that would be loosely regulated by the state. Buddhist monasteries were to be the backbone of vernacular schools, which would be supplemented by government and missionary Anglo-vernacular schools. This plan, although it maintained the fascination and support of a generation of educational officials, backfired. Despite seeking to promote monastery education in line with government goals, it produced conditions in which village and missionary schools thrived, drawing attendance and influence away from the monasteries. Moreover the plan's fairly explicit ideological goals of demonstrating the consonance of Buddhist and colonial ideals as shaped by a concept of religion produced a sophisticated resistance from the Buddhist monks, who exposed religion-making as a threat to the Buddhist *sāsana* or dispensation.

The project of religion-making would later find its impact not in the government's project but in a response of Buddhist elites to the growing influence of missionary and government Anglo-vernacular schools. Seeking to defend Buddhism, now conceived as a religion, these Burmese founded Buddhist Anglo-vernacular schools.[3] However, this earlier historical dead end—the government's attempts to engage the monasteries—highlights the techniques and aspirations of colonial religion-making and the limitations of its reach. In colonial Burma, efforts to shape Buddhism as religion through monastery schools failed because, as the monks articulated, it posed too great a threat to the project of preserving the Buddha's teachings.

■ EUROPEAN FASCINATION WITH BURMESE EDUCATION AND LITERACY

The British perceived the Burmese to be highly educated, an attribute that favored them in a discourse that had constructed education, and literacy in particular, as a marker of civilization and modernity. One of the key aspects of Burmese life that impressed European observers of the late eighteenth and nineteenth centuries was the ubiquity of the ability to read and write. European explorers, diplomats, and missionaries alike were constantly amazed at how common literacy was among men, and often women, of all classes. Michael Symes remarked in 1795 that "a knowledge of letters is so widely diffused, that there are no mechanics, few of the peasantry, or even the common watermen (usually the most illiterate class) who cannot read and write in the vulgar tongue."[4] In this way, the idea of Burmese literacy came to be central to the early European image of Burma.

The origin of this universal literacy, European observers explained, was the institution of the village monastery and the practice of sending all young boys to the monastery to receive elementary training in reading, writing, and basic Pali texts prior to their ordination as novices. The requirement to prepare to take the robes in order to create merit for their families meant that this system educated almost all Burmese males. While few boys stayed on past the initial short period of ordination to continue their education, the system had produced on the arrival of the British one of the most literate populations in the British colonies.

Discussions of Burmese literacy and monastery schools became standard fare for travelers' accounts and colonial reminiscences published back home. Almost every account of Burma published in the second half of the nineteenth century included a few pages on education, with the most famous dedicating whole chapters to the subject.[5] The idea of near-universal literacy was embedded so strongly in the consciousness of Europeans in Burma that it outweighed the quintessential mode of colonial knowledge—the census.[6] In 1872 when the first census of British Burma was taken, the results showed that only 24.37 percent of men and 1.37 percent of women could read and write.[7] Although these figures were higher than those for the rest of British India, the census officials themselves disputed their accuracy, citing instead personal experience that it was rare to meet a Burmese man who could not read and write, over their scientific enumeration methods. The census of 1872 dedicated two full pages trying to reconcile how they could have arrived at what were, to the authors, such clearly false numbers. They speculated on the modesty of the Burmese population in reporting their educational accomplishments, and the laxity of the district administrators in asking the questions, but never questioned the accuracy of the received knowledge that the Burmese as a culture were well educated and valued education.

The British were quick to place the system of monastery education as superior to any other system in the colonies. Burma was "one of the most literate of all the lands of the East," a comparison that could be used both to praise Burmese civilization and to justify further civilizing efforts elsewhere in India.[8] This fascination with widespread literacy did not limit itself to comparison with other colonial possessions; observers compared the Burmese system favorably to those of Europe. Henry Gouger remarked of his time in Mandalay in the 1820s that "my impression was that a larger proportion of the common people could read and write in Burmah than could be found among similar classes in our own country."[9] John S. Furnivall, writing in the 1930s to correct earlier claims, argued that "a hundred years ago the first English Commissioner reported that almost every one could read and write and, even if this report may have been touched with exaggeration, it is certain that the proportion of people who could read and write was then far higher in Burma than in England."[10] The actual literacy rates matter less for our purposes than the enduring perception because conflicting conceptions of literacy and religion lie at the heart of the conflict over education policy.

Education was quickly becoming a key value for Victorian society, one that was central to duties to civilize both its colonial possessions and its underclasses at home. The developing system of mass primary education in England had its origin in the Sunday and charity schools founded in the early nineteenth century to teach poor children to read the Bible and limit the threat of immorality and criminality among the new masses of poor urban youth.[11] As the nineteenth century progressed a consensus developed that education, and literacy in particular, was central to the moral betterment of the individual and the proper regulation of society. The creation of a system of primary education in England was a project of governmentality and the creation of the new responsibility of the state for the self-improvement of the people.[12] The tensions over church authority and state sponsorship of primary education are a prime example of the creation of a category of religion produced as a by-product of the secular social. This is not so much the decreasing authority of religion and the diminished role of the church in society but, instead, an instance of the creation of the secular social that in turn produced religion as a new category of experience and discourse set aside from the legitimate concern of the state for the condition of society.[13] The gradual creation of a system of primary education and the tensions over state or church control meant that these issues and categories were at the front of British minds as they confronted the Burmese education system.

Despite this focus, the educational system in England in the nineteenth century developed unevenly, with a patchwork of different schools and systems for different classes and state funding for schools run by Christian associations. It was not until the end of the nineteenth century that the state attempted a universal system of primary education. In this context, George Brown's claim that "it is a remarkable fact that the Burmese had universal education of a sort long before anything of the kind existed in any European country" is not entirely an exaggeration.[14] In the projects at home those advocating a universal free system of primary education were considered the most progressive. And here, much to their surprise, the British had discovered a culture that had exceeded even England itself in this key index of civilization.

From the British perspective, the Burmese had already accomplished a central goal of the modern state and a great hurdle for the progress of society. The Burmese had demonstrated that they understood the key role literacy played in the improvement of the people and the moral regulation of society and had done this through

religious institutions in ways similar to the process in England. Now colonial officials needed only to instruct them on the proper categorization of their accom-
plishment and offer them their expertise in making the system more efficient and
productive.

■ MONASTERY EDUCATION AND LITERACY:
EVERY LETTER EQUALS A PAGODA

Prior to British colonialism, the monastery was the primary source of education in
Burma, providing training in reading, writing, and reciting Pali and Burmese to all
of the boys of the village prior to their ordination as novices.[15] The training was
meant as a preparation for ordination and as a way of creating merit for students
and their parents. Boys were sent to the monasteries at age six or seven to begin
their education and were given slates to trace the shape of letters as they called
their names aloud.[16] The process of tracing and verbal memorization was repeated
as the students began to learn the first texts in Pali. This method of oral memorization was the most novel and sometimes irritating aspect for European observers.
The sound of a group of boys, each repeating a different section of a text at the top
of his lungs, became the sign of the village monastery and its pedagogy. As one
colonial official put it, "One often hears that the proximity of a pongyi kyaung can
be judged by the babel of voices coming from it... this discordant noise represents
the preparation of lessons."[17] This chaos defied European ideas of pedagogical discipline, but officials were forced to admit that it produced the literacy they
admired.

Boys learned to read by first memorizing the Pali of each text and then memorizing a *nissaya* version that interspersed a Burmese translation with each word of
the Pali text, teaching the meaning of the Pali through the *nissaya* text. In this,
comprehension came through memorization and only at the end of a long process
of learning texts, listening to sermons, and interacting with learned monks.
Memorizing the words and sounds of a text was a process that allowed the student
to interiorize the text for future reference. Beyond the *nissaya*, the meaning of the
Pali was not directly addressed. For the young scholars, questions about meaning
would be posed not to the monks but to less intimidating parents.[18]

Much of what the boys learned in the monasteries was not from texts but from
participation in the daily rituals of the monks. As Jeffrey Samuels has argued,
teaching boys in Theravada monasteries "is largely based on an action-oriented
pedagogy, a system of learning that is centered around doing, performing and
speaking."[19] While the young boys held the status of laity, they participated in all of
the daily rituals of the monastery from morning devotions and the collection of
alms through evening recitations. Boys learned ritual formula including the pre-
cepts and *paritta* texts by participating in these rituals.[20] The very physical and
practical education provided in the monastery was as influential as the practices of
literacy and the assimilation of texts. As Samuels argues, this does not mean that
"these texts have no place in the lives of newcomers to the sangha" but, rather, that
"the pedagogical function of these text has more to do with their performance
than it does with studying their content."[21] Texts were central to monastery

pedagogy, but the goals of monastery education were not limited to assimilating content.

The scholarly culture Europeans admired was represented literally in the treatment of texts. Texts themselves, both palm leaf manuscripts and later printed books, were objects of reverence. They were kept in a special manuscript chest, and students had to pay homage to a book before removing it. Students were reminded of the Dhammaniti proverb translated by one former monastery school student as "Every letter is worth a pagoda," or "One letter means one Buddha."[22] Thus reverence for the texts and reading and copying them were means of paying respects to the Buddha and of producing merit. In monastery education, texts and reading were not simply means of acquiring knowledge but were themselves integrated into the economy of merit and the preservation of the teachings.

Emphasis on texts and reading practices, while similar to European inclinations, was the product not of colonial contact but of a much longer trajectory of reform in Theravada Buddhism. As Michael Charney has demonstrated, these reforms parallel the history and the increasing importance of texts in Sri Lankan Buddhism described by Anne Blackburn.[23] Beginning in the late eighteenth century, royally sanctioned reforms of the sangha increasingly focused on textual memorization and preservation.[24] The purpose of these reforms was the preservation of the Buddha's dispensation or sāsana in the world, and in this they increasingly came to locate the essence of the teachings in memorized Pali texts. These reforms elevated the memorization and recitation of Pali texts to the pinnacle of monastic practice, which in turn strongly shaped the role of literacy and memorization in monastery pedagogy. The consequence was the establishment of curriculum and education as central issues for sāsana reform and the mandate of a pedagogical method that insisted on the precise memorization of texts. This led to the broad system that made literacy a central practice of preserving the teachings.

In addition, part of these eighteenth- and early nineteenth-century reforms was a process of purging monastic curriculum of lay-oriented and practical knowledges. Reformist monks accused their opponents of teaching skills and texts that were directed toward earning a living as a layperson and specialized sciences that are not directly related to Buddhist textual reflection and monastic practice. This discourse established these practices as corrupting forms of knowledge and defrocked monks who were accused of being engaged in teaching them, a set of expectations that would have consequences for the colonial engagement of monastery education.[25]

The practices and priorities of monastery education were organized around the category of sāsana. The Buddhist sāsana, often translated as the Buddha's dispensation, is the life and impact of each Buddha's teachings. The sāsana is at its prime immediately after each Buddha is enlightened but then enters an inexorable decline until the teachings disappear entirely from the world, setting the stage for a new Buddha. In the meantime, it becomes the project of Buddhists, monks and kings in particular, to preserve the sāsana and promote its flourishing at any given time and locale. Thus as a category and a project, it is the ground of possibility for Buddhist efforts of teaching, merit making, and striving toward *nibbana*. While the term *sāsana* comes to stand in for religion in some colonial translations, it is a poor fit for the category of religion promoted by the colonial state; sāsana's claims to universality were not easily provincialized into a system of religious and secular.

Monastery education in Burma did indeed place a premium on literacy as the British perceived. Through the history of reform and the tradition of respect for texts, literacy pedagogy became a central practice of Buddhism and the preservation of the sāsana that had been refined into a core institution of the village. However, literacy in this system was understood primarily not as a means to knowledge or to the content of texts but as a practice of creating merit and preserving Buddhism. In fact, those aspects of previous pedagogy that had focused on lay and practical knowledge outside of the sāsana had been denounced. The rationale was the preservation of the sāsana, a discourse that claimed universal and highest import in both political discourse and the daily life of the village. This was the world to which the British arrived, understanding little of its history or internal logic.

■ THE GOVERNMENT ENGAGEMENT OF THE MONASTERIES

The village monastery system of education was so impressive to the British that when the local colonial administration was forced to consider implementing a system of primary education, it seemed obvious to enlist the monastery schools. In 1864, Arthur Phayre, the chief commissioner of British Burma, faced with pressure from the government in India to create a system of mass education in Burma, proposed engaging the monastery schools in the project by offering the monks free textbooks.[26] He wanted to use the monastery schools as the basis for a near-universal system of primary education that expanded on the current monastery curriculum in areas where European knowledge would be helpful to the people, specifically arithmetic, geography, land measuring, and eventually astronomy and European history. He wrote in 1865, "It is believed that if books on the subjects above mentioned were furnished to the Chief Phongyee of each Monastery, and a qualified Burmese teacher were engaged to superintend the studies occasionally, that the books would be willingly used."[27] Adding European content to Buddhist practices of teaching would both make monastery schools more productive and bring their efforts under the regulation of the colonial state.

Phayre's plan to use the monastery schools as a base for an education system rested on encouraging the existing system and convincing the population that the government shared their educational goals. The gift of books to monks seemed the perfect means of engaging them with a new curriculum. Making donations to monks was one of the most basic acts of Buddhist piety and one that was expected from a sympathetic state. Intellectual materials, in particular the most highly prized new technology of the time, printed books, were especially appropriate donations to monks. The Department of Public Instruction officials quickly discovered, however, that while for the most part the monks were happy to receive the books, since in a Buddhist economy of merit such gifts could rarely be refused, they were slow to employ them in their teaching. The director of public instruction complained that monks "who have taken our books, have let them lie unused in the manuscript chest owing to their indolence."[28] Choosing to store the government's donated books in the place of reverence together with Pali texts in the manuscript chest demonstrated the respect due to precious intellectual artifacts for the monks. It was not likely meant as resistance to the scheme, and the response to this act demonstrates how little the colonial officials understood the role of texts in Burmese Buddhism. To the officials' dismay, the monks never responded with the desired enthusiasm to the gift of books or the offer to participate in the government's system; they did not necessarily share the government's ideas of the purposes of education, nor were they interested in its teaching methods.

While the monastery schools were reticent to engage the colonial system, the lay-run house schools took well to government encouragement. Early colonial discussions put the emphasis on the monastery schools, mentioning house schools as minor classes set up to provide education for girls excluded from monasteries, but Burmese sources indicate that the lay schools had a long history, likely given encouragement under the late eighteenth-century reforms.[29] In 1872, in addition to the free textbooks, the Department of Public Instruction created a series of grants to schools based on the performance of students on new standardized examinations. The lay house schools flourished under this system; their previous volunteer work had now become lucrative, further fueled by government requirements that they charge fees to the parents. Grants to monastery schools were more difficult, given that monks could not accept money in exchange for their efforts. The government attempted to circumvent this by offering the equivalent in gifts of rice or books to the monastery or by making donations to the monastery stewards who dealt with money. They found, however, that "the offer of grants is no inducement to Buddhist monks whose vows forbid them to receive money and the curriculum of the Department is not always approved by those who believe that the sole object of education is to enable their pupils to understand the truths of religion."[30]

Over fifty years the Department of Public Instruction tried dozens of programs to bring the monastery schools into the system, with a determination in the logic of Phayre's original plan—that if only the monastery schools could be modernized, they would create a massive universal primary education system and gain the sympathy of the people. As one report put it, "If anything can be done to encourage the monks to take a greater interest in secular education, which they might easily do without interference with their religious duties, Burma will possess a system of vernacular education such as exists no where else in the East."[31] Yet, according to the statistics they reported each year, all of their attempts were a failure; the number of monastery schools participating never significantly grew, and the growth of lay and missionary schools meant that the monastery schools had an ever-declining influence on the youth of the province.[32]

Despite a prejudice against the monks, doubts of the viability of the system, and the very real failings of its projects, attempts to bring the monastery schools into the colonial education system persisted unabated for more than half a century. The issue remained at the forefront of educational concerns into the late 1930s, when the lay schools offering English education had all but decimated the attendance at monastery schools.[33] Yet they kept trying because they were convinced that the monks shared the government's educational goals. This ambivalence and persistent hope in the monks as educators stemmed from a fundamental misunderstanding of the monastic practices of literacy education.

■ PHAYRE'S RATIONALE AND THE MISTAKEN PURPOSES OF EDUCATION

> They looked on education as the main instrument of freedom.
> —John S. Furnivall, *Colonial Policy and Practice: A Comparative Study of Burma and Netherlands India*

Many discussions of the plan to use the monastery schools as a base from which to build a colonial education system emphasize efficiency and economy as motivating factors for the colonial officials. Monastery schools had the advantage that they required no investment in infrastructure and very little state aid for instructors, economic factors that were frequently used as a rationale for the system in the reports and requests sent to Calcutta and London. However, Phayre's original plan presented a second reason that was a larger and longer motivating factor for many in the Burmese colonial administration. In his early letters to the Home Department in India proposing the system, Phayre expressed deep concern that the only contact the majority of the Burmese had with colonial power was through its coercive aspects: "The people of British Burma as yet know very little of the British Government except as a Police, a Revenue, and Judicial power. . . . The masses of the agricultural population know nothing of the desire of the British Government to educate and to raise them in the scale of civilization."[34] He was worried that the face of the colonial state in British Burma was, to put it in Foucault's terms, purely juridical, whereas the purpose of the state was the improvement of the people. The reason for implementing a system of education was to show the population the true nature of the modern state.

For Phayre this meant not only creating model schools to demonstrate the best in British education but also actively engaging the monasteries to convince the people that the government was not in competition with the monasteries but engaged in the same project with the same ends. His early letters and memos referred to the monasteries as "National schools" and emphasized that the government's educational projects would only succeed if they were seen as augmenting and complementing the monasteries.[35] Colonial officials and British observers had been commenting for decades that the Burmese monasteries were already engaged in one of the most important civilizing projects of modernity; for Phayre all that was left to do was to demonstrate to the monks that they shared a common project and a common goal.

When Phayre saw boys tracing letters and reciting sentences at the top of their lungs he saw education. He, as did generations of officials that followed him, saw monks engaged in the improvement of the people through teaching them to read, a project identical to that of the modern state. Thus to him it seemed only logical to convince the monks that they could become partners in what was now the legitimate concern of the state. For the British government the goal of colonial education was explicitly framed in terms of the "moral and intellectual improvement of the people."[36] As L. E. Bagshawe points out, these two were taken to be fundamentally identical; intellectual improvement was understood in terms of productivity and usefulness in society, and the Protestant ethic had elevated industry as the central moral value of society.[37] Both projects to educate poor children at home and missionary educational projects abroad centered on forming useful and productive subjects. The National Society for Promoting Education of the Poor, which founded schools in England, stated its purpose explicitly as "to confer on the Children of the Poor the Inestimable Benefits of Religious Instruction, combined with such other Acquirements as may be suitable to their stations in Life and calculated to render them useful and productive Members of Society."[38]

These values are reflected in the subjects Phayre chose for the book donation program: geography, land measuring, and arithmetic, topics that were suited to making an agricultural population more productive in its labor. Throughout the annual *Reports on Public Instruction*, education officials lamented the decline of the monastery school because they saw it as the only productive contribution of the monks to Burmese society. They worried that the rise of secular schools served "to deprive the vast army of pongyis of what is perhaps their greatest sphere of usefulness to the community."[39] In the officials' minds, this usefulness was located solely in social contributions, not in the promotion or preservation of the Buddhist sāsana.

Productivity and engagement, however, were not goals of the monastery. The monks whom these education officials decried as detached and indolent were cultivating this detachment. The status monks held and the merit that donations and respect for them produced relied upon their cultivation of detachment from the world. The colonial officials failed to grasp how detachment and intentional disengagement could be a value. They commonly accused the monks of not participating in the government educational system out of apathy—even in those moments when the monks were most actively engaged in resisting the plan.[40] Accusations of apathy, laziness, and indolence, high crimes from a Victorian sensibility, demonstrate how little the education officials understood the purpose and nature of the sangha.

The misunderstanding runs deeper. For the officials of the education department, there was no conflict between teaching the government's curriculum and the religious goals of the monks because they understood education and literacy to be universal projects that work toward a universal good of progress and modernity. Furthermore, they understood the Buddhist aspects of the monks' teaching to be limited within the capacities of religion and confined to the particular. In their minds these aspects made up the *content* of what the students read while having no effect on the universal *practice* of learning to read. Pedagogy and literacy were the secular universal to which religious particularities could be added or neglected without changing the basic practice. The purpose of education was to form modern productive subjects; its religious content could serve to inflect these as productive Buddhist modern subjects or productive Christian modern subjects, but the learning itself was not a religious practice.

Officials from the education department insisted that monks could teach "without interfering with their religious duties," but this meant a recognition of religious duties that were somehow separate from their teaching. It required a logical and conceptual division between activities that were religious and those that were secular. A successful project engaging the monks in a colonial education system would require their recognition of the category of society, whose betterment was the legitimate responsibility of the colonial government. This in turn required a redefinition of the capacities of Buddhism and its location in a sphere known as religion whose responsibilities were for individual moral betterment and soteriology. Buddhism as a religion could operate as an adjunct to the state's projects, as Christian missionaries did, but education was not a religious project or a religious good; it was a social good necessary for the development of a modern, productive colonial society.

Phayre's plan required teaching the monks the proper categorization of their pedagogy. If they could simply learn the correct boundaries of religious and secular, two goals would be achieved at once: the state could further the improvement of the people through the institution of monastery education and the people would learn about the true nature of the modern colonial state. This was simply a matter of asking the monks to recognize the correct and universal categories that should shape their actions and need not, from the state's perspective, threaten their practices.

■ MONASTIC RESISTANCE

The monastic response to the government's education scheme was mixed. A small minority of monks welcomed the books and the new curriculum. Monastic resistance to the plan was much more common and fell into two broad types: those who expressed no open or organized resistance but did not comply with the rules set out by the Department of Public Instruction and those who rejected the plan and organized their opposition along a discourse that labeled the government's education efforts as harmful to Buddhism.

The former consisted of monks who would accept the government's gifts or acquiesce to participation but never allowed themselves or their pedagogy to be shaped by the new rules. These monks were simply not willing to take attendance and keep the records required for registration. These disciplinary acts of pedagogy had no purpose for the monks. Monastery education had its own disciplinary formation, and its ethics and discipline were something the colonial officials much admired, but this discipline operated on a logic very different from that of the modern colonial state. The organizing and surveillance technologies of examinations, records, and attendance did not in any way help to preserve the sāsana. This resistance was about opposing the ethical and disciplinary system that the government's education system was predicated on and not allowing it to supplant the ethical project of the monastery.

The second category of opposition was much more organized and explicitly contested the categories that the government's plan sought to instill. In 1887 a group of monks publicized a statement that teaching math and other subjects on the government's curriculum or accepting a government lay teacher into the monastery was a violation of the Vinaya.[41] This forced the more government-inclined monks to refuse the assistance they had requested and resulted in one monk who had worked with the education department being defrocked. Furthermore, they commissioned a treatise on the types of knowledge contained in the government's curriculum and whether or not monks could teach these subjects.[42] The treatise defined the government's curriculum as *lokāyata* knowledge, knowledge that because it did not assist in teaching people to strive for *nibbana* or a better rebirth instead worked to prevent progress toward these goals as distracting from that teaching. The monastic leaders argued that monks should not participate in the government's education scheme because its teaching did not further the goals of the sāsana and the karmic betterment of their students.

Juliane Schober has argued that the monks' resistance was a shortsighted evaluation of the impact of colonial forms of knowledge that defined opposition to colonial rule in premodern terms and precipitated the decline of monastic authority.[43] Like Donald Smith, she sees in the monk's decision a lack of understanding of the consequences of colonial ideas.[44] I would argue instead that the monks proved acutely aware of the fundamental shifts the government's plan required and their formulation of the problem in terms of *lokāyata* knowledge was an innovative response that sought to preserve the centrality of sāsana as worldview and conceptual framework.

This group of monks rejected the idea that monks could potentially participate in secular acts of teaching without violating their religious goals as the education department had proposed. From the government's perspective the monks were already teaching literacy, which was a secular practice and a social good, and they only sought to add further secular subjects like math and geography. The monks rejected these subjects and said that to teach them would distract from, and thus threaten, the Buddhist projects they should be focused on. Their resistance was not just a rejection of the subjects but also a rejection of the classificatory scheme the government's proposal presumed. The government insisted that the monks could teach the new curriculum without interfering with their religious duties, but teaching in the system required that monks accept the new categories of religious and secular to understand and shape their practices. The monks experienced the category shift the colonial system required as a shift in the nature of Buddhist practice. While the government claimed that it simply wanted to reorganize the system that was already in place, the monks understood the threatening potential of this conceptual change. Religion-making as a technique of the colonial state required not simply a shift toward a more individual, doctrine- and belief-oriented form of religion; it required that the monks and their actions be shaped by new categories. The plan required that the monks' practice be formed not only by the disciplinary procedures of taking attendance and keeping records but also by the recognition of social and religious spheres and Buddhism as a religion bounded off from other aspects of life. However, these boundaries worked against the monastic goal of preserving the sāsana and the Buddha's teachings. As the organized monastic opposition argued, teaching and learning in this system, and I would add being formed by its categories, were not just indifferent to the cause of creating merit and preserving the sāsana; they detracted from and threatened those projects.

In monastery education, learning to read was fundamentally a practice of preserving the sāsana. Learning itself produced merit and kept the Buddha's teachings from diminishing. While the content of the texts was important, the Buddhist aspects of monastery education were not primarily located in the content of the texts. The production of merit and the status of the sāsana did not rest on the boys' comprehension of the content of the texts but, rather, on the continued practice of learning and repeating both the texts and the practices of the monastery. The Buddhist aspect of monastery education could not be partitioned off from a secular practice of literacy; techniques of literacy were themselves Buddhist practices.

The monks resisted the conceptual subordination of the purpose for their pedagogy to a competing claim of universality. For them, their teaching had meaning relative to the category of the sāsana, not subordinated and located in a universal category of religion. The monks were not interested in participating in the creation of Buddhism as a religion because this did not serve their ends. They were not willing to engage a system in which the preservation of the sāsana was a peripheral consequence of a larger project of creating productive, modern colonial subjects. The monks did not recognize the universality of the secular educational project and would not subordinate the project of preserving the sāsana to the colonial categories.

■ CONCLUSION

Even where projects looked similar to the disciplinary and civilizing efforts back home, as was particularly the case with British perceptions of Burmese Buddhist literacy education, local categories and conceptual frameworks were resistant to colonial projects of religion-making. The perception of similarity proved deceptive; the projects were oriented toward very different and ultimately, in the monks' analysis, opposing ends. In this case, the engine of Burmese society's perceived progressive civilization was at its core opposed to the civilizing mission.

The creation of religion as a universal category is a historical process tied to the creation of the secular and social and the processes of governmentality. These historical processes responded to problems originating in Europe, but religion-making was a central technology of European colonialism in Asia and elsewhere. While the project of religion-making created a category of religion that claimed to be both universal and ahistoric, the contests and failures of its implementation in colonial contexts point to how hollow these claims are.

This case is instructive for thinking about the production of religion as a category because of the ways in which the category failed. The monks refused the scheme for primary education and with it the categories of religion and the secular it required. The production of religion as a category required a shift and reformulation of the efforts that count as religious. Locating Buddhist practices and thought within this sphere required reformulating those goals in relation to that category. Religious discourses and projects could not be contained in the category of religion and come out unchanged. The Buddhist goals became provincialized in relation to the universal modern goals of education. Their meaning had to take on a new location in the formation of the subject and collective identity. The education officials only wanted the monks to recognize Buddhism as a religion; the monks, however, understood that the plan required that they reformulate much more. They rejected the new categories because these required a new system of universalities that were in conflict with the monks' concerns for the sāsana and efforts for its preservation.

The creation of religion as a category in colonial contexts runs up against local categories of religious discourses. Religion-making faces the challenge of interpreting and containing those discourses within the new category, disciplining and training their excesses to respond to a new conceptual world. However, new categories reorient and reshape their contents, changing the larger world from which religious projects gain their meaning. Religion-making fails when it is unable to translate local religious discourses into the terms of the new category of religion. The breadth of religious discourses is not just contained within religion but must find a way to become comprehensible in the terms and context of the new category. As the monks point out to us, colonial religion-making is not only a threatening prospect for local religious actors and their authority; it challenges religious projects that take their meaning from local classificatory schemes and locally understood universals.

■ NOTES

1. Philip C. Almond, *The British Discovery of Buddhism* (Cambridge: Cambridge University Press, 1988); Donald S. Lopez, *Curators of the Buddha: The Study of Buddhism under Colonialism* (Chicago: University of Chicago Press, 1995); Tomoko Masuzawa, *The Invention of World Religions, or, How European Universalism Was Preserved in the Language of Pluralism* (Chicago: University of Chicago Press, 2005).

2. Gauri Viswanathan, *Masks of Conquest: Literary Study and British Rule in India*, Social Foundations of Aesthetic Forms Series (New York: Columbia University Press, 1989).

3. Alicia Turner, "Buddhism, Colonialism and the Boundaries of Religion: Theravada Buddhism in Burma, 1885–1920" (Ph.D. diss., University of Chicago, 2009), chap. 3.

4. Michael Symes, *An Account of an Embassy to the Kingdom of Ava: Sent by the Governor-General of India, in the Year 1795* (London: W. Bulmer and Co., 1800), 123.

5. These included Sir James George Scott, *The Burman, His Life and Notions* (New York: Norton and Co., 1963 [1882]), chap. 2; H. Fielding Hall, *The Soul of a People*, 4th ed. (London: Macmillan and Co., 1913 [1898]), chap. 11; Albert Fytche, *Burma Past and Present*, vol. 2 (London: C. K. Paul and Co., 1878), app. G.

6. Bernard S. Cohn, *Colonialism and Its Forms of Knowledge: The British in India* (Princeton, NJ: Princeton University Press, 1996).

7. *Report on the Census of British Burma Taken in August 1872* (Rangoon: Government Press, 1875), 24–25.

8. Kenneth J. Saunders, *Buddhism in the Modern World* (London: Society for Promoting Christian Knowledge, 1922), 3–4.

9. Henry Gouger, *Two Years Imprisonment in Burma (1824–26)*, ed. Guy Lubeigt, Burma Historical Reprint Series (Bangkok: White Lotus, 2002 [1860]), 22.

10. John S. Furnivall, *An Introduction to the Political Economy of Burma* (Rangoon: Burma Book Club Ltd., 1931), x.

11. Phillip McCann, "Popular Education, Socialization and Social Control: Spitalfields 1812–1824," in *Popular Education and Socialization in the Nineteenth Century* (London: Methuen and Co., 1977) 1–40; W. B. Stephens, *Education in Britain, 1750–1914* (New York: St. Martin's Press, 1998), chap. 1.

12. Graham Burchell, Colin Gordon, and Peter Miller, *The Foucault Effect: Studies in Governmentality* (Chicago: University of Chicago Press, 1991).

13. Talal Asad, "The Construction of Religion as an Anthropological Category," in *Genealogies of Religion: Discipline and Reasons of Power in Christianity and Islam* (Baltimore: Johns Hopkins University Press, 1993) 27–54; Talal Asad, "Religion, Nation-State, Secularism," in *Nation and Religion: Perspectives on Europe and Asia*, ed. Peter van der Veer and Harmut Lehmann (Princeton: Princeton University Press, 1999) 178–93.

14. George E. R. Grant Brown, *Burma as I Saw It, 1889–1917, with a Chapter on Recent Events* (New York: Frederick A. Stokes Co., 1925), 90.

15. I use the term *monastery education* to refer to the initial education of lay boys before they were ordained as novices. This is not to be confused with monastic education, the training of ordained novices and monks in the texts of the Pali canon, which was the object of reform and controversy in the eighteenth and nineteenth centuries. For a detailed account of monastery education and its history, see Paul Bigandet, *The Life or Legend of Gaudama, The Buddha of the Burmese, with Annotations*, 4th ed., vol. 2 (London: Kegan Paul, Trench, Trübner and Co., 1911 [1858]), 289–302; U Kaung, "A Survey of the History of Education in Burma before the British Conquest and After," *Journal of the Burma Research Society* 46, no. 2 (1963), 1–125.

16. The monastery schools were supplemented by lay-run house schools in many villages that offered similar training to girls and young boys. These schools were run as acts of merit by respected laymen or -women and taught the same curriculum as the monastery schools outside of the rituals and restrictions of the monastery that limited girls' access.

17. *First Quinquennial Report on Public Instruction in Burma for the Years 1892–93–1896–97* (Rangoon: Superintendent, Government Printing, Burma, 1897), 18.

18. Edward Michael Mendelson, *Sangha and State in Burma: A Study of Monastic Sectarianism and Leadership*, ed. John P. Ferguson (Ithaca, NY: Cornell University Press, 1975), 154.

19. Jeffrey Samuels, "Toward an Action-Oriented Pedagogy: Buddhist Texts and Monastic Education in Contemporary Sri Lanka," *Journal of the American Academy of Religion* 72, no. 4 (2004), 956.

20. Mendelson, *Sangha and State in Burma*, 154.

21. Samuels, "Toward an Action-Oriented Pedagogy," 956.

22. James Gray, ed., *Ancient Proverbs and Maxims from the Burmese Sources: The Nīti Literature of Burma* (London: Trubner and Co., 1886), 34. 153; Heinz Bechert and Heinz Braun, eds., *Pali Niti Texts of Burma: Dhammaniti, Lokaniti, Maharahaniti, Rajaniti*, vol. 171, Pali Text Society Text Series (London: Pali Text Society, 1981), 31. The student's translation is found in Mendelson, *Sangha and State in Burma*, 154.

23. Anne Blackburn, *Buddhist Learning and Textual Practice in Eighteenth-Century Lankan Monastic Culture* (Princeton, NJ: Princeton University Press, 2001); Michael Charney, *Powerful Learning: Buddhist Literati and the Throne in Burma's Last Dynasty* (Ann Arbor, MI: Center for South and Southeast Asian Studies, University of Michigan, 2006), 27–28.

24. Patrick Arthur Pranke, "The 'Treatise on the Lineage of Elders' (Vamsadipani): Monastic Reform and the Writing of Buddhist History in Eighteenth-Century Burma" (Ph.D. diss., University of Michigan, 2004), 27–30; Charney, *Powerful Learning*, 43–44.

25. Pranke, "'Treatise on the Lineage of Elders,'" 5.

26. Peter Hordern, "An Episode in Burmese History: Being a Contribution to the History of Indigenous Oriental Education," *Asiatic Quarterly Review* 4, no. 7 (1892): 34–35; Kaung, "Survey of the History of Education in Burma," 73–75; Leonard Evans Bagshawe, "The 'Moral and Intellectual Improvement of the People': Western Education in Burma to 1880," in *Etudes Birmanes: En Hommage à Denise Bernot*, ed. Pierre Pichard and François Robinne, Etudes thématiques, 9 (Paris: Ecole Française d'Extrême-Orient, 1998), 274–75.

27. Arthur Purves Phayre, "Memorandum on Vernacular Education for British Burma" (Rangoon, 1865), reprinted in Kaung, "Survey of the History of Education in Burma," 83–86.

28. *Reports on Public Instruction in Burma for the Year 1891–92* (Rangoon: Superintendent, Government Printing, Burma, 1892), 71.

29. Kaung, "Survey of the History of Education in Burma," 33–35; Charney, *Powerful Learning*, 54–57.

30. *Third Quinquennial Report on Public Instruction in Burma for the Years 1902–03–1906–07* (Rangoon: Superintendent, Government Printing, Burma, 1908), 3–4.

31. *Report on Public Instruction in Burma for the Year 1912–13* (Rangoon: Superintendent, Government Printing, Burma, 1913), 8.

32. Donald Eugene Smith, *Religion and Politics in Burma* (Princeton, NJ: Princeton University Press, 1965), 64–65.

33. Education Department, *Report of the Vernacular and Vocational Education Reorganization Committee* (Rangoon: Superintendent Government Printing and Stationary, 1936); Kaung, "Survey of the History of Education in Burma."

34. Chief Commissioner of British Burma Lt. Col. Arthur Purves Phayre to Officiating Secretary to the Government of India Hon. R. N. Cust, 26 December 1864, reprinted in Kaung, "Survey of the History of Education in Burma," 83–86.

35. Ibid.; Phayre, "Memorandum on Vernacular Education for British Burma."

36. Dispatch on Education, 1858, quoted in Bagshawe, "'Moral and Intellectual Improvement of the People,'" 273.

37. Ibid. Max Weber, *The Protestant Ethic and the Spirit of Capitalism*, 2nd ed. (New York: Scribner, 1976); John L. Comaroff and Jean Comaroff, *Of Revelation and Revolution: The Dialectics of Modernity on a South African Frontier*, vol. 2 (Chicago: University of Chicago Press, 1997); Stephens, *Education in Britain*.

38. Quoted in John Lawson and Harold Silver, *A Social History of Education in England* (London: Methuen and Co., 1973), 243.

39. *Fourth Quinquennial Report on Public Instruction in Burma for the Years 1907–08–1911–12* (Rangoon: Superintendent, Government Printing, Burma, 1912), 3.

40. *Reports on Public Instruction in Burma for the Year 1891–92*, 5; *Report on Public Instruction in Burma for the Year 1895–96* (Rangoon: Superintendent, Government Printing, Burma, 1896, 4.

41. *Reports on Public Instruction in Burma for the Year 1891–92*, 25; Taw Sein Ko, "Minutes of a Meeting Held on the 13th August 1911 in the Thathanabaing's Monastery to Discuss the Question of Primary Education in Monastic Schools," in *Burmese Sketches*, ed. Taw Sein Ko (Rangoon: British Burma Press, 1913), 266.

42. Minekhine Sayadaw, "Laukāyatādivi Nissaya," in *Laukāyatādivi Nissaya*, ed. Paya Pyu Sayadaw (Rangoon: Di Dout Newspaper Press, 1929) 117–151. Unfortunately the Minekhine Sayadaw died before he finished the treatise, but his draft of the text was

published in the *MahaBodhi News* in 1913. I would like to thank Alexey Kirichenko for bringing this text to my attention and providing me with a copy.

43. Juliane Schober, "Colonial Knowledge and Buddhist Education in Burma," in *Buddhism, Power and Political Order*, ed. Ian Charles Harris (New York: Routledge, 2007), 62.

44. Smith, *Religion and Politics in Burma*, 63.

12 Precarious Presences, Hallucinatory Times: Configurations of Religious Otherness in German *Leitkulturalist* Discourse

Michael Nijhawan

When in October 2008 an ambitious mosque project in Duisburg-Marxloh was inaugurated with much political fanfare, German newspapers titled it "the miracle of Marxloh": Finally the public saw the opening of a mosque that was not accompanied by years of bitter lawsuits, bureaucratic struggles, and deeply divisive public contestations concerning the so-called Islamicization of public space.[1] At the inauguration ceremony, Minister Jürgen Rüttgers announced what might seem a puzzling statement for a leading figure of the Christian-conservative party, known for mobilizing anti-immigrant sentiments during election campaigns.[2] "We need more mosques in this country," he said during the official ceremony, for which he received much applause, "[we need them] not in the backyards, but publicly visible mosques."[3] In calling for such public visibility, the miracle of Marxloh suggests a change of attitudes that comes close to an about-face in national orientation toward immigration. Should Marxloh be regarded as the new symbol for German tolerance, in the same way in which "the miracle of Bern" (*das Wunder von Bern*), a common trope and the harbinger for the Marxloh idiom, evoked the transition in cultural and political acceptance of Germans after the world war?[4] The turn to this national trope made one believe that such a major shift was under way. Admittedly, there is evidence that along with the transnationalization of concepts of immigration and citizenship law, Germany has finally come to terms with the presence of Islam and other "immigrant faiths."[5] The Marxloh effect would then confirm patterns observed in other European cities, where Arab French, Turkish German, or British South Asian Western-educated Muslim leaders have over time managed to win public support for their religious sites and found more acceptance for their respective ethnic and religious communities.[6] Only about two years later, however, in an ongoing national debate following former member of the German Federal Bank, Thilo Sarrazin's, new book *Deutschland schafft sich ab*, public sentiments seem to have shifted again against the acceptance of Muslim immigrants.[7]

But beyond the question of whether or not Islam is now wanted or remains unwanted in Marxloh and other places, there are important subtexts here in the demand to come out of the backyard mosque that need to be tackled in this chapter. First and foremost, this essay will demonstrate that the times of anti-mosque opposition are far from over and the ongoing mobilization of public opinion against "the wearers of the *hijab*" in spaces of local mosque protest as well as in the major feuilletons of not only the German press has significant implications for a politics of religion-making: among other issues, it raises the question of what category of "religion" is produced as tolerable and what that means for subjects who are seen to inhabit forms of religious orientation that transgress the set limits. The recent Swiss public vote against the construction of minarets that was backed by 57 percent of the voters in almost all of the Swiss provinces (cantons) indicates that beyond the political agendas of the conservative to far-Right parties that usually back these protests, the anxiety over "Islamicization" is a predicament shared by a far wider constituency, and not only in Germany or Switzerland.[8] The racist poster campaign that sustained the Swiss vote and which employed the figure of a black burka-wearing, faceless woman surrounded by black minarets towering over a Swiss flag brings me to a second key point. This and other examples show how a visual grammar of racialized space continues to be employed as effective marker of difference in secular identity politics.[9]

Ayşe Çağlar has also emphasized this point in her analysis of German state practices on immigration. Examining public apprehensions against "immigrant ghettos" and the new state policies that are meant to curb the dangers of such "ghettoization," for which the backyard mosque functions as a major trope, she argues against scholars who see Germany advance in the direction of a standardized European model of immigration and citizenship: "The ways in which immigration gains the status of a meta-issue in Germany," Çağlar argues, "[continue to] depend on the rhetoric, metaphor and key terms in which [such] discourses on immigrants are cast."[10] This statement is important for a discussion of how moral and religious difference is publicly negotiated in Germany, which leads to the point that I want to bring up here. In fact, it can be shown that the distrust against specific forms of religious presences has strong undercurrents that are diffusely intersecting with agendas advanced by the political Left and the Right, the elites as well as ordinary Germans. These are undercurrents of an ideological kind, not necessarily apparent at the level of narratives on Islam being wanted but built on hidden assumptions about particular cultural and religious subjects as illegitimate and forever outside the realms of a German, Swiss, or European normative framework. These assumptions and the kinds of affective politics engendered by them produce real social effects for the groups and individuals that are interpellated by the call to step "out of the backyard mosque." This is what this article sets out to investigate. It is not a scenario of state oppression and immigrant victimization. The scenario is much more complex and requires a multilayered analysis of the spheres in which discourses on religious otherness are produced and the kinds of affect that manifest in different local spaces of social interaction. In pursuing this inquiry, I echo the quest made by Brian Goldstone in this volume, in examining what public discourses on religious difference actually accomplish from a perspective of the observable forms of social action and what social effects such discourses have on those who are made to answer for the presumed ill effects of religious otherness and, more precisely, religious violence, fanaticism, and other forms of cultural transgression.

■ THE EFFECTS AND AFFECTS OF GERMAN *LEITKULTURALISM*

The theoretical considerations that I therefore advance in this text evolve around the notions of "culturalism" and "affect" in relation to constructions of religious difference. The notion of culturalism has long been central to a critique of Western discourses on ethnic and religious otherness.[11] Sherene Razack's *Casting Out*, in which she shows how a protracted Orientalist discourse informs new policy initiatives and public debates around religious accommodation or forced marriage in Europe and North America, is a case in point.[12] From a somewhat different vantage point, Yolande Jansen emphasizes the cultural meanings of French *laïcité* and thus, the implicit culturalist assumptions at the heart of a presumably color- and religion-blind French secularism.[13] In the same context, Talal Asad writes about the lingering collective sentiments that have surfaced in France that are not sufficiently explained by references to "public anxiety" or by evoking legitimate concerns with various kinds of violence in the French *banlieus*.[14] Asad draws attention here to what he says are complex cultural and civic processes through which citizens passionately identify with the nation form, its constitutional principles and implicit political theologies.[15]

Focusing on Germany's role within this European framework, I want to be more precise by evoking the idiom of *leitkulturalism*, which is introduced here as a specific reference to the culturalist argumentation that sustains German debates on religious otherness. To the same extent that Jansen is able to distinguish French *laïcité* as a constitutional principle, from *laïcisme* as culturalist idiom with strong politico-theological undertones, I will distinguish the political articulation of German *leitkultur* (which featured in the debate around a new European Constitution) from leitkulturalism as a discursively diffuse but socially effective idiom of mobilizing collective sentiments around a set of norms and values that emphasize the cultural hegemony of Judeo-Christian traditions in Europe. Conservatives have evoked the notion of a German (or European) leitkultur during the debate on Turkey's entry to the European Union.[16] This move has been mostly opposed by the political Left, because it was widely read as a euphemism to allow the further tightening of immigration and citizenship laws in opposition to multicultural models advanced by parts of the Left. At a closer look, however, the debate on religion indicates a much more profound affinity between the two political positions than one is likely to admit. In the following, I try to capture this affinity in the notion of German leitkulturalism and its underlying concept of what counts as reasoned subjectivity and rationality.

In this regard, Wendy Brown makes an interesting point that can be employed for this analysis, despite the obvious differences between leftist politics in Europe and the tradition of political liberalism in the North American context that she is concerned with. Brown demonstrates the subtle ways in which modern liberalism distinguishes different forms of religious subjectivity. She shows how liberalism constructs differences between a "formalist type" of subjectivity characteristic for the modern enlightened subject that emphasizes the consent given to particular cultural modes of expression and an "organicist type" that presumes a blending in of individual motivation with collective beliefs and thus builds on a notion of non-reflexive subjectivity that "affectively predetermines a given course of action or suffering."[17] This has far-reaching implications for the way particular forms of agency and collective expressions of religion are represented in Euro-American publics.[18] Brown's vantage point is not a critique of the "clash of civilizations" argument, which would not be novel. She instead shows how liberal discourse effectively marks and masks specific forms of religious life, their associated practices, and the ideologies that are being exposed through those practices as illegitimate or simply impossible to be incorporated by the modern liberal state.[19] What matters most in such discourses is not so much the specific type of religious tradition (Christianity, Sikhism, Islam, etc.) but, rather, how a type of religious subjectivity is seen to be expressed in particular modes of religious conduct and being.

German leitkulturalism is not immune to such distinctions between kinds of religious subjectivity. The following brief example might serve as an illustration: In February 2001, the German leftist newspaper *die taz* published a satire about "irrational Muslim behavior" on the newspaper's satire page, "The Truth."[20] Following a five-liner in which readers learned that after the horrendous earthquake in Gujarat, India, in January of the same year, some Muslim men went on to publicly destroy television sets after a local imam deemed television responsible for the catastrophe ("God's punishment for moral degeneration"), *die taz* issued a joke it would later argue was fully appropriate in exposing the surreal quality of the incident (people following the "weird" fatwa in an apparently irrational manner). The addition was a German rhyme in which the greatness of Allah was ridiculed with grotesque body imagery.[21] Following public criticism the newspaper received through countless letters and online entries, the author of the satire responded by drawing a parallel between the satire and German pastor jokes, arguing that, after all, "satire is the child of the Enlightenment."[22] He further remarked that satire has a cathartic function, which he rationalized in the following manner: "If Muslims expose the mind-set of infants by destroying sets of television in response to a natural catastrophe, it is only appropriate on our part to use a childish comic and ask: what a strange [*seltsamer*] god is this who chooses such followers?"[23]

In the framework of Brown's model, we see here how South Asian Muslims come to be marked by organicist religious subjectivity (lack of agency, being chosen rather than choosing), which is then paired with an Orientalist imagery of inferior-mindedness. But the example also illuminates the compulsion on the part of the self-declared defenders of Enlightenment values to educate others. And what triggers these compulsions are not mere ideas and opinions but affective dispositions. There are different ways of thinking through such modes of affect. Talal Asad advances a view on affect as a behavioral manifestation of a more profound and widely shared collective sentiment. There are clear indications that this is the case for German publics as well.[24] From a different vantage point, Jasbir Puar develops the notion of "affective politics" by which she tries to chart out the connections between the various forms of symbolic and material violence against racialized bodies, such as those of Muslims and Sikhs in the contemporary "war against terror."[25] Puar, in a broader critique of queer investments in the ideology of American exceptionalism, argues that identity markers that focus on gender, class, and racial difference only insufficiently allow explanation of the transgressive and contagious forms of affect that are powerful precisely because of their ability to bridge these class, gender, and race boundaries.[26] I take the liberty here to single out a specific point that Puar highlights in her critique: the notion that identity can be understood as one of the effects of affect.[27] In the responses to articulations of Sikh and Muslim religion discussed below, this "effect of affect" is enabled by residues of German Orientalist thought and by a legacy of Christian missionary constructions of religious heresy. These are not directly acknowledged but can be traced in the processes of cultural translation that underpin the arguments and actions that I observe in Germany in relation to Ahmadi and Sikh articulations of religion.[28]

■ GHOSTS OF THE PAST, LEGACIES FOR THE PRESENT

Proponents of German leitkultur tend to frame the debate on integration and religion entirely in terms of a post-1960 "guest worker" phenomenon that calls for new policies of integration into a nonlaïcist German cultural tradition in which Enlightenment ideals are paired with Christian normative values and pedagogies. This does not imply that the two churches would be set up against the establishment of mosques and other religious presences—on the contrary, interfaith agendas are often preferred venues for engagement in German tolerance. Yet, as Marxloh and the recent Sarrazin debate illuminate, the public narrative is often one of a new benevolent welcoming of immigrant faiths against a presumed history of religious and cultural homogeneity. But such explanations involve a forgetting of histories, which might be marginal for a discussion of the demographic changes in migration witnessed during the last four decades but which from my vantage point are meaningful to interrogate the normative claims advanced in leitkulturalist discourse. Let me begin with two small details from the historical archive of 1910s and 1920s Berlin. One astonishing story has been excavated and cinematographically rendered in Philip Scheffner's film *The Halfmoon Files* (2007). The film releases the voices of captive soldiers from the French and British colonies in Africa and South Asia that were recorded during World War I by German government agents in conjunction with anthropologists. It sheds a light on the complicities between military and scientific interests in documenting and recording racial others, some of whom, like the Sikh regiments fighting the Germans in Belgium, acquired a reputation of being tough fighters. Among these soldiers features the voice of a Sikh captive, Mall Singh, who provides the film with its leading motif. His hunger-stricken voice, which on the gramophone recordings is reminiscent in style and presentation of the formulaic storytelling genres in the Punjabi vernacular, haunts the filmmaker as a mysterious absence/presence that cannot make sense to a German audience and in the film remains untraceable to biographical time and a place of belonging, a ghostly presence without further anchorage.[29] It was in the same context in 1915 that William II built a wooden mosque in Wünsdorf near Berlin that could be used by South Asian and African Muslims fighting for the British and French, as well as many Tartar Russian and Bashkir Muslims who were also captured by the German army during World War I.[30] The mosque shut down in the 1920s, but shortly after the war, a new mosque project, understood as a continuation of the Wünsdorf mosque, came under construction in Berlin-Wilmersdorf in 1923. It was built by members of the Ahmadiyya Anjuman Lahore under Maulana Sadr-ud-Din as a solid mosque modeled upon South Asian architectural predecessors.[31] It is now considered the oldest mosque in Berlin. Unlike Mall Singh's brief and hallucinatory appearance that remains a mere haunting, the Ahmadiyya missionaries could stay on and found German converts from upper classes who helped to establish the German-Muslim Society. Alongside their partner mosque, the Woking mission in London, the Berlin Muslim community was very active in the years before World War II.[32] The German-Muslim Society was also among the first Muslim organizations in the post–World War II period to be active in the publishing sector, strongly motivated to spread the teachings of Islam to a Western audience.[33]

These are two historical details, but they are important details that evoke different kinds of presences: a hallucinatory presence of a Sikh captive that cannot be written into a meaningful narrative of German history and a marginalized presence of early Islamic missionaries who found accommodation in the German *Kaiserreich* and during the short-lived Weimar Republic and who even had a certain appeal for parts of the German educated classes in Berlin in those times. I shall use these two moments as a blueprint for the contradictory ways in which both communities are captured in the German social imaginary. And as I further argue below, it is the simultaneous occurrence of these seemingly opposed moments of recognition that helps shed a light on the constitutive ambiguities through which German public discourse today responds to specific forms of religious otherness.

In terms of a broader historical perspective, there is of course more to say about how leading members of Sikh and Ahmadiyya communities became enmeshed in colonial politics in South Asia under the British Empire. Both communities strove to secure their status as religious minorities within the empire and did so in seeking modes of cooperation and accommodation with the British, for which the Ahmadiyya elite earned the mistrust and anger of the leading Muslim organizations in the context of the nationalist struggle for independence. In the context of the Partition of 1947 that led to the formation of India and Pakistan as independent nation-states, Sikhs and Ahmadis were tragically implied in cross-border migrations that exiled the majority of each community from the birthplaces of their religions.[34] Subsequently, the question of a separate status, of Sikhs on the Indian side and Ahmadis on the Pakistani side, was tied up with public debates over the secular or nonsecular nature of the new states and the specific rights granted to religious minorities in the postcolonial context.[35] Whereas in the case of an emerging Sikh nationalism, one of the key issues has been the maintenance of boundaries against the assimilatory claims of a hegemonic Hindu political representation, Ahmadis in Pakistan were at the center of a national debate around the standards of Islamic piety, practice, and identity. This was first decided to be in agreement with Pakistan's Constitution, until the riots of 1959 and the ensuing anti-Ahmadi constitutional amendments in 1974 that were finalized in Zia ul'Haq's presidential ordinances of 1984, to the extreme disadvantage of the Ahmadiyya Muslim Jama'at.[36] The national reconfigurations of religious community boundaries and identity narratives led to violence and forced migration, notably in the contest of the Punjab crisis, which pitched a separatist Sikh movement against the Indian state's antiterrorist machinery, and in the anti-Ahmadi legislation that left Ahmadis without protection from rioting crowds and attackers in Pakistan. Both events had the consequence of a transnational dispersal and reconfiguration of religious and political networks in the diaspora, in critical distance from the national politics in India and Pakistan. This had an ultimate impact on the way in which the Sikh and Ahmadiyya presence in Europe established itself and was publicly recognized.

In Germany, where many Sikhs and Ahmadis in the 1980s and 1990s applied for political asylum, the inner life of both communities was essentially defined by these postconflict dynamics until more recent times. The German state, through its legal and police apparatuses, showed a more sympathetic attitude to Ahmadi concerns, whereas the post-1980 Sikh arrival was generally seen with suspicion and underlying fears that Sikh militants would enter the country and run community affairs. In this context, new stories of the descendants of the Sadr-ud-Dins and Mall Singhs who came to Germany and who in large numbers passed through the initiation rituals of the asylum court hearings were written. And it was in those hearings where failed translations and widespread biases against granting asylum to "social welfare spongers" sent many of them into years of sociolegal limbo and some of them into deportation prisons.[37] What needs to be seriously examined, then, is how in these briefly sketched scenarios that bridge the past and present, Sikh and Ahmadiyya religious subjects continue to be written in and out of a German national narrative.

■ PASSING THE "MUSLIM TEST": AHMADIS AND THE GERMAN ANTI-MOSQUERS

In late 2003, at the dawn of Christmas Eve, the conservative mayor of Hessen's capital, Wiesbaden, Hildebrand Diehl, announced that the city, I suppose in appropriate reverence to the religious calendar, wanted to sign a "peace contract" with its Muslim "fellow citizens."[38] It was a hitherto unseen gesture in times of increasing public anxiety about "parallel societies" sprouting in the midst of German cities, with a predominantly Muslim immigrant community presumably immersing itself in moral and political lifeworlds that proponents of German leitkultur have deemed "traditionalist," "antisecular," "oppressive against women," and thus incommensurable with Germany and Europe's secular-democratic order. According to the proposed "peace contract," the Muslim communities of the city would be asked, as a contribution to enhancing the image of Wiesbaden as tolerant and cosmopolitan, to publicly confess their allegiance to the democratic principles enshrined in the German Constitution. Such attempts at demanding a public confession to the secular principles enshrined in German law and the new European Constitution are increasingly common and are being played out in other European and North American publics—noteworthy is the case of Quebec's recent discussion around religious and cultural "accommodations" for immigrants to that province.[39]

Nonetheless, the German preoccupation with restoring the "peace-loving Muslim fellow citizen" deserves some further attention, specifically in the context of local mobilizations against Ahmadiyya mosque projects in various cities in Hessen (and other German provinces), which in fact was the immediate backdrop of Mayor Diehl's announcement.[40] It is indeed no coincidence that the idea of the peace-loving (*friedliebende* or *friedfertige*) nature of Ahmadi Muslims was evoked at a time when a populist anti-mosque movement had largely succeeded in disseminating a public image of Ahmadiyya Muslims as members of a "heretic sect" and as inassimilable immigrants.[41]

Anti-mosque protest as a form of exclusionary body politics is neither new nor specific to the German context.[42] In a similar fashion to the current public mobilization against minarets in Switzerland, there have been several cases over the last two decades in which mosque disputes have mobilized local publics, filled town halls for plenary hearings, and kept German courts busy, specifically if one considers the recent Ahmadiyya mosque projects.[43] Pointing to the "one hundred mosques project" that Ahmadiyya brochures naively advertise, opponents have consistently evoked the fear of an "Islamist sect" that spreads its tentacles across German territory. To be accurate, in the last two decades or so, Turkish Muslim organizations have also been at the forefront of these public protests, and the recent Sarrazin debate has just underlined this point.[44] Attempts to become publicly more visible by moving prayer houses from privately owned apartments and industrial sites at the urban periphery to newly built religious architecture in the city centers and residential neighborhoods have triggered culturalist predicaments on a grand scale. This is what Minister Rüttgers refers to when calling for the "coming out of the backyard mosque." The idea here is that of a transgressive power that comes to be associated with the "backyard mosque" (*Hinterhofmoschee*) as a place of unfathomable otherness, a place where political conspiracies are knotted together and where religious passions are given free rein. The normative claim for "more visible mosques," however, does not sit well with those opposing the construction of mosques as we now see in Switzerland, because the shift from the backyard to the public is read here not as a sign of "normalization" but, rather, as a further proof of what has already been deemed the secretive agenda of an aggressive and uncompromising Islam with the mission of installing the shari'a as universal legal code.[45] It is in this argumentative context that we have seen the beginning of a new type of anti-mosque movement that has acquired the capacity to spill over the boundaries of local publics and cut across established blocs of political affiliation.

In Germany, anti-mosque movements have formed in the city of Schlüchtern, a small city in Hessen's Main-Kinzig district, along with others in Cologne and Berlin. The movements, which have been carried by officially registered public interest groups (*Bürgerinitiativen*), the "pro-Schlüchtern" group as well as the "Interessengemeinschaft Pankow-Heinersdorfer Bürger" (Public Interest Group of Pankow-Heinersdorf's Citizens), have been relatively successful in mobilizing local support in an attempt to force administrators to intervene in the architectural design and intended location in the semiurban cultural geography or to stop the project altogether.[46] The Schlüchtern town administration, for example, seduced by the prospect of keeping its electoral base, went through a juridical struggle to halt the construction of the Ahmadiyya mosque even at the planning stage. In Berlin, where, backed by the Green Party and the Social Democrats as well as the New Left (*Die Linke*), administrative and political clearance has been given to the 2008 opening of the mosque in the city's eastern district, Pankow-Heinersdorf, the public response was substantial, with more than twenty thousand signatures collected by the mosque opponents.

The Schlüchtern dispute is a particularly good example to examine the cultural subtexts in the debate on religious otherness. Schlüchtern, first of all, is not really a Mecca of Muslim pilgrimage.[47] The very presence of Ahmadis in this city is the consequence of state practices of regulating immigration flow through new zoning laws, specifically in the sociolegal domain of asylum seekers and refugees.[48] The idea here is to "share the burden" of receiving incoming new immigrants by modes of spatial dispersal intended to facilitate "integration" into the dominantly white Christian mainstream in these small towns and urban neighborhoods, where immigrants would be less likely to aggregate around their own constituencies.[49] At the peak of incoming asylum seekers in the mid-1980s to early 1990s, German tabloids and members of the conservative political spectrum depicted asylum seekers as social welfare spongers, which had a direct and long-term impact on the image of Ahmadis as well. These sentiments were surely lingering among a significant part of the local public in Schlüchtern and other places, but significantly, in the early stages of the disputes the official concern was rather of an administrative and aestheticist kind.

Thus, when the Ahmadiyya community began their search for an adequate construction site in the small town of Schlüchtern in the early 1990s, negotiations with local town authorities soon let them into a juridical battle through various instances, beginning with the building supervisory authority up to the administrative court in Frankfurt am Main. In these legal battles, it was argued that the mosque would not fit into the cultural landscape of the region and that Islamic architecture would stand isolated and alien in a predominantly Christian environment in rural Hessen. Arguments against noise and traffic were also issued, but it is obvious that the shift of Islamic architecture from hidden and peripheral spaces to the center of a small town was widely perceived as provocative and scandalous. Visible and audible signs of religious difference (notoriously often the minaret and the *adhan*, or call for prayer) have featured as an important hinge upon which public protest unfolds, even though in many cases the organizing idioms of protest discourse would evolve around more technical concerns of town planning, such as parking and traffic concerns; the size, height, shape, and color of buildings; and how they insert architecturally in a particular neighborhood.[50] Other voices claimed that the hundred or so Ahmadi worshippers who would use the mosque for their religious services were mostly not local to the neighborhood and hence "would daily drive forth and back between their homes and the mosque," thus contributing to bad air quality and congestion on the streets. Ridiculous as such an argument might appear, it is increasingly common that presumably color-blind administrative, aestheticist, and infrastructural issues are brought to public consideration and court hearings. In the case of Schlüchtern, it certainly provided a venue for local authorities to use infrastructural concerns as a kind of exit strategy for the mayor's office without, on the one hand, having to align with arguments pushed by extremist, white supremacist groups and not having to face more embarrassment in administrative court hearings that repetitively argued in favor of the Ahmadi claimants, on the other hand.

With the events of 9/11 and the more recent bomb blasts in Madrid (March 11, 2004) and London (July 7, 2005), the contours of public protest changed in such a way that Ahmadis would hence be singled out rather unambiguously as "religious fundamentalists" because of their articulation of religious orthodoxy (building mosques, women wearing the hijab or niqab). If this shift in rhetoric allowed for a translation of latent xenophobic sentiments to Islamophobic ones, the social organization of the movements was still very much the same. In Schlüchtern, the lines between the protectors of German normative values and neo-Nazi groupings were at times difficult to draw, and the conflict was notoriously driven by such right-wing agendas in the city of Cologne, where strong public outrage against the mosque opponents also formed.[51] Despite the fluidity of these boundaries, German anti-mosquers, like their Swiss counterparts, have been adamant in claiming a progressive self-image, demonstratively using sources such as German Turkish feminist author Serap Cileli, who advances a strict secularist argument in forcefully claiming that proponents of a "cultural relativism" were mistaken in their belief in tolerance ("You will kill us with your tolerance") and the peaceful coexistence between Islam and secular modernity.

But there is also a difference between the quotation of secularist arguments and the rhetoric witnessed in the case of the provincial city of Schlüchtern. Consider here that immediately after the terrorist attacks of September 11, 2001, and in the midst of the ongoing dispute around the Ahmadiyya mosque, the pro-Schlüchtern initiative changed its strategy by publicly declaring the city of Schlüchtern a "mosque-free zone." Protesters distributed flyers and mounted visible "no mosque" icons on their Web site, figures that became popular in other cities such as Cologne or Berlin.[52] This imagery expresses the crude populist ideologies shared by a minority of the German population, yet it has also influenced mainstream attitudes in significant ways. Thus, the pro-Schlüchtern group succeeded in the creation of public forums in real and virtual spaces and instigated participatory modes of public protest that ultimately caused political pressure on town authorities and community representatives. The fact that religious symbols are effectively used as civilizational boundary markers can hardly be ignored, too closely linked are the various images and articulations of "Islamicism" as the prime danger of "cultural alienation" (kulturelle Überfremdung).

In a letter that was apparently received and later posted by the Webmaster of the pro-Schlüchtern Internet site, a scene is evoked in which a local inhabitant along with a couple of "his Christian fellows" had met at the site where the Ahmadiyya mosque was to be erected. The letter states that the fellows had gathered at the spot to pray to the archangel Michael so that he might protect this place from being profaned by Muslims. The online version also included an open letter addressed to Ahmadiyya spokesperson Hadayatullah Hübsch (1946–2011), which included the following note: "The construction site where you plan to build the mosque is sanctified in the name of the Trinity, the god of the bible. He has requested that I write this letter. The site is under protection of an angel (the one with the sword).... The one refusing to change his mind will meet final judgment. There will be no mosque on this site, as the Lord does not want it."[53] The letter ends with an explicit warning directed at Mr. Hübsch, a converted German and former leftist activist who, until his recent and unexpected death in January 2011, ran the Ahmadiyya press bureau and served as imam at the Noor mosque in Frankfurt am Main.[54]

The next section will engage in more detail with the semantics of the anti-mosque discourse in reference to Ahmadiyya religious doctrine.[55] Mosque opponents are cognizant of the fact that the community practices a rather purist Quranic discipline of pious conduct, in defiance of the official Islamic world and the various discourses branding them as heretics. Yet this shift from the "marginal-heretic" to the "religious-orthodox" is something that further spurs ideas about the inherent transgressive and "weird" nature of Ahmadiyya Islam. It does not help this context that German converts to Ahmadiyya Islam are known for their political past in the '68er student revolts. This is read as a further indication of ideological radicalism and political unpredictability on the part of the Ahmadiyya leadership. I am not suggesting that the German mosque opponents would evoke the apostasy of Ahmadi Muslims in the same way that various political and religious forces use these grammars on politico-theological grounds. The point I shall raise is this: by employing a language of heresy and sectarianism, the German anti-mosquers enter a scene of translation that constitutes the Ahmadi subject as bearing a stigma and inherent ambiguity. This rendering of religious subjectivity is crucial to the genealogy of Ahmadi identity but also indicative of broader meaning structures of colonial and postcolonial translation that are analyzed by Arvind Mandair in this volume.

▪ TRANSLATING AHMADI HERESY: ORIENTALIST CONFIGURATIONS

Let me return for a moment to the example of the Christian archangel claiming the proposed construction site. The idea that a higher divine agent might intervene in restoring a particular moral-political order or truth is a bizarre reminder of how Ahmadis, as subjects who fall between established categories of religious affiliation, are preconfigured within a historical scenario that juxtaposed Christian missionary and Ahmadiyya, as well as various Hindu, Muslim, and Sikh reformist organizations in the context of religious reformism in British India. This needs some explanation: Avril Powell reports that in what became a widely advertised debate between the Ahmadiyya founder, Ghulam Ahmad, and his native Christian counterpart, H. M. Clark, in the city of Amritsar in 1893, Ahmad appeared to have challenged his opponent to "participate in a *mubahilla*, in which the curse of God would be invoked on whichever spokesman was speaking falsehood."[56] Such rhetorical contests in which divine agency was evoked to restore truth were quite common in the heightened atmosphere of emerging religious nationalisms. Verbal contests were imbricated with martial imagery to which all sides contributed enthusiastically by drawing in popular support from the urban and rural "bazaars." That audiences in Schlüchtern and Berlin today produce such "bazaari" speech events is of course not a linear continuation of the past but an interesting resonance of discursive constellations, of how particular speech events in the present echo colonial speech events of the past, how contemporary forms of cultural translation, crudely distorted in their meaning structure, mirror the logics of prior language events that had evolved around politico-theological issues of proving the sovereignty of the Christian God within the framework of an ethical monotheism.

This paraphrases Arvind Mandair, who examines the legacy of colonial language events in the context of the transformations that Sikh theology underwent during the late nineteenth century, which is also the critical period for the emergence of the Ahmadiyya reform movement. Mandair argues that the Orientalist project of translating Sikh scripture within a framework that posed ethical monotheism (deemed superior) against pantheistic, nondualistic conceptualizations of the divine (indicative of the various forms of Hindu traditions and deemed inferior by E. Trumpp and other Orientalists) was crucial to the extent that this process created a discursive framework in which not only the Sikh elite but of course also the Hindu and Muslim elites have since found themselves entangled.[57] The Ahmadiyya part in this conjuncture is somewhat neglected but, for the purposes outlined here, quite crucial in understanding how actual confrontations between the different groups, notably Christian missionary groups in Punjab, would produce a particular discourse on Ahmadiyya Islam as the "religion with the sword."[58] As it turns out, Mirza Ghulam Ahmad, who was many times at the center of these weeklong debates over the meaning of jihad or the divinity of Christ, had early on defended the purely spiritual meaning of the jihad, while it seems he himself was not shy of throwing out challenges and overt threats to some of his opponents in the course of these public contestations.[59]

My intention here is not to pursue a discussion of the actual content and antagonisms of these debates, which are recorded in Urdu and English archival records. But it is noteworthy that these encounters played a pivotal role in the context of translating and defending religious truth claims, the process of which cannot be fully comprehended without acknowledging the complex epistemic structures set by grand translation projects that Orientalist scholarship had instigated over the years.[60] Mandair's point can therefore be taken further—and I stretch it somewhat freely here—to imply that the very constitution of the Ahmadi subject in idioms of the *jihadi* and the "syncretistic sect" (with all the ambivalence that exists between the two apparently incommensurable ascriptions) bears its imprints on contemporary forms of linguistic and cultural translation.

I mention these issues as an entry to a discussion of Hiltrud Schröter's book Die Ahmadiyya Bewegung des Islam (*The Ahmadiyya Movement of Islam*) in which she portrays the Ahmadiyya Muslim Jama'at as a "heretic Islamist sect of global outreach" characterized by a "blasphemous *Führerkult* with strong aspirations to claim power."[61] This text, so far the only available German monograph on the Ahmadiyya movement of recent origin and published in its fourth edition, is based on what the author calls a "structural-hermeneutic analysis" of Ahmadiyya writings, most of which she consulted in their German translations. The text has been widely used by members of the pro-Schlüchtern group as well as the Interessengemeinschaft Pankow-Heinersdorfer Bürger as a source for their anti-mosque agitation.

In her opening chapters, Schröter refers to early missionary accounts on the Ahmadiyya, and by quoting from these sources she reproduces in minutiae the colonial missionaries' discourse depicting Ahmadis as falling outside of what could ever be an acceptable articulation of religion within the framework of modern reason and secular government.[62] The point is that her interpretations turn theological and cultural discourses of the late nineteenth and early twentieth century, including discourses on race, into a post-Holocaust, post-9/11 "clash of civilizations" scheme in which Ahmadiyya texts are now placed in continuity with Adolf Hitler's *Mein Kampf* and Osama bin Laden's interpretation of the jihad. For instance, in a section in which she analyzes alleged anti-Semistist rhetoric in some of Mirza Ghulam Ahmad's writings, Schröter is aware that the language of race, in particular the negative construal of Jews, is a translation of anti-Semitist literature such as Edouard Drumont's *La France Juive* that traveled with European missionaries to Punjab in the late nineteenth century. She then quotes a longer passage by Drumont that mocks the "Semitic character" of Jews, and despite her previous remarks about the European genealogy of this discourse, Schröter is led to conclude that Ahmad wholeheartedly embraced these messages: "These lines could be literally those written Mirza Ghulam Ahmad," she says.[63] They obviously were not, but within her "structural-hermeneutic framework" such intertextuality is simply taken as a proof in a legal argument that aims at marking Ahmadi religious doctrines as prime examples of anti-Semitist thought today.[64] My intention here is not to ridicule serious academic engagements with articulations of racism and anti-Semitism—quite the contrary—but what can be grasped from Schröter's text is troubling insofar as the regimes of translation that have given birth to such articulations and refractions of anti-Semitism are strangely reversed in their receptivity and logical application. Schröter is very conscious in evoking terms such as *geistige Brandstiftung, Führerprinzip,* and *Endsieg* in her interpretations, which are evocative of German postwar discourse and serve no other purpose than stigmatizing Ahmadiyya religious doctrine as inherently racist, misogynist, and totalitarian in character. This does not end at the level of textual interpretation. In fact, the author claims, without providing any empirical evidence, that the Ahmadiyya principle of *bayat*, or oath of allegiance, is an instrument of absolute control over the individual, which is astonishingly ignorant of the various ways *bayat* is used as a form of submission to the agency of spiritual guides in the context of Sufi Islam and other (Asian) religions (one might add Christian ones too).[65] It does reinforce, however, the general image of the "parallel society," which is characterized as a form of authoritarianism and extreme patriarchal control over children and women.

In the final chapter of the book this is given special attention in a case study of two Ahmadi pupils who had been interviewed by two of Schröter's students. The author's analysis of these interviews reads like an Orientalist text par excellence, a text that denies any interpretive agency to the interviewee, whereas the author herself dissects each and every utterance (she knows what they mean in what they say) in rather self-evident fashion to find the underlying logic of Ahmadiyya ideology being imprinted on the "poor pupils' brains." Examples abound: Maryam referring to her school (the second-tier *Realschule*) as "a very good school" becomes a "very unusual" remark that shows that "the Ahmadi" belongs to a Pakistani upper class that has developed an "aristocratic habitus";[66] the same girl's remark that she can accept a proposed marriage partner only if she agrees with her parents' choice is translated into a "schizophrenic *Latifundienlogik*" (the girl wants to be modern-autonomous and affirmative of ethnic-religious values at the same time; in the author's assessment a kind of double bind).[67] Eveline's "willing obedience" to wear the hijab is deconstructed in such a way that intention is read as mere citation of the oath of allegiance (thus repetitive statement and not an expression of individual autonomy and agency), and terms referring to her bodily practice such as tying the hijab (*Kopftuch gewickelt*) are construed as autosuggestive, false statements of the religious indoctrinated kind: A term such as *gewickelt/tied*, Schröter argues, can be used in reference to diapers but not the hijab, which is why "in reality" Eveline is "disgusted" by wearing the hijab.[68]

Schröter's recourse to feminist arguments barely hides a form of cultural racism that is now more and more common across an international political spectrum.[69] As Sherene Razack notes, this is part of an alarming trend in which feminism, neo-liberalism, and the "clash of civilizations" arguments are fused and mapped upon a broader geopolitical terrain in which the figure of the fanatic Muslim (the misogynist bearded patriarch and the imperiled female) functions as a "principle technology."[70] What seems to be of particular significance in this context is the easy move between anti-Semitist accusations and the portrayal of gendered religious bodies that appear divested of reason and legitimacy. This occurs in full ignorance of the empirical work available in German academic literature that has examined the self-representation of second-generation Muslim women in Germany. Sigrid Nökel, for example, who grounds much of her work on interviews conducted in the Frankfurt am Main region, paints a completely different picture of religiously oriented, hijab-wearing young women, for whom the wearing of the hijab bears different significations, predominantly so in the form of an ethical choice of refashioning their selves and bodies as a conscious and affirmative move of expressing their new hyphenated identities.[71]

Schröter, however, is not concerned with such nuanced work. Instead she is occupied in portraying Ahmadi Muslims as Germany's "heretics." She does so by pushing a discursive scheme that is capable not only of stripping the subject of enlightened forms of reason and agency but also of reinscribing a form of cunning agency that is read as a betrayal of both, the German *Sozialversicherungsgemeinschaft* (the Ahmadi asylum seeker as welfare sponger) as well as religion proper (the Ahmadiyya "sect" betraying Islam and its own reputation as *friedliebende Gemeinde*). It is also not coincidental to find the evocation of disgust as an emotional response to the image of a religiously cultivated Muslim body at the heart of Schröter's writing. The negative remarks on Mirza Ghulam Ahmad's portrayal as the bearded, turban-wearing *mahdi* does fit well into this overall scheme of sectarianism and Ahmadi heresy, but it also stipulates further questions about the figure of the long-bearded, turban-wearing other, which has gained prominence in what Virinder Kalra calls "post Bin-Laden Europe."[72] The next section therefore shifts the focus to articulations of religious otherness in German *leitkulturalist* discourse that problematize this figure of the bearded and turban-wearing religious fanatic, which as I will show in subsequent fashion translates into everyday contexts of stigmatization.

■ DISTANT BEARDS AND PULP MODERNS

In a February 2006 issue of *die taz*, Sonia Mikich, longtime foreign correspondent for the German public broadcasting company ARD and in charge of the critically acclaimed TV journal *Monitor*, published an article titled "Was nun, ferner Bärtiger?" ("What to Do Now, Distant Bearded Man?"), which in circumscribing the moving target of an un/known bearded addressee (read: Muslim fundamentalist) reverses the "blasphemy" allegations that accompanied the Danish caricature controversy.[73] In fact, the text can be read as an ironical rebuttal by a Western-educated, civilized, feminist citizen who seems to be deeply offended by the "blasphemous assault" on European values by radical Muslims. When she writes, "I am offended" (*Ich bin beleidigt*), she initially seems to puzzle the readers by letting us guess whether her irony is directed at the public exchange of arguments that has centered around the question of what and whose "taboos" are being violated. Yet as the text unfolds, the author barely disguises her disgust at the "veiling and nailing of Muslim women," the bombing of Buddha statues, and the whole assemblage of images and events that can be popularly associated with either the Taliban or Al-Qaida. In a response she thinks is similarly particularistic and noncompromising than her accused counterpart, Mikich ironically remarks, "I am very sensitive when my own cultural values are concerned" and "my feelings are absolute and therefore to be expressed in a universalistic manner" (as if Western normative frameworks never came across with sweeping claims to the universal). What happens next is that, line by line, irony gives way to prose in which the repeated evocation of a huffy writer-self ("Ich bin beleidigt") only serves to make the concerns around the "clash of cultures" sound unapologetically more real than ever.

In his "Reflections on Blasphemy," Talal Asad suspects, I think quite persuasively, that the almost obsessive manner in which Western-liberal discourse has been occupied with the presumed blasphemy allegation by the generalized Muslim-as-other in fact points to a more profound anxiety and uncertainty around notions of (constraints on) freedom and societal taboos—remnants of irrational passions and residues of unreason the enlightened self wants to have overcome.[74] "The real problem of blasphemy in Europe lies," Asad argues, "not in the resurgence of religious passions into the public sphere or in the threat posed to the principle of free speech by Muslim immigrants and their offspring. It lies in the repression of the particular contradictions in which Europeans now live and the anxiety that this generates, in the drive to break all limits while at the same time being obliged to maintain them."[75] Mikich's text is obsessed with the configuration of limits and their transgression. Thus when she discovers that there are indeed historical portraits of the prophet Muhammad in an Irish museum, she polemically asks her interlocutor: "What to do now, distant bearded man? Boycotting Irish Butter?" Is this a mere rhetorical figure, and what precisely would be its function? Or can we begin to see in this a subtle way of citing a particular body and a type of ("organicist") subjectivity, unacknowledged in its complex and plural dimensions as the hijab discussion has shown, that, however, becomes profoundly suggestive of how the lines of ethnic and cultural demarcation are being reproduced?[76]

Let me cite here another example, an entry that appeared in the feuilleton of the *Frankfurter Rundschau*, known as leftist counterpart to the other Frankfurt-based national newspaper, the *Frankfurter Allgemeine Zeitung*. Published in April 2004 and titled "Bin Laden on the Subway," the text written by well-known journalist Harry Nutt inserts itself smoothly into ongoing debates about global Islam and the uncanny presence of Osama bin Laden's terrorist networks in pockets of Europe's metropolitan areas.[77] Nutt describes a scene he had encountered in Frankfurt's underground line (U-Bahn). He observed how "two young males of southern origin," which is a standard idiom for nonwhite, immigrant youth, would "provocatively" spread out their legs in the metro compartment, leaving no physical space for other riders to take seats. More than that, they were "expressively loud," forcing other passengers to tune in to their conversations about the latest bin Laden text message they apparently received on their mobile phones (the photo hovering over Nutt's article shows a Nokia mobile phone with a picture that sketches bin Laden's turban-wearing head). Not a single register of modernist, elitist, and paternalistic discourse is left out here by the author; yet what is maybe most astounding is the way Nutt manages to construct a caricature of the two local nonwhite youth.[78] The two youngsters are portrayed as utterly confused characters, suffering from a lack of Ego that turns them into willing receivers of bin Laden's messages: "Bin Laden's will to radicalism meets their desire to demonstrate compelling strength [*durchschlagende Stärke*]." And further: "The only difference between them and Mohammad Atta [one of the September 11 terrorists who resided in Germany] is that the latter would have politely given space to other passengers of the train." Frankfurt's two "Kanak-Germans" were apparently not dangerous, for they were "without mission," "not really blessed by [cunning?] intelligence," in their "macho-style" sitting there like "two desperados"—"pulp fiction, oriental style," Nutt is led to conclude.[79]

Hence, what is represented here is another ironic rebuttal. Unlike Mikich's aversion against the distant undisguised religious fanatic, Nutt focuses on the young hybrid and hyphenated, clean-shaven immigrant youth, the "Kanak-German" machismo as the potential sleeper-terrorist. More interestingly, Nutt evokes the image of a pulp modernism in his representation of Frankfurt's everyday immigrant youth culture. But why "pulp fiction, oriental style"? In a generous reading, Nutt could have meant to fictionalize these real-world characters, turn them into "oriental" doubles of Samuel L. Jackson's and John Travolta's alter egos in the now classic movie. In such a rendering the "oriental" would be a surface of signs worthy of satirical deconstruction. Yet Nutt's text is clearly devoid of all new-noir literary sophistry, which one might have encountered in a French paper and which would have made this a somewhat laughable and enjoyable subject matter. Instead, "pulp fiction, oriental style" condenses a comic body imagery in which the factual and fictive become endlessly reversible, and as if this were a sign for our postmodern times, reversibility is then able to signify the uncanny of terror and violence and its ghostly presence in the everyday. This is played out in a realm of the social imaginary in which the pulp fictionalization of Kanak Germans translates the racist and misogynist slurs of the film genre, where it could be argued they are outlived by the grotesque realities of American consumerist gun culture, into a racial discourse in the guise of educated feuilleton literacy, with its brief excursions into the metaphysical. Similar to Mikich's Western-feminist text, Nutt's does not advance the argument beyond common stereotypes, yet the self-reflexive use of the pulp genre indicates the cultural bias and class distance of the author in reference to the subjects of his essay.

▪ "OSAMA, THROW BOMBS ON OFFENBACH": WRITING THE TURBAN OUT OF MODERNITY

Let me now juxtapose Nutt's text with another incident that occurred around the same time in the Frankfurt subway. I think this example is more suitably telling of how those who fall into the category of a suspicious religious identity are affected in negative ways. The scene I have in mind is based on an incident told by a friend who is a Sikh and a German passport holder in his late twenties. The encounter occurred during the summer in 2004 in the Frankfurt subway and involved a crowd of Frankfurt soccer fans. He happened to note his memories of the event in his diary. Here is a brief excerpt that he shared with me:

> "Die *Eintracht* ist die Größte! Die *Eintracht* ist die Größte!...[The team *Eintracht Frankfurt* is the greatest!...]." Soccer fans on their way to the stadium where they gather to support the local team *Eintracht Frankfurt* can be heard singing in chorus, supported by the regular strokes of a big drum, when I reach the subway platform. As I close in with them, I recognize the song that glorifies the *Eintracht* by cursing the local rival *Kickers Offenbach*. I finally pass the group to reach the platform from where I have to catch my train. The soccer crowd is quick to spot me and almost immediately falls into a new beat while they are shouting: "Osama! Osama! Wirf doch Bomben auf Offenbach! [Osama! Osama! Why don't you throw bombs on Offenbach!]" Other passengers don't seem to notice but I stand perplexed by being thus identified. I don't hesitate for long to quickly leave the crowd behind and avoid any confrontation, as I would sometimes do when youngsters throw words like "Osama," "Shit Taliban," or "terrorist" at me.

Maybe most puzzling is how the soccer crowd, triggered by the image of the turban-wearing, bearded Sikh, instantaneously translates this sign into the monstrous and uncanny head of the global jihad, bin Laden. The one capable of striking down the New York Twin Towers might as well be capable of striking down Kickers Offenbach by dropping a few bombs in the east of Frankfurt. This of course happens in the ritualistic mode of alcohol-induced soccer crowd performance, with fans dressed up distinctively to mark their group membership against their hated local opponent, and so a certain mind-set of drawing exclusive boundaries is playfully put into place. While it is true that hooligan-like behavior can be predictably racist in outcome, in and outside the soccer arena—after all there is a long record of fans shouting racist slurs upon the sight of black soccer players—there is still a degree of surprise and unpredictability in the way a body image in this context stipulates a collective fantasy of terror. Looking at such incidences, it is indeed difficult to frame them within the established parameters of ethnic boundary making, racial profiling, or xenophobic behavior: all of these might account for what is at stake, but none of them captures the quality of transgression on display.

How can the turban be read into this story? Beginning his reflections on the genealogy of the turban within an autobiographic reading of such encounters, which were instigated in a post–September 11 context, Virinder Kalra contemplates how the turban (*dastar* or *pagh*) seems to constantly transgress the discursive and emotional fabric of modernity:

> There is no space for the turban wearer in the plains of the West nor in the cities of South Asia. Whether American modernity or Indian modernity, the turban seems to now stand for an absolute symbol of opposition—eighth century for Muslims and eighteenth for Sikhs—to any tendencies of modernity. Is it possible for the pagh to ever be modern in the western sense, given the way in which the Taliban, be-turbanned and bearded, have been constantly represented as attempting to turn the clock back 1600 years. And given the way that in almost any diaspora context the turban becomes intimately tied with "tradition."[80]

The affiliation with tradition rather than modernity was given special emphasis in German popular discourse in the figure of Aladin, which ties up with Kalra's example of the Air India advertisement that also portrays the turban-wearing "Maharajah" in the servant mode of catering then to white colonial masters and now to multishaded middle- to upper-class Air India passengers. But as Kalra shows in his work, the temporal and spatial circulation of the pagh is much more complex than its docile exoticization. Since its constitutive framings in colonial and Orientalist texts and contexts, the ascribed wild authenticity of the Sikh-as-martial-race that played such a huge role in the draft of the raj's army, it has been imbued with deep ambiguity, based on the idea that once the pagh is "untied" and "untamed," the irrational forces of violence could instantaneously and viciously be unleashed.[81] Thus, Kalra asks: "When did wearing a pagh become a transgressive act? This ties in with so much of the literature on strangeness; this discourse, I would argue, also to some extent renders the turban, as always in a teleological imbalance, unable to resume its role in life-cycle circumstances—i.e. at deaths (where the elder son takes the father's turban), or weddings (where the groom's family all wear turbans), and becomes a symbol universally associated with tradition; a tradition which can never be secularized or modernized, as may have been hoped in the nationalist project, but potentially only erased."[82]

The memory of Mall Singh, then, still haunts us today. Indeed, we have to recognize how this "teleological imbalance" can still be potentially dislocating and render incomprehensible the various cultural and religious locations of the pagh in its everydayness. Could one, on the other hand, imagine that a future German minister would stand up and call for "more turbans in this country"? In fact, it might be just a matter of time until we hear such a call, as the model minority discourse advanced by British and American Sikhs precisely aims at a public recognition of the turbaned Sikh who publicly confesses his being non-Muslim and nonterrorist in conformity with the values of Western democracy.[83] But to the same extent that the call for more mosques has not substantially improved Muslim immigrants' opportunities, any official recognition of turbans would do little to provide sociolegal security and a sense of belonging to the small community of Punjabi Sikhs in Germany. Unlike my friend, who was able to get over the subway encounter rather quickly and in other circumstances would not shy away from approaching individuals who shout racist slurs, there is a noticeable difference when it comes to a majority of Sikhs whom I have encountered in Frankfurt am Main and other places, who are in a much more precarious situation. The move from turban to hat, which in the post–September 11 context has been linked to the discourse of "mistaken identity," in the German context takes on the additional and I would argue even more profound significance of a forced political act of "de-turbanization."[84] In times when border crossers are told by their agents to remove the pagh, cut their hair, and shave off their beards, when at the same time a political faction of exiled Sikhs reemphasizes the pagh as the singular and most important outer symbol of Sikh identity, the pressure is high on Sikhs to either wear or not-wear the turban, be it out of sheer convention, pride, or dignity or because they consider the practices of tying and stylistically covering unshorn hair (*kes*) as part of their daily routines of Sikh religiosity.

Caught in the complex webs of affect described above, the Sikh subject, bearded or clean-shaven, turbaned or de-turbaned, could not be further removed from the kind of scenario journalist Harry Nutt evokes in his fictitious U-Bahn anecdote. Nutt's leitkulturalism remains ignorant of the everyday realities that turn a subway passage into a racist encounter, the walk from a subway station to the local Sikh *gurdwara* into a hide-and-seek game with a patrolling police car, or an often-visited place into a potentially deadly zone.[85] Thus, in the shadows of the Marxloh effect, certain people and the kinds of social experiences they embody remain clearly out of sight. One might argue that they are further pushed back into the backyards of German benevolence. They remain too insignificant and at times untranslatable to become the focus of any serious discussion in German literary and mainstream publics.[86] Thus, the identification of the Sikh turban-wearer through fantastic modes of othering results in a kind of social invisibility that makes people even more prone to the regulative mechanisms of state control than is the case with the official "peace deals" with Ahmadis in times of anti-mosque protest.

∎ NOTES

I am grateful to Anke Allspach, Karine Côté-Boucher, Markus Dressler, Ratiba Hadj-Moussa, Virinder Kalra, Arvind Mandair, Shobna Nijhawan, and Roshanak Shaery- Eisenlohr as well as the two anonymous reviewers from Oxford University Press. Their critiques, comments, and suggestions were instrumental in revising earlier drafts of this chapter. I also thank Elisabeth A. Graves for her fine editing work. All remaining flaws are entirely mine. A few sections of this chapter are based on a revision of my previously published article "'Today, We Are All Ahmadi.' Configurations of Heresy between Lahore and Berlin," *British Journal of Middle Eastern Studies* 37(3): 429–47.

1. Matthias Drobinski, "Das Wunder von Marxloh," *Süddeutche Zeitung*, October 16, 2008, 6.

2. Rüttgers was recently voted out of his office as Ministerpräsident von Nordrheinwestfalen, the provincial state in which the mosque is located. In his 2009 election

campaign, he issued discriminatory remarks about immigrant workers from Romania, whom he deemed unfit for the German labor market.

3. Caroline Jenkner, "Warum das Wunder von Marxloh funktioniert," *Der Spiegel Online*, October 28, 2008, accessed August 3, 2009, http://www.spiegel.de/politik/deutschland/0,1518,586613,00.html.

4. Germany won the 1954 soccer world championships in Bern, Switzerland, which later symbolized the partial rehabilitation of a humiliated German identity. Just a few years ago, Sönke Wortman's film *Das Wunder von Bern* (2003) played in theaters and was widely and sympathetically received by the German public.

5. When Minister of Interior Affairs Wolfgang Schäuble inaugurated the Berlin "Islam Conference" in 2006 (this is a roundtable of experts, who are asked to chart out an agenda for Islamic education in public schools and other issues), he explicitly called Islam a part of German realities. However, when newly elect President Christian Wulff made the same statement in his October 3, 2010 speech commemorating the twenty years of German unification, he faced strong public criticism by conservatives.

6. See the recent issue of the *Journal for Ethnic and Migration Studies* on a comparative perspective on other European cities. For an overview, see Jocelyne Cesari, "Mosque-Conflicts in European Cities: Introduction," *Journal of Ethnic and Migration Studies* 31, no. 6 (2005): 1015–24.

7. In 2010, Sarrazin's book clearly dominated the public debate in Germany. In the seventeenth edition, the book sold within less than a year. It was discussed on numerous talk shows and major newspaper feuilletons as well as on the political terrain. As this issue has surfaced after the original version of my essay has been submitted, it is not possible to engage with the full details of the arguments and the unfolding public debate. However, what is argued in the following text can be directly applied to the culturalist and at times racist logics behind Sarrazin's arguments. It is not surprising that the anti-mosque movements discussed in my text have signed on to many of his key arguments.

Among other topics, Sarrazin compares the success stories of different immigrant groups in Germany, concluding that Turkish and other Muslim immigrants, due to genetic and cultural differences, will show less intelligence and eventually cause a socioeconomic downturn of the country. See Thilo Sarrazin, *Deutschland schafft sich Ab. Wie wir unser Land aufs Spiel setzen* (München: Deutsche Verlags-Anstalt, 2010).

Sarrazin argued earlier that these groups did not contribute much to the German society and economy, apart from "selling vegetables" and "producing headscarf-wearing girls." See Thilo Sarrazin, "Klasse statt Masse," *Lettre International* 86 (2009), accessed January 14, 2011, http://www.lettre.de/archiv/86-Sarrazin.html. Whereas at that time, the incident had already caused a minor public scandal, it was still widely accepted in the mainstream press that Sarrazin "has a point" and was able to stir up a new debate on integration, which after the publication of his scandal-producing book, he eventually succeeded in doing. The *Frankfurter Allgemeine Zeitung* went so far as to evoke his civil courage. See Jasper von Altenbockum, "Zivilcourage bedeuted Risiko," *Frankfurter Allgemeine Zeitung*, http://www.faz.net/s/RubFC06D389EE76479E9E76425072B196C3/Doc~E58C4452870BA4900B453C DB3DAE352A7~ATpl~Ecommon~Scontent.html.

8. The vote that took place on November 29, 2009, had the necessary majority of voters (*Bundesmehr*) and provinces (*Ständemehr*) needed to implement §72, section 3, into the Swiss Constitution, which would now include the line: "The construction of minarets is prohibited." Shortly after the results were released, they were celebrated by anti-mosque protesters all over Europe. See the Web site of the Swiss group supporting the vote: http://www.minarette.ch. While most official responses in Switzerland and the European Union were critical of the vote and raised questions as to whether the vote

could stand in the light of Switzerland having signed the European Union's human rights convention, the very process of amending the complete revision of the Swiss Constitution in 1999, in which the right to religious freedom was enshrined in preamble to the revised text, can easily translate into a constitutional crisis. See, for instance, Martin Otto, "Das Minarett ist der Absinth unserer Zeit," *Frankfurter Allgemeine Zeitung* 283 (December 5, 2009): 38.

9. The "Stopp. Ja zum Minarettverbot [Stop. Yes to the prohibition of minarets]" poster reiterates the visual style and grammar of racial exclusion that were employed in prior advertisement campaigns by the far-Right Swiss People's Party (Schweizer Volkspartei). One of the last posters used, for instance, shows the image of a white sheep kicking a black sheep from the terrain marked by the Swiss flag in almost identical design to press for action against crimes committed by "foreigners."

10. Ayse Çağlar, "Constraining Metaphors and the Transnationalisation of Spaces in Berlin," *Journal of Ethnic and Migration Studies* 27, no. 4 (October 2001): 602.

11. In sociology, "culturalism" is commonly understood as the discursive process of rendering social, ethnic, religious, or racial differences in such ways that individual characteristics and forms of (moral) behavior are subsumed under the larger collective and subsequently explained or categorized on the basis of naturalizing and nationalizing strategies of identification (notions of Arab culture and masculinity as they came up during the Abu Ghraib prisoner abuse would be a prime example of this process). For the purposes of this article, we should think here more broadly in terms of the processes by which various forms of conflict are discursively framed and mobilized in configurations of cultural and religious difference, specifically in such settings in which established hierarchies of majority/ minority configurations have been challenged on the basis of a changing demography in the process of global migration.

12. Sherene Razack, *Casting Out. The Eviction of Muslims from Western Law and Politics* (Toronto: University of Toronto Press, 2008), 108. Razack is specifically concerned with the case of Norway, where there have been new policy initiatives around the theme of forced marriage as bound up with stricter immigration controls and a more profound screening of immigration applicants.

13. Yolande Jansen, "Laïcité, or the Politics of Republican Secularism," in *Political Theologies. Public Religions in a Post-Secular World*, ed. Hent de Vries and Lawrence E. Sullivan (New York: Fordham University Press, 2006), 476.

14. Talal Asad, "Trying to Understand French Secularism," in *Political Theologies: Public Religions in a Post-Secular World*, ed. Hent de Vries and Lawrence E. Sullivan (New York: Fordham University Press, 2006), 507–8.

15. Ibid., 495.

16. The term *leitkultur* was first introduced in Bassam Tibi, *Europa ohne Identität, Die Krise der multikulturellen Gesellschaft* (Munich: BTB Verlag, 1998). Tibi's argument, which can be described as a secular-liberal position that is generally sympathetic to seeing Germany as an immigrant society, was later taken up by a leading German feuilletonist (Theo Sommer, "Der Kopf zählt, nicht das Tuch—Ausländer in Deutschland: Integration kann keine Einbahnstraße sein," *Die Zeit* 30 [1998], accessed May 22, 2008, http://www.zeit.de/1998/30/199830.auslaender_.xml). From there, it entered the political scene, where Christian-Democrats employed the term to mean precisely the opposite, for instance to refer to the denial of the idea that Germany could ever be considered an immigrant society. While both Tibi and Sommer disagreed with the political appropriation of the proposed term, it is clear that the secular-modernist and sometimes blunt assimilationist tones that are laced into their own arguments have strongly facilitated the circulation of the concept. The anti-mosque movement that I introduce further also promotes Tibi's book as an author-

itative academic source; see http://www.moschee-schluechtern.de/texte/tibi_euroident_inhalt.htm.

17. Hent de Vries, "Introduction: Before, around, and beyond the Theologico-Political," in *Political Theologies: Public Religions in a Post-Secular World*, ed. Hent de Vries and Lawrence E. Sullivan (New York: Fordham University Press, 2006), 55.

18. Wendy Brown, "Subjects of Tolerance: Why We Are Civilized and They Are the Barbarians," in *Political Theologies: Public Religions in a Post-Secular World*, ed. Hent de Vries and Lawrence E. Sullivan (New York: Fordham University Press, 2006), 299, 310. The idea of an organicist type of subjectivity or agency could be taken further in cognizance of Asad's critique of Western concepts of agency. See Talal Asad, *Formations of the Secular: Christianity, Islam, Modernity* (Stanford, CA: Stanford University Press, 2003), 67–99.

19. See also Goldstone in this volume.

20. "Mullahs immer klüger," *die taz*, February 19, 2001.

21. It did not take long before this was discussed in online forums such as the Muslim-Markt and chat forums on the *die taz* Web site received numerous letters in protest to what was considered by the editor of the Muslim-Markt as "one of the most degrading remarks against Muslims and the Islam that we have ever come across in the German-speaking context." See "Muslim-Aktion gegen die Taz," June 19, 2008, http://www.muslim-markt.de/Aktion/Sonstige/aktiongegentaz.htm.

22. Michael Ringel, "Wenn die Fatwa droht: Das Taz-Resort, 'Die Wahrheit.' Damit Satire entlarvend wirkt müssen Regeln verletzt werden," *die taz*, June 10, 2008, accessed February 17, 2010, http://www.taz.de/index.php?id=archivseite&dig=2001/02/17/a0100 (my translation).

23. Ibid., (my translation).

24. Talal Asad, "Reflections on Blasphemy and Secular Criticism," in *Religion: Beyond a Concept*, ed. Hent de Vries (New York: Fordham University Press, 2008), 605 ff.

25. Jasbir Puar, *Terrorist Assemblages: Homonationalism in Queer Times* (Durham, NC: Duke University Press, 2007), 205–16.

26. Ibid., 204. A discussion of the new literature on affect is beyond the scope of this essay. For heuristic purposes I will focus on a particular aspect that directly applies to my study of Sikh and Ahmadi subject formations.

27. Ibid., 215.

28. Irene Silverblatt links this genealogy of heresy to the Spanish Inquisition, thereby arguing that heresy accusations were constitutive of racial ideologies as linked to emerging forms of European nationalism. Irene M. Silverblatt, *Modern Inquisitions: Peru and the Colonial Origins of the Civilized World* (Durham, NC: Duke University Press, 2005), quoted in Razak, *Casting Out*, 35. Talal Asad warns against seeing a direct line here between the past and present and argues that contemporary discourses on blasphemy and heresy are based on complex refractions and translations. See Asad, "Reflections on Blasphemy and Secular Criticism," 581.

29. Another documentary film project, *A Prisoner's Song* (dir. Michael Singh, 2009), has further traced Mall Singh's story and could prove that he later returned to his family in Punjab.

30. Manfred Backhausen, ed., *Die Lahore-Ahmadiyya Bewegung in Europa* (Wembley: Ahmadiyya Anjuman Lahore Publications for the Berliner Moschee der Lahore-Ahmadiyya-Bewegung zur Verbreitung islamischen Wissens, 2008), 56.

31. The Berlin mosque was officially inaugurated in 1925. For the history of the Berlin mosque, see ibid.; and Nasir Ahmad, *A Brief History of the Berlin Muslim Mission and the Berlin Mosque Founded by the Lahore Ahmadiyya Movement in Islam*, ed. Manfred Backhausen, Berlin Mosque and Mission, February 2, 2008. http://berlin.ahmadiyya.org/berlin-mission-june06.pdf.

32. A 1920 photograph (reproduced in Backhausen, *Die Lahore-Ahmadiyya Bewegung in Europa*, 30) shows Sikh and Muslim army persona along with members of other Muslim and non-Muslim communities in front of the Woking mosque. Christian missionaries, on the other hand, warned against the "propaganda" of the mission. James Thayer Addison notes the presence of Ahmadiyya communities in two suburban mosques in London (Surrey and Southfields). See James Thayer Addison, "The Ahmadiya Movement and Its Western Propaganda," *Harvard Theological Review* 22, no. 1 (1929): 1–29.

33. Ahmad, *A Brief History of the Berlin Muslim Mission and the Berlin Mosque*, 25.

34. Nankana Sahib, the presumed birthplace of Guru Nanak, is situated in Pakistan, where a small minority of Pakistani Sikhs administers the site. In recent years, Nankana Sahib has seen a resurgence in international pilgrimage, mostly by Sikhs holding European or American passports. Qadian, the founding place of the Ahmadiyya movement, is situated in the Indian Punjab and is similarly a center of international pilgrimage by Ahmadis worldwide.

35. A discussion of the notion of (state) secularism in South Asia is beyond the scope of this article. See Arvind Mandair's discussion in this volume. For a discussion of the anti-Ahmadi campaign in Pakistan, see, for example, Leonard Binder, "The Ahmadiyya Controversy and Its Consequences," in his *Religion and Politics in Pakistan* (Berkeley: University of California Press, 1963), 259–96; Surendra Nath Kaushik, *Ahmadiyya Community in Pakistan: Discrimination, Travail and Alienation* (New Delhi: South Asia Studies Centre, 1996).

36. In 1974, the World Muslim League declared Ahmadis as non-Muslims and excluded them from being recognized under the roof of the *ummah*. See http://www.alhafeez.org/rashid/rabita.html. See also S. Zulfiqar Gilani, "Ahmedis and the Problem of National Identity in Pakistan," in *Religions Minorities in South Asia*, ed. Monirul Hussein and Lipi Ghosh (New Delhi: Manak Publications, 2002), 129–46; and Antonio R. Gualtieri, *Conscience and Coercion: Ahmadi Muslims and Orthodoxy in Pakistan* (Montreal: Guernica, 1989), 35–72.

37. I have explored some of these issues in my article "Deportability, Medicine, and the Law," *Anthropology and Medicine* 12 no. 3 (2005): 271–85. A more detailed analysis of interviews with individuals who went through those hearings, along with interviews that I conducted with interpreters and judges, will be offered in a forthcoming book of mine.

38. Andreas Hartmann, "Vertrag soll Streit um Moschee schlichten," *Frankfurter Rundschau*, December 23, 2004, 29.

39. See Razack, *Casting Out*, 16–17.

40. A more recent example is the cooperation contract signed by the chief of police forces in Berlin's District One, Klaus Kleese, and Ahmadiyya Imam Abdul Basit Tariq. See Sebastian Heiser, "Dialog mit Verspätung. Die Polizei und die Ahmadiyya-Muslim-Gemeinde vereinbaren eine Kooperation—vier Monate später als geplant, weil es Irritationen über den Text gab," *die taz*, November 26, 2007, accessed May 20, 2008, http://www.taz.de/regional/berlin/aktuell/artikel/1/dialog-mit-verspaetung/?src=%20SE&cHash=3e0d578d85.

41. *Friedliebend* here not only connotes being moderate and tolerable but also carries notions of domesticity and assimilability.

42. Several European cities, including London and Marseille, have seen anti-mosque protests. See the contributions in the *Journal for Ethnic and Migration Studies* 31, no. 6, for instance, Jacqueline Cesari, "Mosques in French Cities: Towards the End of a Conflict," *Journal for Ethnic and Migration Studies* 31, no. 6 (2005): 1025–43. For the German context, see René Hohmann, *Konflikte um Moscheen: Eine Fallstudie zum Moscheebauprojekt in Schlüchtern* (Berlin: Humboldt Universität, 2003).

43. Apart from the cases discussed here, there are ongoing disputes in the cities of Cologne, Munich, Neckarsulm, and Oer-Erkenschwick in addition to several smaller cities.

44. Gerdien Jonker, "The Mevlana Mosque in Berlin-Kreuzberg: An Unresolved Conflict?" *Journal for Ethnic and Migration Studies* 31, no. 6 (2005): 1067–81.

45. Thus, the metonymy created among minaret, muezzin, and shari'a was the argumentative mantra used by those backing the Swiss vote against minarets.

46. For "pro-Schlüchtern," see http://pro-schluechtern.blogspot.com/. For Berlin's anti-mosque faction, see http://www.ipahb.de. There are several other populist Web sites relating to both controversies.

47. Schlüchtern is a small town of about 17,500 inhabitants, 1,200 of which are naturalized Germans or foreign passport holders. An estimated one hundred live in and adjacent villages for whom the mosque was being designed.

48. Çağlar, "Constraining Metaphors and the Transnationalisation of Spaces in Berlin," 602 ff.

49. The rationale of this practice is grounded in the 1949 state treaty known as *Königsteiner Staatsabkommen* or *Königsteiner Schlüssel* and is recalculated annually. Originally intended to regulate the funding of academic institutions that exceed the funding potentials of the separate provincial states, thus being in need of federal financial support, the key has been expanded to other areas and since 2004 also applies to the distribution of asylum seekers. It is now recognized as the founding principle of distributing funds and resources between the federal level and those of the state provinces (*Länderfinanzausgleich*).

50. Hohmann notes that for the Schlüchtern town administration the integrity of the city's cultural geography was at stake; no concerns were issued about the particular religious designs of Islamic architecture. See Hohmann, *Konflikte um Moscheen*, 44.

51. In Schlüchtern, the right-wing party "Die Republikaner" launched a successful signature campaign that led to a public vote (*Bürgerbegehren*). In Berlin, members of the extremist National Democratic Party participated in the protest marches and allegedly committed acts of arson on Ahmadiyya property. After right-wing participation in the public protest marches was spotted, members of the Berlin initiative defended themselves by hinting at the broad resonance of their concerns with the German people, which was also expressed in "Wir sind das Volk [We Are the People]" banners, indexing claims to popular sovereignty with specific reference to recent events in German history (the protests in East Germany that contributed to the fall of the Berlin Wall).

52. The "pro-Cologne" initiative has luckily seen a strong countermovement in support of Cologne's reputation as an open and welcoming city. For the mosque opponents, see http://www.pro-koeln-online.de. The popularity of these images has recently been succeeded by interactive online features such as the "Moschee Baba" game launched by the populist right in Austria (FPÖ). The game is unmistakably Islamophobic and had to be taken off the web after an Austrian court declared it unlawful. The game asked players to place visible "stop" signs on appearing minarets and stereotypical figures of bearded Muslims.

53. Anonymous, "Der Engel mit Schwert," November 24, 2002, accessed January 10, 2005, http://www.moschee-schluechtern.de/texte/Michael/021124-mail.htm (site discontinued).

54. Hübsch was a former member of the socialist-anarchist "Kommune 1" and thus was once one of the most widely known radical-leftist activists of the '68 generation. The daily *die taz* has recently devoted an article to Hübsch, drawing specific attention to his spiritual reawakening in a 1970s visit to Morocco. If there is something written between the lines of the admittedly sympathetic text, it is certainly the curiosity if not sheer wonder that Hübsch-the-converted later delivered sermons as imam in Frankfurt's Noor mosque. See Andreas Fanizadeh, "Probier Dich aus! Portrait Hadayatullah Hübsch," *die taz*, January 18, 2008,

http://www.taz.de/1/leben/koepfe/artikel/1/probier-dich-aus/?src=SE&cHash=8fa03342da (accessed June 4, 2008). For an obituary, see Canan Topcu, "Ein Poet und Muslim," *Frankfurter Rundschau*, January 5, 2011, http://www.fr-online.de/frankfurt/ein-poet-und-muslim/-/1472798/5066018/-/index.html (accessed January 14, 2011).

55. The role of Ahmadiyya mosques is not openly articulated in the recent Swiss debate, yet it should be noted that the first mosque with a minaret in Switzerland was built by the Ahmadiyya Muslim Jama'at. On a Swiss TV show broadcast a month earlier than the vote, one of the discussants, Austrian Orientalist Heinz Gstrein referred to the Ahmadiyya "sect" as having established the precedent that others now follow. See *Der Club*, Schweizer Fernsehen, October 28, 2009, http://www.youtube.com/watch?v=qgr4hWGlHx0 (accessed December 5, 2009).

56. Avril Powell, "Contested Gods and Prophets: Discourse among Minorities in Late Nineteenth-Century Punjab," *Renaissance and Modern Studies* 38 (1995): 54.

57. Arvind Mandair, "The Repetition of Past Imperialisms: Hegel, Historical Difference and the Theorization of Indic Religions," *History of Religions* 44, no. 4 (2005): 277–99. Also see his chapter in this volume.

58. For the pre-Partition context, see Spencer Lavan, "The Ahmadiyya Movement: Islamic Religious Reform in Modern India," in *Religion in Modern India*, ed. Robert D. Baird (Delhi: Manohar, 1989), 113–38; as well as Yohannan Friedman, *Prophecy Continuous: Aspects of Ahmadi Religious Thought and Its Medieval Background* (Berkeley: University of California Press, 1989).

59. The founder of the Ahmadiyya movement, Mirza Ghulam Ahmad (1835–1908), announced himself as a *mahdi* (or promised messiah), a renewer of Islam, in a place called Qadian in Punjab, where in the late nineteenth century Indian society underwent sweeping changes during British colonial rule. See Lavan, "Ahmadiyya Movement." Lavan points out that Ghulam Ahmad's claim to prophecy "was neither original nor unusual," as such claims have occurred repeatedly since the beginnings of Islam and with notorious regularity "at the end of an Islamic century, a period associated with the apocalypse" (ibid., 115). For a discussion of the importance of the *mubahilla*, see Powell, "Contested Gods and Prophets."

60. As Powell notes, it is no coincidence that Ghulam Ahmad's opponent, Clarke, bore the name of "Henry Martin," a name that was given to him in reminiscence of "the first Protestant evangelizer of Muslims in north India, best known as the translator of the Bible into Arabic, Persian, and Urdu" ("Contested Gods and Prophets," 46).

61. Hiltrud Schröter, *Ahmadiyya Bewegung des Islam* (Frankfurt am Main: Dr. Haensel-Hohenhausen, 2002), 50.

62. See, for instance, Addison, "Ahmadiyya Movement and Its Western Propaganda."

63. Schröter, *Ahmadiyya Bewegung des Islam*, 52.

64. I should clarify that I am not opposed to the idea of critically scrutinizing actual social and political practices in Ahmadiyya communities. However, Schröter's study does not offer any such insights. Some of the texts she discusses indicate that there exists a latent anti-Semitist ideology in translations of early Ahmadi writings. To conclude from there, however, in the way the author proposes, that Ahmadiyya would propagate anti-Semitist hate speech (*antijüdische Hetze*), which is a criminal act under § 130 in the German penal code, lacks justification.

65. For an Ahmadiyya rebuttal of Schröter arguments, see Hadayatullah Hübsch, "Eine Entgegnung auf Frau Dr. Schröter's Schrift *Ahmadiyya Bewegung des Islam*," 2008, http://mitglied.lycos.de/ahmadiyyaarchiv/islam/artikel/hadayatullah/entgegnung_schroeter.html. Schröter and Hübsch publicly discussed their positions in Schlüchtern's town hall on March 20, 2002.

66. Schröter, *Ahmadiyya Bewegung des Islam*, 121.

67. Ibid., 131.

68. Ibid., 143.

69. See, for instance, Judith Ezekiel, "French Dressing: Race, Gender, and the Hijab Story," *Feminist Studies* 32, no. 2 (2006): 256–78.

70. See Razack, *Casting Out*, 88.

71. Sigrid Nökel, *Die Töchter der Gastarbeiter und der Islam: Zur Soziologie Alltagsweltlicher Anerkenungspolitiken* (Bielefeld, Germany: Transkript Verlag, 2002), 279 ff.

72. Virinder Kalra, "Locating the Sikh *Pagh*," *Sikh Formations* 1, no. 1 (2005): 75–92.

73. Sonia Mikich, "Was nun, ferner Bärtiger?" *die taz*, February 6, 2006, accessed May 28, 2008, http://www.taz.de/index.php?id=archivseite&dig=2006/02/06/a0132.

74. Asad, "Reflections on Blasphemy and Secular Criticism," 606–7.

75. Ibid., 609.

76. Mikich is certainly not alone in this. In her carefully crafted critique of racism within French feminist discourse, Judith Ezekiel, explaining her difficulty in keeping her own distance from the *pro-choix* group in the debate on the hijab, asks: "How can I protest alongside the bearded men keeping watch over the rows of veiled women?" She probably refers to French Islamist groups that have engaged in these debates, some of which must indeed be criticized for their espoused gender practices. However, she also reinstates the image of the bearded Muslim fundamentalist as a kind of archetype here. See Ezekiel, "French Dressing," 258.

77. Harry Nutt, "Bin Laden in der U-Bahn. Eine sonderbare Begegnung im öffentlichen Nahverkehr. Die Adressierungsstrategien der Islamisten und wen sie erreichen," *Frankfurter Rundschau*, April 17, 2004, 15.

78. Ibid. Nutt says: "Die Anzeichen der Verwahrlosung der Beiden wurden während der Fahrt auffällig konterkariert durch das parallelle Zücken zweier topmoderner Mobiltelephone."

79. "Kanak," formerly used as an insult in ascribing primitive otherness to foreigners, has been reappropriated by hyphenated German youth culture as a sociolingual idiom that is more affirmative of their mixed, working-class environments in metropolitan Germany. This idiom has meanwhile achieved literary status and has found entry to German mainstream cultural production. See Feridun Zaimoglu, *Kanak Sprak. 24 Mißtöne vom Rande der Gesellschaft* (Hamburg: Rotbuch Verlag, 2004).

80. Kalra, "Locating the Sikh *Pagh*," 77.

81. Ibid., 80. As Kalra notes, such ideas are not bound to a white Western imagination but are complexly woven into diasporic and nondiasporic South Asian social and political formations as well; the case of martyr Bhagat Singh as hat- (not turban-) wearer being one case in point.

82. Ibid., 89.

83. See Puar, *Terrorist Assemblages*, 191 ff.

84. On this point, see also ibid., 167 ff.; and Kalra, "Locating the Sikh *Pagh*," 77 ff.

85. In one incident of a police raid, a young undocumented migrant died of a heart attack in the Frankfurt *gurdwara*.

86. As my interviews with professionals in Frankfurt social welfare services and migrant services indicate, there is also a profound lack of contact and knowledge about the situation of Sikh and Punjabi legal and illegalized persons on the part of the institutions in charge.

■ INDEX